God, Pharaoh and Moses

Explaining the Lord's Actions in the Exodus Plagues Narrative

PATERNOSTER BIBLICAL MONOGRAPHS

A full listing of titles in this series and Paternoster Theological Monographs
will be found at the close of this book.

PATERNOSTER BIBLICAL MONOGRAPHS

God, Pharaoh and Moses

Explaining the Lord's Actions in the Exodus Plagues Narrative

William A. Ford

Foreword by R. W. L. Moberly

Wipf & Stock
PUBLISHERS
Eugene, Oregon

Wipf and Stock Publishers
199 W 8th Ave, Suite 3
Eugene, OR 97401

God, Pharoah, and Moses
Explaining the Lord's Actions in the Exodus Plagues Narrative
By Ford, William A.
Copyright©2006 Paternoster
ISBN 13: 978-1-55635-321-5
ISBN 10: 1-55635-321-9
Publication date 3/6/2007

Paternoster
9 Holdom Avenue
Bletchley
Milton Keyes, MK1 1QR
PATERNOSTER Great Britain

PATERNOSTER BIBLICAL MONOGRAPHS

Series Preface

One of the major objectives of Paternoster is to serve biblical scholarship by providing a channel for the publication of theses and other monographs of high quality at affordable prices. Paternoster stands within the broad evangelical tradition of Christianity. Our authors would describe themselves as Christians who recognise the authority of the Bible, maintain the centrality of the gospel message and assent to the classical credal statements of Christian belief. There is diversity within this constituency; advances in scholarship are possible only if there is freedom for frank debate on controversial issues and for the publication of new and sometimes provocative proposals. What is offered in this series is the best of writing by committed Christians who are concerned to develop well-founded biblical scholarship in a spirit of loyalty to the historic faith.

Series Editors

I. Howard Marshall, Honorary Research Professor of New Testament, University of Aberdeen, Scotland, UK

Richard J. Bauckham, Professor of New Testament Studies and Bishop Wardlaw Professor, University of St Andrews, Scotland, UK

Craig Blomberg, Distinguished Professor of New Testament, Denver Seminary, Colorado, USA

Robert P. Gordon, Regius Professor of Hebrew, University of Cambridge, UK

Tremper Longman III, Robert H. Gundry Professor and Chair of the Department of Biblical Studies, Westmont College, Santa Barbara, California, USA

To my parents

Contents

FOREWORD

If a Christian understanding of God is fundamentally drawn from Scripture, what should the Christian make of those parts of Scripture, usually in the Old Testament, where God says and does things that seem to be at odds with Christian understanding? This time-honoured question is one that constantly, and rightly, recurs wherever the Bible is seriously studied.

A great strength of William Ford's fine study is that he tackles this question head-on in one of its most demanding forms. Exodus is a foundational book both for the Old Testament in itself, and for the Jewish and Christian faiths that are rooted in the Old Testament. It contains God's self-revelation to Moses at Sinai, the mountain of God, both initially in the burning bush where He reveals Himself as 'I AM', and subsequently when all Israel, delivered from Egypt, gather at Sinai and God gives the Ten Commandments. But what, then, is to be made of the narrative of the exodus which leads to the drowning of numerous Egyptians in the Red Sea? When the text portrays God hardening Pharaoh's heart, is this admirable other than from a narrowly partisan perspective? And why are there so many plagues? Why could not God simply get on with delivering Israel from Egypt if that is what He wanted to do? One may perhaps ask, 'Is the deity portrayed in the text lacking in power to do what he wants?' or 'Is he rather like a cat that has caught a mouse and enjoys playing with it, and only eventually puts it out of its misery when bored with this entertainment?' Could, or should, anyone today believe in such a deity?

There are difficult questions here. On the one hand they relate to questions about the relationship between the presuppositions of faith (the authority and the trustworthiness of the Bible) and the actual practice of textual interpretation. How far may a desire that text mean something acceptable for faith influence, and perhaps distort, the way one reads the text? On the other hand, there are questions of just what is necessary genuinely to see what the text contains and to read it well. Ford is well aware of the complexities of these issues, and handles them with subtlety, sophistication, and self-critical rigour.

His general approach is 'canonical', in that he seeks to interpret the biblical text in its received form, rather than in terms of its possible sources or underlying tradition-history (which is where much modern scholarly effort has been directed). This is based on the premise that the biblical text was shaped in a particular way by those responsible for preserving Israel's traditions so that the enduring significance of what Israel had come to know should be made accessible to subsequent generations who wished to enter into Israel's heritage. Such an approach also enables renewed dialogue both with premodern interpreters and general readers who likewise engage the text in its received form.

More specifically Ford adopts a 'literary' approach, which seeks to be sensitive to the internal dynamics of the biblical narrative. He works seriously with the dramatic dimensions of the text, through asking such questions as 'Who is speaking to whom?' and 'Who knows what and when?' This enables him to make sense of aspects of the text that have often proved elusive to interpreters.

Rather than tackling the question of how one should understand God's deeds and words in the plagues narrative in general theological or philosophical terms, Ford quite simply stays with the question 'How does the biblical text itself explain what God says and does?' He focusses on passages which have tended to receive less attention than they deserve, passages which for some reason never quite 'fitted' within an older style of source-critical approach to the text.

The results are perhaps unexpected, yet clear. Ford has helped me, at any rate, to understand the biblical text in a fresh way that does justice both to critical method and to contemporary faith. I hope that my own experience of having my eyes opened and being enabled to make better sense of a famous and difficult biblical narrative will be shared by many other readers too.

Walter Moberly,
Abbey House,
Palace Green,
Durham.
2006.

PREFACE

This book is based upon a doctoral dissertation entitled *"Whose Explanation? Which Context? A Narrative Theological Study of the Rationale for Divine Action in the Exodus Plagues Narratives"* which was submitted to the University of Durham in 2005. The work has not been significantly amended from the form of the dissertation, and there is some detailed discussion of Hebrew words and phrases which are given in pointed Hebrew script. However the readership of the book may well extend to those who do not read Hebrew. Therefore a list of the most common words with transliteration and translation is provided as an aid in Appendix I. The sections of the book that contain the most discussion of Hebrew are mainly the first halves of chapters 2 and 3 (2.2 and 3.2-3.3), and summaries have been provided at appropriate points.

Translations are my own and follow the Masoretic text (MT) as provided in Biblia Hebraica Stuttgartensia unless otherwise indicated. The majority of the references to God in the passages under consideration use the four letter name of the God of Israel: YHWH. I have used this unvocalised transliteration rather than using 'the LORD' as in many English translations of the text. As this is a work of Christian theology, the term 'Old Testament' is used to refer to the collection of documents also known as 'Hebrew Bible', 'Tanakh' and so forth.

The doctoral work grew out of a fascination for examining theologically 'difficult' passages that emerged in my undergraduate studies, and developed in my Master's year. The path from initial interest in the area to publication has been a long and sometimes confusing one. It is not, however, a path that has been walked alone, and due recognition and thanks needs to be paid to those who have helped in many different ways. Without them this book as it is might never have existed. Such flaws as still remain are, of course, my responsibility. There are too many people to thank individually, and general thanks are gratefully offered for all help, encouragement, comments, criticism, friendship and so forth. However, some deserve special mention.

Academic work could not be done in the absence of practical support. Therefore honourable mention should go to my previous employer PricewaterhouseCoopers for giving me the job without which I would not have been able to fund the doctoral work. I am also grateful for the financial assistance that I have received from the Barry Scholarship in Divinity and the Watkins Hebrew Scholarship. Finally my thanks are due to my friends Chris and Abi Taylor for their gracious hospitality in the last month of my work and beyond.

My interests in the plagues narrative in Exodus first arose during my Master of Studies (M.St.) year at Mansfield College, University of Oxford. My thanks to all in Old Testament and Mansfield, but specifically to my supervisor Paul Joyce, who helped me to focus and develop my undergraduate work.

Both my initial undergraduate study and my Ph.D. work have been carried out at the University of Durham (St Aidan's College and St John's College respectively). My thanks go to all in the colleges, the Theology Department, the Ph.D. process and wider Durham who have helped me in various ways. In particular, as my temporary supervisor, Stuart Weeks increased my knowledge of the ancient Near East, giving me a clearer picture of the story as a product of its time.

The greatest influence on my theological thinking in general, and this dissertation in particular, has to be my supervisor Walter Moberly. As an undergraduate his lectures and seminars awoke my interest in issues such as Old Testament Theology, the character of God and how one reads the scriptures. That interest has been redoubled in working with him on this project. His general guidance, encouragement, and penetrative comments have taught me much and have been greatly appreciated.

I am grateful to Paternoster for accepting the dissertation for publication in their *Biblical Monographs* series. More specifically thanks are due to Robin Parry, Jeremy Mudditt and Anthony R. Cross for their help in converting it from dissertation to book.

Finally, my parents Brian and Ruth Ford are owed a greater debt than I can repay, for first teaching me to read and love the Bible, bringing me up in the Christian faith that remains at the heart of my theological interests, and continuing to support me in innumerable ways, theological, practical and beyond. This book is dedicated to them as a small acknowledgement of this debt.

Abbreviations

AB	Anchor Bible
ANE	Ancient Near East
ArBib	The Aramaic Bible
ASS	All Souls Studies
BDB	Francis Brown, S. R. Driver and Charles A. Briggs, *The New Brown-Driver-Briggs-Gesenius Hebrew and English Lexicon* (Peabody: Hendrickson, 1979, based on the original 1907 edition)
BETL	Bibliotheca Ephemeridum Theologicarum Lovaniensium
BHS	*Biblia Hebraica Stuttgartensia.* K. Elliger and W. Rudolph eds. Stuttgart: Deutsche Bibelgesellschaft, 1990.
BIJS	Bulletin of the Institute of Jewish Studies
BJS	Brown Judaic Studies
BKAT	Biblischer Kommentar Altes Testament
BLS	Bible and Literature Series
BR	Bible Review
BZAW	Beihefte zur Zeitschrift für die Alttestamentliche Wissenschaft
BWANT	Beiträge zur Wissenschaft vom Alten und Neuen Testament
CB	Coniectanea Biblica
CBOTS	Coniectanea Biblica Old Testament Series
CBQ	*Catholic Biblical Quarterly*
CBSC	The Cambridge Bible for Schools and Colleges
CD	*Church Dogmatics.* Barth, Karl. Translated by G. T. Thomson et al. Edinburgh: T&T Clark, 1956-1969.
CFTL	Clark's Foreign Theological Library
COS	*The Context of Scripture: Canonical Compositions, Monumental Inscriptions and Archival Documents from the Biblical World.* William W. Hallo and K. Lawson Younger, Jr. eds. (Leiden: Brill, 1997-2002.)
CSCD	Cambridge Studies in Christian Doctrine
DJD	Discoveries in the Judaean Desert
ET	English Translation
EvT	*Evangelische Theologie*

ExR	*Midrash Rabbah: Exodus*. Translated by S. M. Lehrman (London: Soncino Press, 1951).
FC	The Fathers of the Church
GKC	*Gesenius' Hebrew Grammar*. E. Kautzsch and A. E. Cowley (Oxford: Clarendon, 1990).
HALOT	*The Hebrew and Aramaic Lexicon of the Old Testament*. Edited by Ludwig Koehler and Walter Baumgartner. Translated and edited by M. E. J. Richardson et al. (Leiden: Brill, 1994-2000).
HCOT	Historical Commentary on the Old Testament
HKAT	Handkommentar zum Alten Testament
HR	*History of Religions*
HSS	Harvard Semitic Studies
HTIBS	Historical Texts and Interpreters in Biblical Scholarship
ICC	International Critical Commentary
IBC	Interpretation: A Bible Commentary for Teaching and Preaching
JBL	*Journal of Biblical Literature*
Joüon	Joüon, Paul. *A Grammar of Biblical Hebrew*. Translated and revised by T. Muraoka. Subsidia Biblica 14/I-II. (Rome: Editrice Pontificio Istituto Biblico, 1993).
JHNES	Johns Hopkins Near Eastern Studies
JITC	Journal of the Interdenominational Theological Center
JPST	Jewish Publication Society Tanakh
JPSTC	Jewish Publication Society Torah Commentary
JSOT	*Journal for the Study of the Old Testament*
JSOTSup	Journal for the Study of the Old Testament: Supplement Series
JSR	*Journal of Scriptural Reasoning*
LBI	Library of Biblical Interpretation
LCL	Loeb Classical Library
LXX	Septuagint. *Septuaginta*. Edited by Alfred Rahlfs. (Stuttgart: Deutsche Bibelgesellschaft, 1935, 1979).
MT	Masoretic Text
MGWJ	*Monatschrift für Geschichte und Wissenschaft des Judentums*
NASB	New American Standard Bible
NCB	New Century Bible
NIV	New International Version
NJB	New Jerusalem Bible
NRSV	New Revised Standard Version
NSKAT	Neuer Stuttgarter Kommentar – Altes Testament
OBT	Overtures to Biblical Theology
OTG	Old Testament Guide Series
OTL	The Old Testament Library

OTWSA/	Die Ou-Testamentiese Werkgemeenskap in Suid-Afrika/ The
OTSSA	Old Testament Society of South Africa
PFES	Publications of the Finnish Exegetical Society
Qur'an	*The Holy Qur-ān: English translation of the meanings and Commentary.* The Custodian of the Two Holy Mosques King Fahd Complex for the Printing of the Holy Qur'an
RB	*Revue Biblique*
RSV	Revised Standard Version
Sam. Pent.	Samaritan Pentateuch. *Der Hebräische Pentateuch der Samaritaner.* Edited by August Freiherrn Von Gall. (Giessen: Alfred Töpelmann, 1918).
SHBC	Smyth & Helwys Bible Commentary
SBL	Society of Biblical Literature
SBLDS	Society of Biblical Literature Dissertation Series
SBLSCS	Society of Biblical Literature Septuagint and Cognate Series
SBLSymS	Society of Biblical Literature Symposium Series
SJT	*Scottish Journal of Theology*
SSN	Studia Semitica Neerlandica
TDOT	*Theological Dictionary of the Old Testament.* Edited by G. Johannes Botterweck, Helmer Ringgren and Heinz-Josef Fabry, translated John T. Willis et al. (Grand Rapids: Eerdmans, 1974-).
TgN/TgPsJ	Targum Neofiti/Targum Pseudo-Jonathan from *Targums Neofiti 1 and Pseudo-Jonathan: Exodus*, TgN trans. Martin McNamara, notes Robert Hayward; TgPsJ trans. and notes Michael Maher, ArBib 2 (Edinburgh: T&T Clark, 1994).
TLOT	*Theological Lexicon of the Old Testament.* Edited by Ernst Jenni and Claus Westermann. Translated by Mark E. Biddle. (Peabody: Hendrickson, 1997-).
TNICNT	The New International Commentary on the New Testament
TNIGTC	The New International Greek Testament Commentary
TrinJ	*Trinity Journal*
ThWAT	*Theologisches Wörterbuch zum Alten Testament.* Edited by G. Johannes Botterweck, Helmer Ringgren and Heinz-Josef Fabry. (Stuttgart: W. Kohlhammer, 1973-).
TynBul	*Tyndale Bulletin*
VT	*Vetus Testamentum*
VTSup	Supplement to Vetus Testamentum
WBC	Word Biblical Commentary Series
ZAW	*Zeitschrift für die Alttestamentliche Wissenschaft*

Chapter 1

The Issue and the Approach

1.1 The Issue under Discussion

The story of the exodus is primarily a story about YHWH.[1]

The exodus is often seen as a story about the liberation of Israel. Yet Israel are absent from the action in most of the story.[2] They may form the basis of Moses' commission and the demand to Pharaoh, but they play little active part in the story, in contrast to many other Old Testament stories. Moses, and to a lesser extent Aaron, has a greater role. His story begins in Ex. 2, and he is present at nearly every point after that until the end of the exodus in Ex. 15.[3] However, while he is present, it is as the one spoken to by YHWH, or as the one who speaks the word of YHWH. Apart from this role, little is said about him. In the same way, Pharaoh is present as the one who is addressed by YHWH and who refuses his demands during the plagues. Like Moses, he is one who is important inasmuch as he encounters YHWH. This does not mean that these others are unimportant. The fact that YHWH works with and through human beings will be considered throughout this examination. However, the prime focus in the text is YHWH.

Inasmuch as this story is part of the Old Testament, the fact that it focuses upon YHWH may not be surprising. However there are a couple of notable points concerning the story in relation to YHWH. First it is almost

---

[1] Cf. James Plastaras, *The God of Exodus: The Theology of the Exodus Narratives* (Milwaukee: Bruce Publishing, 1966), henceforth 'Plastaras', 2; Nahum M. Sarna, *Exodus*, JPSTC (Philadelphia: Jewish Publication Society, 1991), henceforth 'Sarna *Exodus*', xiii; William Johnstone, 'Exodus', in John W. Rogerson, R. W. L. Moberly and William Johnstone, *Genesis and Exodus* (Sheffield: Sheffield Academic Press, 2001): 182-276, henceforth 'Johnstone *Exodus OTG*', 183, 205; George F. A. Knight, *Theology as Narrative: A Commentary on the Book of Exodus* (Edinburgh: Handsel Press, 1976), henceforth 'Knight', 8; Laurel A. Dykstra, *Set Them Free – The other side of Exodus* (Maryknoll: Orbis Books, 2002), henceforth 'Dykstra', 95, 115; Thomas B. Dozeman, *God at War. Power in the Exodus Tradition* (New York: Oxford University Press, 1996), henceforth 'Dozeman', 5.

[2] They are present in chapters 1, 5, and 12-15, as well as very briefly in chapters 2, 4, and 6.

[3] In this dissertation, due to the number of references to Exodus, all references will be given without the 'Ex.' prefix, unless stated. Thus Exodus 5:1 will be cited as '5:1' and so forth. Other biblical references will retain their prefix.

unparalleled in terms of the concentration of YHWH's acts and intervention.[4] After appointing Moses as his messenger to the Egyptian Pharaoh and providing him with signs, YHWH strikes Egypt with a series of signs or plagues, cumulating in the plague on the firstborn, as a result of which Pharaoh releases Israel. When, subsequently, Pharaoh pursues Israel, YHWH destroys the pursuing Egyptian army in the waters of the Red Sea.

Secondly, this concentrated portrayal of divine interventions raises difficult moral and theological questions concerning the nature or portrayal of YHWH.[5] This is particularly the case in that section of the narrative that deals with the plagues or signs (Ex. 7-11) which we may call the 'plagues narrative'.[6] We can summarise these issues under two main headings: the length and nature of the plagues, and the interaction of YHWH with Pharaoh, in particular the 'hardening of Pharaoh's heart'.

1.1.1 Length and Nature of the Plagues

The exodus story is one of the longest continuous narratives in the Old Testament. One could compare the Joseph story, and stories about David. A large part of this lengthy story comprises a series of encounters where YHWH sends ten increasingly destructive plagues upon Egypt. These plagues are accompanied by a demand from YHWH to Pharaoh: 'send/release my people that they may serve me'.

However, although later plagues are inimitable (8:15 [19]; 9:11), and indeed unique (9:18; 10:6; 11:6), the series commences with signs, given by YHWH to Moses and Aaron, which the magi of Egypt can copy. As a result Pharaoh is not particularly interested in listening to them, which raises questions as to the reasons for such a commencement.[7] At one point YHWH comments that he could have destroyed the Egyptians with a plague, presumably with the result that Israel could have then left unhindered. However he has not done this for his own reasons (9:15-16). Meanwhile, there is no suggestion that Israel, present only in the narrative from 6:9-11:10 as the object of YHWH and Pharaoh's interaction, are doing anything other than working in the brick kilns, making bricks without

---

[4] The creation story obviously has a number of divine acts in it. Apart from this, one could mention the Elijah/Elisha stories.

[5] Cf. Lyle Eslinger, 'Freedom or Knowledge? Perspective and Purpose in the Exodus Narrative (Exodus 1-15)', *JSOT* 52 (1991): 43-60, henceforth 'Eslinger 'Freedom'', 47.

[6] The issue of the exact boundaries of the plagues narrative will be picked up in chapter 4.

[7] Cf. William H. C. Propp, *Exodus 1-18. A New Translation with Introduction and Commentary*, AB (New York: Doubleday, 1998), henceforth 'Propp', 227.

straw.[8] If Israel is to be freed; freeing them as quickly and painlessly as possible does not appear to be YHWH's aim.[9]

The plagues increase in their power, bringing destruction to the fertile land; suffering; the death of animals; illness; and finally death. Gowan notes that 'few have thought to discuss at all God's choice of death and destruction as his means of getting glory over Pharaoh (14:4). They just accept it, as the author of Exodus accepts it, but in our day we cannot avoid asking how this fits with the whole of scripture's picture of God.'[10]

Yet when we reach 11:10 at the end of the first nine plagues, we find Israel, Pharaoh and Egypt still seemingly in the same position as at the start. We may then ask with Plastaras:

> It might be wondered why the sacred authors chose to tell the story of the earlier plagues at such length (four whole chapters), since they did not achieve their expressed purpose.[11]

To put this another way, with all of the issues noted above, one could ask about the point of the plagues narrative in the exodus story. What is the point of the long description of the first nine plagues? What would be lost if the story skipped from, say, Ex. 5 to Ex. 12?[12] Childs sums up the issue well:

> Only in the plague stories was a tradition retained in which such great miracles, constantly repeated, continued to fail. The fact that ultimately plague X did

---

[8] Cf. David J.A. Clines, *Interested Parties – The Ideology of Writers and Readers of the Hebrew Bible* (Sheffield: Sheffield Academic Press, 1995), henceforth 'Clines *IP*', 197-8.

[9] Cf. Donald E. Gowan, *Theology in Exodus – Biblical Theology in the form of a commentary* (Louisville: Westminster/John Knox Press, 1994), henceforth 'Gowan', 128ff; Eslinger 'Freedom', 56.

[10] Gowan, 128. At this point we should note that the idea of YHWH sending calamities upon people, both Israel and non-Israel, is not unusual. There are a number of instances of YHWH bringing calamities, the most obvious being the Flood (Gen. 6-8). Moreover, passages such as Amos 3:6; Is. 45:7; and Dt. 32:39 appear to set this out quite programmatically. However the wider issue of YHWH bringing calamity in the Old Testament is beyond the scope of this work. For an interesting discussion of this issue, see Fredrik Lindström, *God and the Origin of Evil – A Contextual Analysis of Alleged Monistic Evidence in the Old Testament*, CBOTS 21 (Lund: CWK Gleerup, 1983). His argument is that these and other passages do not show a monistic view. Even if one accepts his analysis, it still leaves the lesser point that YHWH is certainly responsible for some calamities.

[11] Plastaras, 133-34.

[12] Cf. George V. Pixley, *On Exodus – a liberation perspective* (Maryknoll: Orbis, 1987), henceforth 'Pixley *Exodus*', 39-40 who asks a similar question.

accomplish its end, did not remove the difficulty of the earlier one, nor explain the failure. [13]

1.1.2 Interaction of YHWH and Pharaoh

Although we are calling this section the *plagues* narrative, a large part of it is not concerned with the phenomena of the plagues, but rather with the interaction or encounters between YHWH and Pharaoh of which the plagues form a part.[14] YHWH demands that Pharaoh send the people of Israel away, rather than just taking them himself. Such a demand introduces most of the encounters and the plagues are related to Pharaoh's lack of response to this demand. However for each of the plagues before the firstborn Pharaoh's response is to refuse to send Israel. We can continue from the same passage in Childs:

> Indeed the sense of the mystery of Pharaoh's resistance lies at the root of the tradition. Now it is apparent that the essential problem with which we began is not ultimately form-critical in nature, but profoundly theological. The interpreter is still faced with the task of penetrating the mystery of God's power before human pride.[15]

At the end of each plague Pharaoh's response is explained by a narratorial comment on the hardness of his heart. Towards the end of the plagues this hardening is explicitly ascribed to YHWH.[16] Thus he appears to be preventing Pharaoh from obeying his demands, exacerbating the length of the interaction and the effect of the plagues, both in terms of their number and power. Moreover YHWH tells Moses in advance of these encounters that he is going to harden Pharaoh's heart (4:21; 7:3), raising the question of why YHWH would make such demands to Pharaoh at all.

Thus the question of why YHWH would lengthen the plagues is exacerbated by the question of why he would make a demand and then work against that demand by hardening Pharaoh. Discussions have tended to focus, understandably, on the hardening as perhaps the most theologically challenging of these issues. Such discussions vary from short

---

[13] Brevard S. Childs, *The Book of Exodus. A Critical Theological Commentary*. OTL (Louisville: The Westminster Press, 1974), henceforth 'Childs', 149.

[14] The words 'interaction' and 'encounters' are being used in an attempt to avoid pre-categorising the content or the nature of the interactions/encounters between YHWH and Pharaoh before they are studied. Descriptions such as 'contest', 'demonstration', 'negotiations'; 'pedagogical/didactic' would inevitably colour our reading. While there may well be elements of most, if not all, of these present, no single one of them can appropriately function as a summation of the entire process.

[15] Childs, 149.

[16] The specific hardening phrases will be discussed in chapter 3.

excursus in commentaries through articles to a monograph.[17] Therefore we will begin our consideration of the portrayal of YHWH with a summary of representative discussions on the hardening.

1.2 Different Approaches to the Issue

1.2.1 Previous Approaches to the 'Hardening'

A caveat is necessary at this point. As this study will not focus exclusively on the issue of the 'hardening', this summary is intended to be representative of general positions on the issue of the hardening, rather than exhaustive of all scholarly work thereon.[18] The discussions have been grouped into different approaches to the issue for ease of reference. However the lines are necessarily arbitrary, and some works may fall into more than one category or on the borderline of two.[19] The intention of this section is to summarise the different positions here, and in this short space it will not be possible to do justice to all of the arguments.[20]

1.2.1.1 DIFFERENT SOURCES WITH DIFFERENT POSITIONS

The most common approach, certainly until recently, was to approach the problem of the hardening through historical critical methods. The different hardening vocabulary and phraseology were investigated as deriving from different sources, building up a composite picture of how the present text came to be. The most detailed example of this is the monograph by Franz Hesse.[21]

---

[17] This having been said, there are fewer detailed discussions than one might expect.

[18] The discussions mentioned are primarily modern ones. For summaries of early interpretations see Benno Jacob, 'Gott und Pharao' *MGWJ* LXVIII (1923): 118-124; Theresia Heither, *Schriftauslegung – Das Buch Exodus bei den Kirchenvätern*, NSKAT 33/4 (Stuttgart: Verlag Katholisches Bibelwerk, 2002), 85-93; and Lester J. Kuyper, 'The Hardness of Heart according to Biblical Perspective.' *SJT* 27 (1974): 459-474, 465-468.

[19] For example Hesse's discussion deals primarily with the different sources but sees them all, ultimately, as portraying YHWH as the cause.

[20] The issue of the hardening will be considered in more detail in chapter 3.

[21] Franz Hesse, *Das Verstockungsproblem im Alten Testament: Eine Frömmigkeitsgeschichtliche Untersuchung*, BZAW 74 (Berlin: Alfred Töpelmann, 1955), henceforth 'Hesse'. To this we could add, for example, the articles by Wilson, Deist, and Räisänen, as well as a number of commentaries: Robert R. Wilson, 'The Hardening of Pharaoh's Heart', *CBQ* 41 (1979): 18-36, henceforth 'Wilson'; F.E. Deist, 'Who is to blame: The Pharaoh, Yahweh or circumstance? On human responsibility and divine ordinance in Exodus 1-14.', in *Exodus 1-15: Text and Context.* Edited by J. J. Burden. OTWSA/OTSSA 29 (1986): 91-112, henceforth 'Deist'; Heikki Räisänen, *The*

Hesse's comments on the hardening of Pharaoh form part of his overall study of the theme of hardening, considering the possible Old Testament origins of the New Testament issue, considering the hardening both of non-Israel (including Pharaoh) and also of Israel (especially Is. 6).

Although Hesse splits the hardening passages into J, E, P and redactional elements, he still finds tension between divine and human hardening within these individual sources. Thus while J leaves YHWH out of consideration, according to Hesse it is obvious to J that YHWH, who removed the plague, is ultimately involved with the hardening. 'In my opinion, one cannot speak of a relationship of tension between 'self-hardening' and hardening by God in J. For this narrator Jahwe is the secret subject of the apparent self-hardening.'[22] This of course is rather difficult to sustain. Räisänen comments that one 'could just as well claim that J regarded Yahweh as the actual cause of the Fall (Gen. 3).'[23] Hesse finds this tension also in E, and supremely in P.[24] 'In respect of the problem which he faces, P does the only thing that is possible for the theologian: He puts two propositions dialectically next to each other. In this respect theology has not gone beyond him to this day, and will not go beyond him.'[25] Finally he argues that redactional elements such as 4:21 and 3:19 do not progress the matter beyond P at all.[26]

This approach raises the questions of the possible relationships between the assumed sources, and how this may make sense of the text.[27] Thus

---

Idea of Divine Hardening. A Comparative Study of the notion of divine hardening, leading astray and inciting to evil in the Bible and the Qur'an, Publications of the Finnish Exegetical Society 25 (Helsinki, 1976), henceforth 'Räisänen *Hardening*', 53-56. The detailed work by Edgar Kellenberger (*Die Verstockung Pharaos: Exegetische und auslegungsgeschichtliche Untersuchungen zu Exodus 1-15*. BWANT 171 (Stuttgart: Kohlhammer, 2006)) was published as this book was going to press and therefore too late for any engagement.

[22] Hesse, 45. '*Von einem Spannungsverhältnis zwischen »Selbstverstockung« und Verstockung durch Gott kann bei J m. E. keine Rede sein. Für diesen Erzähler ist Jahwe das heimliche Subjekt der scheinbaren Selbstverstockung.*' (Unless otherwise stated, translations from the German are my own. I am grateful to Jenny Moberly for her help with my German.)

[23] Räisänen *Hardening*, 54.

[24] Hesse, 46-51.

[25] Hesse, 48. '*P tut also in der Aporie, in der es steht, das einzige, was dem Theologen möglich ist: Er stellt zwei Sätze dialektisch nebeneinander. In dieser Hinsicht ist die Theologie bis heute nicht über ihn hinausgekommen und wird nicht über ihn hinausgekommen.*' He notes Abot. 3:15 in support of this. Cf. Räisänen's rejection of this view as too modern for P (55).

[26] Hesse, 51-52.

[27] For example, many recent studies explore the model of the later sources (especially the Priestly source) working with earlier sources and adapting the overall picture. The most detailed discussion is found in Fujiko Kohata, *Jahwist und Priesterschrift in*

Childs' excursus on the hardening is structured around J and P, and he concludes that in both cases the hardening is linked to the signs. For J the hardening prevents the signs from revealing the knowledge of God. For P the hardening results in the multiplication of signs.[28] However Childs himself sees source criticism as unable to provide a breakthrough in the problem of the hardening.[29] This, however, has not stopped other discussions. For example Wilson responds to Childs by investigating the function of the different narrative strands of J, E, and P. In J the motif has a literary function but does not give a reason for the plagues, only the next request to Pharaoh. E attributes Pharaoh's actions to YHWH by placing 4:21 at the beginning. Finally P adds 7:3 with אָקְשֶׁה, encouraging the reader to interpret all of Pharaoh's actions negatively.[30] Wilson notes the lack of agreement of scholars on any overall function, and the difficulty of generalising on the use of the hardening motif.[31] These warnings, both implicit and explicit in the source critical approach, need to be heeded.[32] An explanation needs to deal with the variances in form, vocabulary and phraseology to be successful.

1.2.1.2 ONE OVERALL POSITION – YHWH OR PHARAOH

An alternative to the above position is to attempt to find one overall understanding of the hardening, generally with regard to the author or cause of the hardening.

On the one hand, it is argued that YHWH is always responsible for the hardening. Appeals are made primarily to YHWH's initial statements concerning the hardening in 4:21 and 7:3 before the encounters begin, and the concluding phrase 'as YHWH said'. These are seen as indications that while the text may say 'Pharaoh hardened his heart', the reader is to understand that YHWH is ultimately responsible. This then becomes clear at 9:12. The most detailed recent discussion of this is the article by G.K. Beale, which seeks to discuss the hardening in context in a final form approach.[33] In summary his argument has three points at its heart: YHWH

Exodus 3-14. BZAW 166 (Berlin: de Gruyter, 1986), henceforth 'Kohata', who discusses the question of whether P knew the earlier sources. Another recent approach that diachronically considers the changing portrayal of YHWH and divine power in the plagues narrative, is that of Dozeman.

[28] Childs, 170-175.

[29] Childs, 170.

[30] Wilson, 24-27, 27-29, and 29-35 respectively.

[31] Wilson, 19 and 35 respectively.

[32] This is the case even when, as here, one is looking at the final form. Our approach will be discussed at the end of this section.

[33] G. K. Beale, 'An Exegetical and Theological Consideration of the Hardening of Pharaoh's Heart in Exodus 4-14 and Romans 9', *TrinJ* 5 (1984): 129-154, henceforth 'Beale'. Cf. Martin Noth, *Exodus*, trans. J.S. Bowden, OTL (London: SCM Press, 1962),

foretelling his hardening of Pharaoh in 4:21, the phrase 'as YHWH said' referring back to 4:21 and 7:3, and the 'transitive/intransitive' pattern that he identifies in the hardening statements.[34]

Conversely it is argued that Pharaoh is always responsible for the hardening. It is suggested that the attribution of the hardening to YHWH is due to the mindset of the writers who would attribute everything ultimately to YHWH, but in such a way as not to deny the reality and efficacy of proximate causes through human agency.[35] Alternatively 'YHWH hardened' is understood in a permissive sense: YHWH *allowed* Pharaoh to remain hard-hearted rather than *causing* him to be hard-hearted.[36]

The problems with these positions are similar, in that one has to decide which statements to read at face value, and which to 'interpret' in light of the 'face value' statements. That is not to say that the interpretations are not, at least in some cases, subtle. If we had to make a choice one way or the other, 4:21, 7:3 and 'as YHWH said' would favour YHWH as being ultimately responsible. However in light of the issues raised by the source

---

henceforth 'Noth', 68; G. Warshaver, '"The Hardening of Pharaoh's Heart", in the Bible and Qumranic Literature.' *BIJS* 1 (1973): 1-12, 2-3. More famously see Luther's 'The Bondage of the Will', in *Martin Luther: Selections from his Writings*, John Dillenberger ed. (New York: Anchor, Doubleday, 1962), 192, 196-98, and Calvin, 101-102, 194. The discussion is quite subtle, speaking of YHWH using Pharaoh's evil will against him, but Luther notes that the 'as YHWH said' rules out any freewill, and Calvin dismisses the view that the hardening was in any way permissive.

[34] He has other arguments, but these three appear to underpin other discussions. For example in discussing 8:11 [15], he notes the phrase 'Pharaoh hardened' but in view of 'as YHWH said' Pharaoh 'must be viewed as YHWH's agent, who truly hardens himself – however, never independently, but only under the ultimate influence of Yahweh.' (143) cf. 144 on 8:28 [32] and 145 on 9:12, 30 and 9:34-35. While I will be disagreeing with several of his conclusions, it is refreshing to find such a detailed contextual approach. As his approach is both detailed and (to anticipate) comparable to ours, we will interact with it in our discussion of the hardening in chapter 3.

[35] See especially U. Cassuto, *A Commentary on the book of Exodus*, trans. Israel Abrahams (Jerusalem: Magnes Press, 1974), henceforth 'Cassuto', 55-57. Cf. S. R. Driver, *The Book of Exodus*, CBSC (Cambridge: Cambridge University Press, 1918), henceforth 'Driver *Exodus*' 53-54. This causes a problem if the principle is extended to other acts of YHWH, where 'YHWH our God who brought us out of Egypt' becomes 'we brought ourselves out of the land of Egypt' and so forth. Von Rad, commenting on Is. 6, warns against such a move to a general religious truth, asking why Isaiah would be needed (Gerhard Von Rad, *Old Testament Theology*, D.M.G. Stalker trans. from German of 1960 (London: SCM, 1965), Vol II, 152-153). Moreover one could use this point to argue the reverse, that YHWH was indeed seen as behind everything. For different examples of the latter see Hesse, 52-53 and Beale, 143-49.

[36] See especially Benno Jacob, *The Second Book of the Bible. Exodus*, trans. Walter Jacob (New Jersey: Ktav Publishing House Inc, 1992), henceforth 'Jacob *Exodus*', 244-245, 280, 286, 290, 384, 391.

critical approach, we will attempt to find an approach which preserves these differences while remaining one narrative.

1.2.1.3 A CHANGE IN THE POSITION – PHARAOH THEN YHWH

In another approach it is noted that the initial hardening refrains state that Pharaoh hardens his own heart, and then subsequently that YHWH starts to harden at 9:12.[37] This approach can then turn into a variant of one of the two positions in the previous approach. Thus one can understand the progression not as a change of authors of the hardening, but rather as a change of understanding on the part of the reader. Pharaoh's obstinacy becomes more and more outrageous, until it becomes obvious that this unbelievable behaviour must have a cause other than Pharaoh. Probably the most detailed recent discussion of this is found in the article by David Gunn.[38] He sees 4:21 and 7:3 together with the 'as YHWH said' as the hints of divine activity which become explicit at 9:12: 'what was previously implicit has become explicit. Pharaoh's obstinacy makes sense.'[39] Gunn's article is an interesting reading of the encounters, focussing on the richness of the narrative, discussing ambiguity and progression within it, in an approach similar to ours, albeit with different conclusions.[40]

Alternatively the progression is understood as a change in Pharaoh's will or psychology. Initially he starts to harden himself and this self-hardening can be reversed. However at a certain stage he reaches the point of no return. His intransigence has become so habitual and irreversible that he is unable to reverse it even if he wished. This is indicated by the change to '*YHWH* hardened Pharaoh's heart'. YHWH is simply using Pharaoh's own wilfulness against him.[41]

---

[37] The transition is not totally smooth with 9:34 coming after 9:12, but the overall pattern is reasonable.

[38] David M. Gunn, 'The "hardening of Pharaoh's heart": Plot, character and theology in Exodus 1-14', in *Art and Meaning: Rhetoric in Biblical Literature*. David J. A. Clines, David M. Gunn, and Alan J. Hauser eds., JSOTsup19 (Sheffield: Sheffield Academic Press, 1982): 72-96, henceforth 'Gunn'.

[39] Gunn 77; cf. Propp, 336, 353; John I. Durham, *Exodus*, WBC 3 (Waco: Word, 1987), henceforth 'Durham', 96-97, 122.

[40] His summary that ' "Pharaoh's heart was hardened" thus becomes a kind of shorthand for "Yahweh caused Pharaoh's heart to harden" ' (79) unfortunately loses the subtlety in the rest of his discussion. To anticipate our comments in chapter 2, it would be interesting to see how he would discuss the explanation in 9:13-19 or the remonstrative comments in 9:17 and 10:3, which might argue against such an approach.

[41] Cf. Sarna *Exodus*, 23, 36, and Nahum M. Sarna, *Exploring Exodus: The Heritage of Biblical Israel* (New York: Schoken Books, 1986), henceforth 'Sarna *EE*', 64-65. Childs, in particular, is opposed to such a position, seeing it as burdening the text with later discussions (170f).

Fretheim offers a position that comes between these two, albeit somewhat favouring the second.[42] He rejects any attempt at psychologising which aims to 'get God off the hook', but also does not see any glory for YHWH if Pharaoh is an automaton. He prefers a position of limited determinism. YHWH acts and brings in the word of God, and he makes Pharaoh's obduracy of such a character that he is driven to the point of no return, using the image of someone on the river fighting against the pull of a waterfall, and losing.

> *God as subject intensifies Pharaoh's own obduracy.* While initially this does not result in a numbing of Pharaoh's will, it begins to have that effect as events drive toward final disaster. Both need to be said: Pharaoh hardens his own heart, and so does God.[43]

Keil and Delitzsch offer another variant on this approach.[44] They understand the change from Pharaoh to YHWH as YHWH's response to Pharaoh's initial actions. The one who refused to listen to YHWH and learn from him leads himself into judgement, which is expressed by YHWH hardening him as he has hardened himself.

Overall the variants on this progressive approach are more nuanced than the previous one. Once again, the strength of 4:21, 7:3 and 'as YHWH said' would suggest that if one had to make a choice then the change of perceptions might be preferable to the change in psyche. Nevertheless one would still have to explain why the phrase 'Pharaoh hardened' was used at all, and why YHWH interacts with Pharaoh in the way that he does.

1.2.2 An Alternative Approach to the 'Hardening'?

All of the above approaches to the theological issue of the hardening have both strengths and weaknesses, although not all in equal proportions. Another point that most, if not all, of these approaches share to some extent is the tendency to abstract the 'hardening' as a theological issue which needs to be solved. In particular it seems that the author or source of the hardening needs to be defined: is it always YHWH or always Pharaoh, or both (at the same time or consecutively)? This does not mean that they pay no attention to the text in which it is found. For example, Beale is concerned to understand the hardening in context.[45] However while he is

---

[42] Terence E. Fretheim, *Exodus*, IBC (Louisville: John Knox Press, 1991), henceforth 'Fretheim', 96-103.

[43] Fretheim, 98.

[44] C. F. Keil and F. Delitzsch *Biblical Commentary on the Old Testament. Vol I: The Pentateuch*, trans. James Martin, CFTL XXII (Edinburgh: T&T Clark, 1864), henceforth 'Keil', 453-457.

[45] Beale, 130. He does state his surprise that 'apparently no writer in the history of this discussion [on the hardening in relation to predestination and Rom. 9] has ever

interested in context, he is still concentrating on the issue of 'the hardening', due in large part to his interest in Rom. 9:17, rather than the larger issue of YHWH's acts in the plagues narrative.

In light of the above, and the difficulties arising from the various different understandings of the hardening, this work will attempt to approach the issue in a different way. We have noted that the hardening is one of a number of theological issues in respect of YHWH's actions in the plagues narrative. Therefore instead of considering the 'hardening' as a separate issue, we will consider the wider theological issues involved with the portrayal of YHWH in this text. The hardening statements will form an important part of this, but will be considered in relation to the wider issue. Our passage is by far the greatest concentration of references to the hardening of the heart in the Old Testament, but there are other issues present in the text that need to be taken into account as well. While this assertion needs justification, a substantive justification can only be made heuristically by discussing the other elements and showing their relevance. However at this point we can provide one example of how the hardening fits into a wider context, by consideration of the vocabulary used to describe the act of hardening.

1.2.2.1 כָּבֵד, חָזַק AND קָשָׁה IN EX. 1-15

There are three words used in Ex. 4-14 to describe the phenomenon of the 'hardening': כָּבֵד, חָזַק and קָשָׁה.[46] Pharaoh's heart (לֵב) is often the object of these. We do not need to discuss the meaning of לֵב as the centre of a person's will or resolve, except to note that the modern idiom 'hard-hearted' in the sense of 'cruel' or 'pitiless' is not an appropriate understanding here. The three terms have been discussed in relation to Pharaoh's heart. Hesse especially discusses the three terms and other comparable terminology in detail.[47] To avoid going over the same ground, we can note that the nuances of meaning are that חָזַק indicates a heart that is firm or strong, כָּבֵד suggests a heart that is heavy or unresponsive, and קָשָׁה indicates a heart that is stubborn. There does not appear to be any

---

attempted to exegete all of the hardening predictions as they appear in consecutive order throughout their context in Exod 4-14.' (129)

[46] Hebrew citations and translitterations are taken from BibleWorks version 5 (Online: http://www.bibleworks.com/). When discussing the general sense of a Hebrew word, the pointing given will be that of the heading in BDB, excepting verbs only found in a stem or stems other than the Qal. (Citations of specific instances will follow the forms in the text.)

[47] Hesse, 7-14 and 14-20. On the wider use of the terms see e.g. A.S. van der Woude 'חזק' *TLOT* 1, 403-406; C. Westermann 'כבד' *TLOT* 2, 590-602; A. S. van der Woude 'קשה' *TLOT* 3, 1175-1176; Hesse 'חָזַק' *TDOT* IV, 301-308; Stenmans 'כָּבֵד' and Weinfeld 'כָּבוֹד' *TDOT* VII, 13-22 and 22-28; Zipor 'קָשָׁה' *ThWAT* VII 1/2, 205-21.

obvious reason as to why one word is used rather than another in the different hardening statements, and thus there appears to be no material differences between the terms.[48] However the heart is not the only object of these words in our passage, although it is probably the most discussed. In particular there are two other repeated uses that between them pick up all three words. These are the description of Pharaoh's actions in respect of Israel, and the description of YHWH's actions in respect of Pharaoh and Egypt.

Pharaoh, who does not know YHWH (or Joseph), sets work upon Israel. The first Pharaoh sets hard work upon them (קָשֶׁה 1:14) to prevent them leaving. The second Pharaoh tells his men to make the work heavier (תִּכְבַּד 5:9) so that they do not listen to Moses' 'lies'. This policy proves successful, as the people do not listen to Moses because of the hard work (קָשֶׁה 6:9).[49] In all three cases, the main reason for, or result of, this action is to act against Israel's release from Egypt.

The link between these words and Pharaoh's policy towards Israel becomes even clearer in the plagues narrative and beyond. YHWH threatens Pharaoh with a plague, if he keeps 'grasping' Israel (מַחֲזִיק 9:2) and refusing to send them. The institution of the sacrifice or redemption of the firstborn is to be explained by YHWH's actions when Pharaoh 'stubbornly refused to let us go' (הִקְשָׁה 13:15). Finally in the last plague, Egypt press Israel to leave quickly (וַתֶּחֱזַק 12:33, contrast 9:2).

This theme continues when we turn to YHWH's acts. YHWH's first comment to Moses about Pharaoh is that he, YHWH, knows that Pharaoh will not allow Israel to leave except by a mighty hand (וְלֹא בְּיָד חֲזָקָה 3:19).[50] This theme is repeated in 6:1 where YHWH says that now Pharaoh will send them and drive them out because of/with a mighty hand. This phrase becomes epigrammatical for the exodus, remembered as YHWH bringing Israel out of Egypt with a 'mighty hand' (בְּיָד חֲזָקָה). In 13:14 YHWH's 'strength of hand' is contrasted directly with Pharaoh being 'stubborn' in 13:15.

Moreover, as the plagues progress they begin to be defined as 'heavy' or 'very heavy' (כָּבֵד – swarm 8:20 [24]; murrain 9:3; hail 9:18, 24; locusts

---

[48] Perhaps we should restate this in terms of a lack of illumination of the final form of the text. One could explain the different words, as many have, in terms of different sources. However in the final form they appear to be largely interchangeable. There are slight differences in use; thus one could note that the narratorial refrain tends to use a form of כָּבֵד for 'Pharaoh hardened (dulled?) his heart' and חָזַק for 'YHWH hardened (strengthened?) Pharaoh's heart'. However this does not lead to any firm conclusions.

[49] The full phrase includes מִקֹּצֶר רוּחַ 'shortness of breath', which is an idiom for impatience or depression (cf. Mic. 2:7; Job. 21:4; Prov. 14:29; Cornelis Houtman, *Exodus*, Translated by Sierd Woudstra, HCOT, (Kampen: Kok, 1993, 1996), henceforth 'Houtman', I 56; Cassuto, 82).

[50] The exact meaning of וְלֹא בְּיָד חֲזָקָה will be discussed in chapter 3.

10:14. Cf. חָזָק – 'strong' wind 10:19). As with 13:14-15, in 9:2-3 this heavy plague (כָּבֵד) from YHWH is contrasted directly with Pharaoh's action. If Pharaoh continues to 'grasp' Israel, then YHWH's hand will come upon Egypt's livestock, with a very heavy plague. Pharaoh will not act to send the people without this heavy-handed treatment from YHWH, so YHWH will act accordingly. If Pharaoh's hand is heavy upon Israel, then YHWH's hand will be heavy upon Egypt.

Finally, in the Red Sea encounter, YHWH will glorify himself over Pharaoh and his army as they are vanquished and destroyed in the Red Sea (וְאִכָּבְדָה 14:4, 17, cf. v18).

It seems unlikely that these 'other' uses of כָּבֵד, חָזָק and קָשָׁה bear no relation to their use in respect of the 'hardening'. It seems more probable that a deliberate wordplay is intended.[51] In our passage these three words are used primarily for Pharaoh's actions with regard to Israel (grasping, increasing work, hardset against 'sending'); and for YHWH's actions in relation to Pharaoh and Egypt (mighty hand, heavy plagues, hardening Pharaoh, 'glory' over Egypt). Pharaoh's heart is hard or heavy, but so are a number of other things and it forms part of a larger pattern.[52] Thus it becomes more difficult to abstract the 'hardening' as a separate issue. In order to retain these resonances the 'hardening' needs to be read as one element of the ongoing narrative. To this point, and to our approach to the text, we now turn.

1.3 The Approach of this Study

1.3.1 General Approach - Narrative Theology

Our approach to the theological issues concerning the portrayal of YHWH in the plagues narrative will take the form of a narrative theological approach to the final form of the text. It is important for this study that both the theological content and also the narrative form of our passage are interlinked and mutually dependent. The story is more than *just* a story, because of its content, referent and significance. However it is important to recognise that it *is* a story, and not just a series of theological propositions that can be abstracted from their setting. We are concerned with the theology in the story, and thus are seeking to take the story seriously as story. There will be excursus at relevant points where a particular issue needs to be outlined and discussed in detail. However the intention will

---

[51] Cf. Dennis J McCarthy 'Plagues and Sea of Reeds: Exodus 5-14', *JBL* 85 (1966): 137-158, henceforth 'McCarthy 'Plagues'', 141.

[52] Moreover Pharaoh's state (i.e. his 'hardness of heart'), is only of interest inasmuch as it affects how he responds to YHWH's demands concerning Israel. Cf. Hesse, 31.

then be to understand the various occurrences of that issue in its narrative context. Therefore, as regards the hardening of Pharaoh's heart, one key difference in our approach to many of those mentioned earlier is that we will not be attempting to find 'an answer' to the question of who is causing the hardening. Instead we will be trying to understand how these references can be sensibly understood within the narrative of which they form a part. To put it another way, we will not be abstracting the hardening as a separate theological theme; discussing issues of theodicy; or considering discussions of the hardening in post-biblical theology.[53] Our focus is on the text and the role of the hardening within it.

The main focus in the study will be on passages that appear to be giving a rationale for what is going on, will go on, or has gone on in respect of YHWH's actions in the plagues narrative. Its intention is to read these 'explanations' in the plagues narrative in context. Reading them as part of the narrative will involve paying particular attention to where and when they arise, to whom they are addressed, to what they respond, what their function appears to be in that context and how they are received.[54] In the remainder of this introduction we will set out the specifics of our approach,

---

[53] While not wishing to downplay these enterprises, a concentration on the text seems to be the best place to start (cf. Childs, 170-171; Propp, 353). This concentration may yield some insights that can form part of such wider discussions.

[54] Eslinger 'Freedom' also advocates looking to the text and to the explanations and comments within it (47). He argues that the narratorial comments in the text are the best place to start, as the narrator is the one who stands above all the characters in the text (48). The reader should not carelessly assume that the authors voice their opinions through the principal characters in the text, and should be aware of the possibility that the authors might not uphold Israel's views themselves (51ff). Thus his article concludes: 'We can understand why they [Israel] celebrated God's mighty acts in song (Exod. 15); we should also understand and allow that the narrator and the narrative do not.' (59) His article raises questions over our use of two speeches from YHWH as our key texts in the following two chapters.

However Eslinger also points out the lack of any explicit evaluation of the events by the narrator (51). He sees this as leaving the reader to work out the authors' views. Yet while one should not assume that the speech of any principal character is expressing the narrator's views, one might expect a reasonably explicit sign that this is not the case, especially when the character is YHWH. Otherwise the burden of proof must lie on the one who would see the narrator disagreeing. His example of עָצוּם and רַב in 1:7-9 with the precedents in Genesis, and of Gen. 15:13-14 does not necessarily imply that Pharaoh and his reasoning 'are only cogs in the machine engineered and run by God' (53). Moreover the use of the hardening motif in YHWH's messages to Moses (56-58) does not necessarily show that the narrator disapproves of YHWH's actions, however problematic they may be for modern readers. Therefore in this chapter and the next, we will continue with our investigation of statements on the lips of YHWH, as a reasonable way into the theology of the text.

before returning to a couple of more general issues that need to be addressed.

1.3.2 Specific Approach – Chapter by Chapter

1.3.2.1 CHAPTER 2: 9:13-19

Notwithstanding the interest in YHWH's acts in the plagues narrative, one of the longest explanatory passages therein has received very little detailed consideration: the speech of YHWH in 9:13-19, which introduces the seventh plague of hail, thunder and fire from the skies. The reasons for such lack of consideration are uncertain. However, if one wished to speculate, there are two possible reasons that present themselves. Firstly, there is no explicit mention of the hardening of Pharaoh's heart in this speech. Therefore any approach that restricts itself to, or focuses predominantly on, the hardening will not give much attention to this speech.

Secondly, this speech has been viewed as fragmentary from a historical critical perspective. In particular, vv14-16 are seen as a secondary insertion, interrupting the speech that previously would have flowed from v13 to v17. Hyatt comments that 'verses 14-16 constitute a passage curious in its present context. It is too reflective for J, and it comes in awkwardly at this point, since this is not the last plague. Here someone explains the purpose of the plagues, and apparently he has in mind 'all my plagues' (14). We may attribute these verses to a late strand of P.'[55] Noth sees these three verses as corresponding to the whole plagues narrative, but appearing 'too early, for we would now expect it to be followed by the final decisive act of Yahweh.' He also notes the secondary character of the passage in 'the reference to the 'pestilence' in v. 15, i.e. to the secondary section 9.1-7.' However he does continue by noting that 'even if vv. 14-16 are cut out as secondary the announcement of the plague still remains unusually lengthy', referring to vv19-21.[56] Childs puts 9:14-16 together with 9:19-21, 31-32 and 10:1b-2 as sections considered to be 'later than the three sources, often designated as glosses'. 9:14-16 contains 'a theological reflection on the basis of the JE material which is concerned to explain why God has allowed the plagues to continue so long.'[57] He notes that although there is 'rather widespread agreement among the critical commentators' that these passages did not belong to the major literary strands, yet 'there is little consensus as to how to interpret these verses since no one set of forces

---

[55] J. P. Hyatt, *Exodus*, NCB, (London: Marshall, Morgan & Scott, 1971), henceforth 'Hyatt', 117-118.

[56] Noth, 80.

[57] Childs, 141. Cf. Houtman, II 82.

seems at work.'[58] Durham, after giving a brief taxonomy of different opinions as to the makeup of the sources in 9:13-19, argues that the lack of consensus on the makeup of the composite underscores 'both its somewhat patchy appearance and also the fragility of an over-precise assignment of verses and verse-fragments to specific sources without strong evidence for doing so.'[59] Schmidt discusses 9:14-16 and 10:1b-2 as two additions which, differing from their surroundings, have a wider focus than simply the plague in which they come.[60] However they are not independent, instead only being readable in their (jahwistic) context.[61]

Thus we have a speech that is acknowledged to be longer than others. It has an unusual section in the middle of it, containing some kind of overall explanation for the larger plagues cycle, which is often seen as a later addition. However, although these points are made, little more is said about this speech. In particular there is a very little comment on what the speech might mean, *as a whole, and in its context.*[62]

To further justify our use of 9:13-19 in relation to the issues that we have identified for study, we can set out the points above slightly more fully, together with some other points of interest.

On the question of length, and looking at the speech as it stands, it is one of the longest, if not *the* longest, explanations in the plagues narratives. It is set on the lips of YHWH, thus giving an explanation of his own acts.

It picks up several themes that run throughout other explanations of YHWH's behaviour offered in, before and after the plagues narratives. Thus our study of this passage will necessarily bring in these other passages. In particular the demand in v13 (שַׁלַּח אֶת־עַמִּי וְיַעַבְדֻנִי), and the reason in v14 (בַּעֲבוּר תֵּדַע כִּי אֵין כָּמֹנִי בְּכָל־הָאָרֶץ) will require wider consideration. As 9:13-19 is not the first mention of these themes in the canonical order, it will be necessary to return to 5:1-5 in particular in order to deal with the themes as they unfold in the narrative.

However, as well as picking up wider themes, and the unusual offer of mitigation in v19 that will repay investigation, there is the contrast in vv15-16 of what YHWH has done with what he could have done. While there are other explanations that give reasons for why YHWH is acting, this is the clearest explanation set on the lips of YHWH of why he is acting *in the way*

---

[58] Childs, 141.

[59] Durham, 126-127. Cf. Houtman, II 81.

[60] Werner H. Schmidt, *Exodus*, BKAT 2 (Neukirchen-Vluyn: Neukirchener Verlag, 1988, 1995, 1999), henceforth 'Schmidt' , 417-421.

[61] Schmidt, 417.

[62] Thus for example, Houtman gives an overall discussion of 9:13-35 (II 81-85) followed by comments on the individual words and phrases, but he does not focus on the speech as a whole.

that he does, rather than in another way.[63] Thus for an examination of YHWH's behaviour in the plagues narrative, this passage is of fundamental importance.

Therefore chapter 2 will offer an exegesis of 9:13-19. It will start with consideration of relevant individual words and phrases, before moving on to consider the meaning of the speech as a whole, and end with a consideration of the plague of which it forms the introduction (9:20-35).

Considering whether there may be an overall dynamic to, or message of, the speech does not demand that we understand this speech as the work of a single author, or that we see it (or indeed other passages) as a homogenous whole. It would be quite possible to accept that vv14-16 is a secondary insertion into a pre-existing speech, and yet still ask about the function of the amended and expanded speech. The only assumption made regarding such matters is that the redactor was not simply inserting this passage at random with no regard to its effect on the pre-existing material, but rather he had some reason for inserting the speech *at this point*.[64] This assumption should not be taken as making the claim that this work will set out the intention of this redactor, especially considering the hypothetical nature both of him (or her) and of this insertion. The point is rather that, however the text of YHWH's speech in 9:13-19 came precisely into its present state, vv14-16 now form an integral part of that speech. The question in this study is whether analysis of the speech as it stands can be illuminating. This focus is in no way meant to suggest that this is the only appropriate method of investigating this passage, or, more widely, that the approach to the wider plagues narrative followed in this work should be set up as *the* approach.[65]

---

[63] The fact that, as noted above, this section is thought to be a comment on the whole plagues narrative would underline its theological importance, at least in the form of the narrative as we have it.

[64] Schmidt, 417, 418 notes a couple of brief suggestions from Bruno Baentsch, *Exodus, Leviticus und Numeri*, HKAT I.2 (Göttingen: Vandenhoek und Ruprecht, 1903), henceforth 'Baentsch'.

[65] See Johnstone *Exodus OTG*, 252-254 in relation to a literary or 'final form' approach to the plagues narrative in particular, and the avoidance of polarising or absolutizing methods in general. Nonetheless it remains valid for us to focus on the theological affirmations of the text via a narrative approach to its received form.

On this point, Goldingay's comments in his recent Old Testament Theology are also appropriate to mention. After noting the unusual detail in our story, he comments: 'The particular significance of the stories about signs and marvels in Exodus 4-14 is to provide a narrative discussion of theological issues that do not exclusively relate to the once-for-all sequence of events that takes Israel from Egypt to Sinai. Narrative makes it easier to discuss a complicated issue such as the interrelationship between divine sovereignty and human free will, especially an issue that seems to require us to make a number of apparently conflicting statements – as this one does.' John Goldingay, *Old*

In leaving issues of composition history for others to discuss, the intention is not to denigrate them. Instead, by taking an alternative look at the material, the hope is that different and further illumination can be shed upon both 9:13-19 in particular, and the plagues narrative in general, in respect of the theological issues regarding the portrayal of YHWH.

1.3.2.2 CHAPTER 3: 10:1-2

However, there are more explanations in the text of Exodus than simply 9:13-19. Most importantly, starting the discussion with 9:13-19 will leave the matter of the hardening outstanding. Although we are not restricting ourselves to it, this theme is of vital importance in considering the explanations for YHWH's behaviour. As a result we need to test the appropriateness of the exegesis of 9:13-19 offered in chapter 2 as an explanation for the wider plagues narrative in light of the hardening. Therefore the next chapter will concentrate upon the issue of the hardening, both in general, and in discussion of a specific passage: 10:1-2. There are two main reasons for selecting 10:1-2. First, this speech comes immediately after the explanation and plague in 9:13-35, at the beginning of the eighth plague (10:1ff). Secondly, as well as the mention of the hardening (10:1b) and the repetition of the 'know' theme (10:2b), there is YHWH's use of הִתְעַלַּלְתִּי, which suggests something rather different than the explanation given in 9:13-19. Thus in both placement and content, 10:1-2 provides the sharpest test of an analysis of 9:13-19. Therefore exegesis of this passage will help us to amend, refine and develop the points that will have been made in the previous chapter.

1.3.2.3 CHAPTER 4: THE WIDER PLAGUES NARRATIVE

Chapter 2, in discussion of 9:13-19, will set up a thesis concerning the explanation of YHWH's behaviour in the plagues narrative. The comparison of 10:1-2 in chapter 3 will then refine and expand this thesis. After this it will be appropriate to test the refined thesis more widely in chapter 4, by reading through the plagues narrative in light of the thesis and considering whether it forms a reasonable interpretation of the wider story. At this point we should ask the question of what the wider story comprises. Our focus will be upon the plagues narrative in Ex. 7-11 as the place where YHWH's behaviour raises the most theological issues, and this narrative will be considered in some detail. However in such a widening of focus, it might be noted that the plagues narrative in Ex. 7-11 forms a part of the larger exodus story. Several of the issues that we will have considered (YHWH's demand to 'send my people', the theme of knowledge, the hardening of the heart) are first expressed in Ex. 1-6. Thus, in the final form

---

of the text, the reader would be introduced to them at that point. Therefore a case could be made for starting our detailed read-through at Ex. 1, rather than at Ex. 7. However there are a number of issues in Ex. 1-6, such as the name of God in 3:14-16 that would require significant comment. The passages, such as 3:18-20; 4:21-23; and 5:1-5, that are directly relevant to our discussion of YHWH's acts in the plagues narrative will have been covered in chapters 2 and 3. Therefore, for reasons of space, a full discussion of Ex. 1-6 will not be attempted in this work.

One particular passage deserves mention at this point. The enigmatic encounter between Moses and YHWH in 4:24-26 might be held to raise similar questions to those of YHWH's acts in the plagues narrative. However, while this does raise similar issues, it has proven difficult to apply our approach to this passage due to the comparatively 'stand alone' nature of the episode, and therefore the difficulties of reading it in context (though it may, in certain respects, anticipate the passover narrative). This, combined with the large amount of material already present on this short passage, would make any investigation unprofitable in terms of the space required to do it justice.[66]

Concerning the exodus story as it continues after the plagues narrative, there are two main divisions in the text. The story of the exodus from Egypt as such ends at 15:21 after the deliverance at the Red Sea. This is followed by the brief beginnings of the wilderness wanderings, before Israel arrives at Sinai (15:22-18:27), where the covenant and the events surrounding it take place (Ex. 19-24; 25-31; 32-34; 35-40). As the encounters between YHWH and Pharaoh continue after the plagues narrative, we will consider briefly the story of the final plague and the encounter at the Red Sea in light of our thesis. The details of the Passover will be largely ignored for these purposes. The chapter will end with some very brief comments on 15:22-18:27 in light of the points made on the previous story.

1.3.2.4 CHAPTER 5: 1SAM. 4-7 AND THE WIDER OLD TESTAMENT USE OF THE EXODUS

While we will be concentrating on the plagues narrative, with some comments on the story up to Sinai, in the final form of the text we will need to remember that, as well as being part of the wider exodus story, our passage also forms part of a wider scripture that uses this story. In a study that considers the theological issues raised in the plagues narrative, it is appropriate to recognise this importance and to widen the focus once more

---

[66] This underlines the point made in summarising 9:13-19. Our approach is not one that will solve every problem or deal with every passage. However the plagues narrative, as a continuous episode rather longer than 4:24-26, is more suited to it. Thus there will only be a brief comment on 4:24-26 in chapter 3.

to the impact that the exodus story, and more specifically the plagues narrative, has had on the wider Old Testament.

Much could be said on the importance of the exodus story.[67] It is of paradigmatic importance for the Old Testament, for those faiths that hold it as important, and beyond. Any consideration of use outside of the Old Testament is outside the scope of this work. However even restricting ourselves to the Old Testament leaves a vast amount of material. The tradition of the exodus runs through the Old Testament. Hoffmann has listed over 120 uses of the exodus tradition in the Old Testament.[68] It would be difficult to find any other tradition that is more important than that of the exodus.

Thus an examination of all or even many of the references to the exodus in the Old Testament in any kind of detail is also outside the scope of this work. How then are we to proceed? We could focus on those texts that refer to the plagues narrative rather than simply to 'YHWH bringing you/us/them out of Egypt with a mighty hand...'. Two possible candidates might be Psalms 78 and 105, which refer to some of the individual plagues of Egypt.[69]

Ps. 78, for example, lists the plagues in the context of the later ingratitude of Israel in forgetting what he had done for them (vv40-43 and vv56-58 surround and contextualise the list of plagues in vv44-51, and the exodus and conquest in vv52-55). This continues through their time in the wilderness and at Shiloh, until Jerusalem is chosen.

Ps. 105, by contrast, is a psalm of praise to YHWH, which recounts his mighty deeds on behalf of Israel (vv1-6 set out the context of the psalm). As one might expect in such a context, the emphasis is almost wholly on what YHWH does, rather than what the humans do. Thus the section on the plagues in vv26-38 is preceded by vv23-25 which recounts Israel coming to Egypt and becoming fruitful as in Ex. 1. However, v25 states that it was YHWH who turned the hearts of Egypt (הָפַךְ לִבָּם) to hate his people, and to deal craftily with them. Here even the initial treatment of Israel in Ex. 1-2:23 is ascribed to YHWH, although Ex. 1-2:23 makes no mention of this.

---

[67] Cf. Marc Vervenne 'Current Tendencies and Developments in the Study of the Book of Exodus', in *Studies in the Book of Exodus: Redaction – Reception – Interpretation*, Marc Vervenne ed., BETL LXXVI (Leuven: Leuven University Press, 1996): 21-55, henceforth 'Vervenne *Studies*', 21. More widely Vervenne's chapter gives a useful introduction to recent study of Exodus with bibliography. Also on the importance cf. Eslinger 'Freedom', 43-47.

[68] Y. Hoffmann, *The Doctrine of the Exodus in the Bible* cited in Sarna *EE*, 2. Cf. Plastaras, 6-11.

[69] In keeping with our focus on the final form, questions of the different number and order of plagues therein, and possible theories of historical relationship or dependence in relation to the plagues narrative will not be discussed here.

However we will choose to focus on the story of the capture of the ark of YHWH by the Philistines, found in 1Sam. 4-7.[70] The reasons for the choice of this passage are as follows:

1. It is the only place in the Old Testament outside of Ex. 1-15 to make reference to the hardening of Pharaoh's heart (1Sam. 6:6).[71]

2. Like the exodus story, it is in narrative form, rather than being recapitulation, exhortation or other genre.

3. There is a similarity in situation. Something belonging to YHWH is held by foreigners. YHWH acts, by sending plagues, in order to induce them to return it.

4. The focus in at least part of the story is on YHWH's dealings with non-Israel. In 1Sam. 5:1-6:12 Israel do not appear at all, in a way comparable to the encounters with Pharaoh in the plagues narrative. Such a focus is unusual in the Old Testament. Yet this forms part of a wider story concerning Israel (compare 1Sam. 4:1-22; 6:13-7:17 with Ex. 1-6; 12-15).

5. As with the plagues narrative, the rationale for YHWH's acts is often unclear or difficult to comprehend. Thus it raises the same sort of questions.

These similarities suggest that 1Sam. 4-7 would be a good text for comparison. Therefore in chapter 5 we will examine this story. This is not the first work to compare the exodus story and the ark narrative.[72] However the focus here will be on reading the 1 Samuel story in light of the points that will have been made in chapters 2-4 in order to see whether this story can be illuminated by these points.

1.3.2.5 CHAPTER 6: CONCLUSION

Finally, chapter 6 will conclude the study by returning to the issues raised in this original chapter by briefly considering how the points that have been made might feed into the wider discussion of YHWH, his character and his acts.

---

[70] The exact boundaries of the story will be touched on in chapter 5.

[71] Ps. 105:25 is less clear. It will be compared to 1Sam. 6:6 in chapter 5. This story also has mention of the wider exodus (1Sam. 4:8).

[72] As well as comments in commentaries, see e.g. David Daube, *The Exodus Pattern in the Bible*, ASS II (London: Faber & Faber, 1963), henceforth 'Daube' 73-89; Yair Zakovitch, *"AND YOU SHALL TELL YOUR SON" The Concept of the Exodus in the Bible* (Jerusalem: The Magnes Press, 1991), henceforth 'Zakovitch', 52-53; Edgar Kellenberger, 'Pharaoh's Hardening and the Hardening of the Philistines: A Comparison of Ex. 4-14 and 1Sam. 4-6.' An unpublished English transcript of a paper presented at the meeting of the International SBL, Cambridge, 21 July 2003, henceforth 'Kellenberger *Hardening*', 1-3.

1.4 A Couple of General Issues

Before starting our investigation, it is appropriate at this point to say a little more on a couple of issues concerning our method of approaching the text. First, we have largely eschewed conventional historical critical approaches to the text, and perhaps this requires some further comment. Secondly, this dissertation will be addressing issues of theological significance in this text. Such theological issues arise, at least in part, from the fact that this text is read as part of Scripture. Therefore it is appropriate to consider how the text may be approached responsibly in light of this fact.

1.4.1 Matters 'Behind the Text'

Our interest in the final form of the text and how it is read, will exclude four main areas of study.

As noted in the section on 9:13-19 above, issues of composition, whether concerning source-, form- or redaction-criticism will not be investigated in detail. These are issues that, understandably, have received a great deal of interest and discussion over the last couple of centuries. Such discussion forms a reasonable part of many influential commentaries on the text, and the subject of many monographs.[73] However, the issues that we have raised appear in the final form of the text, which is understood as Scripture. Even if their origin could be explained in terms of putative earlier sources and the redaction thereof, this would still leave the reader with the final text.

This, of course, raises the question: 'which text?' Speaking simply of 'final form' or 'final text' might suggest that there is only one version of the story. However there are four main ancient textual traditions or versions of the Exodus narrative: the Hebrew Masoretic Text (MT); Samaritan Pentateuch (Sam Pent); fragmentary Exodus scrolls from the fourth cave at Qumran (4Q11, 4Q13-22); and the Greek Septuagint (LXX).[74] If this were a work concerned largely with issues of the relationship of the different versions to each other, or the historical development of the Hebrew text (whether searching for an *Urtext*, or discussing textual traditions,

---

[73] For example, one influential work is that of Pedersen (Johannes Pedersen, 'Passahfest und Passahlegende.' *ZAW* 52 (1934): 161-175), whose argument is that the plagues narrative grew out of the Passover. For a criticism of this, see McCarthy 'Plagues', esp. 153ff.

[74] It is slightly simplistic to speak of '*the* MT', '*the* LXX' etc, which might imply that there is only one text of each. More specifically, in this dissertation mention of the MT; LXX; Sam Pent and the Qumran exodus texts should be understood as referring to the Leningrad Codex B19^A as set out in BHS; Rahlfs' edition of the Septuagint; Von Gall's edition of the Samaritan Pentateuch; and the Qumran material as set out in DJD IX and XII respectively (excepting any occasions where other scholars' comments on the ancient versions are cited).

recensions and so forth), then a great deal more work would need to be done on the differences between these versions.[75]

However, this dissertation, concerned as it is with the theological problems that have arisen from the text as read, is interested primarily in the received text, rather than raising questions of historical development. Therefore it takes as its starting point the MT and seeks to understand the narrative as set out therein. However this should not be taken as a dismissal of the other ancient versions. At one stage all of the four ancient versions were the 'received text' of at least one community, and all but the Qumran material continue so to be.[76] Therefore this study will take its lead from the approach of BHS and other editions which are based upon one text but bring in variants in the critical apparatus.[77] In keeping with the focus of this work, the versions will be mentioned or discussed primarily insofar as specific variants or interpretations therein are of theological significance for our thesis.[78]

A second area of study on the plagues is the attempt to 'explain' the events in terms of natural phenomena. Some of these even attempt to link the phenomena, or some of them, in a causal chain. The most commonly

---

[75] For further information on the different versions, and scholarship thereon, see e.g. Emanuel Tov, *Textual Criticism of the Hebrew Bible* (Minneapolis: Fortress Press, 1992), henceforth 'Tov'; and S. Talmon 'Textual Criticism: The Ancient Versions', in *Text in Context:* Essays by Members of the Society of Old Testament Study, ed. A. D. H. Mayes (Oxford: Oxford University Press, 2000): 141-170.

More specifically on the LXX of Exodus, see John William Wevers, *Notes on the Greek Text of Exodus*, SBLSCS 30 (Atlanta: Scholars Press, 1990), henceforth 'Wevers'.

For more detailed work on 4QpaleoExod[m] (4Q22) see Judith E. Sanderson, *An Exodus Scroll from Qumran: 4QpaleoExod[m] and the Samaritan Tradition*, HSS 30 (Atlanta: Scholars Press, 1986), henceforth 'Sanderson'. Put crudely, 4QpaleoExod[m] is regarded as being closest to the Samaritan tradition albeit retaining flexibility (Sanderson, chp4; Tov, 97). The other text that contains large parts of the plagues narrative is 4QExod[c] (4Q14).

[76] One could also note that any earlier version of the narrative might well have been the received or 'canonical' version of its community (Johnstone *Exodus OTG, 241*).

[77] A recent discussion of the merits of the 'diplomatic' as against the 'eclectic' approach was given in H. G. M. Williamson, 'Do we still need commentaries?' Presidential paper to the winter meeting of the Society of Old Testament Study, 5-7 Jan 2004.

[78] The main differences that Sam Pent and 4Q22 have to the MT are nine expansions, repeating commands that YHWH has given to Moses to show that they have been carried out. See Sanderson, 196-207, for detailed discussion of these cases. She also provides a complete list of variants between the versions where 4Q22 is extant in her Appendix 2 (325-343). Although my decision to base this work upon the MT was taken for different reasons, it is interesting to note her conclusion that, in a comparison of the variants, 'the statistics have shown that for the book of Exodus [the MT] is by far the best text available to us' (241).

cited example is Greta Hort's article "The Plagues of Egypt".[79] However, there are a number of other examples, scholarly and popular, in article, book and even televisual form.[80]

While this study is focussed upon the plagues narrative, it will not focus on the exact nature of the plagues themselves, but rather upon the dialogue concerning the plagues, generally between YHWH (through Moses) and Pharaoh.

The concern of our study is with why YHWH does what he does, rather than with exactly how he does it. Thus detailed study of the actual plagues would not be particularly relevant to this discussion. Moreover, the text itself does not appear to be particularly interested in the causal links.[81] One point on which the text is clear is that it is YHWH who brings the plagues.[82] Thus Propp dismisses attempts to find rationalistic explanations as intrinsically inconsistent:

> To believe that the Bible faithfully records a concatenation of improbable events, as interpreted by a prescientific society, demands a perverse fundamentalism that blindly accepts the antiquity and accuracy of biblical tradition while denying its theory of supernatural intervention.[83]

Thirdly, in continuity with the previous point, this work will not attempt to address questions of historicity. There is a perennial interest in the exact place of the crossing of the 'Red Sea', the date of the exodus (together with discussions of whether it happened at all) and so forth. However while one may be able to argue that the facts make such a place or such a time more or less likely, it is most unlikely that one could prove, on the evidence that we have, either that the events happened exactly as written, or that they have no basis in history whatsoever. Moreover even if one were to settle this debate one way or the other, this would not resolve the issues of what kind of God this is. Thus, if the exodus happened, one could still raise serious questions about this God from the events.[84] If it did not happen, there is still the text, revered and influential, which will continue to influence people's views of this God. Warrior sums up the issue well:

---

[79] Greta Hort, 'The Plagues of Egypt', *ZAW* 69 (1957): 84-103; 70 (1958): 48-59.

[80] Childs, 167-68 notes earlier attempts, starting with Eichhorn in 1818. Most recently see Colin J. Humphreys, *The Miracles of Egypt. A Scientist's Discovery of the Extraordinary Natural Causes of the Biblical Stories* (London: Continuum, 2003), especially section 3.

[81] The only explicit link between separate individual plagues is found at 10:5, 15. However even this compares the effects of the plagues rather than their causes.

[82] Sarna *Exodus EE*, 75.

[83] Propp, 347-48.

[84] On this see John Goldingay, '"That you may know that Yahweh is God": A Study in the relationship between theology and historical truth in the Old Testament', *TynBul* 23 (1972): 58-93, esp. 58.

People who read the narratives read them as they are, not as scholars and experts would *like* them to be read and interpreted. History is no longer with us. The narrative remains.[85]

Finally, there is still the issue of the world in which the text is set. However, this dissertation will not spend a large amount of time discussing other ancient Near Eastern concepts of deity. This is partly because it is a huge area, studied by others, and I am no expert in this area. The main reason, however, is that it is very difficult to find any close parallels to the story of the exodus in Near Eastern culture. As we will be examining the text in detail, we would need something reasonably close to it in order to be able to compare and contrast properly. However Dt. 4:34 appears to have a point:

'Or has any god tried to come and take for himself a people from the midst of a(nother) people with tests, with signs and with wonders, with battle, with a mighty hand and with an outstretched arm, with great terrors, like all the things that YHWH your God has done for you in Egypt before your eyes?'

This is not to say that there are no examples of groups leaving one country for another.[86] However there are few that explicitly ascribe this to divine action. Initial research suggests three possible comparisons.[87] First there is a passage in the second plague prayer of the Great King Mursili II of Hatti. As part of a confession of guilt for various individual and corporate offences in an attempt to end a plague Mursili explains that he found two tablets:

The second tablet dealt with (the town of) Kuruštama – how the Storm-god of Hatti took the men of Kuruštama to Egyptian territory, and how the Storm-god of Hatti made a treaty concerning them with the Hittites.[88]

The prayer continues by speaking of the Hittites breaking the treaty, but no more is spoken of the movement of the men of Kuruštama. We are given no details as to the circumstances of the move; its methods, or the motivations of the Hittite Storm-god.

---

[85] Robert Allen Warrior, 'Canaanites, Cowboys and Indians: Deliverance, Conquest and Liberation Theology Today', in *The Postmodern Bible Reader*, David Jobling, Tina Pippin, and Ronald Schliefer eds. (Oxford: Blackwell Publishers, 2001): 188-194 , 191.

[86] Kitchen lists examples of people 'voting with their feet' by leaving intolerable conditions in K. A. Kitchen, *On the Reliability of the Old Testament* (Grand Rapids: Eerdmans, 2003), 254.

[87] In conversation with Professor Kitchen at a Society for Old Testament Study meeting I raised this point. Whilst pointing to the above examples of people leaving, he did not suggest any that were ascribed to divinity other than those which I now specify in my main text. This was also the case for other ancient Near Eastern experts with whom I spoke briefly.

[88] 'Plague Prayers of Muršili II' translated by Gary Beckman (*COS*, 1.60: 156-160), 158.

Moving further afield, there is Virgil's Aeneid, where the remnants of the free Trojan people are led by Aeneas to found Lavinium in Italy, via Carthage. This is the removal of a people (or the remains thereof) from one land to found another, which becomes a foundation myth for the nation of Rome. There are also comments on the intent of the gods in respect of this removal. However, there are a number of differences. The comments about the gods' actions are mostly in relation to the journey from Troy (cf. Aeneid I:8–297). Thus it would make a better comparison with the wilderness wanderings, and the forty year ruling in Num. 14 than with the exodus proper. The equivalent for our purposes would be Book II of the Aeneid, whose account of the fall of Troy does not contain the requisite theological reflection. One could in any case question the proximity of the Aeneid to the exodus story in historical, geographical or cultural terms.

Within the Old Testament there is the enigmatic phrase in Amos 9:7:

> 'Are you not like the sons of Cush to me, sons of Israel?' oracle of YHWH. 'Did I not bring up the Israelites from the land of Egypt, the Philistines from Caphtor and the Arameans from Kir?'

As with the Mursili passage, this saying is so short that it is difficult to come to any firm conclusions on it.[89] Excepting this one phrase, there is nothing really comparable within the Old Testament itself. There are instances of YHWH dealing with a foreign ruler through an Israelite (Joseph and Pharaoh in Gen. 41-50; Daniel, his friends and the kings Nebuchadnezzar, Belshazzar and Darius), as well as YHWH acting for his people. However none of these provide a good comparison with the specific events here. Therefore, while we will bring in other OT stories and, rarely, other Near Eastern stories, our main concentration will be on the story of Exodus itself, and how it is to be understood.

Summary of general approach

In light of the above, our approach may be summarised by considering the relevance of the following questions to our study of the plagues narrative:

- *'When?'/'Where?'* These questions, concerning matters of historical detail either of the narrative itself or the text containing it, will not be covered in this work.
- *'How?'/'What?'* These questions will be covered to an extent. Our interest is in how YHWH interacts with people, and what he does. However we will not be looking into the specific details of the plagues, except inasmuch as the text describes them as a whole, or in relation to each other.

---

[89] This is even without raising questions of what Amos is doing with this text, and whether one could use this as a basis for reconstructing a general Israelite belief in a divine exodus for others.

- *'Who?'/'Why?'* These are the key questions that we will be considering: why YHWH does what he does in the way that he does, and what this says about who he is. This will be based upon an analysis of the 'explanations' in the text, giving due attention to their place in the narrative, their speaker, addressee, context and purpose (if such can be determined).

1.4.2 Approaching a Problematic Scriptural Text

How does one responsibly approach a text which forms part of the scriptural portrayal of the God that one worships, yet is 'problematic' in some way for that portrayal? The purpose of this work is to take a closer look at the text, and to examine as best it can how this God is portrayed, and what implications this may have for one reading it, especially in the context of Christian theology.[90] However, even a close reading may find that which it seeks, especially if one is familiar with the text, or thinks one is. This may be the case especially if one holds strong views about the God portrayed in the story, as may well be the case if one follows, trusts and worships him.[91] Alternatively this may lead one to reject certain interpretations as inappropriate. An example of this issue can be seen in certain treatments of the issue of the 'hardening'. Thus some treatments of the hardening appear to arise from the underlying conviction that YHWH could not act in a manner as arbitrary, capricious or unfair as the text appears to portray him as behaving. Indeed this conviction, or at least the problem, is openly stated in some cases: 'the statement that God hardened Pharaoh's heart cannot be taken literally since it would contradict some essential presuppositions about God...'.[92] However one must tread carefully in this area. We are approaching this passage, at least in part, as a problem for those who follow this God. Thus it would not be appropriate to seek to dismiss attempts to read the text as part of a wider whole with an overall perception of YHWH. However the text, and the issues that it raises, require us to approach it in a more open manner.[93]

---

[90] This does not mean that the questions raised are relevant only to Christians reading the text, and it would be gratifying if it were to be of use to a wider audience. However, my own position is that of a Christian approaching the text, and it is this background that has contributed both to the questions raised, and to the formulation of the answers.

[91] Those who are opposed to this God may well be coloured by their pre-understandings, albeit in rather different ways.

[92] Jože Krašovec *Reward, Punishment and Forgiveness – The Thinking and Beliefs of Ancient Israel in the Light of Greek and Modern Views*, VTSup LXXVIII (Leiden: Brill, 1999), henceforth 'Krašovec *Reward*', 80. Cf. Jacob *Exodus*, 246; Cassuto, 55; Driver *Exodus*, 53-54.

[93] There have been attempts that try to understand the story in relation to the wider perception of God, without necessarily rejecting the hardening. Thus Göran Larrson,

To put it another way, if Exodus is read as a part of Scripture, certain preconceptions about God may be imported into the text, which may sit uneasily with the story, and make it difficult to read. One answer to 'if God is X, then why does he do Y?' may be the question 'Is God X?' [94] This may be felt to be inappropriate from a position of faith. However if one holds one's faith as based, at least in part, upon the Bible, then one needs to take its portrayals seriously. This, of course, raises very large issues that are beyond the scope of this work. The point here is to stop any premature closure on such problems by saying 'this *cannot* be the case' and proceeding from this assumption, or by appeal to such concepts as belief, doctrine, orthodoxy or equivalent.

This raises questions about the interaction of theology and objectivity. It is inevitable that one's beliefs will have an effect on one's study. The concern is to ensure that they do not control it, by making certain avenues completely impossible to follow.

Bound for Freedom: The Book of Exodus in Jewish and Christian Traditions (Peabody: Hendrickson, 1999), henceforth 'Larrson', 104, notes the Mekhilta on the Red Sea which has YHWH not celebrating the death of 'his children' the Egyptians. However such understandings still leave the question of what is contained within the text, and whether such attempts can be accepted.

[94] One way to challenge any preconceptions would be to examine readings of the text which give a picture of YHWH that is less comfortably assimilated into a faith context, and consider the validity or otherwise of their interpretations. Two such different pictures of YHWH are given, albeit briefly, in H. W. F. Saggs, *The Encounter with the Divine in Mesopotamia and Israel* (London: The Athlone Press, University of London, 1978), 35-38 and Norma Rosen, *Biblical Women Unbound: Counter-tales* (Philadelphia: Jewish Publication Society, 1996), 159.

Saggs' general concern is to trace out ways in which the Israelites and the Mesopotamians viewed God or the gods, to see how different Israelite religion really was. This comparison is in the light of a dichotomy that he detected in study of the ANE, where Old Testament or Israelite religion were regarded as 'truth', in comparison to other Near Eastern religions which were seen as merely 'data'.

A similar approach to that taken by Saggs can be found in Bertil Albrektson, *History and the Gods – An Essay on the Idea of Historical Events as Divine Manifestations in the Ancient Near East and Israel*, CB 1 (Lund: CWK Gleerup, 1967). For Egyptian equivalents, albeit not directly compared with Israel, see Erik Hornung, *Conceptions of God in Ancient Egypt: The One and the Many* trans. John Baines (New York: Cornell University Press, 1982), henceforth 'Hornung'.

Rosen's concern is the treatment, or lack of it, of women and women's voices within the text or the midrash of the Old Testament. Therefore she set out to write some new midrashim to set out the voices of the Matriarchs, to bring such narratives closer to our interests, and to ask questions that have lain dormant and unnoticed or which 'should not be asked'. However in one particular midrash: 'Bitiah: Memoir of a Tyrant's Daughter (as interviewed in the Jewish Press)', she considers the actions of YHWH in the plagues narrative.

One approach that I find appealing is that of Ellen Davis in her 'bias' that 'no biblical text may be safely repudiated as a potential source of edification for the church.'[95] The importance of the text compels us to recognise and take seriously the difficulties in the text, as part of the text that should not be ignored. However as the problems are problems precisely *inasmuch as* they form part of a religiously authoritative text, this compels us to keep working on the text, rather than rejecting it as judged wanting by our own standards, standards which may themselves need to be scrutinised in their turn. In his discussion of the sacrifice of Isaac in Gen. 22, another 'difficult' yet traditionally authoritative text, Moberly makes a number of insightful comments on the need of the Christian theologian to interact with, and yet not be dominated by, ethical difficulties or 'hermeneutics of suspicion'.[96]

Thus in summary, this story may be a text that was written a long time ago, containing elements which may be problematic for many modern readers. However, it is a story that is still regarded as, in some sense, true by many people. This creates the problems, and it also creates the need to work with the text.

---

[95] Ellen F. Davis, "Critical Traditioning", in *The Art of Reading Scripture*, eds. Ellen F Davis and Richard B. Hays (Grand Rapids: Eerdmans, 2003): 163-180, 164. This work will not attempt to find 'critical traditioning' at work in the exodus text, but it is in agreement with her principles of critical traditioning under the heading of 'critical charity' (177-80). For an alternative comment on faith and problems, see Elie Weisel, 'The Crisis of Hope', in *Die Hebräische Bibel und ihre zweifache Nachgeschichte: Festschrift für Rolf Rendtorff zum 65. Geburtstag,* hrsg. von Erhard Blum, Christian Macholz und Ekkehard W. Stegemann (Neukirchen-Vluyn: Neukirchener Verlag, 1990): 717-724.

[96] R.W.L. Moberly, *The Bible, Theology and Faith – A study of Abraham and Jesus*, CSCD (Cambridge: Cambridge University Press, 2000), henceforth 'Moberly *BTF*'. On these two issues see 127ff and the chapter 'Genesis 22 and the hermeneutics of suspicion' respectively.

Chapter 2

Exodus 9:13-19 – A Key Explanation

2.1 Introduction

9:13-19 stands at the beginning of the seventh plague encounter, the plague of hail (9:13-35). In these verses YHWH gives his spokesman Moses a message for Pharaoh.

This chapter will offer an exegesis of YHWH's speech in 9:13-19 and the rationale that it contains for his actions. It starts with the demand to Pharaoh: 'שַׁלַּח אֶת־עַמִּי וְיַעַבְדֻנִי' (v13), which is repeated in all plagues that commence with dialogue.[1] Following this a reason for the plague is given: '...בַּעֲבוּר תֵּדַע כִּי' (v14). Other plagues have similar reasons given after the initial demand. As these two verses pick up repeated themes, we will consider these in more detail. Where many of YHWH's messages then move to a description of the plague to come, this message, which is longer than others, contains a section in vv15-17 that sets out further rationale for YHWH's acts. The issues in vv15-17, together with the offer of mitigation in v19, are distinctive to this plague and will be closely examined.

Having considered the reasonability of the interpretations of the individual phrases, we will then offer an interpretation of the speech as a single consistent unit. Finally we will examine the context of the speech by reading through the plague encounter which it introduces. The individual meaning of words and phrases and the meaning of the whole are sometimes mutually dependent. Therefore initially certain alternative interpretative possibilities will be left unresolved until the picture has built up to a point where the best interpretation can be selected.

2.2 Individual Words and Phrases

2.2.1 9:13

וַיֹּאמֶר יְהוָה אֶל־מֹשֶׁה הַשְׁכֵּם בַּבֹּקֶר וְהִתְיַצֵּב לִפְנֵי פַרְעֹה וְאָמַרְתָּ אֵלָיו
כֹּה־אָמַר יְהוָה אֱלֹהֵי הָעִבְרִים שַׁלַּח אֶת־עַמִּי וְיַעַבְדֻנִי:

---

[1] Of the ten plagues the third, sixth and ninth have no dialogue before the plague. This will be discussed in chapter 4.

> YHWH said to Moses 'Rise early in the morning, and take your stand before Pharaoh, and say to him: "Thus says YHWH, the god of the Hebrews: 'Send my people that they may serve me!'"'

The speech starts with YHWH giving Moses his instructions and the message that he is to give to Pharaoh. Moses, as YHWH's spokesman, is to start with the messenger formula: 'thus says YHWH' (כֹּה־אָמַר יְהוָה). These are not his words, but YHWH's. YHWH's words to Pharaoh then begin with a stark demand: 'send my people that they may serve me!'

2.2.1.1 שַׁלַּח אֶת־עַמִּי וְיַעַבְדֻנִי – INDIVIDUAL WORDS

During the plagues narrative YHWH makes a single, repeated demand to Pharaoh. The phrase 'send my people that they may serve me' stands at the beginning of every plague that is introduced with a message from YHWH. The wording used is almost identical in every case. This form (including or excluding the אֵת) is used in the second plague (7:26 [8:1]); fourth plague (8:16 [20]); fifth plague (9:1); seventh plague (9:13); and eighth plague (10:3). The first plague (7:16) has the same wording followed by 'in the wilderness'.

As such, this phrase will set the context for the dialogue that follows it. Therefore we need to consider exactly what it is that YHWH is demanding of Pharaoh. What exactly does it mean for Pharaoh to 'send my people', and what are the implications of them 'serving' YHWH?

The demand is often translated 'let my people go' or 'release my people' and understood as a call for the liberation of Israel. Thus the exodus story is later remembered as YHWH bringing Israel out of Egypt, to serve him at Mt Sinai and beyond.

However, we need to consider the second half of the demand ('that they may serve me'), in making sense of it. The original requests to Pharaoh (3:18; 5:1, 3) use the language of festival and sacrifice (זָבַח, חָגַג) in expressing the reason for the request, and it is possible to understand עָבַד in such a cultic sense. One might reasonably assume that these early requests are the basis for understanding the later requests. In this case all that is being demanded is a furlough from work to hold a religious festival in the desert. The presumption in the request is that afterwards they would return to their service of Pharaoh. Whether Israel or YHWH actually had any intention of return is a moot point if this is the case.

However, while this might fit well in context, consideration of the actual words used raises some questions over this understanding. Therefore we will examine each word separately and then consider the phrase as a whole.[2]

---

[2] Discussion of this issue in the commentaries is found at different points, often at 3:18 or 5:3. Their comments on the issue generally will be picked up below. Some translations offered are: Noth 'Let my people go that they may hold a feast to me in the

שָׁלַח 'Send'

The verb used in the demand is the Pi'el imperative of שָׁלַח. This form has the general meaning of dismiss/send away.[3] This can have a positive sense (such as sending away one's guests),[4] or a negative sense (such as banishment, sending away in shame etc).[5] More specifically, it can have the sense of release of slaves;[6] birds;[7] captives;[8] or wives (in divorce);[9] the giving away of daughters;[10] giving people over to sin;[11] letting someone go;[12] and dispersing.[13] Jacob comments on the intensive form here:

> Usually it indicates: "send away, release, dismiss or discharge." If a person was dismissed through the use of this verb, then he ceased to be within the power or sphere of influence of the individual who had dismissed him.[14]

This sense of absolute dismissal does not hold for all uses of Pi'el שָׁלַח. It is used of sending people out to do a job for the sender, where one might assume that they would return.[15] However, this is a rare sense for the Pi'el; although it is regularly found in the Qal.[16]

---

wilderness' (on 5:1, p48 – after this changes from 'hold feast' to 'serve'); Propp (8, 10f) 'release my people that they may celebrate to me' (5:1, 8)/ 'serve me' (7:16); Childs (124) 'let my people go that they may serve me'; Houtman (II 85) 'let my people go so that they may worship me'.

[3] Gen. 12:20; 19:29; Jos. 22:6, 7; 24:28; Jdg. 2:6; 3:18; 7:8; 1Sam. 10:25; 13:2; 1Kgs. 8:66; 2Kgs. 5:24; 6:23; 1Chr. 12:20; Job 14:20. Cf. M Delcor/E. Jenni 'שׁלח' *TLOT* 3, 1330-1334, 1332.

[4] Gen. 18:16; 24:54, 56, 59; 26:29, 31; 30:25; 31:27.

[5] Gen. 3:23; 21:14; 26:27; 31:42; 2Sam. 10:4; 13:16; 1Kgs. 9:7; Jer. 9:15 [16]; 15:1. Note the comparison of Gen. 26:27 with v29 and of 31:27 with v42 where one event is referred to positively and negatively, all using the same verb form.

[6] Ex. 21:26-27; Dt. 15:12-13, 18; 21:14; 22:7. Note that in Jer. 34:9-16, once a slave has been released, one cannot make them one's slave again.

[7] Lev. 14:7, 53.

[8] Is. 45:13; 58:6; Jer. 50:33; Zech. 9:11.

[9] Dt. 22:19, 29; 24:1-4; Is. 50:1; Jer. 3:1, 8; Mal. 2:16.

[10] Jdg. 12:9.

[11] Job 8:4; Ps. 81:13.

[12] Gen. 32:27; 1Sam. 19:17; 20:5, 13, 22; 24:20; 1Kgs. 11:21-22; 20:34, 42; Job 39:5; Jer. 40:1, 5.

[13] Jdg. 19:29; 1Sam. 11:7.

[14] Jacob *Exodus*, 115. He also gives a list of uses (115-116).

[15] Gen. 19:13; 1Sam. 31:9; 2Sam. 18:2. Strictly speaking, this it can only be an assumption, as there is no explicit mention of an expected return. Elsewhere Noah sends out birds from the ark (Gen. 8:7, 8, 10) which did return, but there is no indication that he expected them to return. When the dove does not return (8:12), this shows that the waters have receded.

[16] E.g. Gen. 37:13-14; 42:16; Ex. 2:5; 3:10-15; 9:7; Num. 13:2-3; 22:5; 1Sam. 5:11 (note the different uses of Pi'el and Qal שָׁלַח here); etc.

Eccl. 11:1 speaks of sending one's bread upon the waters as it will be found after many days. This is probably the strongest sense of Pi'el שָׁלַח not referring to removal from one's power. However this certainty may be overstated. Murphy suggests three explanations for the verse, and the most likely two involve either understanding the imperfect of מָצָא with a modal nuance ('you *may* find it'), or seeing the action as nonsensical (bread dissolves in water), which nevertheless will have an unexpected result.[17] In both cases return is not assumed.

Thus, if the absence intended in YHWH's words is only temporary, Pi'el שָׁלַח is an odd form to use. In addition, the imperatival form appears to be far blunter than the previously more respectful cohortative 'let us go' (נֵלְכָה 3:18; 5:3), which one might expect to be continued for a temporary absence; and there is no נָא or בִּי to soften it (cf. 4:13). The initial requests seem to have become demands.[18]

Moreover, although Pi'el שָׁלַח is used to represent the same act as נֵלְכָה, it is also paired with the far more extreme יְגָרֵשׁ (6:1; cf. 11:1), which has a permanent ring to it. Finally in 9:2 לְשַׁלֵּחַ is contrasted with מַחֲזִיק in the sense of 'grasping hold of' or 'holding onto' which suggests a stronger meaning.

עַמִּי 'my people'

Israel do not appear in the plagues narrative except as the object of the encounters between YHWH and Pharaoh, or as those exempted from certain plagues. Their identity in this passage is as 'my people', the people of YHWH. It is inasmuch as they are 'my people' that YHWH demands that Pharaoh 'send' them.

'My people' could mean simply that he is the god of this particular group. Therefore, as his worshippers, they are the ones that should be worshipping him in the wilderness. It would not be unusual for foreign workers to bring their own gods, and Egypt itself had a number of gods within its pantheon. Once again, this idea agrees with the initial message sent to Pharaoh: 'the god of the Hebrews' (3:18; 5:3 cf. 'god of (y)our father(s)' 3:6, 13).

However, once again another meaning suggests itself. In a number of the plagues, YHWH follows the initial demand with a warning along the lines of 'if you do not send my people then I will send/bring a plague upon your people/strike your people' (e.g. 4:22-23; 7:27-29 [8:2-4]; 8:17-19 [21-23]; 9:2-3; 10:4-6). This creates a contrast between Egypt as Pharaoh's people, and Israel as YHWH's people. Pharaoh's actions with regard to YHWH's people are linked to YHWH's actions with regard to Pharaoh's people.

---

[17] Roland Murphy, *Ecclesiastes*, WBC 23a (Dallas: Word, 1998), 106-107.

[18] One could speculate as to whether the tradition might have changed an original Qal to a Pi'el, but all we have now is the final form.

Therefore this demand may be making a more substantial claim. In the same way that Egypt are Pharaoh's people, thus Israel are YHWH's people. If YHWH occupies for Israel the place that Pharaoh occupies for Egypt, then Pharaoh cannot also occupy that position for Israel. Put simply, if Israel are YHWH's people, then they cannot also be Pharaoh's people. Thus, according to this understanding YHWH is making a claim about the ownership of this particular people. 'My people' carries the correlative '(and therefore not your people)'.[19]

וְיַעַבְדֻנִי 'and/that they will/may serve me'

The original request to Pharaoh is for a three day journey so that they may sacrifice (זָבַח) to YHWH (3:18; 5:3) or hold a festival (חָגַג) to him (5:1).[20] After this the purpose is expressed by עָבַד, although language of sacrifice continues from both Moses and Pharaoh (8:4 [8]; 21-25 [25-29]; 10:9, 26).

> The cultic reference is secured by the parallel words used in similar contexts, including *ḥgg*, "celebrate a festival" (5:1; cf. 10:9), and *zābaḥ*, "to sacrifice" (3:18; 5:3,8; 8:4,21,22,23,24,25 [8,25,26,27,28,29]).[21]

Thus we could simply conclude that this is the meaning of the text, and that YHWH is asking for nothing more than a religious ceremony. However, once again, there are some points that may suggest another understanding.

עָבַד and the equivalent noun עֲבֹדָה have already been used in Exodus to depict the condition of the Israelites in Egypt. The previous Pharaoh enslaved them with hard labour (1:13-14). 1:14 is particularly emphatic, with its four-fold use:

וַיְמָרֲרוּ אֶת־חַיֵּיהֶם בַּעֲבֹדָה קָשָׁה בְּחֹמֶר וּבִלְבֵנִים וּבְכָל־עֲבֹדָה בַּשָּׂדֶה
אֵת כָּל־עֲבֹדָתָם אֲשֶׁר־עָבְדוּ בָהֶם בְּפָרֶךְ

---

[19] As there is a dearth of corresponding messages from YHWH to foreign rulers concerning Israel, it is difficult to conclude on this matter. As with שָׁלַח, both meanings are possible.

[20] The assumption here is that the וְ introduces a final clause. Pharaoh is asked to 'send' the people for a specific purpose, whether this is a festival or a change of overlord. If this were to be understood as simply a result 'send my people and they will serve me', it might favour the libertarian understanding of the demand: Pharaoh simply has to release them. However it would raise questions as to why the וְיַעַבְדֻנִי is mentioned to Pharaoh, as this would be irrelevant to him. In the end the function of the וְ would not make a vast difference.

[21] Ringgren, 'עָבַד', *TDOT* X, 385. He also notes Ezek. 20:40; Is. 19:21; Zeph. 3:9-10; Ps. 22:31 [30]; 100:2; 2Chr. 35:3 as similar examples. Westermann, 'עבד', *TLOT* 2, 819-32, sees the use of עָבַד as referring to a one-time 'service of God' as occurring in Ex. 3-12 and 2Sam. 15:8 (829).

As a result, Israel cry out to YHWH from out of their bondage (2:23 מִן־הָעֲבֹדָה) and YHWH says that he has heard the groans of Israel enslaved by Egypt (6:5 מַעֲבִדִים אֹתָם), and has come to deliver them from it (6:6 מֵעֲבֹדָתָם). However Israel would not listen to this message from Moses because of their harsh work (6:9 וּמֵעֲבֹדָה קָשָׁה cf. 1:14). Before this, immediately after the first encounter with Pharaoh, where YHWH's demand is put for the first time (5:1, 3), Pharaoh's response is to increase Israel's work (5:9 תִּכְבַּד הָעֲבֹדָה, cf. 5:11). When they cannot meet the quota with their reduced resources and are beaten, the Israelite foremen go to Pharaoh and ask why he is doing this to his servants (5:15-16 לַעֲבָדֶיךָ), thus defining themselves as Pharaoh's servants.[22]

With all this previous usage connected to Israel's service of Pharaoh, it seems odd that a demand to him for 'simply' a short furlough for a religious ceremony would use עָבַד rather than continuing with חָגַג or זָבַח, which would eliminate any ambiguity. This is especially the case when we remember that both Pharaohs' policies regarding Israel were to increase the workload upon them, to keep Israel under their thumbs and prevent any talk of exodus from Egypt or cessation of work (1:9-11; 5:6-9). Such a man might well understand a request or demand to let Israel 'serve' YHWH as indicating something more than a temporary respite for worship.[23]

The use of עָבַד along these lines is common in the Old Testament. The main sense is that of 'work' (where there is no object), or 'serve' (where there is a personal object). The latter case 'expresses the relationship between an *'ebed* and his or her *'ādôn*, "lord, master". This relationship can take on various forms itself. It can be one of subjugation and dependence, of total claim on a person, or of loyalty. Indeed, all these nuances resonate,

---

[22] The use in 3:12 (תַּעַבְדוּן אֶת־הָאֱלֹהִים עַל הָהָר הַזֶּה) is uncertain. If תַּעַבְדוּן here has the meaning 'serve', we could speculate on how this could be a sign after the event (a criticism raised of seeing תַּעַבְדוּן as the sign here). Inasmuch as Israel are 'serving' YHWH here (more than three days away) they will no longer be 'serving' Pharaoh. However the identity of the sign here is a matter of contention. See e.g. Childs, 56-60; Propp, 203; Keil, 441; Modayil Mani Chacko, *Liberation and Service of God: A Theological Evaluation of Exodus 1-15:21* (Delhi: ISPCK, 2002), henceforth 'Chacko', 104-106; Moshe Greenberg, *Understanding Exodus, The Heritage of Biblical Israel*, Vol II part I of the Melton Research Centre Series (New York: Behrman House, 1969), henceforth 'Greenberg *UE*', 76; Arnold B. Ehrlich, *Randglossen zur Hebräische Bibel: Erster Band Genesis und Exodus* (Hildesheim: Georg Olms Verlagsbuchhandlung, 1968), henceforth 'Ehrlich', 268.

[23] This is supported by Pharaoh's initial response (5:2) where he appears to be asking what right YHWH has to demand this of him. This is different from his practical response (5:4-5) to the more practical request that follows (5:3). This is discussed further in 2.2.2.3 on 9:14.

with one or another feature being more or less emphasized in any given case.'[24]

2.2.1.2 שַׁלַּח אֶת־עַמִּי וְיַעַבְדֻנִי – THE MEANING

We can now put the elements of the demand back together, and examine the two possibilities for understanding the whole phrase.

'Allow my people to go and sacrifice to me'?

First, in light of 3:18, 5:3 and the other uses of sacrificial language, we could understand this as a request for time away from work to hold a religious ceremony. YHWH is saying to Pharaoh 'Allow those who worship me to go into the wilderness to sacrifice to me'. The implication is that Pharaoh is still in control and that they will return afterwards (whether this is true or not). In light of the parallels in the earlier requests, this might be the obvious way to take it.

If this is the case, then YHWH is making a very light demand upon the Pharaoh. However, the reader and Moses are already aware that this is not the ultimate end of YHWH's plans for Israel. YHWH purposes to bring Israel out of Egypt into a good land (3:7-9, 20-22; 6:1-8 etc) and has sent Moses to achieve this. This request appears to be a smoke screen; a way of getting the Pharaoh to allow the people to leave Egypt 'temporarily'. However YHWH, Moses and the reader know that this temporary leave is one from which they will never return.

This raises the question of why YHWH would choose to work in such a way.[25] We could understand it as YHWH choosing to 'work within human frailty'[26] in his dealings with Pharaoh, reflecting the helplessness of Israel's position.[27] Alternatively, or as well, we could note the entertainment in such a story. The evil overlord Pharaoh who refuses to let Israel go is outmanoeuvred and tricked into doing so:

> At the expense of God's dignity – he, after all, does not need to fool Pharaoh – tradition has created an enjoyable story of the Hebrews and their god outwitting a tyrant (cf. 1:15-21). For the sake of drama, even Yahweh briefly becomes an underdog vis-à-vis Pharaoh.[28]

---

[24] Ringgren, 'עָבַד', *TDOT* X, 383. However, as noted above, Ringgren does see the sense in our passage as cultic.

[25] For examples of Jewish commentators' questions concerning this, see Nehama Leibowitz, *New Studies in Shemot (Exodus) Part I*, trans. Aryeh Newman (Jerusalem: Haomanian Press, 1995), 93-95.

[26] Greenberg *UE*, 85. He notes other examples of YHWH similarly working.

[27] Cf. Sarna *EE*, 55.

[28] Propp, 207.

Thus the different encounters and 'negotiations' between Moses and Pharaoh can be seen as two parties trying to outsmart each other.[29]

'Release my people that they may serve me instead'?

The above points notwithstanding, the actual wording of the demand, at least from 7:16 onwards (and including 4:23 and possibly 5:1), suggests that there may be more to the message. The demand begins with a blunt imperative of an intensive verb form that generally has a sense of releasing from one's control. The object of this imperative is 'my people', who are contrasted in some plagues with 'your people'. Combine this imperative of dismissing with the purpose of the demand, which is that Israel 'serve' YHWH (picking up language used by Pharaoh himself concerning Israel's 'service' to him), and this creates a potentially potent cocktail of meaning, with far greater implications than a simple break for worship. Instead it can be seen as a demand for Pharaoh to give up his control of Israel to YHWH: 'Release my people (who aren't your people anyway) from serving you so that they may serve me instead'.[30] This is the expected outcome of the encounters, at least for YHWH and Moses. It is the eventual outcome of the exodus. It is the way it is portrayed elsewhere in the Old Testament as freedom from the house of slaves, of which the hearer or reader would probably be aware.

It is also supported by the contrast in 8:16-19 [20-23] where Israel are first (explicitly) exempted from a plague. YHWH makes the demand upon Pharaoh to 'send my people that they may serve me'. Then he continues 'If you do not send my people, I will send the swarm upon you, your servants and your people...'. There is a parallel in the actions. Pharaoh must *send* (Pi'el) YHWH's *people* who will *serve* him ('his servants'?), if he does not then YHWH will *send* (Hiph'il) the swarm upon Pharaoh, his *servants*, and his *people'*. Furthermore in 14:5 Pharaoh and his officials realise what they have done, and use the very words of YHWH's demand to express their loss of Israel: 'we have sent Israel from our service'.

Moreover, where YHWH speaks to Israel (3:16-17; 6:6-8 etc), there is no mention of serving YHWH as the reason for the exodus, although it is used later as a reason for service (e.g. Ex.20:2). Yet it is a constant refrain to Pharaoh. Thus it could be argued that serving YHWH, in this context, is addressed to Pharaoh, precisely because Israel were serving him. It appears to be a concern of the text that Pharaoh agrees to send the people, thereby agreeing that the people should serve YHWH. Thus, in effect he is to hand over ownership of Israel to YHWH.

If this is the case, then the demand is certainly a demand, rather than a request. The demand, and the dialogue and plagues which follow it, form

---

[29] E.g. 8:21-25 [25-29], 10:8-10. Such passages will be discussed in chp 4.
[30] Cf. Cassuto, 97.

part of an encounter between the two powers of YHWH and Pharaoh with 'whom will Israel serve?' as the question that underlies it. The issue is not simply of the release of Israel for its own sake. Rather Israel are to be released from Pharaoh's service so that they can serve YHWH instead. They will still have a master. The question is which master they will have, and what his service will entail.[31]

> The point of the exodus is not freedom in the sense of self-determination, but *service*, the service of the loving, redeeming and delivering God of Israel, rather than the state and its proud king.[32]

This service to God rather than Pharaoh finds its expression in the covenant at Sinai, which sets out how this service is to operate. 19:4-6 places YHWH's deeds in Egypt at the beginning of his comments to the people.[33] They will be his people and servants, he will be their God, and master (cf. Lev. 25:55). But his mastery will be of a different kind to Pharaoh's, as is indicated in his messages to them (3:8; 6:6-8 etc). Domination and oppression are to be replaced by blessing, but blessing that comes from YHWH's mastery.[34]

---

[31] This contrast is lost in the LXX as it uses λατρεύω to translate עָבַד in YHWH's demands.

[32] Jon D. Levenson, *The Hebrew Bible, the Old Testament, and Historical Criticism: Jews and Christians in Biblical Study* (Louisville, Kentucky: Westminster/John Knox Press, 1993), henceforth 'Levenson *Hebrew Bible*', 144. Cf. the discussion between Levenson, Pixley and John J. Collins on this subject in Alice Ogden Bellis and Joel S. Kaminsky, *Jews, Christians and the Theology of the Hebrew Scriptures*, SBLSymS 8 (Atlanta: SBL, 2000), 215-275.

See also Plastaras, 32 for a discussion of this point: 'By serving Pharaoh, they would remain in servitude, the demeaning servitude which robs man of his dignity. In serving God, they would find true freedom.' Cf. p140.

[33] Cf. Levenson, *Hebrew Bible*, 142-43; Larrson, 34, 127; Michael Walzer, *Exodus and Revolution*, (New York: Basic Books, 1985), 53.

[34] This idea of God's service as positive and normative continues beyond the Old Testament. In the New Testament Christians move from being slaves to sin to being slaves to righteousness or to Christ (e.g. Rom. 6:15-23). For a recent study on this, see John Byron, *Slaves of God and Christ. A Traditio-Historical and Exegetical Examination of Slavery Metaphors in Early Judaism and Pauline Christianity.* (Ph.D. diss. University of Durham, 2002).

Examples of this view in later writers are Augustine's: 'whose service is perfect freedom' and Donne's:'Take mee to you, imprison mee, for I Except you'enthrall mee, never shall be free' (14th Holy Sonnet).

In Jewish tradition, in Abot 6:2 Rabbi Joshua ben Levi comments that no-one is free except the one who studies Torah (cf. Levenson *Hebrew Bible*, 148).

Avoiding Polarisation?

In making this comparison, we are not attempting to create a false polarisation between 'mere worship' and 'absolute service'. Israel's service of YHWH would be predominantly achieved through worship or cultic means.[35] The issue here is what YHWH's demand for 'worship/service' entails for Pharaoh.

Nor is it necessarily a question of two poles of meaning without anything in between. An example of a position that falls between these two is that in Brueggemann's article 'Pharaoh as Vassal: A Study of a Political Metaphor'. He is interested in the intention of Yahweh as a character in the plagues narrative, specifically vis-à-vis Pharaoh, and the wider issue of exodus and liberation. He proposes the thesis:

> In the final form of the text, Yahweh's intrusive action in Egypt concerns the punishment, and finally the nullification, of a recalcitrant vassal who refuses to implement the policies of Yahweh, the overlord.[36]

Using the concept of the 'kingship of God' and more specifically Mendenhall's idea of vengeance as an ultimatum by a sovereign, he notes that YHWH's demands offer no justification or grounds, but simply expect obedience.[37] In light of the previous uses of עָבַד and the contrast in the demand '...serve me', Brueggemann perceives Pharaoh as a vassal who could have retained his own limited authority over the slaves if he had exercised power (for Brueggemann labour practices) over them in a manner congenial to YHWH.[38]

There are some problems with Brueggemann's concept of vassal. He notes the message of release from Egypt in 6:2-8, which is stronger than his understanding of YHWH's demand to Pharaoh, but he sees this passage as

---

[35] Thus Houtman, in disagreeing with Floss that עָבַד is primarily cultic, says:

'It should be remarked that the cult worship of YHWH implies entrusting oneself to him and the recognition of him as Lord. Pharaoh's refusal to let the people go should be seen against that background. Permission for the worship of YHWH entails relinquishing any claim to Israel. 'Service' to Pharaoh can no more be reconciled with 'service' to YHWH than can 'service' to idols (20:5; 23:24, 33).' (I 44).

Cf. Walter Brueggemann, 'Pharaoh as Vassal: A Study of a Political Metaphor', CBQ 57.1 (1995): 27-51, henceforth 'Brueggemann 'Vassal'', 37.

Houtman makes some good points here, showing the importance of worship. However it does raise the opposite question to that posed on עָבַד. If the permission for worship entails Pharaoh relinquishing his authority, why do the initial demands use words such as חָגַג and זָבַח, and make references to a three day journey?

[36] Brueggemann 'Vassal', 31-32.

[37] Brueggemann 'Vassal', 32-33.

[38] Brueggemann 'Vassal', 35. The fact that this is, as Brueggemann notes, a contrast does not make this possible retention immediately obvious. However he does immediately note that such a suggestion is theoretical because of Pharaoh's attitude.

an 'intrusion'. Moreover, although he picks up the use of 'my people', he does not focus on the fact that this is used in speeches to Pharaoh, and often set in contrast to 'your people'. This contrast, together with the sense of 'send' and 'serve' here, makes the idea of a demand that allows Pharaoh to retain control seem odd. We could see Brueggemann as perhaps the most theologically interesting outworking of the 'allow my people to go and worship me' reading, except that he also sees the elements 'let go', 'serve', 'my people' and 'God of the Hebrews' as constituting a 'massive, nonnegotiable contradiction between the rule of Pharaoh and the rule of Yahweh.'[39]

2.2.1.3 שַׁלַּח אֶת־עַמִּי וְיַעֲבְדֻנִי – AN AMBIGUOUS DEMAND?

'Ambiguity'

Therefore we appear to have two possible meanings for this demand. In light of the above discussion, it seems inappropriate to insist upon choosing only one meaning. The language of YHWH's demand could be described as 'diplomatic', as these encounters between YHWH (via Moses) and Pharaoh are, in some sense, exercises in diplomacy. In its narrow scope, it is a demand for a religious festival. However it also has a wider scope, comprising a demand for sovereignty. It is a demand that neither must be understood in the wider scope, nor can be totally restricted to the narrower sense. It contains enough ambiguity that it can be understood in either way, depending upon how one chooses to hear it. Indeed, the fact that there is such an ambiguity in the demand forms an important part of the story. Over the course of the encounters, one is never sure exactly what YHWH and Pharaoh are negotiating, debating and interacting over. By 10:10 Pharaoh is certainly suspicious of Moses' reply, but is the rejection in 5:4 simply an unwillingness to lose valuable work time from the slaves? Thus my suggestion is that this ambiguity in the demand is deliberate. To anticipate later discussion, this sense of ambiguity is a wider theme of the plagues narrative, the perception of which can illuminate other areas as well.

To retain the ambiguity, YHWH's demand will be translated as 'send my people that they may serve me' (referred to in summary as 'send ... serve'). This translation retains the ambiguity, rather than breaking it one way or the other.

'Demand'

In all the discussion over exactly what YHWH is demanding of Pharaoh, we should not forget either the fact that YHWH *is* making a demand of Pharaoh, or the significance of this fact.

---

[39] Brueggemann 'Vassal', 46, cf. points 1 and 2 on p47.

We have noted that the plagues narrative contains some of the most concentrated divine acts in the whole Old Testament. Yet for all this, the story does not depict a God who acts irrespective of the humans involved. The plagues, on the whole, begin with this demand to Pharaoh. YHWH calls upon a human, Pharaoh, to do his will. In most cases, the plague will come if Pharaoh does not obey YHWH's demand.

In the wider traditions of the Old Testament the exodus is remembered as YHWH bringing the people of Israel out of Egypt with a mighty hand and an outstretched arm. Yet in the story he does not just remove his people from Egypt, but demands of Pharaoh that he send them, in order that they may serve YHWH. When Pharaoh refuses time after time, YHWH sends the same demand, time after time.

Thus one can ask why YHWH demanded of Pharaoh that he send the people, rather than simply bringing them out of Egypt irrespective of Pharaoh's position. The powers that he displays, especially towards the end of the story, suggest that he has the power to do this.[40] It seems to be important to YHWH that Pharaoh agrees to send the people.

Moreover, although YHWH is making demands of Pharaoh, Pharaoh is not part of the people of YHWH. Nowhere in the narrative is Pharaoh or Egypt commanded to serve YHWH. They are merely to facilitate YHWH's people in serving YHWH by 'sending' them.[41] Yet even though this is not 'serving YHWH' in the same sense, YHWH is insistent that Pharaoh obeys him.

2.2.1.4 SUMMARY OF 9:13

- The speech to Pharaoh begins with a demand, as do the majority of such speeches. YHWH is concerned that Pharaoh obeys him.
- This demand 'send my people that they may serve me' can be understood in two ways, as requesting leave of absence for a religious festival, or demanding a release of Israel so that they can serve YHWH instead of Pharaoh. It would be inappropriate to insist on breaking the ambiguity.

2.2.2 9:14

כִּי בַּפַּעַם הַזֹּאת אֲנִי שֹׁלֵחַ אֶת־כָּל־מַגֵּפֹתַי אֶל־לִבְּךָ וּבַעֲבָדֶיךָ וּבְעַמֶּךָ
בַּעֲבוּר תֵּדַע כִּי אֵין כָּמֹנִי בְּכָל־הָאָרֶץ׃

'For this time I am about to send all my plagues upon your heart and your servants and your people, so that you will know that there is none like me in all the earth.'

---

[40] This is without even considering what YHWH might have done, which will be picked up at 9:15.

[41] They are also to 'know that…'. We shall discuss the implications of this at 9:14.

After YHWH's demand to Pharaoh, the plague is introduced. Often in YHWH's speeches this is set up as a threat conditional upon Pharaoh's acts: 'Send ... serve me. *If you* do not send them, *behold I* will send...'.[42] However at 9:14 this speech begins to differ from the normal pattern.

2.2.2.1 YHWH'S ACTS

In respect of YHWH's acts there are four main differences from normal:

1. There is no conditionality to YHWH's action. Instead of 'if you do not send, I will send', there is the simple statement 'I am sending'. The plague, it seems, will come irrespective of Pharaoh's actions.
2. The phrase 'I am sending' is preceded by 'this time'. Most of the plague announcements do not have such a reference. This rarity of use suggests that a comparison is being drawn between 'this time' and previous occurrences.
3. Instead of sending one plague, YHWH speaks of sending 'all my plagues'. Taken with the last change this helps to flesh out the comparison.
4. 'All my plagues' will be sent upon Pharaoh's heart; a statement that is not made of any other plagues.

בַּפַּעַם הַזֹּאת אֲנִי שֹׁלֵחַ אֶת־כָּל־מַגֵּפֹתַי (1-3)

In itself the statement 'I am sending' is not difficult to understand, indicating an imminent act of YHWH. The meaning of the reference, and therefore the comparison with other acts, will depend upon the other two phrases 'this time' and 'all my plagues'. There are three possible explanations of the two phrases:

• The reference is to the seventh plague alone. This would make most sense of 'this time'. The problem here is to make sense of the 'all', as it must refer to the plague of hail in some way. One could see it as a reference to the side phenomena of the plague (the thunder, fire etc), as Ibn Ezra and Rashbam suggest.[43] Houtman sees this as fitting the context best, although it is unsatisfactory.[44]

• The reference is to the remaining plagues of hail, locusts, darkness, and probably also the firstborn.[45] 'This time' is more difficult to understand than in the previous case. Moreover some of the plagues have already been sent, therefore 'all' cannot have the literal meaning of 'every one'.

---

[42] This also comes in the speech to Moses in 3:20. Cf. Sarna *Exodus*, 19; Cassuto, 43.

[43] *Ibn Ezra's commentary on the Pentateuch – Exodus*, H. Norman Strickman and Arthur M. Silver (New York: Menorah Publishing Company, 1996), henceforth 'Ibn Ezra', 174; *Rashbam's Commentary on Exodus An Annotated Translation*, ed. and trans. Martin I. Lockshin, BJS 310 (Atlanta: Scholars Press, 1997), henceforth 'Rashbam', 86.

[44] Houtman, II 85.

[45] Cassuto, 115; Jacob *Exodus*, 230.

It may have the sense of 'all remaining plagues'.[46] Alternatively, it may be understood as 'my most severe plagues' in reference to the following plagues.[47] However, either of these seems more satisfactory than 'all' as side phenomena.

- The reference is part of an addition to the plague story (9:14-16), which has the whole of the plagues narrative in view, rather than just the seventh plague, or those following it.[48] In this case, the 'this time' has no real sense at all. However 'all' can be taken literally, as this is an explanation for the entire plagues cycle.[49]

Depending on one's view of the context of 9:14, all of the above are possible. None makes obvious sense of both 'this time' and 'all'. The first makes best sense of the former and least sense of the latter; the third vice versa; and the second makes some sense of both. We will need to wait for the wider context to decide upon the preferred understanding. However, as I am trying to make sense of this speech in context, it makes the third understanding less relevant.

4) אֶל־לִבְּךָ

The phrase 'send X upon the heart' is not used elsewhere. Propp notes Driver's suggestion that the text be emended, and hesitantly follows him, albeit noting that it loses the nuance of Pharaoh's heart suffering in the plagues.[50] Against this suggestion Childs notes that the MT is clear enough.[51] Moreover, this is an unusual explanation, and therefore some variance from normal patterns should be allowed. There is the idiom of setting (שִׁית/שׂוּם) something upon one's heart, which we might understand as 'take to heart'.[52] There is also the idiom of not setting one's heart upon something. Elsewhere in the plagues narrative this is used in respect of YHWH's word, where not setting it on the heart equates to ignoring his sign or his word (7:23; 9:21). Thus, retaining the MT reading, and in keeping with the בַּעֲבוּר תֵּדַע to come, this suggests something along the lines of 'impressing strongly upon'; 'bringing home to'; 'causing to take to heart'.[53] In connection with the 'all my plagues' and 'this time' this reinforces the idea that something different is happening in this encounter.

---

[46] Houtman, II 85; Durham, 128.

[47] Fretheim, 124. This might then have a similar hyperbolic sense to the multiple deaths of 'all' the cattle in the story (see 2.2.7 below).

[48] Schmidt, 417.

[49] Cf. Hyatt, 14.

[50] Propp, 301.

[51] Childs, 129.

[52] E.g. 2Sam. 13:33; 19:20 [19].

[53] Cf. Moberly *BTF*, 85 n23.

2.2.2.2 THE REASON FOR YHWH'S ACTS: תֵּדַע כִּי אֵין כָּמֹנִי בְּכָל־הָאָרֶץ

YHWH has demanded that Pharaoh send the people. It is in this context
that he tells him that he is sending all his plagues upon Pharaoh. Therefore,
when he follows this statement with a reason, one might expect that reason
to be 'so that you will send them' or something similar to link this back to
the demand. Alternatively we might expect a reason based on the situation
such as 'to punish you for your oppression of my people (which I have
seen)'. However these do not seem to be present. Instead, the purpose
(בַּעֲבוּר[54]) of the plague is 'so that you may know that there is none like me
in all the land/earth.'[55]

Moreover this purpose is not unique. 'Knowledge that X' (יָדַע כִּי) and
'knowledge' (יָדַע) are recurrent themes in the plagues narrative. Often this
knowledge concerns YHWH; either knowledge of him, or knowing that he
is X. Furthermore, this 'knowledge' often forms part of a message from
YHWH giving the reason for his acts. Therefore in a study concerned with
YHWH, his acts in the plagues and the understanding thereof, this theme
needs to be considered in more detail.

2.2.2.3 EXCURSUS: יָדַע כִּי/יָדַע IN THE EXODUS STORY

יָדַע occurs twenty-three times in Ex. 1-15. Of these, fifteen are in the
format 'know that...'.[56] The remaining eight are related to knowledge of
things or persons.[57] Moreover, of the twenty-three, fifteen are on the lips of
YHWH. Of these, all but three relate to others knowing things about him.[58]
On the whole, although not completely, יָדַע comes before the plagues
narrative, while יָדַע כִּי comes within them. The uses are set out in
Appendix II.

---

[54] While the ו of וְיַעַבְדֻנִי in v13 may well indicate a purpose, here the בַּעֲבוּר must do so.
All other uses of בַּעֲבוּר as a conjunction have a purposive sense (Gen. 21:30; 27:4, 19,
31; 46:34; Ex. 19:9; 20:20; Ps. 105:45; cf. Gen. 27:10 with אֲשֶׁר). This is also the case
for prepositional usage, as in 9:16 (cf. BDB, 721; Joüon 168e).

[55] הָאָרֶץ here could refer to either the land (presumably the land of Egypt), or the whole
earth. As YHWH's focus is on Pharaoh knowing this, it seems more appropriate to use
'land' here and in other such phrases (e.g. 9:29). Egypt is the area that is affected by the
plagues, and Egypt is the area under Pharaoh's control. However, this should not be
taken as indicating any limitation of YHWH's power ('just' Egypt rather than the whole
world). 'Earth' would be a wholly appropriate translation to retain this sense. Cf.
Brueggemann 'Vassal', 31, Propp, 333. The point here is that while there may well be
nobody like YHWH in the whole earth, those parts of the earth that are outside Egypt
are not of immediate relevance to Pharaoh.

[56] 3:19; 4:14; 6:7; 7:5, 17; 8:6 [10], 18 [22]; 9:14, 29, 30; 10:2, 7; 11:7; 14:4; 14:18 (cf.
16:6, 12; 18:11).

[57] 1:8; 2:4, 14, 25; 3:7; 5:2; 6:3; 10:26.

[58] 3:7, 19; 4:14.

יָדַע in Ex. 1-15

The first use of יָדַע comes in 1:8. A new king arose over Egypt 'who did not know Joseph'. For our purposes we need not concern ourselves over exactly who this king is meant to be, or whether 'new' indicates a new dynasty, or some other event.[59] All, it seems, that we need to know about the king is that he did not know Joseph. This is what marks him out from his predecessors, and this is how he is described. Apart from this he has no name, or other description.[60]

What then, does it mean 'not to know Joseph'? It could mean that he was ignorant of Joseph's existence. However one would then need to ask about the relevance of this statement in context. In light of his subsequent actions, it is more probable that this Pharaoh disregards what Joseph had done for Egypt. Therefore Joseph's deeds do not affect his policy over Egypt, and more specifically over Joseph's kin.[61] Thus we see his change of policy in vv9-22. The king speaks to 'his people' (v9) and perceives the Israelites as a threat to them, and thus oppresses them with hard labour (vv10-14) and worse (vv15-22).

YHWH, who has been notable by his absence during this oppression in 1:1-2:23, appears for the first time in 2:24-25 when the cry of the people rises up. He hears the groans; remembers his covenant; sees the people and 'knows'. Exactly what he knows is not clear. In light of the following explanation to Moses it may be that he 'knows their suffering' (3:7) in the sense of 'understands' (cf. Gen. 48:19). However we understand it, YHWH is introduced as one who 'knows'. Immediately after this, his 'knowledge' translates into action, as he commissions Moses to go to Pharaoh. (3:10 is the consequence of 3:7-9.)

Finally, the new Pharaoh is introduced last in 5:1-18. He is not given any description by the narrator, and is as nameless as his predecessor. Nevertheless, he introduces himself quite well in his initial words and actions in response to YHWH's demand, made to him here for the first time. As this is an important passage for understanding both YHWH's demand ('send...') and his purpose ('know...'), it will be worth examining it in more detail.

---

[59] Cf. Keil, 419; Childs, 15. For a discussion of historical possibilities see James K Hoffmeier, *Israel in Egypt: The Evidence for the Authenticity of the Exodus Tradition* (Oxford: Oxford University Press, 1996), henceforth 'Hoffmeier *Israel*', 122ff.

[60] Cf. Hyatt, 58. Hoffmeier *Israel*, 109-112, suggests that this anonymity is a deliberate move on the part of the author, in a similar way to the omission of the names of the enemies of the Pharaohs in the New Kingdom: 'For the Hebrew writer, there was good theological reason for this silence: the reader learns of the name of God Yahweh and his power as the Exodus story unfolds, whereas his arch-rival, Pharaoh, remains anonymous – a nice piece of irony' (111-112).

[61] Houtman, I 30-31; Propp, 252; Jacob *Exodus*, 10; Greenberg *UE*, 70.

The First Encounter with Pharaoh – 5:1-18

YHWH has heard his people's cry (2:23-25); he has commissioned Moses and dealt with his objections (3:10-4:17); Moses and Aaron have returned to Egypt and have been accepted by the people of Israel (4:18-31). At this point we have the first contact between YHWH and Pharaoh, through the agency of Moses and Aaron.

Moses and Aaron present YHWH's demand: 'Thus says YHWH, God of Israel, "Send my people that they may hold a festival to me in the wilderness"' (5:1).

Pharaoh's response introduces us to him, and contains a question and an assertion: 'Who is YHWH that I should listen to his voice and send (לְשַׁלַּח) Israel? I do not know (לֹא יָדַעְתִּי) YHWH, and I will not send (לֹא אֲשַׁלַּח) Israel' (5:2).

What exactly does Pharaoh mean when he says that he does not know YHWH? His question 'who is YHWH' could be a sign of ignorance, and a genuine request for knowledge. However, as with 1:8, we would need to ask about its function at this point. The use of the אֲשֶׁר after מִי יְהוָה suggests that Pharaoh is questioning YHWH's identity in relation to the demand that he has made.

We can compare other uses of מִי ... אֲשֶׁר such as Jer. 49:19/50:44 'who is the shepherd who can stand against me?' Here the context suggests that this question arises not from ignorance, but rather out of his rejection of the idea that any could stand against him.[62]

It may well be that Pharaoh had not heard of the name of YHWH up to this point. Indeed, if we understand 3:14 and especially 6:3 to be giving the name of YHWH to Israel for the first time, this is hardly surprising.[63] However, as with the above examples, the sense of the construction seems to be dismissal of the one asked about as being not capable of the deed mentioned. Thus it is a dismissal of YHWH, and hence of his demand to 'send'.[64] We could paraphrase the question 'who is YHWH?' as 'who does YHWH think he is …?'

---

[62] The point could also be made about Dt. 4:7-8 where it is unlikely that Moses is asking a genuinely open question about other nations' religious activities. Instead the context (especially 4:5-6) suggests that it is a rhetorical question assuming the answer 'none', showing the uniqueness of Israel (cf. also Dt. 5:26 following 5:25). More widely, Job 21:15 has a very similar use to ours, albeit with מַה instead of מִי: 'what is Shaddai that we should serve him?' Taking things to absurdity, when Solomon says 'who am I that I should build a temple for him?' (2Chr. 2:5), he is expressing unworthiness or incapability rather than asking about his own identity.

[63] For a detailed discussion of this see R.W.L. Moberly, *The Old Testament of the Old Testament*, OBT (Minneapolis: Fortress Press, 1992), henceforth 'Moberly *TOTOTOT*'.

[64] Cf. Houtman, I 462; Propp, 252; Durham, 63; Jacob *Exodus*, 121; Greenberg *UE*, 122; Brueggemann 'Vassal', 36; Driver *Exodus*, 35.

At this point we should pause for a moment to remind ourselves of Pharaoh's position. The story of the exodus is told and retold within religions that have a common view of the one and only, all-powerful God.[65] Even where it is read in a non-religious context, the society may well have the underlying conception of one God (whether believed in or not) rather than many gods. For Pharaoh this would not be the case. The Egyptian pantheon held a myriad of gods, often overlapping with each other, even where one might be exalted.[66] For Pharaoh, this 'YHWH' was not even an Egyptian god, but rather the god of a nation of slaves, represented by two old men from these slaves. Yet they have the effrontery to come before him and his lavish court, replete with his servants, magicians, and others, and make demands of the mighty Pharaoh in the name of this YHWH.

This dismissive view is crystallised by Pharaoh's next sentence: 'I do not know YHWH, and Israel I will not send.' His lack of knowledge of YHWH leads to his lack of obedience to YHWH's demands.[67] Thus in his response Pharaoh twice makes the same connection. YHWH has demanded something, but Pharaoh does not 'know' this YHWH, and as a result he will not obey his demand to send the people. 'Knowing' (יָדַע) YHWH and obeying his demand to 'send' (שָׁלַח) are strongly linked for this Pharaoh.

It is only after Pharaoh's words in 5:2 that YHWH's messages to him start including the theme of knowledge. The messages to Pharaoh before this (3:18; 4:22-23; 5:1) have said nothing about Pharaoh's knowledge of YHWH. They are concerned only with the demand to release Israel. However, from 7:17 onwards, nearly all of the encounters between Pharaoh and YHWH that contain any dialogue raise the theme of Pharaoh 'knowing that …' in relation to YHWH.[68] Thus it appears that this concept of 'knowledge' arises in response to Pharaoh's initial words. Pharaoh does not

---

TgPsJ. 5:2 combines the two ideas: 'The name of the Lord has not been revealed to me that I should listen to his word and let Israel go. I have not found the name of the Lord written in the Book of the Angels. I do not fear him and moreover I will not let Israel go.'

[65] I am thinking here primarily of Judaism, Christianity and Islam.

[66] Hornung, 185-186, notes that in Egyptian religion it was quite normal to address multiple gods as 'greatest god' or 'unique god' without dismissing the other gods. The sense is that each god is unique in his or her own way; that there is none quite like him, or the same as her. Only with Akhenaten does 'unique' god mean that there can be no other gods. One could, of course, raise questions about the view of Pharaoh and Egyptian religion held by the writer(s) of this narrative.

[67] Even with 5:2b alone it would be likely that the וֹ should have the sense of 'therefore'. With the parallel in 5:2a 'who is YHWH אֲשֶׁר I should listen…' it becomes very likely indeed. (Ehrlich, 268, sees the גַּם as creating a cause and effect relationship.)

[68] The first mention of Pharaoh 'knowing' is in 7:5, although 7:17 is the first time that it is made in a speech to Pharaoh.

know and will not act; therefore YHWH will act in order that Pharaoh may 'know...'. Thus Childs:

> The theme of Pharaoh's not knowing Yahweh, which is introduced here for the first time, continues to be picked up and developed within the plague narrative. With considerable relish the biblical writer describes how Pharaoh comes to know who Yahweh is as he demonstrates his power over Egypt (8.18 [22]; 9.29; 11.8).[69]

In response to Pharaoh's initial dismissal, Moses and Aaron try a different tack. They reword the request in far milder terms. The demand שַׁלַּח becomes the request נֵלְכָה נָּא; the focus shifts from a message from YHWH to a request from the slaves because their god, the god of the Hebrews has appeared to them.[70] While this wording comes closer to that of YHWH's message in 3:18, after the initial word and response in 5:1-2 it comes across as a climb-down. If that message had been given immediately, it might have allowed Pharaoh to be magnanimous, or, in light of 3:19, to show up his obstinacy. However, in its context after 5:2 it comes across as an acceptance of Pharaoh's rejection of YHWH's right to make such a demand of Pharaoh.[71] The focus of attention shifts from YHWH to Pharaoh; asking him if he, Pharaoh, would grant such a request to the people.[72] However he refuses again, on the more mundane issue of loss of work (vv4-5).

Thus, in common with his predecessor, and in contrast to YHWH, this Pharaoh is introduced as one who does not 'know'. Moreover, as with both YHWH and the old Pharaoh, this state of 'knowing' or 'not knowing' drives one's actions.[73] The old Pharaoh is introduced as one who did not know Joseph and immediately sets about worsening things for Israel. This Pharaoh's first words are that he does not know YHWH, and he not only rejects YHWH's demand, but also immediately sets about worsening Israel's condition further, by the 'bricks without straw' edict. At this point, as in Ex. 1-2, it is Pharaoh's actions that are described. YHWH's message

---

[69] Childs, 105; cf. Greenberg *UE*, 127.

[70] If הָעִבְרִים here was connected to the term *habiru/hapiru*, this would make it even more mild in comparison to 5:1; portraying YHWH as the god of the slaves or undesirables. However more recently there has been considerable doubt thrown on any connection. See Houtman, I 122-124.

[71] Cf. Moberly *TOTOTOT*, 26; Childs, 105.

[72] Houtman, I 463, sees this as a different strategy, pointing out that in the Old Testament a refusal is often met not with acquiescence, but with a renewed request (Gen. 42:3-14; Num. 20:14-21; 22:5-21; 32:1-24; 1Sam. 17:32-37). However against this we could note that when it is those who speak for YHWH that are met with opposition, they often reply with stronger words, rather than milder ones (1Kgs. 22:19, 28; 2Kgs. 1:12; Jer. 28:12-14; Amos 7:14-17 etc.)

[73] Cf. Fretheim, 27: 'The king of Egypt does not know; God knows. This difference in knowledge has a profound effect on doing (see Jer. 22:16).'

has been given, but he is not, as yet, acting. Greenberg expands on this, describing it as the 'language of redemption turned sour':

> Moses and Aaron had said to Pharaoh, "Thus said the Lord"; the taskmasters said to the people, "Thus said Pharaoh." Moses and Aaron had asked, "Let us go now … and sacrifice to the Lord our God"; Pharaoh twice repeats their request as the reason for the heightened oppression. Moreover, the introductory "Let us go" (nel°ka) is repeatedly echoed in the orders given the people: "Go to your tasks!" "Let them go gather straw"; "Go take straw!" God's demand was "Release my people that they might serve me (weya'abdeni)" (4:23); Pharaoh's scheme was "Let the labor (ha'°boda) bear down on the men, and let them keep at it, and not pay attention to false promises." Pharaoh counters God's claim on Israel's service with his own. This is underscored by the sevenfold occurrence of derivatives of 'abad in verses 9-21, all expressive of subjection to Pharaoh.[74]

Thus it appears that both Pharaohs and YHWH, the figures of power in this narrative, are introduced by what they do, or do not, know; and this is of vital importance to how they act.

יָדַע כִּי in Exodus 1-15

After 5:2 the phrase 'know that' (יָדַע כִּי) starts to appear.[75] There are three main occurrences of this phrase. It is found in the Red Sea encounters where Moses is told that Egypt will 'know that I am YHWH' (14:4, 18 cf. 7:5). It is applied to Israel (6:7; 10:2 cf. 16:6, 12). They will 'know that I am YHWH' as a result of YHWH's actions.

However, it is predominantly found in the plagues narrative, being addressed to Pharaoh or Egypt. It arises in the first plague (7:17); the second (8:6 [10]); the fourth (8:18 [22]); the seventh (9:14, (16), 29); and the tenth (11:7).[76] As noted on 9:13, plagues three, six and nine have no dialogue. The eighth plague has no statement from YHWH to Pharaoh on this issue. However there is the statement to Moses (10:2) and the word from the servants (10:7), which both pick up this terminology. The fifth

---

[74] Greenberg *UE*, 127-128.

[75] 3:19 and 4:14 are two earlier uses of כִּי יָדַע, where YHWH speaks of what he currently knows. However the majority of uses that come after 5:2 are YHWH speaking of humans coming to 'know that X' as a result of divine actions. Cf. Cassuto, 90; Sarna *Exodus*, 36.

[76] 11:7 has אֲשֶׁר rather than כִּי. However אֲשֶׁר appears to serve a similar function to כִּי after יָדַע. יָדַע immediately followed by אֲשֶׁר is only found four times in the Old Testament. Two of the other cases (2Chr. 2:7; Ezek. 20:26), have the sense of 'know that'. Ezek. 20:26 is especially similar, as YHWH states that he will desolate/horrify Israel 'that they will know that I am YHWH' (לְמַעַן אֲשֶׁר יֵדְעוּ אֲשֶׁר אֲנִי יְהוָה). On the difficulty of this verse see W. Zimmerli *I am Yahweh*, trans. Douglas W. Stott ed. Walter Brueggemann (Atlanta: John Knox Press, 1982), henceforth 'Zimmerli *I am Yahweh*', 36.

plague is the only plague with dialogue where there is no mention of knowledge.

While the theme is repeated, the content varies from place to place. Pharaoh will know 'that I am YHWH' (7:5, 17; 14:4, 18); 'that there is none like YHWH our God' (8:6 [10]); 'that I am YHWH in the midst of the land' (8:18 [22]); 'that there is none like me' (9:14); 'that the land is YHWH's' (9:29); and 'that YHWH distinguishes between Egypt and Israel' (11:7).[77]

Ref.	Addressee	Statement
7:17	Pharaoh	בְּזֹאת תֵּדַע כִּי אֲנִי יְהוָה
8:6 [10]	Pharaoh	לְמַעַן תֵּדַע כִּי־אֵין כַּיהוָה אֱלֹהֵינוּ
8:18 [22]	Pharaoh	לְמַעַן תֵּדַע כִּי אֲנִי יְהוָה בְּקֶרֶב הָאָרֶץ
9:14	Pharaoh	בַּעֲבוּר תֵּדַע כִּי אֵין כָּמֹנִי בְּכָל־הָאָרֶץ
9:29	Pharaoh	לְמַעַן תֵּדַע כִּי לַיהוָה הָאָרֶץ
9:30	Pharaoh	יָדַעְתִּי כִּי טֶרֶם תִּירְאוּן מִפְּנֵי יְהוָה אֱלֹהִים
10:2	Israel	וִידַעְתֶּם כִּי־אֲנִי יְהוָה
10:7	Pharaoh	הֲטֶרֶם תֵּדַע כִּי אָבְדָה מִצְרָיִם
11:7	Pharaoh	לְמַעַן תֵּדְעוּן אֲשֶׁר יַפְלֶה יְהוָה בֵּין מִצְרַיִם וּבֵין יִשְׂרָאֵל

However, this still leaves the question of what it means to 'know that...'. This 'knowledge' is portrayed as the ultimate purpose of these acts. There is no mention of any act that this knowledge is meant to cause ('know that X in order that you may do Y'). Neither is it ever explicitly said that Pharaoh 'knows' any of the above points. Moreover the question remains of how this 'knowledge' relates to the demand 'send ... serve'.

יָדַע כִּי in the Wider Old Testament

The phrase 'know that' with some form of יָדַע followed immediately by כִּי occurs over two hundred times in the Old Testament. In his essay on 'Knowledge of God according to the Book of Ezekiel', Zimmerli examines the wider use of his 'recognition formula' ('know that I am YHWH'), and also wider instances of knowledge of YHWH.[78]

In describing this recognition formula his fundamental insight is that the knowledge described is always related to YHWH's acts.

Nowhere does the statement of recognition speak of recognition apart from the divine acts which nourish it. There is no room here for knowledge emerging

---

[77] Chp 4 will contain more detailed discussed of these statements in context.

[78] 'Knowledge of God according to the Book of Ezekiel' in Zimmerli *I am Yahweh*.

darkly from interior human meditation, from an existential analysis of human beings or the world, or from speculation.[79]

As well as proceeding from an act (of God), he suggests that this recognition leads to an act (of the human) as well. He discusses 1Kgs. 18 where, unusually, the event of recognition is described in full detail as well as the divine deed that evokes it. Thus Elijah's request that YHWH be known as God in Israel (1Kgs. 18:36-37) is fulfilled by YHWH's act (v38). However this does not simply lead to the people saying 'YHWH, he is God' (v39), but also to the rejection of the alternative by the slaughter of the prophets of Baal, in which the people assisted (v40). Thus for Zimmerli:

> this example clearly shows that the event of recognition is not an inward, reflective, or spiritual occurrence, but rather manifests itself in open, public prostration before Yahweh. Recognition is not just the illumination of a new perspective; it is a process of acknowledgement that becomes concrete in confession and worship and leads directly to practical decisions.[80]

This, of course, is based upon one example, and we would need a wider sample to confirm the pattern. Zimmerli also notes the example of Naaman, whose confession 'now I know that there is no God in the earth but in Israel' (2Kgs. 5:15) leads to the offer of a gift, and then the request for earth so that he can worship YHWH in Damascus. His one quibble about the temple of Rimmon also relates to practical acknowledgement of YHWH.[81] Soon after our own passage Jethro recognises YHWH, and the sacrifice may be a symbol of this.[82]

On this point of 'knowledge' or recognition leading to action we could add a couple of examples. Jonah's response to YHWH in Jon. 4:2 parodies the idea as Jonah flees from YHWH's commission: 'this is why I was quick to flee to Tarshish, because I knew that you were ...' Jonah's 'knowledge' leads to action, even if it is not the action that YHWH demanded. Gideon asks for a sign so that he may 'know that you [YHWH] will save Israel by my hand' (Jdg. 6:37). The signs are not to gain intellectual assent only, but to get him to act.[83]

One example that might be raised against this point is Ezek. 2:5, where the people will know that a prophet has been amongst them, whether they listen or not. However this is not fatal to the point. The sense may be that the people will be left without excuse; that they will have to acknowledge

---

[79] Zimmerli *I am Yahweh*, 64; cf. Botterweck 'יָדַע' *TDOT* V, 471.

[80] Zimmerli *I am Yahweh*, 67.

[81] Zimmerli *I am Yahweh*, 67.

[82] Zimmerli *I am Yahweh*, 69.

[83] YHWH has more to do before they act (Jdg. 7:2-3, 4-7, 10-11), but the purpose of the signs and the knowledge that Gideon seeks appears to have a fundamentally practical outworking.

that a prophet has been there (i.e. they have been warned), whether they act upon it or not.

This still leaves the question of what it means to 'know that I am YHWH'. Why is it in this form rather than, say 'know YHWH'? Zimmerli suggests that this 'results from the disinclination to have Yahweh's name function as an object ... even within the recognition ... Yahweh himself remains clearly and irreplaceably the subject.'[84]

Understanding יָדַע כִּי/יָדַע in the Plagues Narrative

What can we draw from the above points to help us understand the meaning and implications of יָדַע and יָדַע כִּי in our passage?

The term יָדַע seems to function as an introduction to several of the main characters in the story, and this is followed directly by a record of their action which appears to be based upon this 'knowledge'. In particular the new Pharaoh introduces himself as one who does not 'know YHWH', where this seems to be a dismissal of YHWH in respect of his demand to release the people. Pharaoh does not know YHWH, and he will not release the people. It is after this, and probably in response to it, that YHWH's messages to Pharaoh include his acts, and their purpose that Pharaoh will 'know that...'.

More generally in the Old Testament knowledge of God in this format is based upon divine acts, and leads to human acts as an outworking of this knowledge. Thus we could use 'acknowledge' to render the term. This is not ideal, as it under-emphasises the element of perception and recognition that is a key part to this process (although it does pick up the more practical and official sense of 'recognition', being appropriate action). However, it would remove the opposite danger of seeing 'know' as referring to merely intellectual assent. 'Knowing' something leads, or should lead, to acknowledgement of it.[85]

Therefore the reason for YHWH's actions here is not primarily to gain the release of Israel, or to punish Pharaoh for his misdeeds in respect of Israel. The emphasis on the acknowledgement of YHWH makes such a

---

[84] Zimmerli *I am Yahweh*, 84. Our understanding does not have to rely on Zimmerli. For example Joyce notes that this phrase is often the end product of an action, and is presented without elaboration, and sometimes even the recipients fade into uncertainty: 'the overriding impression is of a terse and cryptic saying'. Paul Joyce, *Divine Initiative and Human Response in Ezekiel*, JSOTSup 51 (Sheffield: Sheffield Academic Press, 1989), henceforth 'Joyce', 94 n. 37, cf. 94-95. However, his cautious conclusion that the central concern is the theocentric revelation of YHWH would still accord with our discussion.

[85] Cf. Brueggemann 'Vassal', 35. Propp, 282 sees knowledge of YHWH as tantamount to recognition of sovereignty. He compares this to ancient Near Eastern treaties where vassals and suzerains are said to "know" one another (albeit this is 'know' rather than 'know that').

'humanitarian' understanding of YHWH's actions rather difficult to sustain. The knowledge of YHWH is an end in and of itself; there are no explicit consequences made in YHWH's speech. However this acknowledgement, at least in part, is shown in listening to YHWH, or obeying him.

In Pharaoh's case he is not called to 'know YHWH', just as he is not called to 'serve YHWH'.[86] However, he is called to 'know that ...' in respect of YHWH. After his initial words in 5:2, this knowledge must express itself in obedience to YHWH's demand, by sending the people. This is a theme that will recur in the plagues narrative. The focus of the implications is theocentric rather than humanitarian. However the implications of this theocentric focus will have a large effect on the humans.

2.2.2.4 SUMMARY OF 9:14

- The introduction to this act of YHWH appears to draw a contrast with previous acts: 'this time I am sending all my plagues...'. The exact meaning of this is still open, and requires study of the rest of the explanation.
- YHWH's stated purpose for his actions is that Pharaoh will know 'that there is none like me in all the earth'. The focus here is theocentric, concerned with YHWH's self-revelation. However, in light of wider usage of 'know that' in the Old Testament and the importance of 'know' in the introduction of Pharaoh and YHWH, 'know that' suggests a practical outworking, perhaps expressed by 'acknowledge'.

2.2.3 *9:15*

כִּי עַתָּה שָׁלַחְתִּי אֶת־יָדִי וָאַךְ אוֹתְךָ וְאֶת־עַמְּךָ בַּדָּבֶר וַתִּכָּחֵד מִן־הָאָרֶץ:

'For by now I could have sent my hand and struck you and your people with pestilence and you would be wiped off the face of the earth.'

If 9:13 follows the normal pattern of introductory speeches and 9:14 shows signs of deviation, then 9:15 is almost unique in content. YHWH appears to be speaking of what he could have done to Pharaoh, with total destruction as a possible outcome.

---

[86] McCarthy, Dennis J. "Moses' Dealings with Pharaoh: Ex. 7,8-10,27." *CBQ* 27 (1965): 336-347, henceforth 'McCarthy 'Moses'', 346, mentions the various elements of Pharaoh 'knowing' (and the expanding nature of YHWH's demands for recognition) briefly, seeing the expressed aim as 'to produce an almost cultic recognition of Yahweh, for the liturgical provenance of the key demand ... is well known'. Cf. Durham, 86. However it is not obvious that 'know that I am YHWH' (as opposed to 'know YHWH') equals belief. Cf. Joyce, 95.

2.2.3.1 כִּי עַתָּה שָׁלַחְתִּי אֶת־יָדִי

The key to understanding this sentence is the translation of the above phrase. The Hebrew phrase 'send/stretch out one's hand' as an idiom for action does not require discussion. However the first three words pose more of a problem. Houtman lists four possible alternatives for this phrase:

Option 1: It denotes a possible action in the past that has not come to pass: 'by now I could have sent...(and struck)'

Option 2: It denotes an action in the future: 'now I will send/am sending...(and will strike)'

Option 3: It is a simple perfect: 'now I have sent...(and have struck)'

Option 4: It is pluperfect in sense: 'now already I had sent... (and stood poised to strike)'[87]

Option 3

If asked to translate the three words out of context, the most probable translation would be the third, taking them as simple perfect: 'Now I have sent...'.

Option 4

Houtman notes that this option is in conflict with the Hebrew text. The use of the pluperfect suggests that YHWH had stretched out his hand to destroy them. The context and following verbs would need to explain why this is a pluperfect rather than a simple perfect as in the last option.

Both of these options present YHWH as having stretched out his hand. If the sense is extended to the following verbs it suggests that YHWH is speaking of the destruction of the addressee as already having happened, which raises problems of sense. These will be discussed in the discussion of וַתִּכָּחֵד מִן־הָאָרֶץ. Thus we move on to two options that are not immediately obvious translations.

Options 1 and 2

Durham, in advocating the second option, notes that translations often favour the first, conditional alternative. However, he claims that the text does not support such a sense:

> None of the usual terms or circumlocutions of conditional expression are present (cf. GKC, ¶ 106*p*, ¶ 112*ff-mm*, ¶ 159*a-k*), nor is there anything in the wider context of the account to suggest a conditional sense.
>
> Yahweh is depicted instructing Moses to report to Pharaoh (in a speech begun with an authenticating messenger-formula) not what he could have done or might do, but what he is doing and is about to do (cf. KJV). This sense is made plain not only by the absence of any conditional terms and syntax, but by the emphatic "*now*" (בפעם הזאת) of v 14 and by the "indeed now" (כי עתה) of v 15, as well

---

[87] Houtman, II 85-86.

as by the assertion in v 17 that Pharaoh continues to tyrannize the sons of Israel and persists in his refusal to obey Yahweh's command.[88]

Although option 1 receives widespread acceptance, there is little detailed support for this case. Therefore Durham's points need to be addressed. The wider use of the phrase within the Old Testament will be examined, to gauge support for both readings. After this the immediate context will be considered.

There are eleven occurrences in the Old Testament of כִּי עַתָּה followed immediately by a verb in the perfect.[89] Excluding Ex. 9:15, these usages break down roughly into two categories: those that deal with an actual event, and those that deal with a possible, yet unreal event.

The first category deals mainly with events in the present or immediate past, such as 'now I know...' (Gen. 22:12), or 'now YHWH has made room for us' (Gen. 26:22).[90] This does not offer much support for reading 9:15 as an actual future action. One could see it as a present that relates to what is to come 'now I am sending...'. However, in light of v14, one might expect this to be represented by, say, אֲנִי שֹׁלֵחַ.

The second category comprises Gen. 43:10; Num. 22:29; 1Sam. 13:13, and Job. 3:13. Of these, the first two follow the normal expression of an unreal possibility, with the use of לוּ or לוּלֵא/לוּלֵי with the perfect (Joüon §167). However, there is no לוּ or לוּלֵי in Ex. 9:15. More relevant for our purposes are 1Sam. 13:13 and Job 3:13 (if we can establish that they are possible, rather than real, actions).

וַיֹּאמֶר שְׁמוּאֵל אֶל־שָׁאוּל נִסְכָּלְתָּ לֹא שָׁמַרְתָּ אֶת־מִצְוַת יְהוָה אֱלֹהֶיךָ אֲשֶׁר
צִוָּךְ כִּי עַתָּה הֵכִין יְהוָה אֶת־מַמְלַכְתְּךָ אֶל־יִשְׂרָאֵל עַד־עוֹלָם: 14 וְעַתָּה
מַמְלַכְתְּךָ לֹא־תָקוּם בִּקֵּשׁ יְהוָה לוֹ אִישׁ כִּלְבָבוֹ וַיְצַוֵּהוּ יְהוָה לְנָגִיד
עַל־עַמּוֹ כִּי לֹא שָׁמַרְתָּ אֵת אֲשֶׁר־צִוְּךָ יְהוָה:
(1Sam. 13:13-14)

Here Saul is being reprimanded for not obeying YHWH's command (v13abα). As a result of this, his kingdom will not endure. Instead another, a man after YHWH's own heart, will be found to rule, because Saul has not obeyed YHWH. (v14).

In the middle of this statement of rejection of Saul, we find v13bβ. As in Ex. 9:15, the issue is how to translate the verb following the כִּי עַתָּה, here הֵכִין.

---

[88] Durham, 127. Interestingly, one of his references to GKC, §106*p*, actually lists 9:15 as an example of conditionality. However we must decide whether this example is reasonable. Joüon does not mention it as conditional, although he has no discussion of 9:15 at all.

[89] Gen. 22:12; 26:22; 43:10; Ex. 9:15; Num. 22:29; 1Sam. 13:13; Job. 3:13; 6:21; Dan. 10:11; Hos. 5:3; Zech. 9:8.

[90] Also Job 6:21; Dan. 10:11; Hos. 5:3; Zech. 9:8.

It would be nonsensical to translate it as an actual future event ('now YHWH will establish your kingdom forever'), as this would contradict v14. Moreover, an eternal kingdom would be an odd result of disobedience.

It would make little more sense to translate it as an actual past event: 'Now YHWH has established your kingdom for ever. But now...' If YHWH has established an eternal kingdom, it seems odd to have this immediately contradicted in v14a. To be fair, one could point to 1Sam. 2:30 to show that YHWH's establishment of something עַד־עוֹלָם does not preclude a reversal of this based on human actions. However, at the point of Saul's indiscretion in 1Sam. 13, his kingdom is anything but eternally established. Moreover, the word order would be strange. One might expect 'Although YHWH has established an eternal kingdom, you have not kept...'. One could compare Nathan's rebuke to David (whose kingdom, in contrast to Saul, was relatively secure). There 2Sam. 12:7b-9 contrasts the generosity of YHWH and the insatiability of David.

It makes most sense to understand the meaning as possible, but unreal 'For now YHWH would have established your kingdom over Israel forever. But now...'[91]

Moreover Job 3:13 uses this form to indicate a hypothetical condition. After lamenting the fact that he was cared for at birth he says:

כִּי־עַתָּה שָׁכַבְתִּי וְאֶשְׁקוֹט יָשַׁנְתִּי אָז יָנוּחַ לִי׃

As he is anything but at rest, this would make little sense as a description of his present condition. Instead, this appears to be a longed for result of the lack of such care. In other words: 'If there had not been knees to receive me or breasts for me to suck, then I would now be lying down...'.[92]

Therefore we have at least a couple of places where, arguably, כִּי עַתָּה plus the perfect, without לוּ or לוּלֵא/לוּלֵי, has a sense of a hypothetical possible action. One could still ask about the appropriateness of the עַתָּה to indicate a past event ('by now'). However, Gen. 43:10 probably requires such an understanding. Judah points out to his father that if they had not delayed, by now they could have returned twice:

כִּי לוּלֵא הִתְמַהְמָהְנוּ כִּי־עַתָּה שַׁבְנוּ זֶה פַעֲמָיִם׃

Alternatively, Davidson suggests that the עַתָּה or אָז in the apodosis of a conditional sentence has shifted meaning from temporal to logical.[93] He notes that this form of apodosis often occurs with no formal protasis, where

---

[91] On this passage Driver notes the normal use of כִּי עַתָּה after לוּ but says that it is 'perhaps too much to maintain that עַתָּה may not refer to a condition *implied*, without being actually expressed. Cf. Ex. 9,15 ... and Job 3:13.' S. R. Driver, *Notes on the Hebrew Text of the Books of Samuel* (Oxford: Clarendon Press, 1890), henceforth 'Driver *Samuel*' 77.

[92] Cf. D. J. A. Clines, *Job 1-20*, WBC 17 (Dallas: Word, 1989), 72, 91.

[93] J.C.L. Gibson, *Davidson's Introductory Hebrew Grammar ~ Syntax* (Edinburgh: T&T Clark, 1994), §122 Rem. 2.

the protasis must be supplied from the context (1Sam. 13:13; Job 3:13; 2Kgs. 13:19; Ex. 9:15; Job 13:19).[94]

Therefore the above evidence suggests that כִּי עַתָּה שָׁלַחְתִּי by itself refers to a past possible action. There is little support for it referring to a future action.

2.2.3.2 וְאַךְ אוֹתְךָ וְאֶת־עַמְּךָ בַּדֶּבֶר

We now move on to the result of YHWH's action. The translation of this phrase is straightforward, excepting that the tense of the verb will depend upon the understanding of the first point above.[95]

2.2.3.3 וַתִּכָּחֵד מִן־הָאָרֶץ

The effect of YHWH's actions will be total destruction. (הִכְחִיד/נִכְחַד) can have the sense of 'conceal' or 'destroy', but the latter is much more obviously the result of plague (cf. Ex. 23:23; 1Kgs. 13:34; 2Chr. 32:21; Zech. 11:8-9, 16 for the sense of destruction). This is even more evident with the addition of מִן־הָאָרֶץ (cf. Gen. 7:23 (with וַיִּמַח) Lev. 26:6 (וְהִשְׁבַּתִּי); Jos. 7:9 (וְהִכְרִיתוּ)). The closest parallel to this passage is probably 1Kgs. 13:34 where Jeroboam's house will be effaced (וּלְהַכְחִיד) and destroyed (וּלְהַשְׁמִיד) from the earth. Therefore the effect of YHWH's action in 9:15, whether past or future, is utter destruction for all the Egyptians.

If we understand 9:15 as a simple past (option 3), this becomes difficult. We need to ask at what point YHWH has 'wiped them out'. To this point the plagues have not been deadly to humans. Moreover, as Pharaoh is able to receive the message, and is therefore not destroyed, we need to consider how this might be understood.

It could be understood metaphorically, i.e. 'you are already wiped out, although you do not realise it'. In support of this one could turn to 8:20 [24] which speaks of the land being 'ruined' (תִּשָּׁחֵת), and especially the words of

---

[94] As a final piece of support for reading it as a past possible action, LXX translates v15 as νῦν γὰρ ἀποστείλας τὴν χεῖρα πατάξω σε καὶ τὸν λαόν σου θανάτῳ καὶ ἐκτριβήσῃ ἀπὸ τῆς γῆς.
Wevers states: 'The verbs are aorist subjunctives and must be translated as potentials and contrary to fact, i.e. as "I might have ... you might have been"', Wevers, 131.
[95] The Samaritan Pentateuch reads ואכה in place of the MT's וְאַךְ. This unapocopated form of the imperfect could suggest that there is a simple waw preceding it, and that the prima facie meaning would be future, rather than a waw consecutive with a past sense. If so, this would support the reading of 'I will send my hand and I will strike...' LXX reads πατάξω, and Vul. *percutiam*, which could also support this (although note Wevers on LXX being subjunctive in force).
However, unapocopated forms of the waw consecutive of ל"ה verbs are frequent, especially in the first person singular (Joüon §79*m*). For example, Neh. 13:25 uses וָאַכֶּה to refer to Nehemiah's past actions. The MT reading, in contrast, is more clearly waw consecutive.

the servants to Pharaoh in 10:7 'do you not yet know that Egypt is ruined
(אָבְדָה)?' Clearly on both occasions there is still enough left to suffer
further plagues, with Pharaoh and his court at the very least not being
destroyed.[96]

However, the wording does not fit well with a metaphorical sense. On
this reading YHWH would have metaphorically sent forth his hand, struck
Pharaoh and his people with plague and wiped them from the face of the
earth. Where הכְחיד/נכְחַד is used in the sense of destruction, it is difficult to
find it used in a metaphorical sense.[97] In particular, the use of plague (דֶּבֶר
9:15) would be difficult to understand metaphorically in light of the actual
plague (דֶּבֶר 9:3) that has befallen the cattle. The land and the livestock may
have been 'ruined' (and yet still be able to bear further plagues). However
the only plague that has directly affected the Egyptian people (and it is
Pharaoh and the people rather than the land or the livestock who are the
ones that have been 'wiped from the land'), is the previous plague. While
this is described as a debilitating condition ('erupting boils with sores'),
there is no mention of any fatalities arising from it, in contrast to the lethal
דֶּבֶר upon the cattle in the previous plague, where every single one died.[98]

Alternatively, we could understand שָׁלַחְתִּי as a simple perfect, but וַתִּכָּחֵד
as a future. Thus YHWH has sent his hand, but the plague has not yet
come. If the plague is still to come then this possibility gives us a meaning
very similar to option 2 where both verbs are future, and therefore we will
subsume this possibility under that option.

Finally, it could indicate a past state that was on the point of happening.
Thus Propp suggests 'For just now I sent ...and struck... so that you were
vanishing from the land' although he rejects this.[99] However even if this
were accepted, it would come close to option 1, and therefore need not be
discussed further here.

---

[96] One could compare the flood story, where YHWH sees that the earth is ruined/corrupt
(נשְׁחַתָה), and thus determines to destroy (מַשְׁחיתָם) it (Gen. 6:12-13).

[97] We do not have to insist upon destruction so total that absolutely nothing remains,
although this might be suggested by מִן־הָאָרֶץ in this case. What does seem clear is that,
even on its own, הכְחיד/נכְחַד as 'destruction' signifies the end of something as a viable
entity. Thus the Assyrian army is wiped out as a force that can attack Judah (2Chr.
32:21), Jeroboam's house is to be wiped out as a dynasty ruling Israel (1Kgs. 13:34, cf.
Ps. 83:5 [4]). Inasmuch as Pharaoh and his people still exist at 9:15 as a force that holds
Israel and with which YHWH is interacting, they do not appear to fit into this pattern.

[98] The fact that livestock seemingly remains from the murrain of 9:1-7 to be rescued
from this plague of hail will be discussed briefly in 2.2.7. The point here is the contrast
between the way the two plagues are described; the first is universally lethal to the
Egyptian cattle (9:6), while the second makes no mention of any fatality. The
assumption, then, is that the second is not as lethal as the first, and cannot be described
as wiping the people from the face of the land.

[99] Propp, 333. Cf. Houtman, I 87 n. 142 who also rejects this.

Therefore option 3 (and with it option 4) seem to be ruled out as viable explanations of this verse. There is no obvious way to make sense of this action of YHWH ('send… wipe out…') as an actual past event (whether literal or metaphorical). Attempts to get around this problem bring us to understandings that follow either option 1 or 2. Therefore from this point we will narrow our focus to these two options.

If we understand 9:15 as warning of a future event (option 2), then we need to ask at what point YHWH carries out this threat. The firstborn and the army get wiped out, and Egypt is 'ruined' as a result of the hail and locust plagues (10:7, 15). However, the people of Egypt as a whole do not get wiped out root and branch by plague.[100] The final defeat of Egypt involves drowning, rather than plague. We could assume that the death of the firstborn was caused by plague, although this is not stated. However even if we grant this, while the final plague is a truly terrible event, it is difficult to extrapolate this to all Egypt being wiped out.

If we understand 9:15 as a possible event in the past (option 1), then we see a variant on the normal plague formula of YHWH striking Egypt with his hand and thus bringing a plague (cf. 3:20). The use of דֶּבֶר recalls the fifth plague of דֶּבֶר upon the cattle (9:3). Thus this could be suggesting a possible extension of that plague from the beasts to the humans as well. The result of this plague is that, instead of simply killing all the livestock, the plague could and would have killed all the Egyptian people as it killed their cattle.[101] However Houtman suggests that the writer is probably speaking in general terms here.[102] In either case, the point is that YHWH could have totally destroyed the Egyptians by this stage. The speech will continue to tell us why he has not done this.

2.2.3.4 SUMMARY OF 9:15

- 9:15 refers to an act of YHWH, not dissimilar in form to other plagues (sending his hand and smiting), except that its result would be the total destruction of the Egyptians.
- It could be a reference to a possible action in the past, a warning of an imminent event, or a description of an actual past happening. The third

---

[100] This sense of וַתִּכָּחֵד is not quite as insurmountable as the problems with option 3, as by the end of the exodus story, Egypt is soundly defeated as a force that can control Israel. However there is still the issue of מִן־הָאָרֶץ. There are no other uses of מִן־הָאָרֶץ following הִכְחִיד/נִכְחַד. However when comparable verbs are used with it, it carries the idea with a sense of total destruction (Gen. 7:23; Jos. 7:9; 1Sam. 28:9; 2Sam. 4:11; 1Kgs. 22:47 [46]; Ps. 104:35 etc.).

[101] Rashbam, 86-87; Propp, 333; Cassuto, 116; Schmidt, 418 (also mentioning 5:3); Hyatt, 118. ExR. XII.1 makes this explicit: 'Take a lesson from the murrain … Had I sent it …'

[102] Houtman, II 87.

option makes grammatical sense but seems impossible to relate to the actual previous events. The second option is possible but not obvious. Both context and wider usage favour the first option.

2.2.4 9:16

וְאוּלָם בַּעֲבוּר זֹאת הֶעֱמַדְתִּיךָ בַּעֲבוּר הַרְאֹתְךָ אֶת־כֹּחִי וּלְמַעַן סַפֵּר שְׁמִי בְּכָל־הָאָרֶץ׃

'However, I have sustained you for this reason: to show you my power and in order to recount my name in all the earth.'

2.2.4.1 הֶעֱמַדְתִּיךָ

Verse 16 introduces another action of YHWH. YHWH is saying that he has done or will do something to Pharaoh, and then gives his reasons for this. However, what does this verb mean?

The Hiph'il of עָמַד has the basic sense of 'cause to stand', and can have specific meanings of present[103]; enable to stand[104]; install/appoint (generally religious)[105]; establish/keep standing[106]; fix (one's gaze)[107]; confirm (covenant)[108]; station[109]; and restore/raise up[110]. Here YHWH is doing this to Pharaoh, and this has been understood in two main ways.

First, there is the nuance of putting someone into a certain position ('install'/'raise up'/'station' etc.). Thus YHWH would be saying that he has put Pharaoh into his current position of authority. This appears to be the way that Paul uses this verse when he quotes it in Romans 9:17, translating it with ἐξήγειρά σε 'raise, bring into power'. The assumption would then be that YHWH is saying that Pharaoh owes his very position to YHWH, and that YHWH has been in control all along, before the events of v15.

Secondly, instead of putting someone into a certain position, there is the nuance of keeping them there ('confirm', 'enable to stand', 'keep standing'). In this case, YHWH would be saying that he has kept Pharaoh in his current position, he has sustained him there. This would be similar to the sense of 1Kgs. 15:4 where YHWH raises up a son, and establishes Jerusalem (cf. Prov. 29:4; 1Chr. 17:14). The LXX favours this understanding, reading διετηρήθης 'you were kept, treasured up', which it also uses in 2:9 when Pharaoh's daughter pays Jochebed to keep

---

[103] Gen. 47:7; Lev. 14:11; 16:7; 27:8, 11; Num. 3:6; 5:18 etc.

[104] 2Sam. 22:34/Ps. 18:34 [33]; Ps. 30:8 [7]; 31:9 [8]; Ezek. 3:24.

[105] 1Kgs. 12:32; 1Chr. 15:16-17; 22:2 etc.

[106] 1Kgs. 15:4.

[107] 2Kgs. 8:11.

[108] 1Chr. 16:17.

[109] 2Chr. 23:10, 19 etc.

[110] 2Chr. 24:13; Ezra 9:9; Neh. 3:1; etc.

(διατήρησόν) Moses for her. The Targums also take this view (Onk. 'preserved'; PsJ 'did not keep you alive to...'; Nf 'kept you alive until now'). Moreover this is the nuance followed by many commentators.[111] The assumption would then be that YHWH is saying that Pharaoh owes his continued position to YHWH, presumably in relation to the events of v15.

2.2.4.2 וְאוּלָם

Linking the two actions of YHWH in v15 and 16a, is וְאוּלָם. This always has the sense of a strong adversative, such as 'however' or 'but'.[112] Therefore what follows in v16 is being contrasted to something. Presumably the contrast is with the statement in the previous verse. Thus the two verses will need to be understood together.

9:15-16aα: Contrast

We now have two possible meanings for the second part of the contrast: 'I have sustained/will sustain you' and 'I raised you up'. We have noted that there are two possible meanings for the first part of the contrast: 'I could have destroyed you' and 'I will destroy you'. In order to determine the best understanding, we need to put the possible halves of the contrast together to see what overall sense they make.

Option	9:15	9:16
A	I could have destroyed you	But for this (reason) I have sustained you
B	I could have destroyed you	But for this I raised you up
C	I will destroy you	But for this I have sustained you
D	I will destroy you	But for this I raised you up

Option D

As a contrast, it is difficult to see how the two statements relate. One would want to replace the adversative וְאוּלָם with an affirmative 'indeed'. The

---

[111] August Dillmann, *Die Bücher Exodus und Leviticus* (Leipzig: S. Hirzel, 1880), henceforth 'Dillmann', 86 '*bestehen lassen*' (allow to remain/continue to exist); Baentsch, 74 '*leben gelassen*' (let live); Schmidt, 346 '*bestehen / am Leben lassen*'; Childs, 125, 'I spared you'; Propp, 301, 'I let you stand'. Driver *Exodus*, 73, noting parallels of Ps. 102:27 and Ex. 21:21, comments that הֶעֱמִיד might have had the sense of ἐξήγειρά in post-exilic Hebrew but not at the time of this text. Houtman, I 349, suggests 'to keep on one's feet' i.e. 'to keep alive', noting 9:11; 18:23 and 21:21.

[112] Gen. 28:19; 48:19; Ex. 9:16; Num. 14:21; Jdg. 18:29; 1Sam. 20:3; 25:34; 1Kgs. 20:23; Job 1:11; 2:5; 5:8; 11:5; 12:7; 13:3-4; 14:18; 17:10; 33:1; Mic. 3:8; cf. Houtman, II 87. It can also be used as a proper name, and mean 'porch', but neither are appropriate here.

sense would then be that this is all part of YHWH's plan, and that
Pharaoh's reason for existence is to be raised up and then destroyed by
YHWH. However, this affirmative sense of וְאוּלָם would be a unique
opposite to its normal adversative meaning.

Option C

As with option D, this does not make much sense at present. If we keep the
sense of הֶעֱמַדְתִּיךָ as past, we would need to read וְאוּלָם as an affirmation,
as in option D: Pharaoh has been spared to this point in order to be
destroyed.

We could understand the sense as a contrast between what YHWH has
done and what he will do: 'I am going to destroy you, but here is why I
have not killed you so far...'. However one would expect עַד־כֹּה or
equivalent to make this clear; especially as such phrases are used repeatedly
in plagues narrative dialogue (cf. 7:16).[113]

We could understand the הֶעֱמַדְתִּיךָ as future, to be consistent with the
future sense of 9:15 in this option. In this case, the contrast would be
between Egypt as a whole which will be destroyed ('you and your people'),
and Pharaoh himself who will be spared (the suffix on the verb is singular)
for YHWH's purposes.[114] There are some Jewish traditions that appear to
be based upon this understanding.[115] However, there are problems with this.
If this is a contrast between the treatment of Pharaoh, and that of his people,
it is odd that v15 includes a direct reference to Pharaoh '...will strike *you
and* your people', rather than just 'will strike your people'. Moreover we
might expect the singularity of Pharaoh's exemption in v16 to be
emphasised by לְבַדֶּךָ (cf. 18:14, 18; Ps. 51:6 [4] etc.) or similar.[116]

Option B

The sense here would presumably be 'I could have destroyed you, but I set
this whole thing up to show you my power [so destroying you wouldn't
have made much sense]'? This is slightly forced in order to make sense of
the contrast, and it implies that destroying Pharaoh was never really a

---

[113] Such phrases include עוֹד, טֶרֶם and עַד־כֹּה. See 2.2.5.1 on עוֹד.

[114] Durham, 125, translates וְאוּלָם with 'in fact', although he does suggest that its
function is to qualify the sweeping statement of v15 (127).

[115] See the note to 9:16 of TgN (38) that it may have known a tradition that Pharaoh was
a firstborn and was saved from the last plague. Alternatively, Jacob *Exodus*, 274, notes
Rabbi Nehemiah's comment that this section was prophetic in respect of Pharaoh's
rescue from the Red Sea. Ginzberg sets this out in book III of the *Legends* (29-30):
'Thus all the Egyptians were drowned. Only one was spared – Pharaoh himself...'. Louis
Ginzberg, *The Legends of the Jews*, (Philadelphia: Jewish Publication Society, 1967).
Pharaoh 'repents', is tortured by Gabriel for fifty days in the sea, and installed as king of
Nineveh; the same king that (unsurprisingly) reacts so quickly to Jonah's message.

[116] This is in addition to the difficulties with understanding שָׁלַחְתִּי as future.

viable option. This does not seem to make a great deal of sense in context, and one wonders why YHWH would make this point, especially to Pharaoh.

Option A

The sense here would be that YHWH could have destroyed Pharaoh in the previous plagues. (This could be a reference to the fifth plague on livestock specifically, or the previous encounters and plagues as a whole.) However, YHWH has chosen to spare Pharaoh from this destruction and to keep him established where he is for YHWH's own reasons; reasons which Pharaoh is about to hear: 'I could have destroyed you, but I haven't, and here is why I haven't:...'.

Option D makes very little sense. Option B possibly could be understood as YHWH boasting about his power. However, it is awkward as a comparison, and it does not make much sense in context. Therefore it is likely that 9:16aα should have the sense of 'sustain' rather than 'raise up'. Option C is possible (albeit difficult), due to the contrast of Pharaoh specifically with Egypt in general. However, it requires a future sense for the perfects in v15 and v16, and raises the question (as above) of when all Egypt gets destroyed by plague.

Option A seems to make the most sense, with a contrast of what could have happened with what actually has happened. Thus, its widespread support amongst modern commentators and translations appears to be justified.[117]

2.2.4.3 בַּעֲבוּר הַרְאֹתְךָ ... וּלְמַעַן סַפֵּר

We now come to the reason for YHWH's preservation of Pharaoh and his people in v16. As in v14 it is introduced with בַּעֲבוּר. Moreover, it deals with similar themes to v14. Although יָדַע is not used, we have YHWH showing Pharaoh his power and recounting his name throughout the earth. However, the method of YHWH's self-revelation is rather different. In v14 YHWH sends a plague to bring Pharaoh to knowledge of himself, whereas in v16 revelation of YHWH is the reason for preservation from destruction. Therefore we need to consider how to understand this, both in its immediate context, and in light of v14.

One way of explaining the difference in methods is to question the comparison between the results in v14 and v16. Do כִּי יָדַע and הַרְאֹתְךָ have the same meaning, or are different results being outlined? The Hiph'il of רָאָה is used only here in the exodus story, in contrast to the more frequent יָדַע. However, יָדַע and רָאָה are often paralleled in the wider Old

---

[117] E.g. Propp, 13; Childs, 124-25; Schmidt, 339-40; Cassuto, 116; Sarna *Exodus* 46; Houtman, II 86; Noth, 80; Driver *Exodus*, 73; Hyatt, 117; RSV/NRSV; NASB; JPST.

Testament where they describe external recognition.[118] Moreover the
content of the revelation seems to be similar. 9:14 speaks of there being
none like YHWH, presumably in his ability to bring plagues like none
other. 9:16 speaks of showing YHWH's power (כֹּחַ), which will lead to the
second purpose of YHWH's actions: to recount[119] his name throughout the
earth.[120] This seems to fit in with the general sense of the previous purpose
and that of v14: further revelation and recognition of YHWH.[121] However
we will need to consider how YHWH shows his power through sustaining
Egypt.

    When used of YHWH, the word כֹּחַ is normally connected to his deeds in
creation, or in the exodus, which are done by his power.[122] It is also
connected with wisdom on a number of occasions.[123] This suggests a
concept of power which is different from simply domination, doing things
'because I can'. If YHWH wished simply to give a demonstration of
overwhelming force, then the possible action mentioned in 9:15 would be
most appropriate. If a god can wipe out an entire race, especially a race that
is not his own, then he is a force to be reckoned with. However, he has
refrained from doing this act, which would seem to show great 'power', in
order to show 'power'. We could explain this seeming paradox in two
ways.

    First, YHWH has avoided wiping Pharaoh out in order to inflict yet more
plagues upon him. A single plague of pestilence that brings total destruction
would show power. However, it could be argued that sending a series of
plagues involving different aspects of the world (control over weather,
animals, disease etc) would be a more effective demonstration. In this case,
the 'power' would be shown in the plagues to come, and possibly would

---

[118] Botterweck, 'יָדַע', *TDOT* V, 461, lists a number of examples including Dt. 11:2; Job
11:11; Ps. 138:6; Is. 41:20 etc. Zimmerli *I am Yahweh*, 31, notes a couple of cases
where the recognition formula in Ezekiel uses רָאָה in place of יָדַע, noting the frequent
parallelism. In our story note 2:25.

[119] Many translations seem to follow the LXX in translating סָפַר in the passive: 'that my
name may be recounted' (διαγγελῇ). While the implication may be that it will be
humans who will recount YHWH's name, the force of the active verb suggests that this
is linked strongly to YHWH's actions. He is causing this recounting by what he is
doing.

[120] As with הָאָרֶץ in 9:14, this could refer to the land or the earth. Here the sense is
wider than simply Pharaoh's focus, and thus it is translated as 'earth'.

[121] The phrase 'show power' with כֹּחַ and Hiph'il רָאָה, is only found in 9:16 in the Old
Testament (Jdg. 16:5 has the Qal, with the sense of 'find out', rather than the Hiph'il
'show'). The only other examples of declaring YHWH's name are in Ps. 22:23 [22] and
102:22 [21], which are not immediately helpful. The concept of recounting YHWH's
deeds is more common.

[122] Ringgren, 'כֹּחַ', *TDOT* VII, 123, 126-127.

[123] Jer. 10:12/51:15; Job 9:4; 26:12; 36:22; (37:23); Ps. 147:5.

have been shown in part in the plagues that have already come. In its favour, this explanation would correspond to that in v14: YHWH shows his power (or is known), by his ability to send plagues upon Egypt. VV15-16 would therefore be explaining why YHWH's plagues have not been as devastating as they might.

Secondly, it is in the act of refraining from destruction that YHWH shows his 'power'. Initially this seems rather less obvious than the first option, raising the question of how one shows power through restraint.

One parallel that may shed some light on this explanation is the speech of Moses in Num. 14. Israel have just rejected the call to go into the land of Canaan, preferring to return to Egypt (Num. 14:1-10). YHWH asks Moses how long the people will refuse to believe in him in spite of the signs that he has performed among them. He says that he will destroy them with plague and make Moses into a greater nation than them (Num. 14:11-12). At this point, Israel's position seems not too dissimilar to that of the Egyptians at 9:16. YHWH has sent signs but they have not been believed.[124] Thus a plague (הֶבֶר) that will wipe them out (cf. 9:15) is coming upon them.

Moses responds that YHWH has brought the people out of Egypt 'by your power' (בְכֹחֲךָ v13) and that if he destroys them, the people round about will say 'YHWH was not able to bring them into the land' (vv13-16). Then he prays 'Now may my lord's power be made great as you said... (וְעַתָּה יִגְדַּל־נָא כֹּחַ אֲדֹנָי כַּאֲשֶׁר דִּבַּרְתָּ לֵאמֹר)' followed by a quotation of YHWH's words to him on the mountain: 'YHWH, slow to anger...' (vv17-18; cf. Ex. 34:6-7). Thus Moses is asking YHWH to make his power great by exercising mercy.[125]

To strengthen the comparison, we can note that the words of YHWH in 34:6-7 are in response to Moses' call for YHWH to 'show me your glory' (הַרְאֵנִי נָא אֶת־כְּבֹדֶךָ 33:18). This may provide a parallel of sorts to 'show you my power' in 9:16. This is especially the case as YHWH's response to this request is to say that he will declare his name to Moses (33:19), which is also the second purpose of 9:16 (although the verb is קָרָא rather than סָפַר).[126]

---

[124] Num. 14:22 speaks of Israel testing YHWH ten times, which resonates strongly with the ten plagues (cf. Abot 5:1-6 esp. 4).

[125] Cf. Gray who, having suggested a meaning of asking YHWH to show his power in another way, continues: 'Or possibly, as v19 would suggest, כֹּחַ rather means *(moral) power*, or *control* by the exercise of which Yahweh pardons; cf. Nah. 1:3.' George Buchanan Gray, *A Critical and Exegetical Commentary on Numbers*, ICC (Edinburgh: T&T Clark, 1903), 157.

[126] One early linking of these passages is found in Romans where Paul combines Ex. 33:19 (Rom. 9:15) with Ex. 9:16 (Rom. 9:17), albeit his point is rather different from the one argued here.

One could object at this point that this reading of 9:16 seems like an attempt to make YHWH's actions more amenable to a modern audience.[127] Would it not be simpler to accept that this is about a contest of power between two forces, or YHWH showing off his greater power? Certainly it would be going too far to suggest that 9:16 is speaking of YHWH showing mercy. The words of 34:6-7 have not been given yet, and Num. 14 is dealing with Moses' intercession on behalf of YHWH's people, which Egypt are not (albeit Israel may be acting a little like Egypt at this point).

Further, as with 9:14, YHWH's acts in sparing the Egyptians are not due to 'humanitarian' reasons. In 9:14 possible humanitarian reasons for YHWH's actions in bringing plagues were to free Israel or to punish Egypt. Here an equivalent reason for YHWH's restraint might be concern for the wellbeing of the Egyptians. However, as in 9:14, this is nowhere indicated in the text, and should be dismissed in favour of the reason given: 'to show you my power...'. TgPsJ. 9:16 brings this point out: 'I did not keep you alive that I might do good to you but to show you...'. As with 9:14, the focus is theocentric.[128] Nevertheless, this theocentric focus has an effect on humans. The question here is what kind of an effect it has, and how we understand YHWH's 'power'.

We can compare this to the discussion on 'send ... serve'. Even in its wider scope of meaning, YHWH is not espousing libertarian principles but rather speaking of a change of masters. Pharaoh is to release Israel from his service so that they can serve YHWH instead. However, the nature of the two masters is contrasted. Pharaoh's mastery leads to suffering. YHWH's mastery is signified by bringing them into a good land. If YHWH and Pharaoh differ in their expression of mastery, then may there not be a similar difference in their expression of power? Pharaoh exercises power over the powerless by increasing his oppressive rule, but such domination is not the only possible model of power. This verse may show that YHWH exercises a different kind of power.

One nuance that arises from this option is the choice of modal verb used for שָׁלַחְתִּי in v.15. Thus far it has been translated as 'could have sent my hand', focussing on the question of YHWH's ability. However, both Fretheim and Cassuto suggest using 'should'.[129] This would suggest that

---

[127] Thus, for example Fretheim's comment (125) that 'God is acting in such a public way so that God's good news can be proclaimed to everyone (see Rom. 9:17).' He notes the use of Pi'el סָפַר in proclamations of good news (eg. Ps. 78:3-4; Is. 43:21); however it can also be used in a less positive sense (10:2, for example, is negative, at least for the Egyptians...).

[128] In Num. 14, and in Ezek. 20 (considered in 2.3.4 below), YHWH's restraint is also for the sake of his Name. Cf. G. A. Cooke, *A Critical and Exegetical Commentary on the Book of Ezekiel*, ICC (Edinburgh: T&T Clark, 1970), 216.

[129] Fretheim, 124; Cassuto, 116.

Pharaoh deserves nothing more than utter destruction, although YHWH is refraining from this for his own purposes. We will continue to use 'could' to translate here, but this indicates that it is not self-evidently about questions of ability alone.

2.2.4.4 SUMMARY OF 9:16

- V16 is either speaking of YHWH setting Pharaoh in his position, before the plagues, or keeping him there in spite of them. Taken with v15, it makes most sense to understand the two as contrasting the possible destruction that YHWH could have wrought upon Egypt, with the reality that he spared them.

- YHWH's reasons for this were not 'humanitarian'. Instead he did it to show his power and extend his recognition. This demonstration of power could be understood either as keeping Pharaoh alive to send more plagues upon him (hence showing more power), or as made in the actual act of keeping him alive.

2.2.5 9:17

עוֹדְךָ מִסְתּוֹלֵל בְּעַמִּי לְבִלְתִּי שַׁלְּחָם:

'Still you exalt yourself over my people, refusing to send them!'

After the concentration on YHWH's actions in v14-16, the focus shifts to those of Pharaoh. We need, therefore, to consider how this shift fits into YHWH's speech. What is Pharaoh doing, and what does it mean in relation to what has just been said?

מִסְתּוֹלֵל

Houtman notes two possible meanings for מִסְתּוֹלֵל: 'exalting oneself', or 'behaving haughtily against' ('opposing'). He favours the latter option, with the image of Pharaoh as a roadblock to Israel's freedom.[130] However, the image of 'lording it' would make sense in context as well. We have suggested that the demand 'send...serve' has at least a connotation of a change of master. If so, then as Pharaoh is 'exalting himself over Israel', he is opposing YHWH's rule over them, and thus opposing their release.

2.2.5.1 עוֹדְךָ AND THE RELATION TO V16

The portrayal of Pharaoh as stubborn is not unique to this encounter. However, we need to consider how this fits with the unusual comments that precede it in v15-16. The connection between the two is made by עוֹדְךָ. As

---

[130] Houtman, II 88. Ehrlich, 294 proposes reading מתעלל (cf. 10:2). However, there is no real need to alter the MT at 9:17 as it makes good sense as it stands.

with וְאוּלָם in the previous verse, this may help to understand how the two statements are to be understood.

The uses of עוֹד with a suffix followed immediately by a participle can be grouped into three different meanings. It is used primarily in a specific phrase in narrative: 'while X was still speaking, Y arrived'.[131] This is not the case here. Alternatively, it is used to show that such and such a situation will or will not remain: 'No longer will ...'.[132] However, 9:17 does not appear to be referring to the future.

Finally it is used to make the point that someone is *still* doing something. Of these cases, the closest parallels to our text are in 9:2, Job 2:3 and 2:9.[133] In Job 2 both YHWH and Job's wife comment on the fact that despite Job's many reverses, he still holds to his integrity. For YHWH this is vindication of his comments to the satan; for Job's wife it is incredulity at his stubbornness.

וַיֹּאמֶר יְהוָה אֶל־הַשָּׂטָן הֲשַׂמְתָּ לִבְּךָ אֶל־עַבְדִּי אִיּוֹב כִּי אֵין כָּמֹהוּ בָּאָרֶץ אִישׁ תָּם וְיָשָׁר יְרֵא אֱלֹהִים וְסָר מֵרָע וְעֹדֶנּוּ מַחֲזִיק בְּתֻמָּתוֹ וַתְּסִיתֵנִי בוֹ לְבַלְּעוֹ חִנָּם: (Job 2:3)

וַתֹּאמֶר לוֹ אִשְׁתּוֹ עֹדְךָ מַחֲזִיק בְּתֻמָּתֶךָ בָּרֵךְ אֱלֹהִים וָמֻת: (Job 2:9)

There is a contrast between the events that have affected Job, together with their expected response, and the response that Job actually makes. One could almost gloss these comments as: 'despite all that has happened, Job has not reacted as one (here either the satan or Job's wife), would expect; rather he still holds firm to his integrity'.

One can compare Job and Pharaoh:

---

[131] Gen. 29:9; 1Kgs. 1:14, 22, 42; 2Kgs. 6:33; Est. 6:14
[132] Zech. 9:8. (This is also the case for Is. 62:4 and Ezek. 34:29 which have passive participles.)
[133] The other text in this category is Gen. 18:22, which is not in direct speech and thus not so relevant.

	Job (the godly)	Pharaoh (the ungodly)
Initial state	Blameless and upright (Job 1:8; 2:3)	Opposed to letting the people go (3:19; 5:2)
Divine action	YHWH sends hand/satan but restrains (Job 1:11-12; 2:5-6)	YHWH sends hand (3:20) but restrains (9:15-16)[134]
Response	Still holds to his integrity (Job 2:3, 9 מַחֲזִיק – cf. Ex.9:2)	Still exalts himself and will not let people go (9:17)

The use in Job 2:9 is most similar of the two, being a direct address to the person in question. One can sense the remonstrating or exasperated tone that his wife uses. We can hear a similar tone in YHWH's words in v17. Despite all that has happened to Pharaoh, he *still* exalts himself. In Job 2:3 there is a corresponding force to the words, although YHWH's statement carries an approving tone, rather than the disapproving tone of Job's wife. In neither case does it make sense to read the statement as purely descriptive, and this is also true of 9:17 (and 9:2).

Let us return to our four options for understanding v15-16, to see how they could fit in with this move in v17.

Options B and D become even more difficult in this context. YHWH would be saying 'I raised you up, and still you are exalting yourself'. This seems to be a relatively superfluous statement. Even if Pharaoh accepted this point, he could well respond along the lines of: 'Fine. You are saying that you raised me, and that I am still raised. Your point is…?'

Option C has difficulties as well. YHWH has just told Pharaoh that he is to be spared the general destruction of Egypt. YHWH then remonstrates with him that he is exalting himself over YHWH's people. This could well serve as a reason for destruction (v15), but it seems odd following a statement that Pharaoh will be spared (v16). There is no obvious progression from v16 to v17 on this reading.

As before, Option A makes most sense. YHWH could have brought destruction upon Pharaoh. Instead he has restrained himself to show Pharaoh his power. However, despite all of this, Pharaoh's reaction has not

---

[134] If we translate Ex. 9:15 as 'I should have…', a further distinction stands out. Job holds on to his righteousness, even though he is being afflicted for no reason. Pharaoh holds on to his unrighteousness, even though he has been spared the punishment that he deserves.

We could also note the similar phraseology in Job 2:3 and Ex. 9:13-14. Satan is asked 'have you set your heart upon my servant Job?', whereas the plagues are to be upon Pharaoh's heart (9:14 cf. 9:21 and 7:22-23 for the exact phrase). Moreover Satan is told that there is 'none like him in all the earth'; whereas Pharaoh is told that there is 'none like me in all the earth' (9:14). There appears to be a similar dynamic here.

been to acknowledge YHWH's power and release Israel. Instead he has chosen to keep himself in a position of power over them.

Moreover, if we accept Option A, it is more difficult to understand v16b (בַּעֲבוּר...) as indicating that YHWH has spared Pharaoh in order to show his power by inflicting more plagues upon him. As with options B and D above, having told Pharaoh that all is going to plan, it would be rather odd for YHWH immediately to remonstrate with him over this. If YHWH wanted to send more plagues, then presumably he would want Pharaoh to keep exalting himself. If this were the case then v17 would make no sense.

The second option makes much more sense of v17. YHWH is showing Pharaoh his power by not exterminating him and his people. However, Pharaoh's response to this is to keep exalting himself over Israel, by not sending them to serve YHWH. Thus he is not obeying YHWH's demand, indicating that he is not convinced by YHWH's power (cf. 5:2).

2.2.5.2 SUMMARY OF 9:17

- Although YHWH has not destroyed Pharaoh in order to teach him something, Pharaoh has chosen to use this restraint of YHWH to continue his own exaltation over Israel, in opposition to YHWH's demand.
- YHWH's words concerning Pharaoh's obduracy, similar in nature to Job 2:3 and 9, suggests that the 'power' spoken of in 9:16 is shown through YHWH's restraint in not destroying Egypt.

2.2.6 9:18

הִנְנִי מַמְטִיר כָּעֵת מָחָר בָּרָד כָּבֵד מְאֹד אֲשֶׁר לֹא־הָיָה כָמֹהוּ בְּמִצְרַיִם
לְמִן־הַיּוֹם הִוָּסְדָה וְעַד־עָתָּה:

'Behold I will rain down tomorrow a very great hail, the like of which there has not been in Egypt from the day it was founded until now.'

We now move to YHWH's response to Pharaoh's response to him. The 'still you' is followed by 'behold I' (הִנְנִי). The brief statement in v14 is now expanded, and we hear of a very great hailstorm, which is unmatched by anything that Egypt has encountered from its very beginnings. This is the first time that such a statement of incomparability has been made. The previous plagues have been heavy (8:20 [24]; 9:3), but this appears to be on a different level of magnitude (cf. 10:6; 11:6). This incomparable plague is being sent to reveal the incomparability of YHWH: לֹא־הָיָה כָמֹהוּ בְּמִצְרַיִם (v18), אֵין כָּמֹנִי בְּכָל־הָאָרֶץ (v14). [135]

---

[135] Cassuto, 115, notes the repetition of this concept 'none like...' after this point, cumulating in the hymn of praise of 15:11 'who is like you, O YHWH'. On incomparability cf. Jacob *Exodus*, 185; Larrson, 76-78.

2.2.7 9:19

וְעַתָּה שְׁלַח הָעֵז אֶת־מִקְנְךָ וְאֵת כָּל־אֲשֶׁר לְךָ בַּשָּׂדֶה כָּל־הָאָדָם
וְהַבְּהֵמָה אֲשֶׁר־יִמָּצֵא בַשָּׂדֶה וְלֹא יֵאָסֵף הַבַּיְתָה וְיָרַד עֲלֵהֶם הַבָּרָד וָמֵתוּ:

'Now, send and bring to safety your cattle and everything of yours outdoors.
Every man and beast found outdoors, and not gathered into the house, upon them
the hail will fall, and they will die.'

The effects of the plague are then set out, and they are far-reaching. Every
single living being that is outside will be struck by hail and will die.[136]
However, these effects are bound up in a call to the Egyptians which, like
9:15-16, is unparalleled in the plagues narratives. YHWH offers the
Egyptians the chance to mitigate the effects of this plague, if they bring
their livestock and servants indoors. (Although the animals and humans can
be saved, the crops will still be destroyed. Therefore the effects may be
mitigated rather than avoided completely.) After YHWH's response to
Pharaoh's response to him, the Egyptian people are offered a choice of
responses to YHWH. The wider implications of this mitigation will be
discussed in 2.3.3 and 2.4.5.

2.3 The Meaning of 9:13-19?

The previous section has discussed the relevant individual words and
phrases in 9:13-19, considering factors such as grammar, context and wider
usage to come up with the most satisfactory translations and interpretations.
However, making sense individually is only the first stage. In order for our
interpretations to be judged successful, they must be able to combine to
make overall sense as a coherent single message. We could attempt to put

---

[136] The *casus pendens* that starts v19b (כָּל־הָאָדָם וְהַבְּהֵמָה ... עֲלֵהֶם) arguably
emphasises the universal destructive potential of the plague. There is, of course, the
problem that the animals of the Egyptians appear to have been killed already in the fifth
plague (9:6) e.g. Hyatt, 100; Ehrlich 294. However this does not invalidate the point of
the narrative here. At the least, the Egyptian servants in the fields were in danger of
death, and could have been saved. Rather than focussing on this discrepancy, or trying
to find a cunning way around it (such as differentiating the terms used, or suggesting
that the Egyptians stole the Israelites' cattle after the fifth plague), we should
concentrate on the point that the text makes. The Egyptians have the chance to save
כָּל־אֲשֶׁר לְךָ בַּשָּׂדֶה (whatever that may be), or to leave it to die.
The same point is true for the plague on the firstborn, where the firstborn of the cattle
appear to die yet again (12:29). The point is that *every* living Egyptian firstborn from
that of the greatest being – Pharaoh - to that of the lowest - servants/prisoners (contrast
11:5 and 12:29), and livestock - will die. It is a plague immeasurable in grief (even
compared to this one), for amongst all the Egyptians אֵין בַּיִת אֲשֶׁר אֵין־שָׁם מֵת (12:30).
On the probable use of hyperbole in the text, see Propp, 347; Cassuto, 111; Fretheim,
121; Keil, 480.

other of the options together to form single messages in contrast to the
options that we have selected. However, this would be laborious. Moreover
if the case has been sufficiently made in the previous section, this is
unnecessary. If the case has not been made, then we need to return to the
previous section before continuing.

The interpretation to be put forth argues that this message from YHWH
to Pharaoh makes sense as a whole and in context. Its purpose is to
announce a change in YHWH's actions towards Egypt and to explain this,
in order to provoke the correct response from Pharaoh.[137]

2.3.1 The Warning of a Change (vv13-14)

Moses is sent to Pharaoh with the standard demand from YHWH: 'send my
people that they may serve me' (v13), which contains its ambiguity of
meaning. As he has done several times already YHWH calls upon Pharaoh
to respond appropriately. This demand forms the context for the rest of the
message. YHWH is not simply telling Pharaoh of what he has done and
what he will do; he is calling upon him to act.

However, instead of the normal conditional response 'if you do not send
... I will send...' (e.g. 7:27 [8:2]; 8:17 [21]; 9:2), Pharaoh is told that this
time YHWH is sending all his plagues upon him and his people, so that he
will know that there is none like YHWH (14 cf. 7:17). This knowledge is
more than simply intellectual acquiescence. For Pharaoh truly to 'know that
...', he must acknowledge it as well. The implications of this flow from
their very first encounter in 5:1-2, where Pharaoh will not 'send' the
people, because he does not 'know' YHWH.

Instead of offering Pharaoh a choice of 'Pharaoh sending (Pi'el) Israel'
or 'YHWH sending (Hiph'il) plague', YHWH then explains to him why he
is sending 'all his plagues' (vv15-18).

2.3.2 The Explanation of this Change (vv15-18)

YHWH contrasts the plagues that he has sent upon Pharaoh with another
option open to him – total destruction. YHWH could have destroyed
Pharaoh and Egypt with one plague of pestilence (v15). Presumably, he
could have exempted Goshen, having already demonstrated the ability to do
so (8:18-19 [22-23]; 9:7). Then he would be able to bring his people, Israel,
out of Egypt as he had promised.

---

[137] The suggestions that this message announces a change in YHWH's acts, or that this
message puts Pharaoh's survival to this point in perspective are nothing new. Cf.
Greenberg *UE*, 150-51; Keil, 489; Cassuto, 116. The difference here is the attempt to
explain the reasons for it, and the way that the whole speech hangs together.

However, YHWH has not done this. Instead he has sustained Pharaoh, keeping him (and his people) alive (v16). Until this plague there has been no mention of the death of Egyptians, only animals. He has done this, not out of some humanitarian impulse, but rather as part of his program of self-revelation to Pharaoh, and beyond him to all the earth. This preservation from previous death thus has a similar aim to that of the plague that YHWH is about to send. Compare the similarities of v14 'you will know that there is none like me in all the land/earth', and v16 'show you my power and to declare my name throughout the earth'.

However, Pharaoh's response to YHWH's actions is less than impressive. He should have learned/acknowledged that 'I am YHWH' and thus obeyed his command to release Israel. Instead he has responded to YHWH restraining his [YHWH's] own power over Egypt ('you and your people' v15) by maintaining his [Pharaoh's] own power over Israel ('my people' v17). He has maintained the sentiment of 5:2 'Who is YHWH that I should listen to his demand to release Israel? I do not know YHWH, and Israel I will not send.' Therefore YHWH's strategy in v16 has fallen upon deaf ears (or a hard heart). Thus, as there is an ambiguity in the demand 'send ... serve' allowing two different interpretations of it, there is also an ambiguity in YHWH's past actions set out in v16. He has restrained himself in order to show Pharaoh his power by so doing. However, Pharaoh has taken it another way. He has continued to exalt himself over YHWH's people, in the manner of 5:2. Thus for him, YHWH's actions, far from demonstrating power, have confirmed his original views of YHWH as one who can be ignored. YHWH's use of power (through restraint) is so different from Pharaoh's concept of power (through domination), that for him it appears as weakness.

If Pharaoh will not respond to that strategy, YHWH will respond by changing it. This time, he will send a different kind of plague or plagues upon Egypt (v18, cf. v14). This plague will be something 'the like of which has never occurred before in Egypt'. One can presume that the possibility for ambiguity and self-deception on Pharaoh's part are therefore lessened. These plagues to come will be harder to ignore.

Thus we have returned to the beginning of YHWH's speech, and the reason for the plague to come is set out.

2.3.3 The Response to this Change (v19)

Finally, although Pharaoh has not responded to YHWH's restraint (v16) beforehand, he is given the chance to take it up once more. This plague cannot be stopped (see v14 above). However it can be mitigated with regard to the humans and livestock. If Pharaoh and his people are willing to follow YHWH's word, then this incomparable plague will be lessened; perhaps to the status of one of the earlier plagues.

In one sense it is a welcome sight to the reader to see this genuine alternative offered. Childs contrasts this with the inevitability of previous plagues.[138] However, we have noted that this plague (unlike most others) is inevitable. There is no 'send or I will send', it is simply 'I will send'. Thus the choice that Pharaoh had to avoid previous plagues has changed to a choice that he has (together with his people) to mitigate this plague.[139]

However, as Houtman notes, there is a sting in the tail.[140] Pharaoh and his people can preserve their livestock and servants, but only by obeying the word of YHWH. If Pharaoh agrees to 'send' in order to save his possessions, he is accepting YHWH's word that he will be sending a plague, and acting upon that acceptance. This would make it more difficult to maintain his opposition when YHWH next tells him to 'send' Israel out, in order to 'save' his people and his land from another plague. Pharaoh can keep either his cattle or his resistance and independence; not both. Moreover, any of Pharaoh's people who do obey YHWH's word are showing a split in the opposition to YHWH, and potentially undermining Pharaoh.[141]

In other words, as with the sustenance (הֶעֱמַדְתִּיךָ) in v16, this offer of mitigation is not simply due to YHWH being 'nice'.[142] This is the only plague where such mitigation is offered, and one would expect something similar in the firstborn plague especially if this was primarily to prevent the loss of life. One could imagine an offer to the god-fearing Egyptians to partake in the Passover, put the blood on their doors, and maybe even join Israel in leaving Egypt as part of the 'mixed multitude' (12:38). However, there is no such offer.

---

[138] Childs, 158.

[139] This contrast would not be appropriate for Childs, as he does not see the conditional at the beginning of most of the plagues as a real conditional, as Pharaoh's refusal is assumed (147, contrast Fretheim, 99). However one could equally assume Pharaoh's refusal to this word of YHWH also (albeit perhaps not his people's refusal). Moreover, just because one assumes that Pharaoh will refuse, it does not make the conditional irrelevant unless it is impossible for Pharaoh to refuse. It is interesting that it is only at this point, where YHWH starts hardening Pharaoh (at least explicitly), that this offer is made.

[140] Houtman, II 82; cf. Noth, 81.

[141] Houtman, II 82. There is no purpose given for the mitigation, as there is for the plague (v14) and the previous restraint (v16). However, if we accept that 'knowing that...' involves acknowledgement through action, then this acceptance of YHWH's word is, in effect, acknowledging him.

[142] Sarna *Exodus*, 46, suggests that here YHWH is showing concern for the needless loss of human and animal life, and notes a rabbinic comment on his compassion, even when angry. However, this does not sit well with YHWH's actions in the rest of the plagues, especially the last.

Let us not, however, reduce this offer into merely a cunning plan of YHWH. The following text shows us that there was a real alternative, and any Egyptians (including Pharaoh) could have saved their livestock (vv20-21, 25a). This follows the pattern that we have seen throughout YHWH's words. In v13 the call is for Israel to serve YHWH, not to go free. However, that 'service' will be of a different, more beneficial kind than their service to Pharaoh. In v14 YHWH sends the plague for the sake of his self-revelation. However, Pharaoh's acknowledgement of him as the result of this must include sending the people of Israel. In v16 Pharaoh and Egypt have been spared from destruction, which is a real benefit for Egypt, and this is done to show Pharaoh YHWH's power. In all these cases beneficence is inextricably linked to one's engagement with, and response to, YHWH.

2.3.4 9:13-19: A Responsive God Seeking Response?

Our reading of the whole explanation moves between YHWH's acts and Pharaoh's acts; YHWH's responses to Pharaoh and Pharaoh's responses (or lack of them) to YHWH. The demand to Pharaoh to respond appropriately to YHWH (v13) is followed by YHWH's announcement of his coming action, which is intended to make Pharaoh respond in a certain way by acknowledging YHWH (v14). This action of YHWH is explained as a response to Pharaoh's lack of response to YHWH's previous actions (vv15-18). Here the statement of YHWH's power in vv15-16, showing that Pharaoh's survival is due to YHWH, is followed by a remonstration concerning Pharaoh's behaviour, as he has not responded appropriately (v17). Finally Pharaoh is given the chance to respond again, in terms of the offered mitigation (v19).[143]

We are seeking to explain YHWH's actions in the plagues narrative. Therefore at this point, we should consider briefly if this is a model that can be supported by wider Old Testament examples.[144] We could suggest a reasonable number of passages in respect of this picture. For now we will consider only two, which have links to our passage: Amos 4:6-12 and Ezek. 20.

---

[143] YHWH has a possible response to Egypt in terms of destruction, which he does not take (v15), and Pharaoh has a possible response to YHWH in terms of listening to YHWH which he does not take (v17 cf. later on Pharaoh's response to v19). The passage makes clear that these are realistic possibilities.

[144] The majority of our work will be to consider this model within the plagues narrative. However at this point it is worth considering whether there is wider Old Testament support, as this model is rather different than one that might be constructed out of these verses, such as the idea of a determinist God who 'raised up' Pharaoh and is effectively controlling him.

Amos 4:6-11 lists a series of calamities that YHWH has sent upon Israel: cleanness of teeth (hunger); lack of water; crops struck with blight, mildew, and locust; pestilence 'after the manner of Egypt'; death by sword; overthrow like the divine overthrow of Sodom and Gomorrah. Each of these is followed by the words 'and/but you did not return to me', presumably YHWH's reason for sending the plagues. Even without the reference to the plagues of Egypt, we can see similarities. 9:17 echoes in the continual refrain of Israel's lack of response. As with Num. 14, here Israel appear to be put in the position of Egypt. These divine actions have not received the correct response from Israel. Therefore, because of this, YHWH will act definitively: 'Therefore thus will I do to you, and because I will do this to you, prepare to meet your God, O Israel!' (Amos 4:12).[145]

In Ezekiel 20, the prophet responds to a request for him to enquire of YHWH with a recapitulation of Israel's history in judgement upon Israel. Time and again YHWH acts favourably towards Israel, so that they may 'know that ...'. However each time Israel respond inappropriately to him. They refuse to get rid of their idols from Egypt; they reject YHWH's good laws; they desecrate his sabbaths. As a result each time YHWH purposes to destroy them. However he acts for the sake of his name and the way it will be perceived in the nations, and thus Israel are not destroyed. 'I said I would pour out my anger upon them to spend my wrath on them in the midst of the land of Egypt. But I acted for the sake of my name, that it would not be profaned in the sight of the nations ...' (Ezek. 20:8-9; cf. 13b-14; 15-17; 21-22).

However, finally, YHWH no longer restrains himself (Ezek. 20:23-26). He gives them 'laws that are not good', specifically relating to the firstborn, to horrify or devastate them 'so that they will know that I am YHWH' (20:25-26 contrast v11), and scatters them amongst the nations. Even the final restoration of Israel is done for the sake of YHWH's name (Ezek. 20:44), in contrast to what Israel's deeds have deserved. YHWH's treatment of Israel differs in moving from beneficence, through restraint, then devastation, to the final restoration but in each case the reason remains the same.[146]

---

[145] This assumes that Amos 4:6-12 is one unit rather than two or three, with v12 unconnected to vv6-11. Stuart argues for the interconnectedness: Douglas Stuart, *Hosea-Jonah*, WBC 31 (Dallas: Word Books, 1998), 336-337. He also notes the increase in severity of the disasters which, to anticipate, is a feature of the exodus plagues as well. Cf. A. G. Auld's comments on Gese's similar views in A.G. Auld, *Amos*, OTG (Sheffield: Sheffield Academic Press, 1995), 50.

[146] Corrine Paton "'I myself gave them laws that were not good': Ezekiel 20 and the Exodus Tradition' JSOT 69 (1996): 73-90, discusses Ezek. 20 and Exodus, albeit with the concern of whether Ezekiel knew the Exodus traditions, and the implications of Ezek. 20:25-26.

2.4 The Response to YHWH's Words

2.4.1 9:20-21

We now see the responses of the Egyptian officials to YHWH's word. Those who 'feared YHWH's word' gathered their servants and livestock into the house (v20). Those who 'did not set YHWH's word upon their hearts' abandoned their servants and livestock (v21).

In the plagues narrative there are a number of different phrases used to depict reactions and attitudes to YHWH. We have already seen the importance of the repeated יָדַע and כִּי יָדַע, and the link between knowing, acknowledging and action. Here we have two different terms used to explain the actions of the two groups of officials.

Fear (יָרֵא) as a term used to describe people's attitudes to YHWH is an important theological term in the Old Testament. Moreover it occurs several times in the exodus story (1:17, 21; 9:20, 30; 14:31). In the first two cases, the midwives' fear of God leads to their refusal to kill the Israelite boys, and YHWH rewards them for this. As with 9:20, the 'fear' leads to an action that involves saving the lives of beings dependent upon them. In both cases this necessitates taking a position which is in opposition to Pharaoh, their master (although this is less evident in the case of Pharaoh's officials). This moral restraint is a feature of those who 'fear God' in the Old Testament, both in Israel and beyond.[147] In the last case the Israelites' response to YHWH's acts at the Red Sea (saving them and destroying the pursuing Egyptians), is to 'fear YHWH and trust in him and in his servant Moses' (14:31). In 9:20 the wording is slightly different, as the officials feared the word of YHWH. This reflects the fact that they are responding to a particular word of YHWH (v19) rather than showing a more general reverence for him.

In none of these cases does it make sense to understand 'fear' as 'terror'.[148] If the midwives had been terrified of anyone, Pharaoh would seem to be a good candidate; yet their 'fear' of God led them to act against such terror. In 14:31 paralleling trust with terror would not make good sense.

---

[147] Moberly *BTF*, 92-94. This forms part of his wider discussion on 'fear of God' in 80-96.

[148] Jacob *Exodus*, 275, suggests that הַיָּרֵא אֶת־דְּבַר יְהוָה does not refer to Egyptians who believed in YHWH. Instead it denotes those who were frightened of the word that Moses brought. However this is an unnecessary polarisation. In the demand to Pharaoh 'send … serve', Pharaoh is not being called upon to serve YHWH, but he is called upon to respond correctly by sending Israel. Thus here the officials do not need to follow YHWH in order to respond appropriately to his word.

We have already compared Job to Pharaoh on v17. We can return to him again, as a paradigmatic example of one who 'fears God' (Job 1:1, 8; 2:3), where this term is linked to being blameless and upright, and turning away from evil. The question raised in the first two chapters is 'does Job fear God for nothing?' YHWH's response in 2:3 is that Job *still* maintains his integrity, even though he has been attacked for no reason.[149]

This understanding of 'fear' as the basis for moral deeds is strengthened when one considers the cause of the alternative action.[150] If fearing YHWH's word leads to obedience and saving one's slaves and livestock, then not setting YHWH's word upon one's heart leads to abandoning them. If the resulting actions are opposite, this suggests that the causes of these actions are also opposite. That is, fearing YHWH's word is equivalent, or at least comparable, to setting it upon one's heart. Elsewhere, Is. 57:11 combines not fearing YHWH and not setting him on the heart, along with not remembering him, and being false to him.

The phrase 'to set upon one's heart' means to pay attention to something, to be concerned about it, with the result that it affects one's actions.[151] We might say 'take it to heart'. Thus not to set something on one's heart is to ignore it, with the result that that one's actions are unaffected by it.[152] At the end of the first plague, Pharaoh turned away, entered his house, 'and did not set it upon his heart, even this!' (7:23). This comes just after the statement that his heart was hard and he would not listen to Moses and Aaron.

In other words, there appear to be a diversity of terms used for the actions and stance of Pharaoh and the Egyptians, the meanings of which overlap. 'Knowing', and 'fearing' lead to one set of actions. 'Not setting upon one's heart', 'hardening', 'not listening' lead to another, opposite set. In all cases, one's attitude to YHWH is the reason for one's actions.

2.4.2 9:22-26, 31-32

This is the description of the plague itself, and its effects. Except for noting the power of the plague, and the exemption of Goshen, these sections can be passed over for our purposes.

---

[149] See Moberly's discussion in *BTF*, 84-88.

[150] Cf. Ehrlich, 295.

[151] Dt. 11:18; 1Sam. 21:13 [12]; Job 22:22; Song. 3:8; Dan. 1:8. Cf. 'set heart upon', e.g. Dt. 32:46; Job. 1:8; 2:3.

[152] 2Sam. 18:3; 19:20 [19]; Is. 42:24-25. Cf 'not set heart upon', e.g. 1Sam. 9:20; 25:25.

2.4.3 9:27-28

Now Pharaoh responds to the plague with words of repentance, admission of sin and guilt, and confession of YHWH as right/righteous (הַצַּדִּיק).[153] He promises not to delay the exodus any further, simply requesting the end of the plague. He seems to be saying all the right things.

However, we can question whether Pharaoh is serious in his 'repentance'. Elsewhere in the Old Testament, simply making the confession 'I/we have sinned' does not always indicate genuine repentance. It can be motivated by fear (Shimei, 2Sam. 19:20 [19]), or be temporary (Saul to David, 1Sam. 26:21, cf. 24:16-22 [15-21] and 27:1). Pharaoh's repentance could fit into both categories.

Furthermore, a confession of sin should be accompanied by appropriate penitent action to remove this sin before YHWH can be expected to act. Thus at the beginning of the story of Jephthah, the people cry out to YHWH in their need and confess their sin, he is unmoved, and reminds them that they have forsaken him and turned to other gods. Therefore they should ask those gods to help them (Jdg. 10:10-15). It is only when they remove the foreign gods from amongst them that YHWH can bear their suffering no longer (Jdg. 10:16). After this Jephthah emerges with the spirit of YHWH to defeat the Ammonites (Jdg. 11:29, 32).[154] Pharaoh, however, wants the plague to be removed before he obeys YHWH by sending the people, rather than obeying first.[155]

2.4.4 9:29

Notwithstanding Pharaoh's seriousness or otherwise, Moses does agree to intercede with YHWH so that the plague will stop. The reason for the cessation of the plague is given: 'so that you will know that the land is YHWH's (לְמַעַן תֵּדַע כִּי לַיהוָה הָאָרֶץ).'

Once again the reason concerns knowledge of YHWH. In 9:14 'all' YHWH's plagues were to be sent 'so that you will know that there is none like YHWH in all the land'. In 9:16 YHWH had preserved Egypt 'to show you my power and to recount my name in all the land'. Here the knowledge comes by the removal of the plague.[156] However, what does the knowledge signify?

---

[153] Cf. Schmidt, 347.

[154] Also compare 1Sam. 7:2-13 with 1Sam. 4:1-11; cf. 1Kgs. 8:47-50; Jer. 3:25-4:2.

[155] This does not mean that we have to see Pharaoh as insincere in his offer when he makes it. The question is not so much sincerity as seriousness: will Pharaoh stand by it?

[156] The comparison between the purposes in 9:14 and 9:16 is strengthened by this verse. If the plague that was sent to gain recognition is then removed to gain recognition, the text is clearly dealing with different actions of YHWH with a similar goal.

First, the removal is a demonstration of YHWH's power.[157] The plagues are sent upon Pharaoh and his whole people and land without exception (7:27-29 [8:2-4]; 8:16-19 [20-23]). However YHWH can also completely remove these plagues, to the extent that not one creature remains (cf. 8:6-10 [10-14]; 8:27 [31]; 10:19). The land is his, inasmuch as he demonstrates his total power and control over it.[158]

However, as with 9:16 it is worth considering the implications of YHWH revealing himself through the removal of a plague. In other words, YHWH is to be known to the Egyptians not only as one who sends plagues (9:14), but as one who removes them as well (9:29), and as one who has refrained from greater possible destruction (9:16). This knowledge through removal lends further support to understanding 9:16 as speaking of power through restraint. In case we might think that these are aberrations from the norm, let us consider YHWH's methods of self-revelation to Pharaoh. Only twice is the sending of a plague announced to him as the means of YHWH's revelation (7:17; 9:14). In other places the revelation is linked to the removal of the plague (8:6 [10]; 9:29), or the exemption of Israel or Goshen from it (8:18 [22]; 11:7).[159] What Egypt and Pharaoh are learning is not, primarily, that YHWH sends plagues, but that he does not send them on his people, and that he ends them when asked.[160]

In other words, would it be fair to say that the picture of YHWH that Pharaoh is meant to receive is not primarily of a god who shows himself in the power of destruction, but rather of one who refrains from greater destruction?

2.4.5 9:30

However, Moses follows this message of future acknowledgement with the bleak statement that he knows that Pharaoh and his officials do not yet fear YHWH. This colours our understanding of Pharaoh's previous 'repentance'. One could simply note with Durham that Moses shows 'understandable scepticism' in light of Pharaoh's past refusals (cf. 8:25 [29]).[161] However, Moses claims that he 'knows' Pharaoh does not yet fear. The importance of יָדַע in this passage suggests that something stronger is meant, especially following the use in v29. Here the term appears to be a deliberate contrast with the more 'standard' use in the previous verse.

---

[157] Cf. Propp, 326.

[158] Cf. S. Bertman, 'A note on the reversible miracle.' *HR* 3 (1964): 523-37, although he does not mention these signs.

[159] Cf. Childs, 171.

[160] Perhaps this should be nuanced as 'He ends them when his representative asks'. Pharaoh always asks Moses to intercede, rather than speaking to YHWH directly.

[161] Durham, 129.

Moses will continue to play his part in order that Pharaoh may 'know...'. However to the same extent that Pharaoh will 'know...' (eventually), Moses 'knows' (now) that Pharaoh does not yet fear YHWH.

Jacob notes the suggestion of Ibn Ezra and Ramban that this means 'you will not fear YHWH (i.e. release Israel) before I spread my hands'.[162] 'Fearing YHWH' is expressed by actions, and the action that YHWH demands of Pharaoh is to release Israel. Moses is thus saying that Pharaoh will not do what he is told before the plague ceases. Regarding this suggestion, we have noted that fearing YHWH relates to actions. Moreover, we have also noted on 9:27-28 that Pharaoh is not good at backing up his words with actions. However, there is one particular action that has been specifically linked to fear of YHWH.

The use of 'fear' reminds us of the division in vv20-21 between those who feared YHWH's word and showed this by moving their possessions, and those who did not. This would be an obvious test of 'fear of YHWH'. If Pharaoh left his servants and livestock out in the field (which Moses could check), it would be reasonable proof that he did not yet fear YHWH. The text is silent on whether Pharaoh did follow YHWH's words or not.[163] Although one cannot be sure, the joint use of 'fear' and the strength of 'know' makes it a plausible reason.

If we follow this speculation, what would it mean for the understanding of the encounters? We have noted the oddity of the mitigation in v19, and the fact that it is not renewed in later plagues. However, we should bear in mind that at this point in the narrative, nobody (except perhaps YHWH) knows that such a mitigation will not be renewed for any further plagues.

Now in v30 we learn that Pharaoh has not taken up this offered mitigation. He may call out *in extremis*, and promise anything to stop the plague, as it is too great to bear (v28aβ) and YHWH will respond to him. However, Pharaoh will not act unless he is in such a position.

Just as in v17, he has used the restraint of YHWH to further entrench himself, to show that he does not fear YHWH. Therefore, the principle of 9:13-19 suggests that Pharaoh has cut off the opportunity of any further mitigation. If he will simply use such opportunities as v19 in the same way as he had used the restraint of YHWH (v16) to exalt himself, and prevent Israel from leaving (v17), then further opportunities cannot and will not be given. For the reader who does know the events to come (in contrast to the characters), the shadow of the final plague, which has no escape for any Egyptians, looms at this point. Pharaoh will learn that 'YHWH distinguishes between Israel and Egypt' (11:7). Pharaoh has cut off the chance for a distinction within the Egyptians, whether god-fearers or not.

---

[162] Jacob *Exodus*, 278.
[163] Houtman, II 90.

2.4.6 9:33-35

Moses is proved correct in his comment in v30. Once again Pharaoh reneges on his promise and hardens his heart when the plague ceases.

In light of the discussion of vv13-19, we should note that Moses has agreed to ask YHWH to remove the plague so that Pharaoh will know 'that the land/earth is YHWH's' (v29). It is the removal of the plague (as in 8:6 [10]) that will bring this knowledge.

However, the text shows that it is when Pharaoh sees the respite caused by the removal, at the very point when he should acknowledge YHWH (9:29; cf. 8:6 [10]), that he chooses to harden his heart (9:34; cf. 8:11 [15]). That which is meant to bring acknowledgement of YHWH actually brings more rejection of him and his demand.

To bring out the force of this, perhaps one should translate 'And Pharaoh saw that the rain, the hail and the thunder had ceased, *yet* he added to his sin and hardened his heart, he and his servants'. One can almost hear the '*still* you exalt yourself' of v17 echoing here. Once more YHWH's method of showing power has allowed an ambiguity in how Pharaoh perceives and responds to it (the cessation of the plague could be seen as YHWH's power, or it could be seen as the fact that the plague has ended and therefore of no more concern). Once more Pharaoh has chosen to misunderstand YHWH's power as weakness, and reinforce his own position.

2.5 Concluding Remarks

The interpretation put forward in this chapter sets out a chain of responses between YHWH and Pharaoh in their encounters. YHWH's interactions with Pharaoh have been deliberately restrained. Rather than acting unilaterally, he has been looking for a certain response from Pharaoh. However, Pharaoh has refused to give it, preferring to use that restraint to exalt himself over YHWH's people. As a result YHWH changes or increases his methods of interacting with Pharaoh. This passage is the clearest explanation of this pattern, although it can be seen in other places in the plagues narrative. These will be discussed in chapter 4.

However this explanation and this passage do not cover all of the 'explanations' given in respect of the plagues narrative. Passages that speak of YHWH 'hardening Pharaoh's heart' in particular need to be considered to see how they impact upon it. Therefore the next chapter will deal with the following explanation in 10:1-2, which appears to have a rather different feel to it.

Chapter 3

Exodus 10:1-2 – A Contrasting Explanation

3.1 Introduction

When advancing a thesis such as is found in the previous chapter, it is appropriate to consider potential arguments against it or problems arising from it. Within our narrative arguably the sharpest questions are raised by the passage which follows. Immediately after 9:13-35 comes a message from YHWH to Moses which appears to give a very different understanding of these events.

וַיֹּאמֶר יְהוָה אֶל־מֹשֶׁה בֹּא אֶל־פַּרְעֹה כִּי־אֲנִי הִכְבַּדְתִּי אֶת־לִבּוֹ וְאֶת־לֵב
עֲבָדָיו לְמַעַן שִׁתִי אֹתֹתַי אֵלֶּה בְּקִרְבּוֹ: 2 וּלְמַעַן תְּסַפֵּר בְּאָזְנֵי בִנְךָ
וּבֶן־בִּנְךָ אֵת אֲשֶׁר הִתְעַלַּלְתִּי בְּמִצְרַיִם וְאֶת־אֹתֹתַי אֲשֶׁר־שַׂמְתִּי בָם
וִידַעְתֶּם כִּי־אֲנִי יְהוָה:

YHWH said to Moses 'Come to Pharaoh, for I have hardened his heart and the hearts of his servants in order that I may set these my signs in his midst; and in order that you may recount in the ears of your son and of your son's son how I toyed with the Egyptians and [recount] my signs which I set among them, and you will know that I am YHWH.'

There are two main 'problem areas' in 10:1-2 for our thesis:
1. The hardening of Pharaoh's heart (10:1). This is a recurrent theme in the plagues narrative in a similar way to the themes of 'send ... serve' and 'know...' discussed in the previous chapter, and, as noted in the chapter 1, one that has exercised the minds of many of the readers of the text.
2. הִתְעַלַּלְתִּי (10:2). While several other passages have comments on YHWH's hardening of Pharaoh, some of which give reasons, this passage gives perhaps the most problematic reason for YHWH's acts.[1] The exact translation of this word will be discussed later, but however one understands it, it has unpleasant connotations.

---

[1] 9:13-19 has the regular 'send ... serve' and 'know' elements but also has the unusual 9:15-19. In 10:1-2, in comparison, there is not only the regular 'hardening' but also the unusual הִתְעַלַּלְתִּי. This is one reason why these two seemingly opposed passages were chosen for detailed study. They contain some of the most extensive rationales for why YHWH acts as he does (rather than why he acts at all). Furthermore their proximity to each other raises the issues more acutely.

Combining these two points raises a serious question regarding our thesis. In 'hardening' Pharaoh, YHWH appears to be stopping him from responding appropriately, which according to our reading of 9:13-19 is YHWH's aim. Moreover he is doing this in order to 'deal harshly with' Pharaoh, or 'toy with' him which exacerbates the contrast with the image of the God who shows power through restraint, seeks response, and is himself responsive. The image here seems to be closer to Gloster's words:

> As flies to wanton boys are we to the gods,
> They kill us for their sport. (*King Lear*, Act IV, Scene I).

Therefore this chapter will examine the general issue of the 'hardening of Pharaoh's heart' and also the issue of הִתְעַלַּלְתִּי. As previously noted, the hardening forms only part of our passage and the rationale. Therefore it will not be possible to devote as much attention to it as could be wished. We are examining it in light of the thesis proposed which will inevitably guide our discussion. Had we started with 10:1-2 (or 4:21-23, 7:3 etc) then the discussion might be different. Nevertheless in no sense is this intended to 'explain away' hardening as a 'problem', but rather to interact with it in order to test, amend, and refine our thesis.

There are other elements in 10:1-2 which have not yet been mentioned: YHWH's signs (mentioned twice); recounting to descendants; and the final reason 'that you will know that I am YHWH'. These are not 'problematic' as such for our thesis. These will come into our discussion later in the chapter.

3.2 10:1 and 'the hardening of Pharaoh's heart'

To deal with 10:1 we need to consider the issue of the 'hardening of Pharaoh's heart' more generally, and then return.[2] This long approach is necessary due to the importance and difficulty of the issue both in 10:1 and beyond. In light of the comments in chapter 1 the importance needs little comment. The difficulty arises not only from the implications of the heart being hardened, especially by YHWH, but also from the variety of terms and phrases used to describe this phenomenon (כָּבֵד, חָזַק and קָשָׁה; 'Pharaoh hardened'/'YHWH hardened' etc). These factors have given rise to the many different understandings of this phenomenon as set out in chapter 1.[3] Rather than focussing on these discussions, we will focus on the statements as part of the narrative. Thus, in line with our general approach, we will pay particular attention to the contexts of the different statements concerning

---

[2] There is little discussion of 10:1-2 as such in the secondary literature, probably because most of the issues will already have been raised in earlier hardening passages.

[3] Furthermore, as noted in chapter 1, the terms used to describe the phenomenon of 'hardening' are also used in the passage with other senses ('heavy', 'grasp', 'glory' etc).

the hardening. There are two main contexts in which these statements occur.

The first context, as in 10:1, is as part of messages of YHWH to Moses.[4] In them YHWH tells Moses that he [YHWH] will harden, or has hardened, Pharaoh's heart.[5] These messages fall mainly outside the plagues narrative. 7:14 comes at the commencement, but 10:1 is the only one to come in the midst of the encounters. The second context is as a narratorial refrain which concludes the sign of the serpent staff, and each of the first nine plagues.[6] Three statements occur in this context as we are variously told that 'Pharaoh hardened his heart', 'Pharaoh's heart was/remained hard' and 'YHWH hardened Pharaoh's heart'. This is then followed by the statement that Pharaoh did not listen to Moses and Aaron, or that he did not send the people. Some of these statements conclude with 'as YHWH said'. We will investigate both of these contexts in turn.

3.2.1 First Context of Hardening References: YHWH's Statements to Moses

We have noted that most of these messages fall outside the plagues narrative. As such they will not form part of the read-through in the next chapter, in contrast to the hardening refrains. However as they are of importance for any understanding of the plagues narrative, we will consider them in some detail here. Our primary concerns are with their function as messages in their own context, and their relation to the plagues narrative and the actions therein.

3.2.1.1 THE GENERAL FUNCTION OF THESE STATEMENTS

There are a series of messages given to Moses about the encounters with Pharaoh.[7] YHWH's initial message to Moses is short and simple: 'I am sending you to Pharaoh to bring my people, the sons of Israel, out of Egypt' (3:10). There is no mention of Pharaoh's reaction, or indeed of any problems. It is Moses who starts to raise problems, primarily concerning his own ability and the reception that he will get. In answering them, YHWH gives the next picture of the encounters to come in 3:18-20. Moses will give the message, but YHWH knows that Pharaoh will only respond to a mighty

---

[4] 4:21; 7:3; 7:14; 10:1; 14:4, 17.

[5] 7:14 is an exception where YHWH states that Pharaoh's heart remains hard.

[6] 7:13, 22; 8:11 [15], 15 [19], 28 [32]; 9:7, 12, 34, 35; 10:20, 27; cf. 11:10 and 14:8. 11:10 appears to be a summary of the initial plagues, and 14:8 comes during the Red Sea encounter, so these do not correspond quite as well.

[7] 3:10, 18-20; 4:21-23; 6:1; 6:28-7:5; 7:14; 10:1-2; 11:1, 9; 14:4, 17.

hand.[8] Therefore YHWH will send his hand and Pharaoh will respond correctly. Here we have forewarning of Pharaoh's obstinacy, but no suggestion that YHWH is responsible for it. Then in 4:21-23, a passage whose immediate context is difficult to ascertain, YHWH tells Moses that he, YHWH, will harden Pharaoh's heart and Pharaoh will not send the people. After the first encounter with Pharaoh, in response to Moses' complaint YHWH tells him that now he, YHWH, will act (6:1) and tells him to go and tell Pharaoh to send the people (6:10-11, 29). Once again there is no suggestion of problems. Moses responds that Israel has not listened, and therefore asks why Pharaoh should listen to his ineloquence (6:12, 30). In reply, YHWH makes him as 'god' to Pharaoh with Aaron as his prophet (7:1 cf. 4:16) and gives him the most detailed picture yet of what will happen (7:2-5). Moses will speak as YHWH has commanded him; Aaron will proclaim it to Pharaoh; YHWH will harden Pharaoh; YHWH will increase his signs; Pharaoh will not listen; YHWH will lay his hand upon Egypt and bring Israel out with signs and judgements; Egypt will know that he is YHWH when he brings Israel out. At this point we are informed that Moses and Aaron did what YHWH commanded (7:6).

---

[8] Ska puts forward a compelling argument for understanding וְלֹא in 3:19b as 'except' or 'unless' (Jean Louis Ska, 'Note sur la traduction de welo' en exode III 19b', *VT* XLIV (1994): 60-65). He discusses cases where there are two consecutive negatives, and the וְלֹא does not connect two identical forms (say two verbs or nouns) where the first is positive and the second negative. Instead it is part of an expression that modifies a verb. In Ex. 8:22 [26] the context requires the understanding that the Israelites *would* be stoned if they sacrificed. Compare Is. 32:1-3. Moreover in 1Sam. 20:2 the *Qere'* text contains two negatives, and the context requires the sense that Saul does nothing *without* telling Jonathan. Compare Ezek. 16:43 (61-64). Therefore he concludes that in several cases where וְלֹא follows a negative, it has a positive sense, although the rarity of cases prevents the formation of a general rule. He notes that with the exception of Is. 32:1-3 the texts above have a similar context, that of a dialogue, where the וְלֹא has a precise rhetorical function. The deliberator seeks to persuade the addressee of his knowledge, and speaks of the future. Moreover the function of the וְלֹא is to address a potential objection of the addressee (e.g. Moses might say 'I know that there is no way in which Pharaoh will let Israel go' and God responds 'I am well aware of that, but he *will* let you go if I act with a strong hand'). Therefore in a double negative situation, the second negative וְלֹא takes on the force of an affirmation, enabling one to translate 'except' in 3:19.

The owner of the mighty hand is not explicit in the text. It could be a symbol of human might or force, it could be Pharaoh's hand, or it could be YHWH's hand. The last requires a verb to be supplied such as 'unless *compelled/influenced* by a mighty hand'. Despite this it is preferable for two reasons. First it fits best into context. YHWH's hand is what is required (v19), and therefore YHWH's hand is what will be sent (v20). Moreover, the phrase associated with the exodus in the Old Testament is YHWH bringing Israel out of Egypt 'with a mighty hand'.

If there is any kind of pattern here it appears to be that YHWH's initial messages to Moses are quite basic, and he gives more details in response to Moses' objections. Thus 7:1-5 is far more detailed than 3:10. These messages are effectively summaries of the encounters to come, which give different levels of information depending upon the context, with the later ones generally having more details than the earlier ones.

A summary should give the overarching sense of what will happen, but it would not be expected to give all the precise details. More detailed messages would give further details, and the description of the events would give further details still. Thus 3:18-20; 4:21-23 and 7:1-5 expand the simple message that Moses is to go to Pharaoh, by giving details of his reception and what YHWH will do. (There is no indication in 3:10 that Moses' mission will meet with any problems.) In a similar way, the plagues narrative itself expands the summaries by setting out *exactly* how Pharaoh reacts and what YHWH does. After 4:21 and 7:3 the reader may be surprised at the message in 8:11 [15] that 'Pharaoh hardened his heart' (although 3:19 and 5:1-18 may have suggested something similar). However, he may have been surprised at 4:21 by the mention of *YHWH* hardening Pharaoh, which had not been brought up in previous messages. Just as 4:21 does not invalidate the earlier messages, so understanding 'Pharaoh hardened' as '*Pharaoh* hardened' in the plagues narrative need not invalidate 4:21 and 7:3. In other words, if 4:21 and 7:3 are understood as summaries it does not necessarily follow that they must be understood as stating that *on every occasion* that Pharaoh's heart is hardened, it is YHWH that is responsible for it. Attempting to argue the reverse leads to some difficult readings.

For example, if we assume that 4:21 does mean that YHWH is always responsible, we would need to read 5:1-18 (and especially 5:2) as YHWH hardening Pharaoh, although there is no indication of this in the passage. The narrative speaks of Moses and Aaron before Pharaoh, and Pharaoh's responses. As in 1:1-2:23 Pharaoh is present and powerful, whereas YHWH is conspicuous mainly by his absence. To argue that 4:21 should control our reading of 5:1-18 would lose the sense of the narrative. Often in Old Testament narratives, the narrator is sparing with his comments. However in this narrative he is unusually forthcoming with statements about YHWH working behind the scenes. Might one not expect something similar to, say, 9:12, in respect of 5:1-18? Yet there is no comment on any hardening.[9] What we have is rather different. In his complaint to YHWH about the encounter, Moses asks YHWH why he sent him to speak in his name. Since that time Pharaoh has brought evil. There is no mention of YHWH controlling Pharaoh (which concept Moses has heard about in 4:21). His

---

[9] Cf. Gunn, 74. He sees the previous mention of 4:21 as creating uncertainty for the reader as to what is happening.

complaint seems rather to say that because YHWH has sent him to Pharaoh, Pharaoh has reacted negatively (in a way which he would not have done had YHWH not sent Moses). Thus YHWH is responsible for provoking Pharaoh by Moses' message, and is therefore responsible for the evil. Moses' complaint is not about YHWH's actions ('why did you harden him?') but rather about his *lack* of action in backing Moses up.[10] In reply YHWH does not attribute Pharaoh's reaction to divine hardening (contrast 10:1). Instead he focuses on what he, YHWH, will do now, not mentioning the past.[11] Thus there is no reason to read prior divine hardening into this exchange.[12]

3.2.1.2 3:18-20; 4:21-23; 7:1-5 IN THEIR CONTEXTS

Furthermore, we do not need to see all of these 'summaries' as having exactly the same message, albeit in more or less detail. They come at different points, in different contexts and may be in response to different issues. How then may the different contents of 3:18-20; 4:21-23 and 7:1-5 relate to the plagues narrative?[13]

3:18-20 comes as part of YHWH's response to Moses' second objection in his initial encounter with YHWH. The encounter in 3:1-4:17 has four objections from Moses (3:10, 13; 4:1, 10), each one with a response from YHWH (3:11-12, 14-22; 4:2-9, 11-12), before Moses asks to be excused and YHWH gets angry (4:13-17). Immediately before 3:18-20, YHWH has told Moses that Israel will listen to him, in response to his objection. He then moves on to contrast Israel's behaviour with that of Pharaoh, who will only respond to force.

Thus in 3:18-20 there is a distinction between Moses speaking, and YHWH sending his hand to perform signs with the result that Pharaoh will release Israel. Moses is given no signs for Pharaoh here. In fact he has yet to receive any signs for Israel at this point. The words in 3:18 are only spoken by him in this form (or close to it) in 5:3, and never again. There are no signs in chapter 5, but thereafter his speeches to Pharaoh are always accompanied by signs. Therefore perhaps we can see 3:18-20 contrasting the initial encounter between Pharaoh and Moses (v18 as a summary of the

---

[10] Thus Moshe Greenberg, 'The Thematic Unity of Exodus III-XI', *Fourth World Congress of Jewish Studies Papers*, Vol 1 (Jerusalem, 1967): 151-154, henceforth 'Greenberg 'Unity'', sees Moses as doubting YHWH's power and authority, indeed everything that is implied by his Name, as Pharaoh does in 5:2 (153). Indeed McCarthy 'Plagues', 140 sees the differences between Ex. 5 and 7-10 as great enough to establish that Ex. 5 comes from a variant tradition within J. While this is not our approach, it does bring out the differences.

[11] Cf. Childs, 106-107.

[12] Contra Beale, 135-136.

[13] This is not an attempt sharply to differentiate and draw distinctions, but rather in a heuristic way to suggest possible differences of focus and emphasis.

events of chapter 5, and v19 as Pharaoh's response), with the subsequent actions of YHWH (v20 as a summary of chapters 7f).[14]

This could explain why there is no mention of 'hardening' here. As the narrative stands chapter 5 gives a situation where YHWH is noticeably absent. The only players are Moses (and Aaron) and Pharaoh. Moses' rejection by Pharaoh appears to be based on nothing but Pharaoh himself.

4:21-23, by contrast, comes in a message from YHWH to Moses on the return to Egypt. There appears to be no obvious reason for YHWH giving him this message, no word or deed from Moses to which YHWH is responding. Moreover it comes just before the difficult and oft-studied 4:24-26. Therefore the context in which the message is given is of less help to us here. However the context to which the message refers may be of more help. It looks to a point when plagues I-IX are over.[15] 4:21 sums them up, leading up to the message for Pharaoh. Pharaoh is to be told that he has not responded to YHWH's demand, and therefore YHWH is sending the firstborn plague (4:22-23). There is no comment on what will happen after or as a result of the firstborn plague (i.e. Israel leaving; contrast 3:20 and 7:4-5). The focus is wholly on the last terrible plague, the result of Pharaoh's lack of correct response.[16]

The contrast seems to be between the initial acts (chapters 7-10?) which are to be performed by Moses, and the final act of YHWH (chapters 11-12?). Therefore chapters 7-10 are seen here as part of the 'unsuccessful' acts. This may explain why the signs are attributed to Moses here, rather than YHWH as in 3:20. Moses' efforts are unsuccessful, whereas YHWH is successful. In concentrating on the final effective act, the earlier ones are shifted slightly away from YHWH, to Moses.[17] However they are still the signs that YHWH has given to Moses, so this does not divorce YHWH from them, it merely shifts the focus. It may also explain the change in terminology from 3:18-20. In 3:19 Pharaoh will not be shifted, but YHWH's signs do shift him. The plagues cycle is viewed as a cumulative process (or at least as a single process). In 4:21-23 a distinction is made

---

[14] If so one could see 6:1 as a recapitulation of this distinction in 3:20. In response to Moses' complaint that nothing has happened, YHWH is reminding him of what he has already told him in 3:20; 'now' comes the time when YHWH will act and Pharaoh will drive Israel out.

[15] Noth, 47; Driver *Exodus*, 31; Greenberg *UE*, 109-110.

[16] In light of this we can return to the context in which 4:21-23 is given. Mention of the killing of the Pharaoh's firstborn son by YHWH (symbolising and anticipating the Egyptian firstborn) is immediately followed by the salvation of Moses' son from death by YHWH through blood (symbolising and anticipating Passover and the Israelites?). Cf. Michael Fishbane, *Text and Texture – Close Readings of Selected Biblical Texts* (New York: Schocken Books, 1979), henceforth 'Fishbane *Text*', 71.

[17] Chapter 4 will spell out the differences in the plagues narrative between the first nine plagues, and the final one.

between the last plague and the rest. As a result, a reason is needed why the initial signs of YHWH will not succeed (as 3:20 suggests that they will), and YHWH's hardening of Pharaoh is introduced. Both 3:18-20 and 4:21-23 see the initial mission of Moses as unsuccessful, in contrast to the subsequent work of YHWH which is successful. Therefore the joint message that comes from them both is that Moses will not be able to affect the Pharaoh, but YHWH certainly will.

7:1-5 is the conclusion to a period of interaction between YHWH and Moses (5:22-7:5), coming after Pharaoh has worsened the situation in response to YHWH's demand delivered by Moses.[18] Israel have effectively rejected Moses and his message (5:20-21; 6:9). At this point YHWH tells Moses to return to Pharaoh again (6:1, 10-11, 29), to which Moses responds that, if *Israel* will not listen, it is unlikely that Pharaoh will. He brings up once more the issue of his own incapability, but unlike 3:11 and 4:10 he can now appeal to the preceding events (6:12, 30). As in 3:10-4:17, YHWH answers by moving the focus to himself. Along with this focus on YHWH comes an escalation in the position of Moses. In 3:18-20 he has no signs, he simply speaks to Pharaoh and YHWH acts. In 4:21 he has signs (albeit unsuccessful ones); here he is 'god to Pharaoh'.[19]

The focus on the events is probably the widest of the three. Moses will speak; YHWH will harden, and will make his signs great; Pharaoh will not listen; YHWH will put his hand upon Egypt and lead out his people with 'great judgements'. This last act or acts will cause Egypt to 'know that I am YHWH'. The idea that 'Egypt will know...' occurs only here and in the Red Sea encounter (14:4, 18).[20] This suggests that the focus here may be on YHWH's actions in the Red Sea (vv4-5) and his previous actions in the plagues. The firstborn could be part of v3 or vv4-5, although probably the latter in light of 3:20 and 4:22-23. However unlike these two it appears that the focus is on the Red Sea rather than the firstborn. In 3:20 *Pharaoh* would send them, which suggests the firstborn plague (12:31-33). Here *YHWH* will bring them out, suggesting perhaps the last encounter (14:1-31).

The overall impression in 7:1-5 as with 4:21-23 is that YHWH is responsible for the hardening in the plagues. However, as noted above, it

---

[18] Cf. Greenberg *UE*, 169.

[19] It is difficult to know what exactly to make of this phrase. Suggestions are that Moses would function with divine authority before Pharaoh (Childs, 118); that Moses would be the highest authority of the Israelites (Jacob *Exodus*, 172-73); or that Moses will instruct Pharaoh as God instructs his prophets (Cassuto, 89 – cf. 4:15-16). Childs' suggestion seems most likely, but, however we understand it, Moses' position here is extremely high.

[20] 11:7 with its second person plural may indicate the wider Egyptians rather than just Pharaoh and his court; however the form of 7:5 and 14:4 and 18 is much closer. Cf. Childs 139-40.

would be unsafe to assume that this must mean that YHWH will be responsible for every single hardening event.[21]

3.2.1.3 TWO POSSIBLE OBJECTIONS

At this point a couple of objections may be raised. If 4:21 and 7:3 should not be read as saying that all hardening is ultimately caused by YHWH, then why does YHWH say that he will harden, and indeed emphasise it? Is this interpretation of these verses as 'summaries' not effectively trying to weaken the link with the plagues narrative or to downplay them, perhaps because they are not conducive to this thesis? More specifically, in these messages YHWH makes a point of emphasising that it is *he* who will be hardening Pharaoh with an emphatic אֲנִי before the verb (4:21; 7:3; 10:1; 14:17 'And I, I will harden...'; cf. 3:19).[22] Moreover several of the earlier plagues conclude with the statement 'as YHWH said', which would appear to refer back to these comments and underline them.

Initially we should respond that in no way is this reading trying to downplay the fact that YHWH's messages to Moses predominantly speak of YHWH as hardening Pharaoh (3:19 and 7:14 are exceptions). We need to respect the wording of the text here, just as we need to respect the wording of the hardening refrains.[23] Therefore we will look more closely at both of these objections to consider their significance. On the first point,

---

[21] As an example of an alternative reading of 7:3, we could understand וְהִרְבֵּיתִי as 'increase' or 'make great' rather than simply 'multiply' (cf. Gen. 3:16; 15:1; 34:12; Jdg. 20:38), thus dealing with the nature of the plagues rather than their number. The initial plagues are not particularly 'great', while the later plagues are much more so (cf. 9:14; 9:18, 10:6 etc.). It is immediately after the point where YHWH is said to harden Pharaoh (9:12) that the plagues begin to become uniquely powerful. Thus we *could* understand 7:3 as referring to the later plagues, which are truly 'great' and where YHWH is clearly hardening Pharaoh. (The issue of the increase in the plagues and the change at 9:13-19 will be discussed further in chapter 4.) Furthermore we could then note that 10:1 speaks of YHWH hardening in the past (9:12?) whereas 7:3 speaks of him hardening in the future (perhaps 9:12 but certainly not 5:1-18).

This is not to argue that 7:3 *must* be referring only to the plagues after 9:12, but rather to cast doubt on any certainty that it *must* be referring to every plague. The fact that the details are summarised leaves open different possibilities for understanding.

[22] A participial verb form would require a personal pronoun to indicate the subject. However in 3:19, 4:21 and 7:3 the perfect or imperfect are used which, having their own suffix or prefix, do not require the וַאֲנִי. Therefore this must be significant in its presence. In 14:17, where a participle is used, the emphasis is given by וַאֲנִי הִנְנִי מְחַזֵּק. 10:1 is slightly different and will be picked up below.

[23] Thus if every hardening refrain in the plagues narrative had the phrase 'YHWH hardened Pharaoh's heart', 4:21 and 7:3 should be read as saying that YHWH will harden continually. The issue here, as with the wider issue of 9:13-19 and 10:1-2 and the viewpoints that they represent, is that there are seemingly multiple 'explanations' in one narrative which do not easily agree with each other.

what does it mean that YHWH is giving these messages to Moses and emphasising his involvement in the process via the hardening. What does this emphatic 'I' mean? On the second point, what is the function of the 'as YHWH said' and to what does it relate?

First Objection: וַאֲנִי

The emphasis upon YHWH suggests a contrast with another ('I, and not somebody else'). If this is the case, then there are two obvious contenders: Pharaoh and Moses.

The above objection, and quite possibly some other readings of this verse, might assume that the contrast is between Pharaoh and YHWH ('I am hardening Pharaoh, he isn't hardening himself'). These messages would then be a statement to Moses that YHWH is ultimately behind all the obstinacy of Pharaoh.[24]

However, the וַאֲנִי may also be a contrast with Moses. Moses is to perform the signs, but YHWH will be acting also. Having told Moses what he is to do, YHWH then informs him what he, YHWH, will do for his part. If so, it would change the focus from being a statement on the issue of divine and human 'hardening' to being a statement about the different roles that YHWH and Moses are to play.[25] This is appealing for a number of reasons.

First it deals with an issue already raised in the text (in Moses' objections), rather than an issue that has arisen in theological reflection upon it.[26] Moses, often unsure of his ability to fulfil YHWH's commission, is told that YHWH will be working as well as him. The context is one of reassurance, and the comments on hardening should be understood in this light.[27] One could compare this to YHWH's statements 'I will be with you/your mouth' (3:12; 4:12) which have a similar function: Moses is not facing the power of Pharaoh alone; YHWH is present and working. In what we might call a division of labour, YHWH sets out the jobs to be done, assigning some to Moses, and some to himself.[28]

This can be contrasted with YHWH's messages to Pharaoh. Pharaoh is told 'you do X, or I will do Y' or 'because you have not done X, I will do Y'. Moses, however, is told 'you do X, and I will do Y'. An adversative relationship is contrasted with a co-operative one. Moses' task is to go to

---

[24] Cf. Wilson, 29; Beale, 133f; Propp, 353.

[25] Cf. Houtman, I 527, on 7:3; Durham, 87.

[26] Cf. Childs, 173-174, who argues against the hardening in the text being primarily an issue of theodicy.

[27] The observation that YHWH encourages Moses is not new to this thesis of course. Houtman mentions this point several times (e.g. I 486 on 5:22; I 491 on 7:1-5) cf. e.g. Jacob *Exodus*, 244; Cassuto, 74 on 6:1; Keil, 457.

[28] Cf. Fretheim, 76.

Pharaoh, speak YHWH's words and perform YHWH's signs (10:1a, cf. 4:21a; 7:2 תְּדַבֵּר אַתָּה; 14:2; 16). YHWH will carry out the plagues, and influence Pharaoh.

Secondly, this contrast between YHWH and Moses would fit the wider use of the emphatic וַאֲנִי in the Old Testament. A common use of וַאֲנִי before the verb is to contrast one action or state (of the speaker) with a preceding one (often not of the speaker). Jer. 1:18 can be compared with 10:1-2. Both Jeremiah and Moses are spokesmen of YHWH who doubt their competency in speaking (3:11; 4:10, Jer. 1:6).[29] However, YHWH has already acted to strengthen or harden a person, albeit in Jeremiah's case it is the prophet who is made 'hard' (Jer. 1:18; cf. Ezek. 3:8-9), whereas for Moses, it is Pharaoh who is made 'hard' (10:1). Furthermore Gen. 6:17 can be compared with the messages to Moses before the plagues begin. Noah is given his instructions to build the ark (Gen. 6:14-16), and after this YHWH will bring the flood upon the earth (v17). In both cases the וַאֲנִי contrasts YHWH's action and the action of his agent.[30] Dt. 31:23 and 1Sam. 16:3 (cf. v1) are similar examples that use וְאָנֹכִי. In the last three cases the context is clearly one of reassurance, where YHWH's acts have a motivational effect.[31] In all cases, the aim of the speech is to get the agent of YHWH to do something.[32]

While there are other examples that fit this pattern, this is not the only use of וַאֲנִי, although it appears to be the most prevalent. However, it is reasonable to conclude that there is a common pattern throughout the OT of וַאֲנִי being used to contrast the following state or action with that which precedes.[33]

---

[29] Cf. Deist, 98 and Hyatt, 83 on Jer. 1 and Ex. 4:10-12.

[30] Jer. 1:17 has a corresponding emphatic וְאַתָּה.

[31] Noah's state is unclear, but Samuel is afraid of Saul, Jeremiah doubts his competency, and Joshua is told to 'be strong and courageous'.

[32] This contrast pattern is also found in wider usage of וַאֲנִי in the OT: between humans, 'You do …, I will do…' (Gen. 22:5; 33:14; 42:37; Num. 23:15; Jos. 8:5; 1Sam. 14:40; 19:3; 20:20; 2Sam. 14:8; 1Kgs. 1:14; 18:24; Jer. 40:10); distinguishing between the actions of the speaker and a third party (2Sam. 19:39 [38]; 1Kgs. 5:9 [4:29]; 12:11; Ezra 7:28; Neh. 5:15; 12:38); combined with וְאַתָּה, וְאַתְּ or וְאֵלֶּה to sharpen the distinction (Jdg. 11:27, 35; 2Sam. 13:13; 24:17); or in adversative forms (Dt. 32:21; cf. 2Sam. 12:12 (YHWH's responsiveness); 2Sam. 11:11; Amos 2:9-10 (as part of the larger passage); Jer. 2:21; Hos. 11:3; 1Sam. 17:45; 24:18 [17] etc.)

Especially in the Psalms, וַאֲנִי is used to distinguish the actions of the speaker from others. Often the distinction is between enemies or evildoers who gloat or do evil, and the speaker who trusts in YHWH, follows YHWH's law, or is in need of his help (Ps. 13:6 [5]; 26:11; 30:7 [6]; 31:7 [6], 15 [14], 23 [22]; 35:15; 38:14 [13]; 40:18 [17]; 41:13 [12] etc. cf. Jos. 24:15; Jer. 17:16; Jon. 2:10 [9]; Mic. 7:7; Hab. 3:18).

[33] Cf. Durham, 87; Houtman, I 527; and Childs 90-91 on 7:3. In 7:2 there is a corresponding emphatic אַתָּה. In 4:21f the LXX retains the force of וַאֲנִי with ἐγώ, and

In saying this we should not downplay the importance of the first mention of the hardening being an attribution to YHWH. Even if it is not a deliberate attempt to close the issue of who is doing the hardening, it is still a text that needs to be considered, and it certainly causes problems for those who wish to see the 'hardening' as a progression from Pharaoh's actions to YHWH's actions. The emphasis in these messages to Moses is definitely on YHWH, whoever is being contrasted (or even if there is no explicit contrast at all).

Second Objection: כַּאֲשֶׁר דִּבֶּר יְהוָה

This phrase is found at the end of several of the narratorial refrains, which conclude the individual plagues:

7:13	Pharaoh's heart remained hard, and he did not listen to them, as YHWH said
7:22	Pharaoh's heart remained hard, and he did not listen to them, as YHWH said
8:11 [15]	He hardened his heart, and did not listen to them, as YHWH said
8:15 [19]	Pharaoh's heart remained hard, and he did not listen to them, as YHWH said
9:12	YHWH hardened Pharaoh's heart, and he did not listen to them, as YHWH said to Moses
9:35	Pharaoh's heart remained hard, and he did not send the sons of Israel, as YHWH said by the hand of Moses.

Beale describes this phrase as 'probably the most significant in the whole plague narrative complex, especially as it pertains to the *cause* of the hardening.'[34]

His argument is that this phrase has the sense of promise-fulfilment, with an exact correspondence to the words previously spoken. It refers back to 4:21 and 7:3, which state that YHWH will harden Pharaoh. Therefore it indicates that the concluding formulae are to be understood as YHWH hardening Pharaoh. His argument has two parts to it. Firstly he discusses the wider use of the phrase כַּאֲשֶׁר דִּבֶּר יְהוָה; then he looks at the previous words of YHWH to consider the referent of this phrase.

Wider Use of 'as YHWH said'

Beale notes that the phrase is used approximately 200 times in the Pentateuch, of which 95 refer to 'acts to be accomplished or having been

---

also adds a οὐ to v22, which is not in the MT. This strengthens the comparison with Moses. Cf. Wevers, 53.

[34] Beale, 140. His argument on 'as YHWH said' is found on pp140-141.

accomplished in exact correspondence with the way in which Yahweh previously said they would'.[35] He notes that in many cases this is in the same concluding formula as 7:13, except that צִוָּה often replaces דִּבֶּר. In some of these cases the context is of promise-fulfilment where the previously spoken word had of necessity to occur. He suggests that our usage probably should be understood in this sense. Therefore we shall examine the examples that he provides for this context of promise-fulfilment, to see what light they shed upon the use in Ex. 7-11.[36]

We can break these examples down into more specific categories.

1. YHWH acts/will act as he said/says he would (Gen. 21:1a, 1b; Dt. 1:11; 12:20; 26:15).

    Here YHWH is acting explicitly to bring about what he has promised. Thus this is different from YHWH predicting or influencing what someone else (e.g. Pharaoh) will do.[37]

2. Conscious obedience (Gen. 24:51; Dt. 26:19).

    Here humans agree to follow YHWH's word.[38] Once again this is different from Pharaoh, as his actions are certainly not in conscious obedience of YHWH. Moreover there is no sense that YHWH is influencing the people's reactions.[39]

3. Humans fulfilling YHWH's promises (Dt. 2:14; 10:9; 18:2; 31:3).

    Here YHWH's promises, not set down as direct orders to anyone, are fulfilled by human actions. However, this will presumably come about, as in the last category, by obedience.[40]

---

[35] Beale 140, cf. 141 on 7:13.

[36] He gives as examples (note 53) Gen. 21:1a, 1b; Dt. 26:15; 18:2; 10:9; 2:14. (Also where the phrase refers to future fulfilment he notes Gen. 24:51; Dt. 1:11; 6:3; 10:9; 11:25; 12:20; 26:19; 31:3.) Of the examples cited on the wider 200 (note 51), many of them simply have כַּאֲשֶׁר, and thus are of less comparative use. We will also draw in some of these examples, and those cited as the predictive sense in note 52, as appropriate.

[37] Beale is arguing that the purpose of this phrase is to show that YHWH himself is doing what he promised, and thus that *he* is hardening Pharaoh. However the distinction being made here is that the uses above *explicitly* state that YHWH is the author of the fulfilment of his word, whereas our texts do not.

[38] There are a number of other examples that we could mention of the phrase being used in this way, such as Gen. 12:4; Num. 5:4; 17:5 [16:40]; 27:23; Dt. 1:21; 2:1; Jos. 4:8; 11:15; Jdg. 6:27; Job 42:9. In our text we could note the use of כַּאֲשֶׁר צִוָּה יְהוָה (e.g. 7:6, 10, 20; 12:28, 50). However these are used of Moses, Aaron and Israel, who do obey YHWH.

[39] One could contrast Bethuel and Laban, who recognise YHWH's hand at work (Gen. 24:12-14, 50) and obey his wishes, with Pharaoh, who sees but hardens his heart instead of obeying (9:34).

[40] Thus the Levites will receive their portion from YHWH (Dt. 10:9; 18:2). However this is due to the other tribes obeying the commands of YHWH, by bringing sacrifices

4. Conditional promises (Dt. 6:3; 11:25; 26:15-19).
    YHWH promises something to Israel, for example that they will live
    long (Dt. 6:3), or that YHWH will cause others to fear Israel (Dt.
    11:25). However, this promise is conditional on their acting in a
    certain way (in both Dt. 6:3 and 11:22 this will come about if they
    obey his commandments). However, if Israel disobey him, another
    set of promises (or threats) will come about (e.g. Jos. 23:15; 2Kgs.
    17:23; Jer. 27:13; 40:3). This is closer to the demand to Pharaoh to
    release Israel, with the warning of what will happen if he does not
    (cf. 10:3-4).[41]

Therefore, in comparing the above usages with the occurrences of 'as
YHWH said' in Exodus we have a problem. While in a more general sense
these examples speak of YHWH's words being fulfilled, they do not speak
of them being fulfilled in a comparable way. In our narrative YHWH
himself is not acting (1st category), at least not explicitly, except in 9:12.
Instead Pharaoh is behaving as YHWH said he would, but he is not doing
this in any kind of conscious obedience to YHWH (2nd, 3rd, and 4th
categories). Instead he appears to be acting against YHWH. In none of
Beale's above examples do we have an example of humans behaving like
Pharaoh.

One could respond that the model here is YHWH controlling Pharaoh's
action via the hardening of his heart, and that therefore it would fit into the
first category above. Let us accept this assumption for the sake of
discussion. This would create a model where the speaker (YHWH) says
that someone (Pharaoh) will do something. Subsequently that person does
it, *and it is directly due to the speaker that this happens* (i.e. due to divine
influence on Pharaoh). However, this is still not a good match with any of
the examples cited heretofore.[42]

However, Beale notes that his argument does not depend upon this, as he
moves onto the second part, where he is on stronger ground. The phrase 'as
YHWH said' must refer to a previously spoken word (or words) of YHWH.

The only places where YHWH has said anything about Pharaoh's lack of
response are:

---

and giving from them to the Levites; rather than YHWH creating miraculous food for
the Levites after the fashion of the manna. This would also apply to Joshua in Dt. 31:3.

[41] Dt. 26:15-19 combines an unconditional promise of YHWH to give the land (vv1, 15)
with a request for YHWH to bless the land (v15). This follows (and appears to be
dependant upon) the confession of obedience re tithes (vv13-14), and leads into a
rehearsal of the promises of both Israel (vv16-17) and YHWH (vv18-19 – as he said).

[42] To be fair to Beale, this discussion takes up only two pages of an article that seeks to
examine all the hardening language in context. Thus he could not be expected to discuss
the wider context in great detail.

a)   3:19 (I, I know that Pharaoh will not allow you to go, except with a strong hand);

b)   4:21 (I, I will strengthen his heart and he will not send the people);

c)   7:4 (I, I will stiffen Pharaoh's heart and I will make great my signs and wonders in the land of Egypt. And Pharaoh will not listen to you and I will set my hand...)[43]

Beale notes that when we refer back to the spoken word in 4:21 and 7:3 we find three essential details:

a)   the heart of Pharaoh was to be hardened;

b)   this hardening was to result in Pharaoh "not listening" or "letting Israel go"; and

c)   *the subject of this hardening was to be Yahweh himself.*

If we look for exact correspondence, the formula is used five times to refer to Pharaoh not listening (which matches 7:4 most closely); and once (9:35) to refer to Pharaoh not sending the people (which matches 4:21 most closely, but possibly also 3:19). So far, Beale's case is strong.

However we now run into a problem. Beale claims that this formula denotes an act 'in which the essential details of the act are performed in exact correspondence with the previously spoken word of Yahweh'.[44] The word of YHWH (4:21; 7:3) is that he, YHWH, will harden Pharaoh so that he will not listen or release Israel. Beale notes that in 7:13 (where he discusses this point), his points a) and b) above are present, but c) can be assumed because of the 'exact correspondence' with 4:21/7:3.

However in only one of the six occurrences of the formula is this exact correspondence upheld (9:12). The remaining cases have either 'Pharaoh's heart remained hard', or even 'Pharaoh hardened his heart' (8:11 [15]). We could assume from this, as Beale does, that this "exact correspondence" shows that YHWH is the ultimate cause of the hardening in all six cases. However, against this one could point out that, with the exception of 9:12, there is *not* an "exact correspondence" between YHWH's words about the hardening, and the narrator's summaries. In one case (8:11 [15]) it is explicitly not the same as it speaks of *Pharaoh* hardening his heart.[45] In order to create this 'exact correspondence', we have to change the *prima facie* meaning of the text. This raises the question of whether this argument is assuming that for which it is arguing. The correspondence made between

---

[43] Elsewhere YHWH speaks of Pharaoh releasing the people (e.g. 6:1) but these are not relevant here.

[44] Beale, 141.

[45] Moreover, to anticipate, as Beale understands the Qal as 'Pharaoh's heart remained hard', this again appears to be different from YHWH intervening to harden it. One could argue that this is over subtle as he sees the Qal in each case as referring back to a previous hardening by YHWH. However once again this blurs the exact comparison between YHWH's word and the act, weakening the dependence of this phrase on 7:3.

what YHWH said and what happened has to be strong in order to be able to infer that the subject of the hardening is YHWH where this is not stated. However, the stronger the correspondence posited, the more of a problem it becomes when there is *not* an exact correspondence.

However, if we are not to accept Beale's argument, we need to suggest an alternative that better fits the passage. One way to solve this would be to define the limits of the antecedent of 'as YHWH said' more clearly. We can pick up the 'division of labour' point made above. The explanations in 3:18-20, 4:21-23 and 7:1-5 set out separate acts (Moses goes and speaks/performs signs; YHWH hardens/sets his hand; Pharaoh refuses to release/releases). The phrase 'as YHWH said' is immediately preceded by a reference to what Pharaoh has done (or has not done). Therefore one can assume that it is definitely referring to this. Less clear, however, is whether it is also referring to the phrase that comes before that, concerning the hardening of the heart.

In other words, we could understand that 'as YHWH said' focuses on *Pharaoh's* acts (not listening/not sending), rather than focussing either on YHWH's acts ('hardening') or on both of them together. When YHWH ascribes the 'hardening' to himself, he appears to be contrasting his actions with those of Moses ('you speak and I, for my part, will harden'), rather than contrasting them with Pharaoh ('you speak and I, and not Pharaoh, will harden'). This alternative is appealing, as it does allow us to maintain the exact correspondence between deed and preceding word. YHWH said that Pharaoh would not listen, and that Pharaoh would not send; and Pharaoh is doing exactly that.[46]

If the formula is referring back specifically to Pharaoh's actions, what is its function? Presumably it would be showing that YHWH anticipated this reaction from Pharaoh all along (and told Moses).[47] Pharaoh's actions are not catching YHWH by surprise. That Pharaoh will not respond appropriately is the one constant in all three speeches from YHWH up to this point (3:19; 4:23; 7:3-4), whereas the reasons for this vary.[48] Moses gets reminders of this from YHWH (7:14; 10:1). In the narratorial refrains the focus is more on the reader, perhaps to reassure them in their turn. The reader thus gets more reassurance than Moses, who has to wait until 10:1 for YHWH to provide him with another message or summary.

---

[46] Moreover, we have argued that the hardening relates to what Pharaoh does, or does not do; rather than simply to his mental state. Therefore it is not surprising that 'as YHWH said' would also refer to his actions. Thus the 'division of labour' in YHWH's messages refers to Pharaoh's actions as well: Moses will do X; YHWH will do Y; Pharaoh will do Z.

[47] Cf. Fretheim, 100.

[48] The other constant is that Moses must go to Pharaoh, but this is not relevant to the point in question (see above on 3:10).

3.2.1.4 SUMMARY OF THE 'SUMMARIES'

On a number of occasions YHWH speaks to Moses concerning the coming encounter or encounters with Pharaoh. In these messages YHWH summarises what will happen, setting out what Moses is to do, what YHWH will do, and often what Pharaoh will do. Several of these summaries include the comment from YHWH that he will harden Pharaoh's heart, as part of this 'division of labour'. Depending on the context and the focus of these statements, the details given can vary to some degree. As the later statements tend to be more detailed than the former statements, so the encounters within the plagues narrative (and the hardening incidents within them) are more detailed again. To these we now turn..

3.2.2 Second Context for Hardening References: Concluding Narratorial Refrains

The plague of hail ends with Pharaoh sinning and hardening his heart (9:34), followed by the statement that Pharaoh's heart remained hard (9:35). At the end of the plague of locusts, which contains 10:1-2, we hear that YHWH hardens Pharaoh's heart (10:20). One of these three statements is used to conclude each of the first nine plagues and the serpent staff sign before them. These, and the patterns noted in 3.2.2.1-3, are set out in Appendix III. Closer attention to these refrains suggests that there is a pattern in their use, corresponding to the actions in the plague that they conclude.

3.2.2.1 PHARAOH HARDENED HIS HEART

On three occasions Pharaoh is said to 'harden' his own heart (8:11 [15], 28 [32]; 9:34; all Hiph'il כָּבֵד). Where this refrain is used, it concludes a plague where Pharaoh has agreed to let Israel go if the plague is averted or ended, albeit with conditions (8:4 [8], 21-24 [25-28]; 9:27-28). If the hardening describes Pharaoh's stubborn stance towards YHWH's demand, then Pharaoh's agreement that Israel may leave could be described as a 'softening' of Pharaoh's heart (or position).[49] However, as in 9:34, when the plague is removed Pharaoh reneges on his agreement. Thus he makes an active move against releasing Israel, which is described as 'hardening' his own heart.[50]

3.2.2.2 PHARAOH'S HEART WAS/REMAINED HARD

The phrase 'Pharaoh's heart was hard' occurs five times (7:13, 22; 8:15 [19]; 9:7, 35; cf. 7:14). In each case the Qal of חָזַק is used, except 9:7

---

[49] Alternatively we could follow Gunn and use 'weakening'; cf. Gunn, 75ff.

[50] We could perhaps describe this as making his heart 'harder'.

which has Qal כָּבֵד. In contrast to the previous refrain, where this phrase is used it concludes a plague where there is no sign that Pharaoh has changed his attitude at all during that plague. He does not negotiate with Moses and Aaron (if he encounters them at all) and makes no offer to send the people. His position appears to be unchanged from the hardening at the end of the previous plague.[51]

Therefore it seems that the Qal has the nuance of 'Pharaoh's heart *remained* hard', as opposed to a deliberate hardening of a heart that has 'softened'.[52] The refrain is responsive to what Pharaoh has done (or not done) during the plague.[53]

There are two cases that need further discussion.

If Pharaoh's heart *remains* hard at 7:13, this suggests that it has been seen to be 'hard' already. The obvious precedent is 5:1-5 with its aftermath in 5:6-21. Although the vocabulary of hardening is not used there, Pharaoh is certainly hard-set against Israel leaving, both because he does not recognise YHWH's authority, and also because he does not want to lose his workers. Thus the meaning of 7:13 is that Pharaoh has not been swayed from his original position by this initial sign.[54]

9:35 follows immediately after 9:34. Thus while we could understand it as saying that Pharaoh remained hard in v35 after hardening himself in v34, the statement seems a little superfluous. Interestingly these are followed by 10:1 which contains the third hardening message 'YHWH hardened'. This

---

[51] Moreover, in contrast to the previous refrain which comes after a respite, this refrain comes immediately after Pharaoh has seen the difference between Israel and Egypt, either in the ability or inability of his representatives to copy YHWH's representatives, or in the effect of a plague (7:12, 22; 8:14-15a [18-19a]; 9:6-7a). 9:35 is discussed briefly below.

[52] Beale comes to the same conclusion on different grounds. He notes two possibilities for understanding the perfect Qal חָזַק: either aoristic action or perfective action. The former would refer to a definite past action and would have a passive sense; the second would 'conceive of the subject (Pharaoh's heart) as in a given condition resulting from a preceding action.' He gives four reasons for preferring the latter: the unusual nature of a transitive-passive sense for the Qal of חָזַק; the word order in the Hebrew designating the heart as subject; the use of Hiph'il or Pi'el stems in contrast to show the heart being worked upon; and the unique use of a verbal adjective (כָּבֵד) in 7:14, which could continue the sense of 7:13 (139). Moreover, he describes a 'transitive-intransitive' hardening pattern in the plagues where a hardening act is followed by a hardened condition (5:2 and 7:13; 8:11 [15] and 8:15 [19]; 8:28 [32] and 9:7; 9:34 and 9:35). 9:12 does not fit but he explains this as the first explicit identification of YHWH as agent (148-149). Cf. Hyatt, 102, on this usage not being passive or reflexive. Schmidt, 343, prefers to leave the question open.

[53] Rashbam, 73, notes the contrast between Pharaoh not being moved and Pharaoh being moved and restiffening himself again.

[54] Cf. Beale, 139, albeit we disagree on the cause of the hardening in 5:2.

could suggest that the three are broadly the same. However the context of 10:1 as a speech to Moses rather than a narratorial refrain needs to be taken into account. In light of the comments on 'summaries' above, we cannot assume that 10:1 is referring solely to 9:34-35.[55] With regard to 9:34 and 9:35 as yet I am unable to see how the two are to be read together in their current context. The only other similar double mention of Pharaoh's position is at 7:22-23.

3.2.2.3 YHWH HARDENED PHARAOH'S HEART

On three occasions later in the plagues, YHWH steps in and 'hardens' Pharaoh (9:12; 10:20; 10:27 – all Pi'el חָזַק). These instances span the two different circumstances noted above. Once YHWH 'hardens' when there has been no change in Pharaoh's position, and twice he 'hardens' Pharaoh when he has 'softened'. This does not immediately fit the distinction noted above. However the context offers help with understanding.

The problem is 9:12, where mention of YHWH's hardening appears redundant as Pharaoh has not 'softened'; thus we might expect 'Pharaoh's heart *remained* hard.' However, this occurs immediately after an act of the magi. Previously in all such cases, Pharaoh's heart is said to remain hard. Here it may be suggested that the elimination of the magi from the scene may have rendered this position impossible; thus YHWH steps in to bring about what would have happened previously, by 'strengthening' (חָזַק) his position so that this does not (have to?) affect him (cf. 8:15 [19] especially).

In 10:20 by contrast, the plague has been removed. In all three previous cases, the plague's removal led to Pharaoh hardening his own heart (8:11 [15]; 8:28 [32]; 9:34). The first and last cases are explicitly linked to him seeing the respite yet rejecting the 'knowledge' it contained. Thus once again, YHWH steps in to bring about what would have happened previously. Pharaoh sees the respite and YHWH hardens him. Finally, there is the oddity of 10:26-27 where Moses makes a demand that Pharaoh cannot accept. Previously Pharaoh had compromised with Moses'

---

[55] Thus although it follows the two narratorial hardening statements in 9:34-35 we should distinguish the context. This argues against the idea that the juxtaposition of the three hardening statements indicates that, in effect, they have the same meaning (contra Propp, 336). Indeed if 10:1 is a summary, it may not be appropriate to ask 'to what exact point is YHWH referring here?' By this point we know that YHWH has hardened Pharaoh (9:12) and that at least some of his servants have refused to listen (9:21).

Moreover, if we did assume that 9:34-10:1 all have broadly the same meaning, this raises the question of how one understands this single message. For example, Jacob *Exodus* argues that 10:1 has the same semantic range as the previous uses (246). He translates the passage as 'I have permitted his will to remain firm' (280). However, Gunn notes 'as for the hardening [in 9:34], the formula is immediately placed in the context of YHWH's causality' (77). Thus the position could be argued either way, leaving us little wiser as to any overall meaning.

demands (8:24 [28]) but then reneged. However, in the previous plague of locusts, before the plague takes place, Pharaoh had refused Moses' counter-demand outright (10:10-11). There is no mention of hardening in 10:10-11 (from either Pharaoh or YHWH), but the effect is the same as when hardening occurs: Pharaoh refuses the offer. Once again we could see YHWH following Pharaoh's previous actions. As Pharaoh did in 10:10-11, so YHWH does in 10:26-28. As a result, Pharaoh rejects the counter-offer and drives them out.

3.2.3 Summary of the 'hardening'

- As noted in chapter 1, the words used for the hardening (כָּבֵד, חָזַק and קָשָׁה) are also used in the exodus story with other meanings.
- There are two main contexts for mention of the hardening of Pharaoh's heart. The first, mainly pre-plagues narrative, is YHWH's statements to Moses where YHWH states that he will harden Pharaoh's heart. These statements act as 'summaries' of the encounters with Pharaoh, setting out what Moses, YHWH and Pharaoh will do.
- The second context is the narratorial refrains that conclude each plague. These fall into three groups, stating that Pharaoh hardened his heart, that Pharaoh's heart remained hard, and that YHWH hardened Pharaoh's heart. These different refrains arise from Pharaoh's actions in the plague that they conclude.

3.2.4 Return to 10:1

It is now possible, in light of our discussion on the hardening comments, to offer some preliminary comments on 10:1. 10:1 is one of a number of messages from YHWH to Moses setting out what Moses is to do, and what YHWH will do or has done. Some of these messages also mention what Pharaoh will do. 10:1 appears to be a 'summary' of the position, much as the previous messages were. The 'division of labour' motif continues from the earlier messages. Moses is to go, YHWH has hardened, and YHWH will set his signs (cf. 3:18-20; 4:21-23; 7:1-5). However, 10:1 is unusual on a couple of counts. First it is a message to Moses during the plagues narrative, whereas most of the other messages come before or after it. Secondly YHWH speaks of what he has done, rather than what he will do, and this is the reason for Moses to go: 'Go *because* I *have* hardened'. However this second difference presumably flows from the first. Instead of being a summary in advance, this is a summary in the midst of the events, and YHWH tells Moses that he is doing what he said he would.

3.3 10:2 and הִתְעַלַּ֫לְתִּי

In 10:1-2 the hardening is not an end in and of itself, but rather a means to an end. Moses is told that YHWH has hardened Pharaoh so that he may set his signs in his midst, and so that Israel may recount these signs and how YHWH 'הִתְעַלֵּל'ed Pharaoh. Once again, there appears to be a difference in explanation from that of 9:13-19, which spoke of restraint and remonstration. Here the message is of hardening and הִתְעַלֵּל. To give a sense of the difference, some examples of translations of הִתְעַלַּ֫לְתִּי in commentaries and translations follow. Any further interpretative remarks follow the respective translations in parentheses.

- '*quae fecerim in Aegypto*' (Calvin, 193), cf. KJV/NKJV;
- 'busied myself with'/'dealt severely with' (Fretheim, 127);
- 'deal ruthlessly with' (Cassuto, 123 – the idea of retribution), cf. NIV;
- 'ὅσα ἐμπέπαιχα τοῖς Αἰγυπτίοις' (LXX – 'ridicule/make fun of/deceive/trick');
- 'made a mockery of' (Sarna, 48 – humbling and humiliating Egypt); cf. NASB; JPST;
- 'made fools of' NRSV; NJB;
- 'made sport of' (Hyatt, 123 – dealing ruthlessly or wantonly), cf. RSV;
- 'toyed with' (Childs, 126; Jacob, 280);
- '*quotiens contriverim Aegyptios*' (Vg. 'grind, wear down, diminish, treat contemptuously');
- 'amused myself aggravating' (Durham, 131-132);
- 'lorded it' (Propp, 336 – acting with capricious power);
- 'deal with gruesomely' (Houtman, II 102);
- 'have to do with a person, generally in a bad way, to do him harm' (Keil, 493);
- 'deal with wantonly'/'play a dirty trick on' (*HALOT* II, 834);
- '*jemanden übel mitspielen*' ('play with someone wickedly'/'use a person ill') (Baentsch, 79 - through derision, or ill-treatment as here); cf. Dillmann, 90 '*einem übel mitspielen*';
- Schmidt, 348 n2 '*mutwillig umgehen mit*' ('treat maliciously/wilfully'), and '*jmd. übel mitspielen*' although he also has '*nach Gutdünken handeln*' ('act as one sees fit/at one's own discretion').
- 'abuse/mistreat someone' (Roth, 'עָלַל' *TDOT* XI, 139-46, 141);

Thus we have a spectrum of meaning from the innocuous 'did/busied myself with', through 'deal harshly with' and 'make a fool of/toy with' to 'abuse, mistreat, deal with wickedly'.

The form here is Hithpaʻel.[56] There are five other uses of the Hithpaʻel of this verb in the Old Testament, all of which, as here, have ב marking the object:

- One refers back to this passage (1Sam. 6:6).
- One refers to the sexual abuse of the Levite's concubine in Gibeah (Jdg. 19:25).
- One refers to Balaam's donkey's treatment of his master (Num. 22:29).
- Two refer to the potential treatment of conquered kings by their enemies (1Sam. 31:4/1Chr. 10:4, Jer. 38:19)

We will look at these to gauge any range of meanings and consider which of them, if any, are helpful comparisons to 10:2.

3.3.1 1SAM. 6:6 – REFERRING TO THE EXODUS הֲלוֹא כַּאֲשֶׁר הִתְעַלֵּל בָּהֶם

The use in 1Sam. 6:6 refers back to the exodus and, in light of הִתְעַלֵּל, presumably to this very passage. Being dependent on 10:2, it is difficult to use it to refine the meaning here, except to note that both nations were experiencing plagues from YHWH. 1Sam. 6:6 will be discussed further in chapter 5.

3.3.2 THE LEVITE'S CONCUBINE (JDG. 19:25) וַיִּתְעַלְּלוּ־בָהּ כָּל־הַלַּיְלָה

Jdg. 19 contains the story of the Levite's concubine. She is thrown out of the house to the mob of evil men, who spend the night sexually abusing her. Trible uses the word 'torture' to translate the term here.[57] In this situation it is clear that the word is being used to describe something morally repugnant, and quite terrible.

We could see links between Pharaoh helpless in the hands of almighty YHWH, and the concubine helpless in the hands of the mob. However, this would be to miss out on an important element in the text. Pharaoh is not a helpless concubine. He is the one who has said that he does not 'know' YHWH, and is exalting himself over YHWH's people. YHWH's spokesmen are two elderly Hebrew slaves, in contrast to the power of Pharaoh and his court, and their god is the god of a slave people, who are under the power of Egypt (cf. 5:2).

3.3.3 BALAAM (NUM. 22:29) וַיֹּאמֶר בִּלְעָם לָאָתוֹן כִּי הִתְעַלַּלְתְּ בִּי

To avoid death from the opposing angel, Balaam's donkey turns from the road; then presses against the wall, crushing Balaam's foot; and finally refuses to move altogether. In his anger Balaam beats the donkey. When the

---

[56] עָלַל is also found in other stems where it has the general meaning of 'deal with (severely)' (also 'glean' and 'gather') (*TDOT* XI, 140-41; *HALOT* II, 834). However we will restrict the analysis to the six hithpaʻel uses as the closest match.

[57] Phyllis Trible, *Texts of Terror*, OBT 13 (Philadelphia: Fortress Press, 1984), 76.

donkey asks why he has done this, Balaam responds that the donkey has 'הִתְעַלֵּל'ed him, and that if he had a sword he would kill the beast.

This suggests something far milder than the previous example. Balaam may think that the donkey is being rather recalcitrant, but the worst that happens to him is that his foot gets hurt. Otherwise he is simply made to look stupid.

The vehemence of his threat to kill the donkey may suggest that his use of הִתְעַלֵּלְתְּ may be hyperbolic and disproportionate to the situation (cf. Jon. 4:9 where he claims he is 'angry enough to die' because he loses his shelter, or v3 where YHWH questions the appropriateness of his anger). This would give a sense closer to the previous case: Balaam is accusing the donkey of abusing him.

However, the context is rather different from the previous case. The donkey has no power over Balaam; rather Balaam has the power to beat it when it displeases him. Thus 'abuse' would be a curious word to use, even hyperbolically. The more probable explanation is that he is simply accusing the donkey of making a fool of him. The 'great seer' (Num. 22:6, 15-17) cannot even control his own donkey. Thus Milgrom explains it as 'made a mockery of'.[58]

How does this usage fit the context of Exodus? There are some points of comparison between Balaam and Pharaoh:

a)   Both of them are figures that are intending to harm or obstruct Israel.[59]

b)   There is direct divine action in both cases (unlike the previous examples). However this action is seemingly contradictory (telling Balaam to go and then sending an angel to oppose him, compared to telling Pharaoh to let Israel go and then 'hardening' him which prevents this).

c)   Both lack perception as to the reason for this action, whereas the concubine (and the kings) are all too aware of what is happening and why. The הִתְעַלֵּלְתְּ, although bad at the time, is in contrast to death. In Balaam's case this is his lack of perception as to why the donkey is behaving thus. Its 'abuse' is actually saving him from death (Num. 22:33). In Pharaoh's case YHWH has already told him that he could have destroyed Pharaoh (9:15). However instead he is choosing to restrict his power in order to show his power. This 'abuse'/'toying with' may be the alternative to death.

---

[58] Jacob Milgrom, *Numbers*, JPSTC (Philadelphia/New York: Jewish Publication Society, 1990), 191.

[59] Moreover in some Jewish traditions, Balaam becomes one of Pharaoh's counsellors (along with Jethro and Job). See Judith R. Baskin, *Pharaoh's Counsellors – Job, Jethro and Balaam in Rabbinic and Patristic Tradition*, BJS 47 (Chico, California: Scholars Press, 1983).

However, Pharaoh has refused to see this (9:17); like Balaam his
perception is lacking.

However, while Pharaoh is not a helpless concubine, neither does he
play master to YHWH's donkey. Pharaoh may initially perceive him to be a
god who can be ignored, but this miscomprehension is soon removed. Once
again the relational dynamics are wrong.

3.3.4 THE FATE OF CONQUERED KINGS (1SAM. 31:4/1CHR. 10:4, JER. 38:19)

פֶּן־יִתְּנוּ אֹתִי בְּיָדָם וְהִתְעַלְּלוּ־בִ/פֶּן־יָבֹ[וֹ]אוּ ... [וּדְקָרֻנִי] וְהִתְעַלְּלוּ־בִי

When it is clear that he has lost the battle with the Philistines, Saul tells his
armour bearer to run him through so that he does not fall into the hands of
the Philistines who will run him through and וְהִתְעַלְּלוּ him. Among the
commentators, Driver suggests 'mock' or 'abuse'[60] and Brueggemann has
'humiliated and tortured'.[61] Zedekiah fears being given into the hands of
the deserters, who would הִתְעַלְּלוּ him. This is his reason for not
surrendering to the Chaldeans, although Jeremiah promises him that it will
not happen if he surrenders. McKane suggests that 'playing with' or
'making a toy of' is more than simply 'mocking' or 'jeering'.[62]

These present a closer match to our situation. If we pick up the
underlying message in YHWH's demand, the encounters between him and
Pharaoh concern the issue of whom Israel will serve, and whether Pharaoh
will acknowledge YHWH by sending them. The image given by הִתְעַלֵּל in
this circumstance is of the victor proving to their opponent (and presumably
to the wider world) that they have beaten them. Perhaps a similar image is
found in the entreaty of the psalmist 'do not let my enemy triumph over
me' (Ps. 13:3 [2], 5 [4] cf. 41:12 [11]), or the idea of one's enemies being
put to shame (בּוֹשׁ – Ps. 25:2-3; 35:26; Is. 26:11; Jer. 17:18 etc).

In 1Sam. 31 the verb for 'run through' (דְּקַר) is used for both
alternatives. Thus Saul knows that he is going to die. His choice is whether
to die of his own accord, or at the hands of his enemies. When they find
him, his enemies do indeed mock him, albeit posthumously (1Sam. 31:9-
10). Pharaoh's later responses (9:27-28; 10:16-17) give an example of this
kind of defeat. However, as we have seen with 9:27-28, these words arise *in
extremis*. When the plague is removed Pharaoh's actions belie his previous
comments.

This would make sense of the Septuagint rendering. In all of the above
examples except Jer. 38:19, the LXX translates הִתְעַלֵּל with ἐμπαίζω, which

---

[60] Driver *Samuel*, 228.

[61] Walter Brueggemann, *First and Second Samuel*, IBC (Louisville, Kentucky: John
Knox Press, 1990), 207.

[62] William McKane, *A Critical and Exegetical Commentary on Jeremiah*, ICC
(Edinburgh: T&T Clark, 1996), 957.

has the sense of 'ridicule/make fun of/deceive/trick'.[63] Jer. 38:19 has καταμωκάομαι 'to mock'. If the potential fate of Saul and Zedekiah are similar then these two verbs would give a sense of 'ridicule' or 'mock' here.

One interesting use of ἐμπαίζω with YHWH as subject is in Ps. 103:26 [Heb. 104:26] where YHWH forms the mighty Leviathan (cf. Job 41) to 'play with' him. The Hebrew verb used is שָׂחַק which appears to have a milder meaning than הִתְעַלֵּל (cf. Jdg. 16:25; 2Sam. 2:14; 6:21 etc.). However, perhaps this may give one way of understanding 10:2. To Israel Pharaoh would have been seen as a great force. However, in comparison to YHWH, whom Pharaoh does not recognise, this great power is nothing but a plaything.[64] Alternatively we could consider 1Sam. 17:45-47 where David comes against the mighty warrior Goliath, in the name of YHWH. David's comments on what he will do to Goliath and the Philistines (v46) might well be summed up with הִתְעַלֵּל, although this is not used. Of the different uses of הִתְעַלֵּל, therefore, this seems to be the most useful comparison to YHWH's acts against Egypt.

With this in mind, we can return to 10:2. YHWH's acts are to be remembered as הִתְעַלֵּל, as mocking, humiliating, shaming Egypt.[65] One image that this does not convey is that of punishment or just reward for actions. None of the above examples are obviously retributive[66], and this is not given as a reason for YHWH's actions. The one difference in the uses of הִתְעַלֵּל ascribed to YHWH is that they do have an explicit reason given. Here Moses and Israel will 'know that I am YHWH'. In 1Sam. 6:6 YHWH's הִתְעַלֵּל is linked to Egypt sending the people. As in 9:13ff, we have the same themes.

---

[63] It can have the sense of 'treat harshly' (1Macc. 9:26; 2 Macc. 7:10), and is paired with 'beat' in Prov. 23:35. Cf. also Gen. 39:14 Potiphar's wife on Joseph 'playing with' them.

[64] This could also apply to the small nation(s) of Israel/Judah continually faced with the might of Egypt (to a greater or lesser extent) as a powerful neighbour. Yet this weak nation had a strong god whose power, the prophets proclaimed, was greater than that of Pharaoh (cf. Ezek. 29:3-4; 32:2 for other images of Pharaoh not dissimilar from Leviathan).

[65] One could ask whether this word refers to the hardening, to the plagues or both. However this question is probably unnecessary. It is difficult to say more than that it refers to YHWH's acts in respect of Egypt as a whole.

[66] One could suggest that the deserters were taking revenge on Zedekiah but this would be speculation.

3.4 9:13-19 vs. 10:1-2 – Summarising the Differences

A comparison of our preliminary remarks on 10:1 and 10:2 with our discussion of 9:13-19 shows us that we have two rather different rationales for YHWH's actions.

	9:15-16	**10:1-2**
YHWH's action	*Sustain* Pharaoh and his people from destruction	*Harden* Pharaoh and his servants
1st reason	*Show* you (Pharaoh) my power	Set my *signs* on them (Egypt)
2nd reason	*Recount* my name in all the world	*Recount* to your son and son's sons how I הִתְעַלֵּל'ed Egypt and the signs I set on them
3rd reason	(cf. 9:14 *You* [Pharaoh] *will know* there is none like me)	*You* [Israel] *will know* that I am YHWH

Set out like this, we may be able to compare and contrast.

YHWH's Actions

In both cases YHWH's actions appear to be lengthening the process. In other words, if the speeches are 'explanations', they appear to be explaining why the process has gone on so long.

However, the explanations of YHWH actions appear rather different. Is YHWH's previous use of lesser plagues to be understood as restraint to get a response, or as playing with Pharaoh?

1st Reason

In both cases, the first reason is some form of demonstration. We have noted the potential paradox of YHWH demonstrating power by restraining power in 9:16. 10:1 speaks of setting signs on Egypt.

2nd Reason

This is followed by the second reason. This involves a human response of recounting (סָפַר) YHWH's name or his deeds. In 9:16, the audience is spatial: YHWH's name will be heard throughout the whole world. In 10:1-2 it is temporal: the story will be handed down throughout Israel's generations.[67] However, this distinction is not totally clear cut. The only place which obviously refers to this passage is 1Sam. 6:6 where the speakers are Philistines.

3rd Reason?

The pattern is not exact at this point. There is an equivalent to 10:2b in 9:13-19, but it comes in 9:14, rather than after 9:16. However, inasmuch as we have argued that 9:14 is a summary that is expanded in 9:15-18, it is arguably comparable to the final reason in 10:2.

Therefore we have two important rationales for YHWH's acts in the plagues narrative. They have certain similarities. Both refer to YHWH's actions as lengthening the encounters. Moreover, both outline similar purposes. YHWH will act to demonstrate something, so that by it he will be spoken of universally (either temporally or spatially), in order that people will acknowledge him. However with these similarities there is a substantial difference in the way that YHWH's actions are understood. On the one hand they are seen as restraint rather than destruction; on the other, they are seen as 'toying with' people. (הֶעֱמַדְתִּי(ךָ is contrasted with הִתְעַלַּלְתִּי.[68]

We will move on to examine the immediate context of 10:1-2, as done with 9:13-19, to see if this sheds any light on the differences.

3.5 The Passage in (Immediate) Context (10:3-20)

The first point that we notice when considering the context is the unusual nature of the pre-plague encounter with Pharaoh.

First there is the presentation of YHWH's message to Pharaoh. Normally YHWH's message to Pharaoh is given in his speech to Moses: 'Go to Pharaoh … and say to him "…" '. There is then no record of Moses or Aaron giving this message to Pharaoh; the narrative continues with Pharaoh's reaction. The assumption is that Moses has repeated the message verbatim, and this does not need repetition.[69] However on this occasion

---

[67] Sarna *Exodus*, 48, suggests that Ps. 78 and 105 are examples of such recounting.

[68] In light of this we might wish to question whether our interpretation of 9:13ff is correct. Might this latter passage not suggest that 9:16 (say), should be interpreted as 'I raised you up'? This would emphasise the power and control of YHWH, and could fit well with the imagery of 'toying with' Pharaoh. Pharaoh, like the mighty Leviathan (Ps. 104:26), is merely the plaything of the almighty YHWH.

However, in our discussion of 9:16 as part of the wider speech, we noted that this reading causes problems when taken with 9:15 and 9:17. We would need to find a way to make sense of this reading of 9:13-19 in its context. Therefore we will leave such reconsideration until we have exhausted other avenues.

[69] Ann. M. Vater, 'A Plague on both our houses: Observations in Exodus 7-11', in *Art and Meaning: Rhetoric in Biblical Literature* ed. David JA Clines, David M Gunn, Alan J Hauser, JSOTSup 19 (Sheffield: Sheffield Academic Press, 1982): 62-71, sees the text

YHWH's speech only contains the command 'Go to Pharaoh' before giving this explanation to Moses. The reader hears the content of his message to Pharaoh when Moses speaks it to Pharaoh (10:3-6a).[70]

The message itself starts with what appears to be an exasperated remonstration from YHWH to Pharaoh in the style of 9:17: 'How long will you refuse to humble yourself before me? Send my people that they may serve me' (10:3).[71]

The message 'If you do not send ... I will bring...' is then presented to Pharaoh (10:4-6). However, unlike the other plagues where the description of the message is followed by the description of the plague, here there is a response before the onset of the plague.

The servants of Pharaoh take it upon themselves to add their voice to that of YHWH, Moses and Aaron: 'How long will this one be a snare to us? Send the men that they may serve YHWH their God. Do you not yet know that Egypt is ruined?' (10:7). The echoes of YHWH's words are several, although nuanced as coming from Pharaoh's servants rather than YHWH's servants. There is the question of 'how long' (cf. 9:17; 10:3) these encounters will continue; there is the reiterated demand 'send ... serve'; and there is the question of whether Pharaoh 'does not yet know' that Egypt is ruined (cf. 9:29-30).

Apparently as a result of this advice, Pharaoh calls back Moses and Aaron for negotiations before the plague occurs, the only time that he does this. He offers to send them, but questions who will be going. On learning that all will go, not just the men, he accuses Moses of plotting and drives him out (10:8-11). It is only at this point that the plague comes (10:12-15). Then, as in 9:27-28, Pharaoh calls Moses and Aaron, admits his sin and

---

presenting Moses 'as a "silenced messenger", whose own voice melts into the words of God' (65).

[70] The Samaritan Pentateuch and 4QpaleoExod[m] have an extended version of YHWH's speech, which contains the words in vv3-6. Whereas the majority of the expansions of this type repeat the words of YHWH to Moses in the context of Moses' speech to Pharaoh, here the position is reversed. However, inasmuch as it brings this speech into line with the others, there has to be a reasonable argument that this represents a tidying up of an anomaly rather than an original lost by the MT. All of these expansions could also be understood as showing that Moses did exactly as he was commanded, or, uniquely in this case, that what Moses did had been commanded by YHWH. See Sanderson, 197-198.

[71] Joüon notes that the translation would literally be 'How long have you refused to humble yourself before me?' However the action is presumed to continue from the past up to a moment in the future. Thus it becomes 'How long will you refuse?' cf. 16:28; Ps. 80:3 [2] (Joüon §112e; cf. GKC §106h).

asks them to intercede with YHWH to remove the plague (10:16-17).[72] YHWH removes the plague as asked, but then hardens Pharaoh's heart and Pharaoh does not release the people (10:18-20).[73]

In contrast to the encounter in 9:20-35 which resonated with YHWH's message in 9:13-19, here the encounter in 10:3-20 (and especially 10:3-10) reads strangely after the message of 10:1-2.

YHWH has just spoken of hardening Pharaoh and toying with him, yet in the encounter that follows, YHWH reproaches Pharaoh for his lack of response, and Pharaoh is arguably more responsive than at any point previous to this. He responds to a mere warning of a plague, rather than the plague itself. Moreover it is the servants, spoken of as hardening themselves or being hardened (9:34; 10:1) that echo YHWH's words (10:7).[74]

Thus in considering how 9:13-19 and 10:1-2 relate, we also need to consider how 10:1-2 relates to what follows. The point is made most sharply by the juxtaposition of 10:2 and 10:3. YHWH, who is 'toying with' Pharaoh (v2), is expressing exasperation over Pharaoh's intransigence (v3). The reader is tempted to respond 'He will refuse to humble himself as long as you keep hardening him!'

This juxtaposition of seemingly contradictory phrases is not unique. Immediately before it there are the strange comments on hardening in 9:34-10:1 which use each of the three hardening phrases in turn. Assuming that we do not simply assume that they are identical in meaning, we need to suggest a way of understanding them in context.

We have already discussed the dynamics of 9:15-17, where YHWH's comments about his power and control are followed by a remonstration over Pharaoh's continued obstinacy similar to 10:3. Earlier in the story YHWH answers Moses' comments about his ineloquence (4:10) with the statement that is it he, YHWH, who gives or takes away the ability to speak. Then Moses is told that he has to go to Pharaoh; YHWH will be with him and tell him what to say (4:12). However Moses then asks YHWH to act without him (4:13 'send by the hand you will send').[75] The divine anger

---

[72] He makes no explicit statement that the people may leave (contrast 9:28). However, as he appears to be capitulating in the face of the plague, such a statement can probably be assumed, whatever one may think of its value in light of previous promises.

[73] 10:3-20 will be examined in more detail in chapter 4. The issue here is its relation to 10:1-2.

[74] Cf. Fretheim, 97-98. Contrast Propp, 336 'incongruity'.

[75] Moses' reply is normally translated as 'send someone else'. This quite possibly expresses Moses' wish, and gives a good English idiom, especially as Keil notes that בְּיַד probably means a person rather than a hand as such (1Sam. 16:20; 2Sam. 11:14; 12:25; 1Kgs. 2:25). Nevertheless, it loses the focus on YHWH, and thus its sense as a reply to 4:11-12.

that follows this comment (anger which has not arisen from any of Moses' questions) suggests that this is not an appropriate response to make. YHWH's comments about his power are meant to motivate Moses to go, not give him an excuse to get out of going.[76]

In all these three cases (10:2-3; 9:15-17; 4:11-14), YHWH's focus on his amazing power is followed immediately by a call for human action. YHWH's power and human action, at least in these cases, are not mutually exclusive. In 10:3 there would be no point in remonstrating with Pharaoh if there was no chance of his responding correctly. Thus, 'toying with' and 'hardening' do not appear to preclude human response.

However there is a difference between the two earlier passages and the juxtaposition of 10:2-3 (and 9:34-10:1). Both 9:15-17 and 4:10-14 form part of a single encounter. Therefore if we assume that YHWH's speech to Pharaoh (9:15-17) and his responses to Moses (4:10-14) are meant to make sense, then these comments cannot be contradictory and must make sense in relation to each other. In this passage, by contrast, we have a comment from the narrator (9:34-35); followed by a message from YHWH to Moses (10:1-2); followed by a message from YHWH to Pharaoh, given by Moses (10:3-6).[77] The messages are set in different contexts and given to different recipients. Moreover, the explanation in 9:13-19 is one of the messages given to Pharaoh, whereas the explanation in 10:1-2 is one of the summaries given to Moses. This fact may suggest a way to approach the differences.

YHWH has just said that he has the power over speech; and previously he has said that he will send his hand upon Egypt (3:20). Moses' response to these comments appears to be 'then [in light of your power], send by the 'hand' that *you* will send. [Why do you, the powerful YHWH, need *me* to go?]'

[76] That it is a refusal rather than just humility seems evident from the anger that this generates. YHWH has worked through Moses' objections patiently, constantly bringing the focus back to himself. However, here the focus is not returned to YHWH for the first time, but rather he gets angry with Moses and provides Aaron. Interestingly YHWH is never said to get angry with Pharaoh, although we may detect a hint of exasperation in 9:17 and 10:3 amongst other places. The only other mention of anger in the encounters is from Moses in 11:8 when he leaves Pharaoh. In both cases, extended negotiations have broken down. Moses has just refused to go to Pharaoh; and Pharaoh has just refused to speak to Moses ever again on pain of death. It seems that while negotiations and discussions are permissible, refusal is not.

[77] Another example of this would be 4:21-23 where Moses is given a message which *contains* a message to Pharaoh (v22-23). Read as one single message, 4:21-23 gives us similar problems, as YHWH appears to be saying that he will harden Pharaoh and then punish him for it. However, as above, if the message of 4:22-23 has any real substance to it, then the sense must be more complicated than that.

3.6 Whose Explanation? Which Context? What Response?

In itself the observation that the explanations in 9:13-19 and 10:1-2 are given to different people is nothing new. Jacob notes that the lengthy explanations to plagues VII and VIII are for Egypt and Israel respectively.[78] Durham comments on the differences in the 'proof of presence' motif between Egypt and Israel.[79] In his comparison of 9:14-16 and 10:1b-2, Schmidt notes that these two explanations should be read in context as the complementary word of God to Pharaoh and Israel.[80] Janzen notes the shift in focus at 10:2 from Egypt 'knowing' to Israel 'knowing', as does Gunn.[81] However, I have not come across any extended consideration of the implications of this observation. For example, what does it mean theologically that YHWH has different things to say to different people, and how might this affect our overall thesis?

3.6.1 Pharaoh

The majority of the interaction in the plagues narrative is between YHWH and Pharaoh. He receives a message from YHWH via Moses at the beginning of most plagues, and interacts with Moses at the end of most. We have seen that YHWH's message to Pharaoh is predominantly a demand to release YHWH's people so that they may serve him. This is followed by a warning of the plague that will come if he does not; a plague that will cause Pharaoh to 'know' or acknowledge YHWH.

Pharaoh is the absolute ruler who presently controls YHWH's people.[82] He stands opposed to YHWH's demand for his people to serve him, as he does not think much of YHWH (5:2; 9:17). YHWH's acts are a means of disabusing him of his perceptions: '*In this* you will know that I am YHWH' (7:17). YHWH's tone to him is adversative ('send ... or I will send ...'), and remonstrative ('how long...?', 'until when...?'). His comments emphasise Pharaoh's responsibility to 'send' the people.

---

[78] Jacob *Exodus*, 187, 194.

[79] Durham, 135.

[80] Schmidt, 417.

[81] J. Gerald Janzen, *Exodus*, (Louisville: Westminster/John Knox Press, 1997), 71; Gunn, 83-84.

[82] It would be too crude to see Pharaoh as a 'god', due to the complexity of Egyptian religious thought. The relationship of Pharaoh with the gods of Egypt is not easy to describe. Hornung shows that, although having attributes of deity, and could be addressed as such, being elected by them (p193), and able to take on their roles (p192), Pharaoh was not simply identified with the gods e.g. Horus (pp140-142). One could however ask whether the Israelite writer of the narrative might, nevertheless, have understood Pharaoh to be worshipped as a god in Egypt.

3.6.2 Moses

In one sense there is a good deal of interaction between YHWH and Moses in the narrative. Where YHWH sends a message to Pharaoh he sends it via Moses. However, these messages are for Pharaoh, and Moses appears to be simply the mouthpiece of YHWH in these matters. Moses also intercedes with YHWH to end the plagues, but this is simply reported as a fact, without further detail. Direct messages to Moses in the plagues narrative are rare.[83]

In contrast to the mighty Pharaoh, Moses is the representative of a slave people or, more specifically, of the god of a slave people.[84] He is uncertain of the response that he will receive from either Israel or Pharaoh, and doubts his ability to be YHWH's messenger. This forms the context for YHWH's encounters with him in 3:10-7:7 as previously discussed.

By 10:1-2 seven plagues have passed since YHWH's last word to Moses (7:14). These have had no obvious effect on Pharaoh. His response is either to ignore YHWH (7:22-23); to 'mock' Moses (or is it YHWH?) by reneging on his promises (8:25 [29]); or to show a lack of respect for YHWH by treating any mitigation or restraint as a chance to assert his power and to be obstinate (9:17, 30). Moses continually performs his function of announcing plagues during this time. He is even willing to continue to intercede with YHWH to end the plagues when Pharaoh promises to release the people, even though he does not believe Pharaoh's words (9:30).

This is the only time during the plagues narrative when YHWH has a message for Moses. This raises the question of why he chooses to speak to him at this particular point. We have seen that YHWH's previous messages to him have often been in response to objections that he raises or setbacks that he faces (3:10-4:17; 5:22-7:5). After these YHWH speaks to Moses when Pharaoh ignores the first sign (7:14 after 7:8-13), once again here and then at the end of the ninth plague when Pharaoh comprehensibly breaks off negotiations and Moses storms out in a rage (11:9 after 10:28-29 and 11:8b). At least one purpose of YHWH's words is to encourage or reassure Moses so that he will go to Pharaoh as instructed.[85] In light of these prior examples, we could ask whether there is a comparable situation at 10:1-2.

---

[83] As we have seen, most of the interaction between YHWH and Moses comes before the plagues narrative.

[84] The messages and 'explanations' are given to Moses, although he is accompanied by Aaron. Therefore 'Moses' is used as shorthand.

[85] This purpose can be seen in YHWH's words: 'I will be with you, and this will be a sign...' (3:12 cf. 4:11); 'that they may believe that [I] appeared to you' (4:5); 'now you will see what I will do' (6:1, cf. 3:19-20); 'I will make you as God to Pharaoh' (7:1); 'Pharaoh has not listened so that ...' (11:9). This is without mentioning the warning of Pharaoh's state, including the hardening.

While there is no message from Moses to YHWH, 10:1-2 is preceded by something rather unusual.

Almost immediately before this statement from YHWH, Moses has said that he, Moses, knows that Pharaoh does not yet fear YHWH (9:30). The fact that Moses speaks personally ('I [Moses] know...'), rather than as YHWH's representative here is unusual in the plagues narrative.[86] This is followed by a comment from YHWH to Moses (rather than to Pharaoh), which is also uncommon in these encounters. Therefore it is worth considering whether these two peculiar statements are connected.

If there is a connection, the most obvious suggestion is that YHWH is responding to Moses' words. Moses has heard YHWH's great ultimatum to Pharaoh (9:13-19). He has seen that Pharaoh disregards even this call, and the offered mitigation (9:20-21), and finally the effects of this plague 'never before seen' (9:18, 34). Even after this, Pharaoh does not fear YHWH, and will not obey YHWH, and Moses knows this. YHWH previously told him that he knew that Pharaoh would not obey, unless compelled to do so by a mighty hand (3:19). Even the above, it seems, is not mighty enough. One could imagine him asking 'what more can YHWH do that could convince Pharaoh?' or more pointedly 'what is the point of my going back to Pharaoh if he won't even respond to that last message?'

It is at this point that Moses is told by YHWH to go to Pharaoh once more, and give him yet another message. However this message is preceded by a message of reassurance to Moses, which speaks of why Pharaoh is still obstinate.[87] It is not that YHWH has failed. YHWH is in charge, despite the way things may appear. Moses just has to continue to do his part.

The above does depend upon understanding 9:30 as expressing similar sentiments to the situations above, which is not explicit. However, inasmuch as the comment is made to Pharaoh, rather than YHWH, one would not expect Moses to cry out in the manner of 5:22-23. In the plagues narrative, the focus is on Pharaoh, not Moses, and Moses' state is less obvious than before.[88]

---

[86] Admittedly he does negotiate with Pharaoh. However his statements, although sometimes referring to YHWH in the third person, correspond to YHWH's own words, e.g. 'you will know that there is none like YHWH our God' (8:6 [10]). Here it is what Moses knows, which is different.

[87] Cf. Jacob *Exodus*, 243-44.

[88] Thus we get no explicit comment on Moses' feelings between his objection of inadequacy (6:30) and his anger just before the last plague (11:8). Interestingly when Pharaoh is first encountered it is in a section predominantly concerned with YHWH's dealings with Moses. As such we get no explicit comment on Pharaoh's position (5:1-18 has no comment on the hardness of his heart) even though the comments that he makes (5:2, 4-5) suggest to us that he is as hard-hearted then as he is later. When the focus is mainly on Pharaoh (7:8-11:10), Moses is portrayed in a similar way to Pharaoh in 5:1-18 and we have to deduce his state from his comments.

3.6.2.1 A Comparison of Moses and Pharaoh

In the above analysis YHWH speaks to Moses in order to encourage him when he is facing reverses. YHWH speaks to Pharaoh in order to warn him when he is obstinate. In both cases, YHWH's messages are in response to human reluctance to follow his words, and their intention is to elicit a correct response from the listener.

At this point we can mention another similarity between 9:13-19 and 10:1-2. They both begin with a command, and this command sets the context for the explanations that follow.

Pharaoh is told (repeatedly) to 'send ... serve'. YHWH's words after this relate to what he will do either *if* Pharaoh does not send (e.g. 10:4), or as in 9:13-19, *because* Pharaoh has not sent. Moreover these words come at the beginning of the individual plagues, where the preceding comment is the narrator's refrain at the end of the previous plague that Pharaoh's heart has been hardened (by whatever agency), and that he has refused to listen to/obey YHWH.

Moses is told (repeatedly) to 'go to Pharaoh', and it is only inasmuch as he goes that Pharaoh will be told to 'send'.[89] For most of the plagues narrative he receives no further comment, as YHWH has dealt with him previously on this subject (3:1-7:7). However on occasion he does receive a further message from YHWH.

Viewed in this light, the messages from YHWH do not appear to be setting out a flat overall rationale for the plagues narrative, which can be dug out and compiled into one explanation. Instead their purpose is to elicit a certain response from the hearer. Knowledge is imparted, but that knowledge should have practical consequences.[90]

There is another similarity. In both cases this reluctance is addressed by changing the recipient's perception, in particular as it relates to YHWH and his actions. Pharaoh is obstinate, seeing YHWH's restraint as an opportunity to keep himself dominant over Israel. He sees himself in charge of affairs, and YHWH points out to him that this is not the case. It is YHWH who has chosen to keep Pharaoh alive, for his own purposes (9:13-19). Moses, by contrast, initially doubts his own abilities and is told that YHWH will be with him, will tell him what to say and will even make him God to Pharaoh (3:12; 4:11-12; 7:1 etc). When Pharaoh's actions appear to belie YHWH's words, YHWH's response is to say that he, not Pharaoh, is in charge of events (6:1; 10:1-2; cf. 3:18-20; 4:21-23; 7:3-5; 11:1, 9).

---

[89] The message in 7:16 connects the two more clearly: YHWH has sent (שְׁלָחַנִי Qal) Moses to Pharaoh to tell him to send (שַׁלַּח Pi'el) the people. Cf. Cassuto, 97.

[90] Thus it is not enough for Pharaoh to say 'I have sinned, YHWH is righteous' (9:27). He has to act upon this. More widely, one needs only look at the usage of the exodus tradition in the wider Old Testament to see how many of the occurrences are linked to a call for Israel to do something as a response. This will be picked up in chapter 5.

Pharaoh focuses on his own superiority as against YHWH's inferiority. Moses focuses on his own inferiority, Pharaoh's superiority and (on occasion) YHWH's lack of action. In both cases YHWH's message is designed to shift their attention from themselves onto him and his deeds. It is as a result of this change of perceptions to a focus on YHWH and his power that they will, or should, respond appropriately to YHWH by obeying him.[91]

Returning to the question of how one understands 10:1-2 in relation to 9:13-19 and to its immediate context, we can now describe more accurately the problem that it poses. YHWH deals with Moses (predominantly) in Ex. 3-7 before the main encounters with Pharaoh where Pharaoh is simply a figure of oppression in the background. In contrast in Ex. 7-11, Pharaoh is the main recipient of YHWH's attentions and Moses recedes into the background somewhat as YHWH's representative. However in 10:1-2 the focus shifts from Pharaoh to Moses briefly as he receives a message from YHWH, which recalls the language of the messages in Ex. 3-7. 10:1-2 comes across as one of YHWH's summaries to Moses, in a similar way to 3:18-20, 4:21-23 or 7:1-5. By contrast, 9:13-19 is a message to Pharaoh, as is 10:3-6. If 9:34-35 is addressed to anyone, it is to the reader.

We can go further than this. There are two main contexts for mention of the hardening: the narratorial refrains, and YHWH's statements to Moses. The reader hears about the hardening after every plague, with different refrains being used. Moses only hears about the hardening in YHWH's messages to him both before and during the plagues, as YHWH summarises the process to him, telling him what he is to do, what Pharaoh will do and what YHWH for his part will do. The emphasis here is on YHWH hardening Pharaoh's heart, part of the focussing on YHWH's acts. However in the messages to Pharaoh, he is reproached for his own obstinacy, but the language of hardening is *never* used. The focus is on his own stubbornness.

The demand to Pharaoh to 'send...' is an oddity inasmuch as YHWH is insistent that Pharaoh must agree to send Israel, rather than YHWH simply taking them himself. The language in YHWH's messages to Pharaoh follows this theme, emphasising Pharaoh's personal responsibility and the plagues that will befall him and his people if he does not act. The language in YHWH's messages to Moses emphasises YHWH's control over events.

---

[91] This reading might answer the critique that the final form of the text (perhaps as a result of the changes of the Priestly writer), in promoting the power and actions of YHWH, is effectively demotivating, disempowering or removing the focus from the humans. (For this view see Pixley *Exodus*, 27, on 4:10-12 'All responsibility for the revolution is credited to heaven.' More widely see xviii-xx and 36-39.) In light of 4:14 especially, the correct response to hearing of YHWH's power is *not* to abrogate one's own responsibilities (cf. 9:17).

Nevertheless, even in these messages the actions of the humans are still important.[92]

To put it another way, describing these statements from YHWH as 'explanations' or 'rationales' might suggest that they are designed to give one overall intellectual understanding of YHWH's actions. However, their function is more than this. We might choose to describe them as 'motivations' or 'arguments', as they seek to gain a response from their addressee. Moreover, the response sought is *precisely* that which the recipient does not want to do, based on their perspective at the time. YHWH speaks to Moses when he is discouraged, and to Pharaoh when he is stubborn. Moses does not wish to go to Pharaoh and Pharaoh certainly does not wish to send Israel, yet these are the commands of YHWH, which form the reason for the explanations, 'send ... because you have not, I will ...' (9:13-14); 'Go to Pharaoh because I have...' (10:1). By changing their focus and understanding, the message is intended to change their actions.

Thus as we read the text, we are listening to conversations between YHWH and individuals, and seeing their understanding of the situation develop, based on YHWH's words and actions, and their response to them.

3.6.3 Israel

YHWH's words to Moses in 10:1-2 contain a message to Israel. Israel, as a people, do not feature directly in the plagues narrative from 6:9 to 12:1, except as a subject of negotiation between YHWH and Pharaoh. In 10:2 Moses is to recount to his descendants what YHWH has done to Egypt and they will know that he is YHWH.

The verb and suffixes in 10:2a are singular, suggesting that Moses is the one to recite. This is followed by 'you [plural] will know that I am YHWH'. However presumably this was not intended to restrict the recounting to Moses (rather than any parent). Instead it probably indicated that the message would originate from him, or that Moses represents Israel. Thus it becomes a tradition for Israel to recount to their children. The Israel addressed here will be Israel as receiver of the tradition, rather than Israel as slaves in Egypt. Thus the context of Israel as slaves is less important for understanding this 'explanation' compared with that of Moses and Pharaoh who are being addressed directly in their specific context. However, a fundamental part of Israel's self-understanding is that they *were* slaves in Egypt. This is stronger than simply something that happened to some

---

[92] Thus, for example 3:20, where YHWH expands the standard 'YHWH brought us out with a mighty hand' to say that his mighty hand will cause *Pharaoh* to send them out. Verse 20, 'I will send **my** hand, and I will strike Egypt with all **my** plagues which I will do', is focussed upon YHWH in everything except for the last action 'and *he* will send them.'

ancestors, as it is to be repeated to each generation that 'YHWH brought *us* out…'.

Israel's response to YHWH's words and deeds is to remember these events. The Egypt and Pharaoh with whom YHWH is 'toying' were the slavemasters and tormenters of Israel, the iron-smelter from which YHWH rescued them (Dt. 4:20; 1Kgs. 8:51; Jer.11:4). Therefore Israel were not likely to be concerned with whether Pharaoh was learning about YHWH as he should (9:16). The slaves at the brick-kilns or their descendants would probably applaud the idea of a pestilence that wiped out Egypt and allowed them to go free (9:15). As with Moses, their concern was more likely to be whether the delay in release was due to YHWH's lack of power, rather than his restraint.[93]

The 'hardening' comes up in the messages to Moses, whereas הִתְעַלַּלְתִּי is found within this message to Israel.[94] We have noted that it is difficult to understand הִתְעַלֵּל as deserved punishment or equivalent (although there are 'explanations' to Moses which suggest that YHWH acts in judgement e.g. 6:6; 7:4; 12:12). In light of the above, we can offer a couple of reflections on the use of הִתְעַלַּלְתִּי in 10:2.

3.6.3.1 'BEING A PHARAOH TO PHARAOH'?

The one that YHWH is oppressing is, as noted above, the Pharaoh who was exercising despotic power over Israel, 'mocking them' (8:25 [29]); and 'lording it over them' (9:17).[95] However, this passage states that eventually Israel will recount that, ironically, whatever Pharaoh was doing to Israel, YHWH was doing to Pharaoh, in 'toying with him' or 'abusing him' (thus 'mocking him' and 'lording it over him'?).[96] In other words, the use of הִתְעַלֵּל in 10:2 may suggest that YHWH was 'being a Pharaoh to Pharaoh'. This would fit in with YHWH's continual threat of acting against 'you, your servants and your people', if Pharaoh will not allow 'my people' to serve 'me' (cf. 8:16-19 [20-23]). YHWH is doing to Pharaoh as he does or has done to Israel:

'With the faithful you show yourself faithful; with the blameless you show yourself blameless, with the pure you show yourself pure; but with

---

[93] Thus one can note psalms of praise on this subject such as Ps. 105 and Ps. 136. To the reader it may seem odd to juxtapose 'smiting Egypt' and 'his steadfast love endures forever'. However perspectivism in some form is inescapable.

[94] In our narrative the hardening is never mentioned in the messages to Israel, as it is never mentioned to Pharaoh. While Israel as later readers will, of course, come across the hardening of Pharaoh's heart, they will come across it in messages to Moses.

[95] We have noted Ehrlich's proposal of reading מתעלל for 9:17 (294). This, if adopted, would make the contrast even clearer. However the sense of tyrannous power still remains with the MT reading. Pharaoh was 'playing with' Israel and/or 'treating them harshly'.

[96] Cf. Jacob *Exodus*, 244; Gunn, 78.

the perverse (עִקֵּשׁ) you show yourself perverse (תִּתְפַּתָּל)' (Ps. 18:26-27 [25-26]; 2Sam. 22:26-27; cf. Job 5:13). Greenberg notes that Rashi glosses עִקֵּשׁ here with 'Pharaoh' in his comments.[97]

One could push a little further and suggest that YHWH's 'hardening' of Pharaoh is in response to Pharaoh's 'hardening' of Israel. This is not just in reference to the 'hard' work placed upon them (תִּכְבַּד 5:9), but the reason for it. Pharaoh judges, correctly, that the 'bricks without straw' policy will turn Israel against Moses and Aaron, and 'harden' them against their message (cf. 5:21 and especially contrast 6:9 with 4:31).

To return to our original quotation from Lear, we can now question its applicability here. This questioning is not so much on the grounds of content; הִתְעַלֵּל may well give the impression of 'flies to wanton boys'. Instead we need to distinguish the context of Gloster from that of Pharaoh. Gloster's position is more similar to that of Israel in 2:24-25 or 6:9. There is no real sense in which Gloster is being 'done by as he has done'; Edmund, Regan and Cornwall are not 'being a Gloster to Gloster'. However Pharaoh is not so innocent.

Interestingly the words of 10:1-2, to be recounted to one's sons, are only used once in the wider Old Testament, and then by non-Israelites in 1Sam. 6:6. Israel's standard phrase of remembrance is 'YHWH our God brought us out of Egypt with a mighty hand…'. Perhaps one reason why this phrase is used here is that this 'explanation' for Israel is being given to Moses, who has had first hand experience of being 'toyed with' by Pharaoh. Therefore the choice of YHWH's words, even in the speech ostensibly for Israel may be influenced by Moses' situation. We could, perhaps, paraphrase it as 'You think that you are being played with by the mighty Pharaoh. However in time to come you will tell your son that Pharaoh was being played with by me'.

3.6.3.2 PHARAOH AS SYMBOL OF ULTIMATE EVIL?

Pharaoh is portrayed as the oppressor of Israel, whose name is never given.[98] Whatever the reason for this anonymity, one effect of it is to make him an almost symbolic figure of oppression, indeed evil to the reader. If one sees Pharaoh and his forces as the ultimate forces of evil, the idea that they have 'got what was coming to them' is not so problematic. Thus we can note Origen's homily on the ten plagues where he compares the defeat of Pharaoh and his powers to Christ leading the powers of darkness in triumph (Col. 2:15; Eph. 6:12).[99] A sharper comparison might be the

---

[97] Greenberg *UE*, 85

[98] Cf. Gunn, 74.

[99] *Origen Homilies on Genesis and Exodus*, trans. Ronald E. Heine, FC 71 (Washington: The Catholic University of America Press, 1981), henceforth 'Origen', Exodus Homily

reaction of a survivor of a Nazi death camp (or their descendants) to the news that Hitler or Eichmann were dead. However, this would be a memory in the recent past, rather than something that has moved into distant history.

3.6.3.3 SCHADENFREUDE, OR MORE? 'SIGNS' IN 10:1-2

In light of the above two points, we could understand הִתְעַלַּלְתִּי in the context of Israel as *Schadenfreude*, albeit understandable *Schadenfreude*. However there is one more element in the message that may nuance it further. YHWH's immediate purpose in hardening Pharaoh and his aides is to set 'my signs' (אֹתֹתַי) in their midst. Moreover, Israel are to recount how YHWH toyed with Egypt, and the signs that he set on them. In the discussion of 9:13-19 and the comparison with 10:1-2 above, we have noted that YHWH's acts have a purpose, or purposes. These purposes relate to the responses of the humans that encounter his acts. Therefore the plagues are not ends in and of themselves. Instead they should act as signs, pointing beyond themselves to something else.[100]

The word 'signs' is used primarily in dialogue with Moses.[101] For Pharaoh, the same acts are called 'smiting/striking/plagues' or 'sending (of the hand)' i.e. the image of an assault of some kind.[102] The division is not absolute. Pharaoh is told that they are signs (8:19 [23]) and Israel are told that YHWH will smite (12:12), but the overall emphasis differs between the two.

However, although the word is used predominantly when addressing Israel, the plagues are never said to be signs 'for you' (i.e. for Israel) explicitly. The signs for Israel are the blood on the doorposts (12:13), the eating of unleavened bread (13:9) and the redemption of the firstborn (13:16). These are all signs that involve human action rather than simply sitting back and watching YHWH at work. None of these refer to the first nine plagues.[103] Instead the signs in 10:1-2 are to be set in the midst of the

---

IV, 267-270. To be fair to Origen, he also suggests that there was profit for Pharaoh in the scourgings. Thus he picks up the Pharaonic side of the interaction (e.g. 255).

[100] These signs are often twinned with 'wonders' (מוֹפְתִים), which denotes 'signs that confirm, warn, inspire fear or prognosticate', and is used especially of the exodus (Helfmeyer 'אוֹת' *TDOT* I, 167-188, 168 cf. 169 on other synonyms of אוֹת with regard to the exodus). See William Johnstone *Chronicles and Exodus: An Analogy and its Application*', JSOTSup 275 (Sheffield: Sheffield Academic Press, 1998), chp 10 for further discussion of 'signs and wonders'.

[101] 3:12; 4:8-9, 17, 28, 30; 7:3; 10:1-2.

[102] 7:17, 27 [8:2]; 8:17 [21]; 9:3, 14, 15; 10:4.

[103] There are also signs found before the plagues narrative (3:12; 4:1-9, 30). However these are signs to Israel to prove specifically that YHWH is with Moses, rather than anything wider.

Egyptians, or upon them.[104] This would suggest that the signs are actually for the Egyptians. The plagues are not meant to destroy Egypt outright, as YHWH has already said (9:15-16). Instead they are to be signs from YHWH.[105]

Initially the signs are to be set among Egypt (10:1bβ). At this point the implication is that they are intended for Egypt,[106] although the word 'signs' is not used when speaking to them. Thereafter Israel are to recount the signs that YHWH set upon Egypt (10:2a). Thus the image that we have here is Israel as bystanders or observers, who see that YHWH sets signs upon a third party. This is supported by the recollections of these 'signs' elsewhere in the Old Testament. The signs are often paired with YHWH's 'mighty hand' which was not laid upon Israel, although they see it. The emphasis is that they were signs performed upon Egypt, in the eyes of Israel.[107]

What is the relevance of the point that Israel are seeing signs set upon someone else? Presumably YHWH's dealings with Pharaoh are being held up to them as a message. As with other points in our passage, this message could have more than one meaning.

First there is the message that YHWH is totally superior to the mighty Pharaoh. This is brought out with הִתְעַלֵּל and the fact that Pharaoh and his forces cannot stand before him.

Secondly, however, there is the message that YHWH sets terrible signs upon people, especially if they do not respond to him. Pharaoh is being held up as a warning to Israel here as one who ignores the signs that YHWH sends upon him.[108] If this is not the case, we need to make sense of why YHWH is concerned that Moses should recount to Israel the signs that YHWH set upon a non-Israelite. If these were simply punishments or power then one could explain it as YHWH dealing with Pharaoh because of Israel or 'because he can'. However, he is giving this foreign ruler plagues that point beyond themselves to something else. This image of Pharaoh is picked up strongly in the Qur'an. The main portrayal of Pharaoh is as one

---

[104] The concept of setting signs upon a person or people is rare elsewhere in the Old Testament. It is mainly used to refer to the plagues (Ps. 78:43; 105:27; Jer. 32:20). Elsewhere YHWH sets a sign for the nations (Is. 66:19). These seem to suggest that the sign is for those upon whom it is set.

This seems different from setting someone or something *as* a sign, which are intended for others (e.g. Ezek. 14:8, Ps. 74:4).

[105] Cf. Helfmeyer 'אוֹת', 171.

[106] Thus Sarna *Exodus*, 48; Fretheim, 127.

[107] Dt. 4:34; 6:22; 11:3; 34:11; Jos. 24:17; Neh. 9:10; Ps. 135:9; Jer. 32:20-21. There are other occurrences which simply note that YHWH brought Israel out of Egypt with 'signs', which are ambiguous as to the recipient of the 'signs'.

[108] Cf. Plastaras, 136.

who is sent signs and a message from Allah, but who rejects them.[109] This is the reason that he is drowned in the Red Sea.[110] In relation to our comments on 9:34, where Pharaoh hardens himself at the point when the plague is removed, we can see this point made here also (7:135; 43:48). Therefore one message of these signs to Israel may be 'you saw what happened to Pharaoh when he did not heed my signs. Do not be like him!'[111]

One may protest that this goes against the general idea of the exodus as freedom for Israel. One could suggest that the signs are to be read as signs of YHWH's favour towards Israel, so that they should follow his covenant with them. However, while this may be true, it does not explain why these signs were for Pharaoh (rather than for Israel directly). We have seen in Num. 14 that Israel could act like Egypt at times.

This is not to suggest that the use of the exodus tradition is primarily as a cautionary tale to Israel in the style of Hilaire Belloc: *'Pharaoh, who didn't listen to YHWH and was drowned in the Red Sea'*. The primary use would still be of thanksgiving, as in Ps. 136:10-15 'his חֶסֶד endures forever', and all that this thanksgiving entails.[112] However, I suggest that this use of 'signs' in 10:1-2 nuances הִתְעַלֵּל from being simply jingoistic celebration of the death of another, to something more sobering.

The last element of the message is that, having recounted the signs, they will 'know that I am YHWH'. Thus in recounting the story, they are not simply to laugh at Egypt, but rather to consider how *they* should respond and acknowledge YHWH.

3.7 Concluding Remarks

10:1-2 as an explanation is rather different from that of 9:13-19, which was discussed in the previous chapter. This has required us to expand and refine our original thesis in light of the problems and differences that this has raised. In concluding this chapter it seems appropriate briefly to consider this thesis in light of the other attempts to understand YHWH's actions, in

---

[109] Sura 3:11; 7:103-36; 8:52-54; 23:45; 29:39; 43:47. For further discussion of Islamic understandings of Pharaoh and the hardening of the heart see Vincent J. Cornell '"I am Your Lord Most High": Pharaoh and the Sin of Hubris in the Qur'an' and the responses thereto in *JSR* 2.2 (2002). n.p. [cited 18 August 2004]. Online: http://etext.virginia.edu/journals/ssr/issues/volume2/number2/

More generally, the whole edition is devoted to theological discussion of the issue of the 'hardening', albeit without detailed engagement with the text of Ex. 1-15.

[110] Sura 20:78; 28:40; 51:140. (Although cf. 10:90-92 where Pharaoh repents at the Red Sea and is saved as a sign for others.)

[111] Cf. Propp, 354, who notes this suggestion. On Israel's knowledge see Durham, 99-100, 109, 130.

[112] On this see chapter 5.

particular the hardening. Therefore we can return to the taxonomy of interpretations of the hardening set out in chapter 1 to check whether our expanded thesis has recognised and worked with the strengths of each position as was our intention.

Although we could not go into detail on the subject, we noted that the historical critical approaches have highlighted differences in the text concerning the understanding of the hardening motif, making any single understanding of the hardening difficult. The concept of differences in understanding has formed an important part of our thesis, although we have chosen to group and explain the differences by context and addressee rather than by original source, tradition or redaction. Where 9:13-19 is an explanation given to Pharaoh, 10:1-2, as an explanation given to Moses, is rather different. There are, however, underlying similarities in the responses sought. However the explanations do not stop with Pharaoh and Moses. Israel, as hearers and readers of the story, are also addressed.

The explanations that focus upon the role of YHWH in the hardening process have some strong arguments, predominantly YHWH's initial messages and the phrase 'as YHWH said'. By recognising that the initial messages are given to Moses, and that the emphasis on YHWH's acts creates a 'division of labour' motif, we have seen how, for Moses, this is the way that YHWH explains Pharaoh's actions, and reassures him so that he will continue to carry out his role. Moreover a focus upon the role of YHWH is another underlying similarity in the messages to Moses and Pharaoh.

The importance of Pharaoh's own responsibility, will, actions and responses has been maintained, primarily in the messages to him from YHWH, where a focus upon divine power can be followed immediately with a call for human action.

Finally, the fact that the hardening refrains seem to progress from Pharaoh hardening to YHWH hardening fits into our wider theme of the responsiveness of YHWH set out in the previous chapter, without needing to explain it as a progression of Pharaoh's psyche or of the reader's understanding. This progression and the responsiveness it shows will become even more important in the next chapter as we read through the plagues narrative as a whole and see how the story and the themes therein develop.

Chapter 4

Reading the Plagues Narrative and Beyond

4.1 Introduction

In the previous two chapters we have examined two important passages in the plagues narrative, which offer seemingly rather different rationales for YHWH's actions. The first explanation in 9:13-19 picks up a number of wider themes in the plagues narrative, setting up a pattern of responses, both from YHWH and Pharaoh. Initially 10:1-2 might seem to contradict this. However, appreciating that this is a message to Moses (whose situation is very different from that of Pharaoh, the addressee in 9:13-19) and partly to Israel, allows us to perceive a similar function to the previous message. Both messages are given as part of divine demands that require a response from the recipient. In both cases there are different possible responses, and YHWH's message is a response to their acts, designed to get the recipients to focus on him and thus obey him, something that they may not want to do.

The next step is to consider the wider plagues narrative in light of our refined thesis and the issues raised thus far. Thus doing we can further test the thesis, expand or refine it, and see how it illuminates the wider text.[1] The chapter will take the form of a read-through of the text, with discussion of relevant sections. As our focus is on YHWH's actions in the plagues narrative, the discussion will centre on the encounters between YHWH and Pharaoh in Ex. 7-11. The chapter will conclude with some brief comments on the remainder of the exodus story. It was noted in the previous chapter that 10:1-2, inasmuch as it is an explanation to Moses, is unusual in Ex. 7-11 where Moses speaks as YHWH's representative. YHWH's interactions with Moses come primarily in Ex. 3-7. However where similarities or

---

[1] There are, of course, other themes and issues that could be raised from the rich and deep passage under consideration. Thus for example Zevit mentions three different approaches to the plagues: historical or causal links, which were mentioned in chapter 1; the individual plagues as polemics targeted at individual Egyptian gods which will be discussed briefly at 12:12; and finally the plagues as linked to creation. (Ziony Zevit, 'Three Ways to Look at the Ten Plagues.' *BR* 6.3 (1990): 16-23, 42-44, henceforth 'Zevit'). The link with creation is also made by Fretheim as a key element in his commentary (Fretheim, 12-14 etc.; Propp, 345, offers criticism). Childs, 165, notes rabbinic moves to explain the 10 plagues for 10 sins against Israel (Mek. Beshallah 7). In all these cases, attempts are made to explain the specifics of each of (or most of) the individual plagues. Our concentration, as in previous chapters is on the explanations and encounters rather than the events of the plagues themselves.

contrasts can be seen between YHWH's interactions in 7-11 and 3-7, these will be noted accordingly. We will pick up the story at 7:8, where the main encounters with Pharaoh begin.

4.2 The Plagues Narrative (7:8-11:10)

4.2.1 Serpent Staff (7:8-13)

YHWH tells Moses that Pharaoh will ask for a wonder (מוֹפֵת), at which Aaron is to throw down his staff, so that it becomes a serpent (7:8-9). Thus it happens (7:10).[2] This recalls the similar sign that Moses was given to establish himself before Israel (4:1-5, 8 את, 30). However, there is a difference here. Whereas the people believed (4:31), Pharaoh has an answer to this wonder. He summons his wise men and sorcerers and they do as Aaron has done (7:11-12a). However, Aaron's staff devours their staves (7:12b). As a result, Pharaoh's heart is hard (וַיֶּחֱזַק) and he does not listen to them, as YHWH said.

4.2.1.1 PART OF THE PLAGUES NARRATIVE?

Our study is not concerned primarily with either separating out different units of text, or comparing the literary form thereof.[3] The more relevant question here is not 'where does the plagues narrative start?' (e.g. 6:28; 7:8; 7:14?), but rather 'what is the function of 7:8-13 in the wider story?'

This is the first encounter with Pharaoh since 5:1-5. Then there was a demand, but no sign. Here there is a wonder, or sign, but no demand; in fact no conversation takes place at all. Pharaoh, it is said, will ask for a wonder, and Moses and Aaron are to provide one for him. As with the initial message in 3:18, this is ostensibly deferential to Pharaoh, yet the encounter closes with a suggestion that Pharaoh's power is not all it seems.

Thus it is not totally comparable to the plagues narrative, due to the lack of verbal interaction.[4] Perhaps the best way of thinking about it is as an introduction. Three themes in particular are introduced here, apart from the giving of signs itself. We have discussed already the hardening of Pharaoh's heart and his refusal to listen 'as YHWH said'. The one remaining theme is the role of Pharaoh's magicians.

---

[2] Fretheim, 113, notes the irony that Pharaoh asks for a wonder and will get more than he bargained for. Cf. 5:2 where Pharaoh 'does not know YHWH'; soon he will know more than he wishes.

[3] On this, see for example McCarthy 'Moses', especially 338f.

[4] The closest match would be VI, the only (other) plague where nobody speaks to Pharaoh at all.

4.2.1.2 EXCURSUS: THE MAGICIANS

This is the first of five encounters with these Egyptian wise men, priests, sorcerers or magicians, who provide Pharaoh's initial answer to Moses and Aaron.[5] They are called upon by Pharaoh to answer the signs and wonders of Moses and Aaron; and initially they are able to copy them.

After the words of YHWH to Moses, this comes across as somewhat odd. YHWH is the one who gives sight and speech, or takes them away (4:10-11). YHWH is the one who will not only tell Moses what to say (4:12), but has also given him signs (4:21; 7:9 cf. 4:1-5). However, the sign that YHWH gives to Moses and Aaron is one that can be copied by Egyptian magicians. As a result, Pharaoh is less than impressed.

One approach is to suggest that Moses and Aaron were simply using magic tricks that were available in Egypt. References to wax crocodiles and snakes that can be made rigid by applying pressure give us some possible background to the story.[6] However, we need to be careful here. The narrative speaks of a staff that turns into a serpent and then back again, rather than a serpent that changes form. This makes an easy comparison more difficult. Moreover this raises the more interesting question of *why* YHWH would give a sign that could easily be copied, rather than one that would show his supremacy clearly.

The point is brought out in the Midrash Rabbah, which has Pharaoh mocking Moses and Aaron:

'So these be the signs of your God! It is usual for people to take goods to a place which has a shortage of them; but does one import murics into Apamea or fish into Acco? Are you not aware that all kinds of magic are within my province?' He then asked for children to be brought from school and they also performed these wonders; moreover, he called also his wife, and she did thus ... Even children of four and five years of age whom he called did likewise.[7]

---

[5] 7:11-12; 7:22; 8:3 [7], 14-15 [18-19]; 9:11. Here they are described as מְכַשְּׁפִים, חֲכָמִים and חַרְטֻמִּים. This latter phrase, which continues in the later encounters, is only found in the OT in the context of a foreign ruler's court, as those whose abilities are contrasted with an Israelite leader (Joseph; Gen. 41:8, 24; Moses; and Daniel; Dan. 1:20; 2:2); cf. Houtman, I 533. Later tradition expanded the role of these magicians, naming them Jannes and Jambres for example. See Hoffmeier *Israel*, 88-89 for details of possible Egyptian origins of the word, where they are described as chief lector priests. We will continue to use 'magicians' to describe them, whilst being aware of the limitations of the term.

[6] Cf. Propp, 348 who sees the first type as 'fairly remote'; Sarna *EE*, 67; Kitchen, 249 n11.

[7] ExR. XI. 4-7. A note suggests our equivalent would be 'coals to Newcastle'. Cf. Greenberg *UE*, 98-99, 141-42 on Sekel Tob.

This oddity has led to some suggestions that the magicians' seeming ability to copy the signs is simply based on trickery and deception.[8] This would maintain a distinction between YHWH's 'true' miracles, and Pharaoh's 'false' miracles. However, this is not supported by the text. The phrase כֵּן ... נַם־הֶם וַיַּעֲשׂוּ suggests that the magicians did *exactly* what Aaron had just done, and the text seems to have no problems with this.[9] Indeed, such an attempt is 'a form of rationalisation – of course, within the framework of orthodoxy – which misses the point of the conflict by attempting to remove its ambiguity.'[10] As with the demand to Pharaoh (וְיַעַבְרֻנִי ...שַׁלַּח.), this initial sign (and those immediately following it) has a form of ambiguity that needs to be appreciated and retained in order to make sense of it.

However, within this ambiguity there are a few differences that may be illuminating.

First, there is a difference in the method of performing the miracle. Aaron's act is described as a מוֹפֵת, a wonder or sign, in line with the usage throughout the text.[11] However, the magicians are described as doing the same thing בְּלַ(הֲ)טֵיהֶם, by their secret arts.[12] Aaron's act is a sign, something to point beyond itself. Its function is presumably to validate Moses and Aaron's right to speak in the name of this YHWH. In light of 5:2 it may be the first step towards bringing Pharaoh to a knowledge of YHWH. However this is not explicit. In contrast to this, the magicians' act, although the same act as that of Aaron, is done through concealed arts; the effect of which is to maintain Pharaoh's intransigence, and make him unresponsive to the sign. Thus signs and sorcery can look very similar.[13]

---

[8] Houtman, I 535 notes some of these. Cf. John J. Davis, *Moses and the Gods of Egypt: Studies in Exodus* (Winona Lake, Indiana: BMH Books, 1986), 91-92.

[9] Cf. Noth, 72.

[10] Childs, 152. He continues, rightly, to note that this is a contest of power. This makes it a little odd when, on his discussion of the third plague of gnats, he comments that 'this is the first explicit indication of how the author settles the question of the *true* and *false* miracle' (156, emphasis mine). It is not clear how the magi's lack of power shows them to have been false hitherto. Cf. Durham, 108-09.

[11] Cf. Houtman, I 535. We have seen that the 'plagues' are also described as 'signs' to Moses and Israel. However we will continue to use the word 'plagues' in this chapter to describe these acts.

[12] This phrase occurs four times in all (7:11, 22; 8:3 [7], 14 [18]). In the latter three cases the form is בְּלָטֵיהֶם from לוּט, to conceal or cover, hence 'secret arts' (cf. Cassuto, 95). In this case, the form is בְּלַהֲטֵיהֶם, which may be a variant form of this (GKC §77f). Alternatively it may be from לָהַט to blaze/burn, and thus have the sense of 'dazzlings'/'delusions'. In either case the point will stand that these acts stand counter to the signs that reveal things, whether by concealing, or dazzling. Cf. Houtman, I 534.

[13] Thus the Qur'an describes Pharaoh as one who sees the signs as sorcery:

Secondly, however, there is the final comment in 7:12b that Aaron's staff swallowed theirs. It is debatable how much to make of this. It most naturally reads as an indication that YHWH's power is greater than that of the magicians.[14] However, there is no message attaching to it saying that Pharaoh will 'know that...' as a result of the staff swallowing (cf. 9:14, 29). Pharaoh could take note of this final difference, but he does not; and it is not sufficiently blatant to compel any such recognition.[15] At this stage there are indications, but nothing more.

The end result of this wonder is not surprising for two reasons. First, from the perspective of Moses, he has been told by YHWH that Pharaoh will not listen to him, and this has been linked to YHWH's hardening of his heart (cf. 4:21; 10:1-2). Perhaps here we see the fleshing out of this summary. The text suggests that the reason for Pharaoh's lack of response is his ability to copy, albeit imperfectly, what YHWH has given Moses to do. He was not impressed in 5:2, and he remains unimpressed and hard-set against YHWH's demands at 7:13.

Secondly, from Pharaoh's perspective, we have noted YHWH's comments in 9:13-19 (albeit not yet given at this point in the story). There YHWH explains that he has restrained himself from what he could have done, and gives his reasons for this. Thus it is not surprising that the initial signs are less distinguishable than they might be. The plagues narrative is introduced, not with an awe-inspiring, unarguable proof of YHWH's incomparability, but rather a 'wonder' that can be understood in a number of ways.

As with his demand to Pharaoh ('send ... serve'), YHWH seems concerned that Pharaoh responds correctly, rather than either ignoring him

---

'To Moses We did give Nine Clear Signs: Ask the Children of Israel: When he came to them, Pharaoh said to him: "O Moses! I consider thee, Indeed to have been Worked upon by sorcery!"' (Sura 17:101). The focus in the Qur'an's stories of Moses before Pharaoh is generally upon the initial encounter of the serpent staff (7:122; 10:75-92; 20:56f; 26:10-69; 40:23-27; 51:38-40).

As another example, Barth also makes use of this passage to comment on the similarity between that which is from God and that which is human (CD I.1, 249; I.2, 342-43; 4.3, 565). Cf. also Rashbam, 70 where Pharaoh's heart stiffened because he believed Aaron had acted through sorcery. This may get us closer to Childs' comment on true and false miracles, albeit that it is their purpose, not their status that is contrasted here. One could also contrast their source ('sorcery' vs. 'as YHWH said') but the text gives no indication that the signs were false – e.g. שֶׁקֶר or equivalent. As in our reading of the wider plagues, it is not so much the plagues themselves as what they signify that is at issue. Nobody denies the plagues' existence. The question is what they mean, and how to respond to them.

[14] Indeed Philo, *Mos.* 1:110, sees it as clear evidence.

[15] Contrast the Qur'anic retellings of the story where the magi tend to confess God's power at this point rather than in the third plague. (Sura 7:122; 26:10-69).

or compelling him. We can see a similar pattern in the initial signs to Israel. Moses is given signs to prove his credentials as the one sent by YHWH (4:1-9). He has been given a sign that YHWH is with him (3:12); now the people will be given signs to make the same point.[16] However these signs, at least the first two, are not necessarily conclusive. YHWH gives the two signs and says that the people will believe (should believe?) as a result of the signs (4:8-9). However he then follows this with the statement 'if they do not believe...' and gives a further sign. However, although these signs do not compel belief or acknowledgement, they are still given in place of signs which, arguably, would be more compelling. The last sign (over which no doubt is raised) is given only if or when the first two fail.

Childs summarises the issue in 7:8-13 well:

> Now by introducing this element of ambiguity right at the outset, the author makes it clear that the witness of the plague stories does not lie just in a naïve display of supernatural fireworks. The issue at stake is on another dimension. How can Pharaoh be made to discern the hand of god? The so-called 'supernatural' element was in itself not enough. The divine sign is made to look like a cheap, juggler's trick, which a whole row of Egyptian magicians can duplicate with apparent ease.[17]

4.2.2 *1: River of Blood (7:14-25)*

We now come to what is generally seen as the start of the ten plagues proper. Moses and Aaron get the message from YHWH to give to Pharaoh (7:14-18); then they are told to bring the plague and do so (7:19-21). However the magi also turn water into blood, and Pharaoh is unimpressed, leaving his people to dig around for water (7:22-25).

4.2.2.1 MESSAGE

In 7:14, YHWH tells Moses that Pharaoh's heart is hard (כָּבֵד).In light of 7:13 and the meaning of 'remains hard' it seems probable that YHWH's use of the adjectival form is referring to this continual state; Pharaoh's heart remains hard. This is the last word from YHWH for Moses until 10:1-2. Moses is given several messages for Pharaoh, but there is nothing addressed to him. In the light of the other messages to Moses in 10:1; 4:21 and 7:3 it is remarkable that here YHWH does not ascribe the cause of Pharaoh's 'hardness' to himself. There is no emphatic אֲנִי, and the first person verb is replaced by an adjective. One could read this as indicating implicitly to Moses that YHWH has hardened Pharaoh, in line with his

---

[16] Cf. Num. 16 where Moses' role as YHWH's spokesman is also questioned. Moses' words to Israel are 'by this you shall know that YHWH has sent me to do these things' (Num. 16:28). The same wording appears in Zechariah (2:13 [9], 15 [11]; 4:9; 6:15).

[17] Childs, 152. Cf. Propp, 227.

previous words (4:21; 7:3). Alternatively, we could refer to 7:13, which we have argued is not a direct reference to YHWH's action. In this case, although Moses has been told that YHWH will harden Pharaoh's heart, this is not stated to be the case, at least not yet. Like 10:1, and in contrast to 4:21 and 7:3, this refers to a present state rather than a future one. Unlike 10:1 (בֹּא ... כִּי־אָנִי) this 'hardness' is not given as the reason for Moses to go to Pharaoh.[18]

After giving his last word for Moses until 10:1, YHWH sets out his first message for Pharaoh since his rejection of the initial demand in 5:2-5.[19] Moses is to meet him on the banks of the Nile (7:15) and give him the following message (7:16-18):

יְהוָה אֱלֹהֵי הָעִבְרִים שְׁלָחַנִי אֵלֶיךָ לֵאמֹר שַׁלַּח אֶת־עַמִּי וְיַעַבְדֻנִי בַּמִּדְבָּר

(v16a)

The wording of the demand has varied slightly from 5:1 and 5:3. The reference to the wilderness is still present (for the last time). However the verb has changed from the straightforward חָגַג to the more ambiguous עָבַד, which becomes the standard reason for the release of Israel (cf. 9:13, 10:3). However the announcement of the plague is slightly different from the usual message to follow.

וְהִנֵּה לֹא־שָׁמַעְתָּ עַד־כֹּה [17] כֹּה אָמַר יְהוָה בְּזֹאת תֵּדַע כִּי אֲנִי יְהוָה
הִנֵּה אָנֹכִי מַכֶּה בַּמַּטֶּה אֲשֶׁר־בְּיָדִי עַל־הַמַּיִם אֲשֶׁר בַּיְאֹר וְנֶהֶפְכוּ לְדָם

(vv16b-17)

Here, instead of the normal demand and conditional threat pattern, 'Send ... or I will send' (cf. 10:3-4), there is something that has a number of similarities to the message in 9:13-19.

1. Pharaoh is told that he has not listened up to this point (7:16b עַד־כֹּה; cf. 9:17 עוֹדְךָ; 10:3 עַד־מָתַי), referring to the demand, which he has refused (5:2), and the wonder which he has ignored (7:13-14).

2. If Pharaoh will not respond to these methods, then YHWH will bring a plague upon him. It will be by means of this that Pharaoh will 'know that I am YHWH' (בְּזֹאת תֵּדַע 7:17, cf. 9:14).[20] As with 9:14, the knowledge/acknowledgement will come through the sending of the plague itself. These are the only two places in the plagues narrative

---

[18] We could speculate that Moses has only heard YHWH speak of himself as the one who will harden Pharaoh. Therefore he might well understand 7:14 as being caused by YHWH, in line with the other messages. However this might be another example of the summary phenomenon where Moses is told something but not everything. We have to wait until 10:1 before Moses is told explicitly that YHWH has hardened, and that is after YHWH has explicitly started hardening (9:12). May there be an ambiguity in the messages to Moses, as there is the message to Pharaoh?

[19] The sign in 7:8-13 could be seen as a message, but this 'message' does not have any practical response demanded.

[20] Cf. Childs, 128, who notes the use of בְּזֹאת in 1Sam. 11:2.

where knowledge for Egypt is linked to sending plagues, rather than
removal, restraint or exemption (cf. 9:16; 9:30).

3.   Moreover this 'knowledge through plague' is explicitly linked to the
      fact that Pharaoh has disregarded previous messages from YHWH.
      (7:16a; 9:16).[21] If a message and wonder will not suffice, then Pharaoh
      will get a plague (7:17). If restraint in plagues will not suffice, then
      Pharaoh will get 'all my plagues', plagues the like of which Egypt has
      never seen (9:14, 18). Finally, as with 9:13-19, the plague is not
      conditional upon Pharaoh's refusal of YHWH's demand. Pharaoh has
      refused to listen, and the plague *will* come.

In summary, Pharaoh is informed that, due to his refusal to respond
correctly, a new phase in the encounters is beginning.[22] YHWH then
outlines the plague, and it comes (vv18-21).[23] However, as with the serpent
staff encounter, the magicians are also able to turn water into blood by their
secret arts (v22). There is no explicit equivalent of Aaron's staff
swallowing their staffs. However, commentators have noted the irony that
although the magicians are able to copy Aaron, they are not able to (or at
least they do not) turn the blood back into water. Arguably, therefore, their
acts only worsen the plague.[24]

This copying is followed by an exact repetition of the wording of 7:13
(7:22). Once again, the magicians' ability to copy the sign leaves Pharaoh
unimpressed; he does not listen to them, as YHWH said. However this is
followed by a second comment on Pharaoh's reaction. He turns, goes into
his house and does not set his heart even upon this (וְלֹא־שָׁת לִבּוֹ גַּם־לָזֹאת).
Once again we find comparisons with 9:13-35.

1.   These are the only two conclusions to individual plagues where there
      is more than one comment on Pharaoh's heart (7:22-23; cf. 9:34-35).

---

[21] 14:4, 18 also have knowledge of YHWH related to a plague, albeit specifically to
YHWH being 'glorified' (Niph'al כָּבֵד) over Pharaoh and his might.

[22] Houtman, II 8-9, notes that so far it has all been Pharaoh, and it is not obvious if
YHWH has any real clout.

[23] As previously noted, Sam. Pent. and 4QpaleoExod[m] have a long addition which
essentially repeats v16-18 to show that Moses and Aaron did as YHWH said
(Sanderson, 197; Propp, 293). We need not mention such additions to each plague in
turn.

[24] Cf. Durham, 98. Houtman, II 26, does not see this, regarding this plague as a
stalemate, and thus a reversion from 7:12. There is certainly no explicit comment on the
magicians' inferiority here. See comments on the next plague for Pharaoh's response.

Once again the problem could be raised of how the magicians could really perform
such a miracle. Moreover one could also ask where they got water in order to turn it into
blood, if Aaron had turned all the water in Egypt into blood already. Childs, 165-66;
Houtman, II 30 and Propp, 325, cite examples of this. However, as before in 9:19 and
7:11, such rationalisation need not concern us.

2. Moreover, the language of setting one's heart upon something occurs only in these two encounters. In 9:21 those who do not set their hearts upon the word of YHWH are contrasted with those who feared the word of YHWH (9:20); something that Pharaoh does not yet do (9:30).[25] Here Pharaoh remains hard, and does not set his heart on 'even this'. Thus our 'nexus' of terms grows stronger. Hardening is equated with not setting the heart upon the matter, which results in not listening. This is opposed to fearing or acknowledging YHWH (9:20-21, 14).

3. As a final comparison, Pharaoh does not set his heart on 'even this' (גַּם־לָזֹאת).[26] YHWH had said that 'by this' (בְּזֹאת) Pharaoh would acknowledge him. However Pharaoh, who has not responded to words or wonders (7:16), does not respond even to this escalation in YHWH's actions, as he does not respond even to the escalation to the plague 'never before seen' (9:34-35).

4.2.2.2 EXCURSUS: STRUCTURE AND PROGRESSION IN THE PLAGUES?

This raises the question of why these two plagues (I and VII) in particular have such similarities, and whether this reflects anything more widespread in the plagues narrative. In both cases, the speeches from YHWH appear to mark some watershed or change in proceedings. YHWH has acted in a certain way; Pharaoh has not responded appropriately; therefore YHWH's response to Pharaoh's response will be to increase his acts, in order that Pharaoh will acknowledge him. Why should the first plague of ten have a summarised version of this, and the seventh plague of ten have an extended version? Is there anything in the wider context that would explain this 'change' and why it would be mentioned at these points?

One theme common to both contexts is a change in the 'hardening' of Pharaoh. YHWH has mentioned this matter to Moses previously as something that will happen in the future (4:21; 7:3). However the first time that it is mentioned as occurring is at 7:13, which immediately precedes the first announcement of a 'change'. Similarly, the first mention of YHWH hardening Pharaoh comes at 9:12, just before the announcement of a 'change' in 9:13-19. This might then have some connection to these explanations. However, this point should not be pushed too far. Firstly, we have noted that the phrase in 7:13 has the sense of 'Pharaoh's heart

---

[25] Also we noted that in 9:14 'all' YHWH's plagues will be sent upon Pharaoh's heart, in order that he will acknowledge YHWH. While the language is not identical, the concept seems similar, albeit that YHWH is impressing it upon Pharaoh (causing him to set it upon his heart?) rather than Pharaoh setting his heart upon it. 'Setting one's heart upon' (cf. 1Sam. 4:20; Job 1:8; 2:3; Ps. 62:11 [10]; Ezek. 40:4) seems to have a reasonably similar sense to 'setting upon one's heart' (see examples given at 9:14).

[26] Jacob *Exodus*, 258, lists other uses of גַּם־לָזֹאת.

remained hard' and therefore this would not suggest a change on the part of
Pharaoh. Secondly, even if this point were accepted, then one would wish
to ask why the hardening had changed at that point.

Another way to explain these similarities would be the question of
whether there is any wider structure to the plagues. This is especially the
case in terms of the explanation at 9:13-19. One could attempt to account
for the explanation in 7:16-17 by arguing that this is the beginning of the
plagues proper, and therefore some sort of 'change' is not surprising. This
is less obvious at 9:13-19, as seven is not an obvious breaking point in the
cycle. One might expect it, for example, at the end of the nine plagues,
before the last plague on the firstborn.[27]

One structure that has been suggested is the division of the first nine
plagues into three triads, with the tenth plague forming a single plague at
the end. This is based primarily on comparisons of the initial words of
YHWH to Moses in each plague to go to Pharaoh:

	1st plague of triad	2nd plague of triad	3rd plague of triad
1st triad	Go to Pharaoh in the morning as he comes out to the waters. Take your stand to encounter him on the banks of the River. (7:15)	Go to Pharaoh (7:26 [8:1]).	No words (8:12 [16])[28]
2nd triad	Get up early in the morning and take your stand before Pharaoh as he comes out to the waters. (8:16 [20])	Go to Pharaoh (9:1)	No words (9:8)
3rd triad	Get up early in the morning and take your stand before Pharaoh. (9:13)	Go to Pharaoh (10:1)	No words (10:21)

The wording is not exact, but there are repetitions that suggest that some
kind of pattern has been created.[29] This is not a new suggestion. The

---

[27] Thus Noth, 80, sees this explanation as coming too early, expecting it before the last
decisive act of YHWH.

[28] YHWH speaks to Moses and Aaron, but he does not tell them to give Pharaoh a
message before the plague, as is the case in the other six plagues.

[29] Thus, the wording of the first plague in each triad differs in each case, but each
contains a reference to the morning (בֹּקֶר), and to taking one's stand (וְהִתְיַצֵּב/וְנִצַּבְתָ).
The second plague is briefer, although the 'explanation' in 10:1b-2 takes the place of the
message.

division into three triads can be traced back to the Talmud,[30] and the comparison of the opening words to Rashbam.[31]

This raises the question of what relevance, if any, such a structure would have. Childs cautions against the tendency to use a 'clear and unified structure' as a reason for discounting different sources in the plague narrative, especially as there is no consensus on what this structure might be.[32] He notes the 3:3:3 pattern, but questions to what extent it is accidental or intentional.[33] Propp takes a more positive line, ascribing it to the redactor.[34] Durham notes the danger of polarising between fragmentary or formulaic approaches, when there appears to be elements of both.[35]

In respect of the above, this work does not intend to build an argument mainly upon a putative structure.[36] Neither does it seek to raise questions of author(s), authorial or redactorial intent. Childs offers a better criterion of what use the above structure could be: 'But perhaps the decisive question is not that of intentionality, but in what way this structural observation aids in illuminating the final composition.'[37] He himself does not see that it brings the major themes into any sharper focus. However, there may be more to be said when we return to our original question of the links between the first and seventh plagues.

The fact that the vast majority of commentators at least recognise the reasonability of the above noted pattern, whatever importance or lack of it they may ascribe to it, can give one some confidence in exploring its possibilities in terms of illuminating the text. This is relevant, as another question that might be raised is why we are concentrating on this structure, rather than others. For example, McCarthy has proposed a literary structure that would divide the plagues from the serpent staff to the darkness (7:8-10:27) into a concentric pattern of two groups of five.[38] Thus the staff (#1) has characteristics linking it to the darkness (#10) and so forth. The firstborn is a separate literary unit. He argues for thematic parallels that support this structure. However he does note that 'of all the thematic ideas

---

[30] Fishbane *Text*, 74; Jacob *Exodus*, 180.

[31] Cf. Propp, 321. Cassuto, 92-93, notes Abarbanel also. Cf. Zevit, 18. On this structure, cf. Greenberg *UE*, 171-172; Sarna *Exodus*, 38, esp. n.19, and *EE*, 77; Keil, 473; Hoffmeier *Israel*, 146-147.

[32] Childs, 130, lists examples of this.

[33] Childs, 149-50.

[34] Propp, 321.

[35] Durham, 96. More widely on this position see Greenberg 'Unity'.

[36] The discussion of structure was deliberately left out of chapter 2 to ensure that the argument concerning 9:13-19 would be constructed without relying upon it. In contrast, having made that argument, it is now appropriate to see if our position can be illuminated by it.

[37] Childs, 150

[38] McCarthy 'Moses', 336-347.

and phases of Exodus 7,8-10,27 only the expressed purpose of all Yahweh's dealings, namely, that he be acknowledged as supreme god is not used in a way which reinforces the concentric structure.'[39] While this may not be a problem for McCarthy's purposes, it is a major concern of this discussion. Therefore McCarthy's scheme is not greatly helpful to us.[40]

Returning to the question of the similarity between 7:14-17 and 9:13-19, we have already noted the theme of progression of some kind within YHWH's acts. If we link this observation with the structural observation above, we can see that both 'watersheds' come at the beginning of different 'triads' in the nine plagues. Does this indicate a more structured system of progression in the plagues? Might this set the changes in YHWH's action, and the concurrent changes in the hardening in some form of context?

In suggesting a theory of progression, we are not claiming that the individual plagues show a straight line of increasing severity, one following the next. Rather there are different phases in the encounters that are marked out by speeches from YHWH (7:14-17; 9:13-19). Within these phases are multiple plagues that have similar characteristics in terms of severity.[41]

One specific example raised against increases is that the plague of blood is more severe than its immediate successors, the frogs and gnats, and indeed some of the later plagues.[42] However, while it may have been symbolically profound, 7:24-25 suggests that it may have been more of an irritation than a devastation. The Egyptians had to dig for water, suggesting that there was some around. Moreover, Pharaoh did not take it seriously (7:23), in contrast to later plagues.[43]

---

[39] McCarthy 'Moses', 343. He also noted that the use of the different hardening terms is not woven into the pattern.

[40] Jacob *Exodus*, 179-80, in addition to mentioning the 3:3:3 (+1) pattern, also suggests an alternative pattern of 5:5, but running from the blood river to the plague on the firstborn. Thus the fifth plague on the cattle is the end of the first section; a 'lesser death' in comparison to the 'greater death' of the firstborn, which ends the second section. However, we will restrict ourselves to discussing one scheme overall.

[41] So, for example, McCarthy suggests the idea of some progression in the plagues, moving from primitive magic, through an increase in the dignity of YHWH's representative, up to gaining admissions from a living god, although the seeming purpose of the plagues, the liberation of Israel, is not fulfilled ('Moses', 338, 344-36). Propp, 318, suggests that the redactor has put the milder 'P' plagues first in order to create 'an impression of mounting severity throughout the cycle'. Cf. Jacob *Exodus*, 183, on different stages in the process.

[42] Durham, 103, notes this point. However, he is not concerned about increasing severity, but rather the cumulative effect.

[43] Cf. Childs, 154: 'To this extent there is a slight exegetical basis for seeing some relation between the tradition of the first plague and the natural seasonal reddening of the Nile, which modern critical commentators never tire of citing.'

At this point we need to inject a slight note of caution. If this were to be a cast-iron structure that clearly set out such progression consistently, we would expect the fourth plague of the swarm, as first plague of the second triad, to be comparative to the two we have discussed. While there are some elements of progression that can be seen,[44] the message from YHWH there does not contain the elements that we have noted above. The same could be said for the last plague, which on this scheme would be a progression. There are some elements here, but not as above.[45] However, this is not catastrophic to our analysis. We are not looking to set up a cast-iron formulaic structure that can be clearly and indisputably traced throughout the cycle. The stories combine some similar elements whilst allowing for variety in length, content, and so forth, and this is part of what makes the whole cycle a good story. As we continue looking at the various plagues, we will keep this overall structure in mind, especially where the 'triads' begin and end. We will then see what it brings forth from the continuing narrative, and consider how YHWH's plagues progress and how this relates to Pharaoh's actions. More generally we will pick up any wider examples of development in the encounters, as the story continues to develop.[46]

4.2.3 II: Invasion of the Frogs (7:26-8:11 [8:1-15])

The second plague commences with a message from YHWH that introduces the 'standard' demand (שַׁלַּח אֶת־עַמִּי וְיַעַבְדֻנִי) 7:26 [8:1], cf. 9:13; 10:3 etc.). References to the wilderness now disappear from the demand, although they continue in the negotiations.

This is followed by the first conditional threat from YHWH. If Pharaoh will not release them, then YHWH will strike (נֹגֵף)[47] his territory with frogs, in its entirety (7:27-29 [8:2-4]).

The threat is carried out, and frogs come out of the Nile. (8:1-2 [5-6]). Once again, the magicians copy the sign (8:3 [7]). As with the two previous encounters with the magicians, while they can copy what is done, yet there is an indication that this copying is not a satisfactory reply. As in the last plague, they can increase the plague, but there is no indication that they can

---

[44] This point will be discussed further at IV. To anticipate this: the plagues begin to be permanent in effect; are described as כָּבֵד; and explicitly exempt Israel.

[45] The tenth plague does share some of the same features as I and VII. The plague is not conditional. Moreover there is a change of some kind as it will be effective (11:1, 4-7). However, there is no comment on Pharaoh's lack of response to previous plagues as the reason for this 'change'.

[46] For a rather different interpretation of the development in the narrative see Gunn. Cf. also Brueggemann 'Vassal', 42; Krašovec *Reward*, 67, 76.

[47] Durham, 101, 103, notes that נֶגֶף is used of the actions of YHWH in the OT, most often in a context of punishment. However, it is never used of the actions of any other god. Cf. Driver *Exodus*, 72.

remove it. Pharaoh himself acknowledges this in his reaction.[48] For the first time he summons Moses and Aaron, rather than leaving them to take the initiative (8:4 [8]). Moreover instead of his heart remaining hard following his magicians' copying of the sign, he calls on Moses and Aaron to call upon YHWH to remove the frogs. If they do this, then he will release the people to sacrifice to YHWH. This appears to be a substantial shift in Pharaoh's position. The one who did not acknowledge YHWH (5:2, cf. 7:13, 22-23) now calls on him, through his representatives, to remove the plague. He would be unlikely to admit to such a loss of face if he had the means to annul YHWH's acts.

Moses then asks Pharaoh to name a time when YHWH will remove the frogs, and Pharaoh appoints the next day (8:5-6 [9-10]). Moses agrees to this, couching both replies in respectful language (עָלַי הִתְפָּאֵר, כִּדְבָרְךָ). Childs suggests that Moses' words are more than simply polite language. Moses is giving Pharaoh an advantage in letting him name the time.[49] YHWH then does as Moses asks (8:9 [13]), who does as Pharaoh asks (8:6 [10]).

However, as with 7:8-13, the seeming power of Pharaoh is subverted. The reason for Moses' words, and YHWH's action in removing the plagues, is not to show that YHWH and Moses are obedient to Pharaoh. Rather this is done so that Pharaoh might know that there is none like YHWH (לְמַעַן תֵּדַע כִּי־אֵין כַּיהוָה אֱלֹהֵינוּ 8:6 [10]).[50] As in 9:13-19 and 10:1-2, the initial perspective or perception of the significance of events is changed. In all cases, seeming exaltation of Pharaoh actually leads to exaltation of YHWH.

Therefore in one sense Pharaoh has already admitted that 'there is none like YHWH', at least in respect of this plague, as he cannot remove it. However he promises a more practical acknowledgement of YHWH, by agreeing to his demand, if he removes the plague. Pharaoh is responding in the language of YHWH's demand. 'Send the people, or I will send a plague' becomes 'remove the plague and I will send the people'.

Having considered the means of gaining the acknowledgement, we need to consider its meaning. What does it mean to 'know that there is none like YHWH our God'? Firstly, as noted above, it requires acknowledgement of

---

[48] Cf. Durham, 104. Ibn Ezra, 157; Noth, 72. Houtman, II 42, in contrast to his view on the previous plague, sees Pharaoh's response as realisation that the magi can only increase the plagues; thus the reader is delighted by his actions.

An alternative reason may be that Pharaoh, who previously went into his house to ignore them, is now personally affected by the frogs in even his house. However there is no explicit reason given for his action.

[49] Childs, 128, 156.

[50] Cf. Propp, 326.

the power that YHWH has over the plague. He can remove it, and the forces of Egypt cannot.

However, there is another possible sense here. In 7:17, the acknowledgement was to come through the bringing of the plague (cf. 9:14). However here it comes from the removal of the plague (cf. 9:29). YHWH does not wait until Pharaoh has released the people before he removes his plague; rather he responds to a request for relief by bringing relief (8:9 [13]; cf. 2:23-25). Pharaoh, in contrast, responds to a request for relief from suffering by increasing that suffering (5:3, 6-9, 17-18); thus attempting to silence that request (5:9). Just as Pharaoh and Egypt are unlike YHWH in their inability to remove the plague, so they are unlike him in their methods of dealing with the powerless.[51]

YHWH then removes the frog infestation, albeit with the darkly humorous twist that the frogs die and the land stinks (8:9-10 [13-14]). However, just as in 9:34, it is *at the moment* when Pharaoh sees that the respite has arrived, that he hardens his heart (8:11 [15] וְהַכְבֵּד ... וַיַּרְא).[52] Thus his response to a respite that is meant to bring him to an acknowledgement of YHWH (8:6 [10]; cf. 9:29) is instead to harden his heart.

As in 9:34, the concluding refrain of self-hardening is totally appropriate here. Pharaoh has had the chance to acknowledge YHWH. Indeed, he has started down that path when he summons Moses and Aaron, and asks for intercession, 'softening' his heart. Yet at the point when he should complete this acknowledgement, he reneges on the deal, thus actively hardening his heart (or position) on this issue. This active reneging or hardening is in contrast to 7:13 and 7:22-23 where he simply remained hard-set against sending the people, with no 'softening' in the encounters at all.[53]

Thus Pharaoh takes the respite arising from YHWH's removal of the plague as an excuse to uphold his position. We can feel the remonstration in 9:16-17 starting to build force. YHWH is unlike Pharaoh in his treatment of those weaker than him, but it seems that Pharaoh chooses to see this as

---

[51] LXX gives the content of the acknowledgement as οὐκ ἔστιν ἄλλος πλὴν κυρίου, thus giving it a monotheistic or universalistic claim (cf. Propp, 296; Wevers, 110). However this does not seem to fit the context as well as the MT sense above, which deals with YHWH's incomparability on multiple counts.

[52] Propp, 296, discusses the odd Hiph'il infinitive absolute here.

[53] In light of 9:27-28 and 10:16-17, it should not be assumed that Pharaoh is being either totally genuine or deliberately false in his offer in 8:4 [8]. As there, he gets the order of 'repentance' wrong, seeking remission of the plague before responding appropriately. However, this is a comparative 'softening' from a position where he paid no attention at all to the previous sign (7:22-23).

weakness.[54] Thus his perception of YHWH is not sufficiently changed from 5:2, and he is unresponsive to YHWH's acts.

4.2.4 III: Gnats out of Dust (8:12-15 [16-19])

This is the first of the three plagues with no initial dialogue between Moses/Aaron and Pharaoh. Aaron is told to strike the dust, and it becomes gnats 8:12-13 [16-17]. The magicians try to copy him, as in the three previous cases. However, this time they are unable to do so (8:14 [18]).[55] As a result they inform Pharaoh that 'this is the finger of (a) god/divine finger' (אֶצְבַּע אֱלֹהִים הוּא). However Pharaoh's heart remains hard (8:15 [19]), in a conclusion that replicates 7:13 and 22.

Pharaoh receives no word from YHWH via Moses and Aaron in this plague, but he does not have to. His magicians take their place on two counts.

First they fail to replicate the miracle. Thus they prove that there is a limit to their 'arts'. It is important for the significance of this encounter that we do not understand the magicians as faking their results in the first three encounters. While in these previous cases they provide a reason, albeit not perfect, for Pharaoh to disbelieve YHWH, here that reason is removed, as they cannot even copy the plague. As with 7:17 and 9:14, the power of YHWH's actions is being increased.

Secondly they confess to Pharaoh that there is something greater than human power or ability at work here. The phrase 'the finger of god' is ambiguous in meaning.[56] It is not an explicit confession that this is Moses and Aaron's god at work, as would be made by acknowledging 'the finger

---

[54] In light of the suggestion in the previous chapter of YHWH 'being a Pharaoh to Pharaoh' in 10:2, we could speculate whether Pharaoh is understanding 'YHWH as Pharaoh' here. In other words, he is judging by his own standards where power equals oppression and respite equals weakness.

[55] The verse starts וַיַּעֲשׂוּ־כֵן (as 7:22; 8:3 [7]). Thus it appears that the magi will be able to copy as they did before. However this perception is proven to be wrong (וְלֹא יָכֹלוּ).

[56] Reference to the 'finger of God' is found elsewhere in the OT for the inscription on the stone tablets (Ex. 31:18/Dt. 9:10 contrast Is. 2:8/17:8), and for the creation of the heavens (Ps. 8:4 [3]). Cf. Lk. 11:20 which, as here, deals with the question of the source of miraculous power: 'But if by the finger of God [in contrast to 'by Beelzebub'] I drive out demons, then the kingdom of God has come to you.' See B Couroyer 'Le Doigt de Dieu.' *RB* 63 (1956): 481-95, for discussion of the usage in the Bible. He argues that the term has Egyptian magical origin, referring to Aaron's staff. Even if his point is accepted (see Childs, 129 against this), it would still have a similar meaning of the magi admitting that Aaron's staff is more powerful then theirs; thus still an ambiguous confession. More generally, cf. Houtman, II 57, for references to discussions of 'finger' and what 'finger of god' might mean.

of YHWH'.[57] In the mouths of presumably polytheistic magicians one could easily understand this as 'this is the finger of a god/the gods/a divine finger.'[58] Thus they would be acknowledging that this feat is beyond their power, and therefore accrediting Moses and Aaron with being more than simply magicians themselves. However, this could be understood, perhaps, as one of the Egyptian gods or another force. The confession allows a degree of ambiguity, which almost appears to be a backward step from 8:4 [8]. However, we should note that as magicians, rather than YHWH's representatives, this might be the furthest that they were able to go.

It is also unclear whether this confession is meant to suggest anything more than a confession of defeat: 'this is beyond us!'[59] Critically, in contrast to the servants who perform a similar confessing function in 10:7, the magicians do not suggest any response to this turn of events. One could hear an unspoken 'This is the finger of god – therefore you should propitiate/obey him...', and perhaps Pharaoh might have, if he had 'ears to hear'. However the indeterminacy in the phrase would allow Pharaoh to hear it differently.[60] Pharaoh is as unmoved by their failure as he was by their 'success' in copying Aaron, and his heart remains as hard as it was at 8:11 [15].

4.2.5 IV: The Sending of the Swarm (8:16-28 [20-32])

The fourth plague begins as the first (7:15). Moses is told to take his stand before Pharaoh by the waters (8:16a [20a]). The form of the message is similar to that of 7:26-27 [8:1-2], with the demand and threat conditional on its refusal (8:16b-17 [20b-21]). In this case, the frogs are replaced by the swarm (הֶעָרֹב). It need not concern us whether this refers to a swarm of

---

[57] Cassuto, 106. Chacko, 175, notes Kaufman's point that they do not say 'their god is greater than ours'.

[58] Propp, 328, cites 9:28; Ezek. 1:1; 8:3; 40:2; Job 1:16 for this sense of אֱלֹהִים as 'divine'.

[59] Cf. Greenberg *UE*, 156. Thus Keil, 483, suggests that they are protecting their own reputation: it was a god that has beaten them, not Moses and Aaron. Cf. Ehrlich, 289, who sees the magi as effectively saying that the previous plagues were from human sources (cf. 9:27 '*this time* I have sinned'?). Ibn Ezra, 162, suggests the magi see it as due to an arrangement of the stars, comparing it to 1Sam. 6:9. Rashbam, 79, has 'natural disasters' (our 'act of God'?), rather than Moses and Aaron's sorcery. Cf. Larrson, 63.

[60] One could compare this contrast between 8:15 [19] and 10:7 with the difference between the serpent staff encounter and those that follow. There, a sign is given, and the swallowing of the other staffs could show the greater power of YHWH. However (as in 8:12-15 [16-19]), there is no demand made and no obvious response is required from Pharaoh.

wild beasts[61], or a swarm of flies.[62] The point of the text is that this swarm will invade the living space of all Egypt.

However, the message then differs from that of the preceding plagues. YHWH makes a distinction between his people, and between Pharaoh's people, so that the swarm will not enter Goshen and his people Israel will be spared (8:18-19 [22-23]).

4.2.5.1 EXCURSUS: EXEMPTION OF ISRAEL

This is the first mention of a theme that runs throughout the rest of the plagues narrative, cumulating both in the distinction of the Israelite firstborn from death in the tenth plague through the Passover, and also in Israel's passing through the Red Sea on dry land where the Egyptians are drowned. It is not mentioned in every plague thereafter but the general theme is maintained.[63]

In contrast, the first three plagues have no such mention. One could assume that YHWH would want to shield his people from all the plagues.[64] However, this suggests an overly humanitarian view of YHWH's action here. We have noted his lack of action in Ex. 1-2 and 5. Moreover, in light of 9:15, it would have been much easier for Israel had he unleashed one terrible plague upon Egypt (exempting Goshen), after which they could leave. Presumably while this process of encounters and plagues is ongoing Israel are still suffering hard labour making bricks without straw. The text gives us no warrant to suppose that their lot gets any easier from 6:9 until the exodus itself. YHWH's main aim in this process does not seem to be to release Israel as quickly and easily as possible. Therefore it does not seem

---

[61] Durham, 114, notes Philo and the Haggadah holding this view.

[62] This appears to be the modern consensus, e.g. Propp, 328, Cassuto, 107.

[63] There is no mention of an exemption of Israel from the sixth plague of boils (9:8-12). However, Greenberg notes that the magi were unable to stand before Moses and Aaron. This assumes that the latter two could stand and therefore that these Israelites at least were free from boils (*UE*, 174 n.1).

Moreover if 9:15 is understood as the possibility of extending the cattle plague to humans, where the boils could have been fatal rather than irritating, this would suggest that 'your people' in 9:15 would exclude Israel. However this is more speculative.

There is also no mention of an exemption of Israel from the eighth plague of locusts. It seems unlikely that this lack is meant to mark a sharp distinction between it and the plagues surrounding it. Even if it did, it would only mean that any crops in Goshen would be of no use to the Egyptians once the Israelites had left. (If Israel had no time to leaven their dough (12:39), they presumably would have no time to harvest crops! In contrast Israel's portable livestock and servants are necessary, and therefore preserved, cf. 10:25-26. Alternatively Greenberg *UE*, 174 n.1, suggests that they were not farmers.)

Neither of these exemptions is to be insisted upon.

[64] Examples of this view are cited in Childs, 143ff; Propp, 313; Greenberg *UE*, 174; Houtman, II 29.

unreasonable to suppose that Israel could have been affected by the first three plagues.[65] We need not insist on it. As with so many elements of this story, the text is uncertain and allows us to draw our own conclusions. The important point is that from this point onwards Israel are explicitly and publicly exempted from most, if not all, of the plagues.[66] If one sees Israel as always exempted and thus does not see this as a change, one still needs to explain why it is mentioned and focussed on from this point.

Moreover, the reason for the exemption of Israel is not given as YHWH's concern for Israel, but rather as another means of educating Pharaoh in acknowledging YHWH.[67] Goshen will be spared from the swarm 'so that you will know that I am YHWH in the midst of the land' (לְמַעַן תֵּדַע כִּי אֲנִי יְהוָה בְּקֶרֶב הָאָרֶץ 8:18 [22]). Thus, as with the removal of the plague of frogs (8:6 [10]), the knowledge of YHWH that Pharaoh will receive is not linked to the sending of the plague, but rather to a limitation of the plague, in this case exemption from it.

The contrast is drawn sharply in 8:17-19 [21-23] between Israel and Egypt, Pharaoh and YHWH. If Pharaoh will not send (שִׁלַּח Pi'el) YHWH's people (עָם) to serve (עָבַד) YHWH, then YHWH will send (שָׁלַח Hiph'il) the swarm upon Pharaoh, his servants (עֶבֶד) and his people (עָם), and his houses. However YHWH will exempt Goshen and thus make a 'distinction' between his people and Pharaoh's people.

The word פְּדֻת in 8:19 [23] causes some problems. Ehrlich pithily sums up the problem: 'פְּדֻת *ist ein Unwort*'.[68] Elsewhere in the OT it has the sense of 'redemption'.[69] Here, however, that sense is problematic. Following 8:18 [22] (וְהִפְלֵיתִי) one might expect a similar theme of separation or distinction.[70] Targum Onkelos, and the rabbinic commentators understand פְּדֻת as combining the two ideas. Israel is redeemed inasmuch as they are separated from the lot of the Egyptians, or alternatively it is their

---

[65] One could also point to the wanderings in the wilderness that they are about to endure, which elsewhere are portrayed in less than comfortable terms (e.g. Dt. 8:2-4, 11-16).

[66] Cf. Childs, 157.

[67] Neither is it a question of moral judgement. Israel are not obviously spared because of their piety (contra Philo *Mos.* I.143).

[68] Ehrlich, 290. (It is difficult, in an English translation, to keep the pithiness of *Unwort*.)

Three recent discussions of this verse are those of A. A. Macintosh 'Exodus VIII 19, Distinct Redemption and the Hebrew Roots פדה and פדד', *VT* 21 (1971): 112-114, henceforth 'Macintosh'; G. I. Davies 'The Hebrew Text of Exodus VIII 19 (EVV. 23) An Emendation', *VT* 24 (1974): 489-492, henceforth 'Davies'; and R. Althann 'פְּדֻת in Exodus 8:19', in *Exodus 1-15: Text and Context*. J. J. Burden ed., OTWSA/OTSSA 29 (1986): 73-79, henceforth 'Althann'. Cf. Houtman, II 63, for other discussions.

[69] Ps. 111:9; 130:7; Is. 50:2.

[70] Some ancient versions do give this sense, with LXX reading διαστολήν, and Vulgate *divisio*; cf. Macintosh, 548.

redemption that distinguishes them from Egypt.[71] However, Davies points out a problem, inasmuch as redemption in Hebrew and English 'is not brought about *between* X *and* Y, but *of* X *from* Y. Yet it is the proposition *byn* which is used in this verse (twice).'[72] In terms of understanding the text, the idea of 'distinction' or 'separation' needs to come in, and emendations that have been proposed seek different ways of doing this.[73] For our purposes, we need not determine exactly how the text should be read. Davies notes that all explanations which do not translate פָּדֻת as 'redemption' are based upon positing a *hapax legomenon*.[74] Therefore, one could say, it is down to the ingenuity of the scholar to decide. For our purposes, the important point is that this element of 'distinction' is brought in, either by emendation, cognates, or by an ambiguous or double meaning of the word. The wider events of the exodus are remembered as a redemption (6:6, Mic. 6:4 etc), and at this point the means by which this is done is by distinguishing Israel.

As with the new element of 'distinction' in the plague, there is a new element in the acknowledgement that it is intended to bring. Its purpose is that Pharaoh will 'know that I am YHWH *in the midst of the land*'.[75] It was not unusual in the ancient Near East for deities to strike their own lands with plagues, or to act to defend their cities. What is unusual here is that a foreign god, a god of a slave race, a god who is not known to Pharaoh (5:2), has the ability to inflict any number of different nature plagues upon Pharaoh's land of Egypt.[76]

This also nuances our understanding of the 'my people'/'your people' distinction. One could read this as saying that Israel are YHWH's concern, whereas Egypt are Pharaoh's concern, and YHWH has no real influence over them. However, this is the god who has been plaguing Egypt, and who is to be acknowledged in the midst of the land. Thus, as with the language

---

[71] Cf. Macintosh, 549-50; Propp, 328-29.

[72] Davies, 489.

[73] Thus Dillmann and others have suggested פלח (see Davies, 491, for criticism); Davies suggests פרדת, which has been corrupted by haplography (491); Althann suggests בדד (75). Macintosh suggests leaving the MT and understanding it as derived from the unattested פדד by means of an Arabic cognate (550).

[74] Davies, 490.

[75] This could also be translated 'know that I, YHWH, am in the midst of the land' (cf., Houtman, II 63, for different translations). However the first translation retains the 'know that I am YHWH' from 7:5, 17 etc with the additional point that this is now shown to be true in the midst of Egypt. However, there is little overall difference between the translations. LXX (and Targums) read 'I, YHWH, am the Lord of all the earth' (Propp, 297; Wevers, 117). As at 8:6 [10] while this claims more, it does not fit as well into the context. (See 4.2.5.3 below on 8:21 [25]).

[76] Cf. Durham, 114.

of 8:6 [10] and 8:8 [12], this seeming respect for Pharaoh may contain a sharper message for those that have 'ears to hear'.

Keil notes that this may be a response to the magicians' incomplete confession in 8:15 [19] of the 'finger of (a) god'. This distinction of Israel and Egypt lessens any thoughts that these events could be the work of an Egyptian deity.[77] Whether or not we follow this point, the plague is intended to bring about a change of perceptions. This foreign god of the slaves is to be acknowledged as in the midst of Egypt, just as in 10:2 this 'god of the Hebrews' is the one who will be remembered as 'toying with' the mighty Pharaoh.

However, this claim from the foreign YHWH is linked not to his ability to send plagues, but to his ability to exempt his people from them. As with the acknowledgement of 8:6 [10], there are two possible senses for this claim.

On one level this may relate to YHWH's total control over the plagues. Just as he can totally remove them, when the magicians cannot; so he can also exempt his people from them. The swarm is not a plague that YHWH simply lets loose to travel uncontrolled across the land; there will be no swarm in Goshen. He is YHWH in the midst of the land, and can control the plague completely, rather than being a foreign god only able to fling plagues from Horeb. Moreover, while YHWH can protect his people, Pharaoh cannot protect the Egyptians.

On another level, as his ability to remove plagues showed him to be a different character from Pharaoh in respect of the powerless, so here his concern for his people also marks him out as different from the Pharaoh who disregards the plight of his own people in refusing to release Israel (7:23-24; contrast 2:24-25 with 10:7-10). Although the purpose of the exemption is explained as a demonstration to Pharaoh (rather than to help his people), the means by which he demonstrates to Pharaoh is by exempting his people.[78] This dynamic is comparable to the mitigation offered to the Egyptians in 9:19. It is not done primarily to help the Egyptians, but to demonstrate the importance of obedience to YHWH. However, this obedience itself leads to mitigation and thus relief. The difference is that Egypt only received one chance at mitigation, which they had to act upon; and Pharaoh destroyed any chance of a repetition of this. In contrast Israel are automatically exempted from most, if not all, of the future plagues by YHWH's power, not by their own actions (excepting the final plague).

---

[77] Keil, 484. This is not the first time that YHWH has been associated with Israel before Pharaoh (5:1, 3; 8:6 [10] etc). However this increases the distinction.

[78] I would therefore agree with Cassuto (108) that there are two reasons for this exemption, but disagree over their relative priorities.

4.2.5.2 THE PLAGUE – A CHANGE IN THE ENCOUNTERS?

After this, the plague comes: a heavy (כָּבֵד) swarm enters the land and the
land is ruined (תִּשָּׁחֵת) (8:20 [24]). If we look to the 3:3:3 structure of the
plague cycle, we notice that this is the start of the second triad. Can we see
here a similar shift in the method of encounters between YHWH and
Pharaoh as found in 7:16-17 and 9:13-19?

If there is a shift, it is a less obvious one than in the first and seventh
plagues. There is no summary of how YHWH has previously acted (9:15-
16; 7:16a). Neither is there an explicit statement that Pharaoh has refused to
respond appropriately (7:16; 9:17). Nor is there a statement that *because of
this*, something new will happen (7:17; 9:18). Moreover the plague is
expressed as a threat conditional on Pharaoh's response, rather than the
unconditional plagues of 7:17 and 9:14. Finally, there is no change in
respect of the 'hardening'. Therefore I have some sympathy with Houtman,
who sees plagues I-VI as not ascending in difficulty or effect, in
comparison with the difference between I-VI and VII-X, which is
striking.[79] However, there are some changes that can be observed.

First, in this 'triad' there are no magicians to copy the plagues. Their
failure and confession could be said to mark the end of the first 'triad' and
any form of possible competition between the power of Pharaoh and that of
YHWH. Pharaoh can no longer respond in like kind. Yet Pharaoh will not
admit defeat even when his side is beaten. Thus something new is
required.[80] Moreover, the plagues appear to move from irritation to serious
hardship. The swarm ruins the land (תִּשָּׁחֵת הָאָרֶץ 8:20 [24]); the livestock
are killed (9:6); and people are directly afflicted for the first time (9:10).
The first two are described as כָּבֵד (8:20 [24]; 9:3). Finally, this is the point
at which Israel begin to be exempted from the effects of the plagues.
Therefore one can see some progression in the style of the encounters;
albeit not as extreme as the changes at 7:14-17 and 9:13-19.

4.2.5.3 RESPONSES IN WORDS

As with the frog invasion (8:4 [8]), Pharaoh summons Moses and Aaron as
a result of the plague and allows them to go and sacrifice to YHWH (8:21

---

[79] Houtman, II 20.

[80] The magicians' failure admittedly comes at the end of the previous triad. However
this is consistent with the overall pattern. The 'change' in the encounters between
different triads occurs both in the last plague of the preceding triad and the first of the
next. The magicians fail but still P does not listen (III) and then Israel is exempted from
the כָּבֵד plagues (IV). The magicians bow out and YHWH hardens (VI), and then
YHWH brings the incomparable plagues (VII). There is no involvement of servants (in
contrast to VII and VIII) and Pharaoh ceases negotiations (IX), and then the last, terrible
plague occurs (X). All reflect increasing lack of response from Pharaoh, and subsequent
response from YHWH.

[25]). However this time he tells them to sacrifice to YHWH in the land (בָּאָרֶץ). To this Moses replies that it is not appropriate to sacrifice to YHWH in Egypt as the Egyptians would consider it an abomination, and would stone them. Therefore he reiterates the request for a three day journey (8:22-23 [26-27], cf. 5:3). Pharaoh agrees to this, on the condition that they do not go far (8:24 [28]). Moses agrees to this on the condition that Pharaoh does not renege on his promise as he did before. (8:25 [29]). This exchange can be viewed on different levels.

On one level, the demand relates to the sacrifice. Pharaoh cleverly picks up Moses' words in 8:18 [22] that YHWH is 'in the midst of the land', and says in effect 'Well, if he is in the midst of the land, you don't need to go into the desert; worship him here (and stay under my control).'[81] Moreover, Moses has dropped the 'three day journey' from the demand (8:16-17 [20-21]), so Pharaoh may see it as a negotiable point.[82] However, Moses knows that he needs to get the people out of Egypt in order to worship/serve YHWH 'on this mountain' (3:12), and so he parries Pharaoh's stroke, and ripostes by pointing to Pharaoh's own people as a problem. This is an oddity, as we might expect the offence to come from YHWH or Israel, rather than Egypt. However, objections from a slave race would probably have less effect than pragmatic considerations as to the behaviour of the Egyptians, and the loss of slaves by stoning. Thus, on this level, Moses is being as clever as Pharaoh in getting what he really wants. The 'trick' of the three-day journey (cf. 3:18) is maintained.

However we can view this differently. This view is not to invalidate the above picture, which is engaging and skilfully drawn.[83] However, while Pharaoh is picking up YHWH's language, he is missing the sense of it. YHWH has just shown that he is 'YHWH in the midst of the land', but he has shown this precisely by *separating* Israel from Egypt ('my people' and 'your people'), while Pharaoh is trying to keep them together. Moreover, the acknowledgement that 'I am YHWH in the midst of the land' is for Pharaoh to make, not Israel (לְמַעַן תֵּדַע כִּי); and the way that he is to make it has been outlined to him from the beginning 'release/send my people...' (cf. on 5:2), not 'keep them...'. Furthermore Moses, in effect, points out that the Egyptians do not yet acknowledge YHWH 'in the midst of the land' as they would stone the Israelites for sacrificing to him, a sacrifice that they consider to be an abomination.[84] Therefore sacrificing in the land

---

[81] Propp, 329 and Greenberg *UE*, 157, note Abarbanel suggesting that Pharaoh is being very clever here.

[82] Cf. Houtman, II 59.

[83] Childs, 135-36.

[84] Whether the Egyptians would have done this or not is a moot point. Durham, 115, notes Gen. 43:32; 46:34 for wider examples of this Egyptian attitude of abomination to

is not appropriate. Interestingly however, both Moses and Pharaoh are implicitly agreeing that YHWH can be worshipped anywhere, not just in the wilderness.[85]

Pharaoh has chosen to interpret the statement in 8:18 [22] in a certain way. This is a possible reading of a statement that, like others, can be taken in more than one way. However, Moses' reply shows that, although there are different possibilities for interpretation, they are not all equally appropriate or correct. Thus ambiguity does not equate to total subjectivity.

The wider ambiguity in the demand 'send ... serve' is coming under strain at this point. Pharaoh concedes the point, either because he understands the point above, or (more probably) because his bluff is called and he wants the plague to end. However his condition is 'only (רַק) you shall not go far' (8:24 [28]). If we understand 'three days' to indicate a short indefinite period of time,[86] this comment would be superfluous if Pharaoh really believed that they would only go for three days. Thus his condition suggests that he has his suspicions, but chooses to keep the process going and maintain the ambiguity for now.

Moses reacts in a similar manner. He does not explicitly accept the condition that they will not go far, but he agrees to go and intercede with YHWH to remove the plague. As with the plague of frogs, he stands in the place of YHWH to Pharaoh (8:9 [13] cf. 7:1), to the extent that he can speak for YHWH (cf. 8:27 [31]). However, Moses has his own condition: 'only (רַק) let not Pharaoh add to the mockery/deception (הָתֵל) by not sending the people to sacrifice to YHWH' (8:25 [29]).[87]

הָתַל is used more widely in the Old Testament, meaning variously 'mock', 'deceive', 'trifle with', and 'make a fool of'.[88] One could see a similarity, both in sound and in meaning, to סָלַל in 9:17, where Pharaoh 'lords it' over Israel by not sending them. This is followed by the similar עָלַל in 10:2, where YHWH does something similar to Pharaoh.

The reference to a previous 'mockery' (תָּלַל) is presumably a reference to Pharaoh reneging on his promise after the plague of frogs was removed (8:4 [8], 11 [15]). As with Pharaoh's condition, if Moses really believed that this time Pharaoh would keep his promise, then this comment is

---

Israel, at least in the eyes of the biblical writers. Propp, 329, suggests that this would have been more likely in the first millennium.

[85] Propp, 329.

[86] E.g. Jos. 2:16, 22; Jon. 3:3.

[87] Cf. Propp, 331.

[88] Always Hiph'il, as here, or Hoph'al: Gen. 31:7; 1Kgs. 18:27; Jdg. 16:10, 13, 15; Job 13:9, 19; Is. 44:20; Jer. 9:4 [5]. Childs, 129, defines it as trifling with a person in a less than serious manner.

otiose.[89] He too has his suspicions that Pharaoh will once again renege, but his intercession to YHWH and his remonstration with Pharaoh show that he still believes that there is a possibility that Pharaoh will do as he should. One does not remonstrate if remonstration is deemed to be pointless.

The ambiguity in the demand (שַׁלַּח...וְיַעַבְדֻנִי) shows signs of straining on both sides, but it holds for now.

4.2.5.4 RESPONSES IN ACTION

After this, Moses goes out and keeps his side of the bargain, and the swarm disappears totally (8:26-27 [30-31]). However, once again (גַּם בַּפַּעַם הַזֹּאת) Pharaoh reneges, hardens (וַיַּכְבֵּד) his heart, and does not send the people (8:28 [32]). The mockery is increased.[90]

4.2.6 V: Death of the Livestock (9:1-7)

As in 7:26 [8:1], Moses is commanded to go to Pharaoh and give him the now standard demand (9:1). However, this time the counter threat is spelt out a little. If Pharaoh refuses to send them and still grasps hold of them (וְעוֹדְךָ מַחֲזִיק בָּם), then the hand of YHWH will be on the livestock of the Egyptians, manifesting itself as a very heavy plague (דֶּבֶר כָּבֵד מְאֹד).[91] Thus the imagery of the strong hand returns (cf. 3:19-20; 6:1). If Pharaoh's hand holds Israel strongly (מַחֲזִיק), indeed *still* holds Israel (עוֹדְךָ cf. 9:17), then YHWH's hand will descend heavily (כָּבֵד) upon Egypt's livestock, 'measure for measure' (9:2-3).[92]

---

[89] Cf. Childs, 157. While he sees Moses as not trusting Pharaoh, he sees Pharaoh as clutching at straws. I prefer to see the double רַק as indicating that they are both negotiating distrustfully at this point. So far, Pharaoh has not used the more submissive or penitent language of 'sinning' that the later, more terrible plagues provoke (9:27-28; 10:16-17).

[90] This plague and the previous one are often seen in source critical terms as doublets due to the similarity of the nature of the plague (insects). Whatever their origin, in their final form they have very different messages: the failure and confession of the magi on the one hand; the exemption of Israel on the other.

[91] Childs, 157-58, notes that Pharaoh's responsibility is maintained, not destroyed, despite the hardening in 8:28 [32], which he ascribes to YHWH. While his view of 8:28 [32] differs from ours, his comments on responsibility agree with the comments made on 10:3 following 10:2.

[92] The use of the participle form of הָיָה here is unique in the OT. G. S. Ogden 'Notes on the use of הוֹיָה in Ex. IX 3' *VT* 17 (1967): 483-484, notes that one might expect an imperfect here, to bring out the future sense of הָיָה. He suggests that this form has been 'manufactured' to agree with a wider pattern in Moses' statements about what YHWH would do if Pharaoh refuses (7:17, 27 [8:2]; 9:3; 10:4), which all have participial forms.

However, we can suggest a possible additional reason for its use here. In light of the parallelism between Pharaoh and YHWH noted in 9:2-3, might this odd participial form

However, it is not quite measure for measure. In light of 8:16-19 [20-23] we might have expected 'if your hand is still upon *my people*, then my hand will descend upon *your people*, with a terrible plague' to get the exact comparison.[93] However this is not the case. The plague only falls upon the livestock of Egypt.[94] We are reminded of YHWH's similar words in 9:15, that he could have send his hand, and struck Pharaoh and his people with plague (דֶּבֶר) and wiped them out. Yet he sustains them instead (9:16). Is this the point at which YHWH begins to exercise this restraint, or begins to sustain Egypt, so that the plague only falls on the livestock? How will Pharaoh respond to this?

As with the swarm, the plague will be heavy (כָּבֵד 9:3, cf. 8:20 [24]), and it will exempt Israel (9:4, cf. 8:18-19 [22-23]). YHWH then brings this about. All of the livestock of Egypt die, while not one of the Israelites' livestock is killed (9:6). The distinction is absolute.

In response to this, Pharaoh sends (Qal שָׁלַח) ... but only to investigate YHWH's claim of distinction.[95] He sees that is it so. However at this point, the point at which he sees the sign that YHWH has sent, he is unresponsive to it and does not send (Pi'el שִׁלַּח) the people (9:7). Once again, the sign that was meant to bring acknowledgement, only brings unresponsiveness (cf. 8:8 [12]; 9:34). The situation is slightly different here. The issue is the exemption of Israel from the relevant plague, rather than respite for the Egyptians from it.

Another oddity in this plague is that there is no language of acknowledgement (יָדַע). However, we do not need the same word each time, just as Moses and Aaron do not need to speak each time (8:15 [19]). In 9:2-3 there is the comparison between the strength of Pharaoh's grasp and the heaviness of YHWH's hand.[96] Thus the lesson for Pharaoh may be

---

have been 'manufactured' in order to give a good parallel to the participle מַחֲזִיק describing Pharaoh's action? As Pharaoh does, so YHWH does.

[93] One might argue that this is balanced by a similar inequality. YHWH's hand brings death, whereas Pharaoh's hand only brings suffering. However the Pharaohs' treatment of Israel appears to have deadly intent behind it (5:21; cf. 1:16-22).

[94] 4:22-23 achieves a similar effect by the substitution of 'son' for 'people', which does give a parity. However, to achieve a similar parity here, YHWH would have to describe Israel as his 'livestock', which would not be an appropriate term. For further discussion of 'son' in 4:22 see e.g. Childs, 102; Propp, 217.

[95] Cf. Durham, 118.

[96] This may have overtones of 7:16-17 and 9:14-18, where, if Pharaoh has not responded appropriately ('still' 'up to now' etc), YHWH will act more strongly. If we look to the 3:3:3 pattern, we might have expected this comment on Pharaoh's previous behaviour to have come in plague IV, as it starts the second triad, as the equivalent of 7:17 and 9:17. Moreover it is in this plague that Pharaoh picks up on the issue of exemption, rather than in the last plague where it was introduced. However this would only be a problem if we were looking for a cast-iron structure. Between them, these plagues (IV and V) express

that if he thinks himself strong, YHWH is stronger (and with that strength comes the ability, and the intention, to exempt his people). However, Pharaoh's heart remains unresponsive. He is not impressed by the death of cattle, and thus it will take something more ominous to move him. As with the lack of further mitigation after the seventh plague, for those who know the story, the shadow of the firstborn death to come looms larger.

4.2.7 VI: Erupting Boils and Sores (9:8-12)

As with the gnats plague (8:12-15 [16-19]), there is no dialogue in this plague, although the sign is to be performed in front of Pharaoh (9:8). As the dust became gnats (8:12-13 [16-17]), so now the soot becomes boils (9:9-10).[97]

Once again, the magicians take the place of Moses and Aaron in witnessing before Pharaoh (9:11); this time even more powerfully than in 8:15 [19], albeit silently. Then they were unable to replicate Aaron's act; now they are unable even to stand before Moses and Aaron because of the boils. Why do they appear here, after an absence of two plagues? Having failed to replicate the dust to gnats, and confessing as they do to Pharaoh, it would have been pointless for them to try to replicate the heavier (כָּבֵד) plagues that follow (IV and V). However, this is the first plague that directly targets humans, showing that YHWH can affect them as well as wider nature. Thus the magicians return, showing that even they are not immune to this debilitating condition. Instead they suffer the humiliation of not being able to stand before Moses and Aaron. Pharaoh's equivalent to Moses and Aaron are not only defeated (8:15 [19]); they are broken. They never appear again.

While this disease is debilitating, it is not as terrible as the disease that befell the livestock. It is not described as כָּבֵד, as the last two plagues were, and, more to the point, it is not fatal. The swarm has 'ruined' (שָׁחַת) the land; the דֶּבֶר has killed the cattle; thus we might expect this affliction to kill the Egyptians. Yet, as with the previous plague, our expectations are

---

the idea of an escalation or 'change', although, as noted above, this is not as clear as at 7:16-17 or 9:13-19.

[97] There were Egyptian equivalents to the exodus story where it was the Hebrews who had the skin disease, and who were driven out by Egyptians as lepers. A large part of Josephus' *Against Apion* is concerned to rebut various versions of this: (*Ag. Ap.* 1:73-104 Manetho's history; 1:105-287 Josephus' counter-arguments; 1:288-302 Chaeremon; 1:302-320 Lysimachus; 2:1-32 Apion's story). References taken from H. St.J. Thackeray, *Josephus I The Life; Against Apion*, LCL (London: William Heinemann Ltd, 1961). For a summary of Josephus' argument see John Barclay, *"The Politics of Contempt: Judeans and Egyptians in Josephus' Against Apion."* [cited 30 August 2004]. Online: http://josephus.yorku.ca/pdf/barclay2000.pdf On the general issue cf. Propp, 350; Jacob *Exodus*, 219, 272.

not fulfilled. Returning to 9:15-16 once again, this continues to bear out YHWH's point. He has already proved that he can send deadly plague (דֶּבֶר), but he only sends it upon the cattle. He has now proven that he can afflict humans, but he does so with a lesser, albeit excruciating, condition. Pharaoh and Egypt are sustained.[98]

At this point, the concluding refrain alters, and YHWH is cited as hardening Pharaoh's heart for the first time. It is not immediately obvious why this change takes place here.[99] It follows directly on from the retirement of the magicians from the story, and this may have some relevance. Perhaps YHWH is now taking the place of the magicians in strengthening Pharaoh's resolve against the signs.[100] However, to understand this move, we will need to move on to the explanation in the next plague.

4.2.8 *VII: Unparalleled Fury from the Skies (9:13-35)*

We now return to our original study of 9:13-19 and what follows, to view it in terms of the wider narrative.

4.2.8.1 THE 'EXPLANATION' AND THE NEW SITUATION

Moses is given a message for Pharaoh: 'all' of YHWH's plagues are coming upon his heart, so that he will know that there is none like YHWH in all the earth. YHWH could have stretched out his hand and destroyed Pharaoh and his people, but he sustained them to show them his power and that his name might be known throughout the land. However, Pharaoh has not responded appropriately. As a result, a storm like none other is about to come, that will mean death to anything in the open. Therefore Pharaoh and his people should go and bring in anything belonging to them outside (9:13-19).

On the assumption of the model of arrangement of the plagues into the three triads plus one, our explanation in 9:13-19 comes at the beginning of the third and last triad of plagues, those 'the like of which have never

---

[98] Houtman, II 76, sees the possibility of people and animals dying from the disease in this plague, although it is not mentioned. His comments are a guard against seeing this plague as merely irritating 'boils' (the description often given to this plague). However, in light of the fact that the text is not slow to inform us of death (4:23; 9:19 etc), it is not obvious that this plague was fatal. Even if it could be life threatening, this plague would be distinct from plagues that are intended to kill.

[99] Even if, in the light of 4:21 and 7:3, one sees this as merely making explicit what was previously implicit (e.g. Childs, 158), one still needs to ask why it is made explicit at this point. *Something* changes here.

[100] Cf. Greenberg *UE*, 160, who notes Ramban's suggestion of this.

occurred before'. Moreover, immediately prior to this Pharaoh is hardened by YHWH for the first time (9:12).

This suggests that there will be some change in the encounters between YHWH and Pharaoh after this point. 'This time' could be referring to the final triad of plagues, and possibly the firstborn as well. Here YHWH is sending 'all' his plagues upon Pharaoh (9:14). 9:15-16 have detailed what YHWH could have done, but has chosen not to do. The previous two plagues have shown that this is no idle boast. However, even after the last two terrible yet in some way restrained plagues, Pharaoh has refused to acknowledge YHWH, but treated YHWH's restraint as a reason to continue exalting himself. Therefore, as in 7:14-17, YHWH is changing the way that he deals with Pharaoh.[101] There is a genuinely new situation here, and *this new situation* is the reason why such a comparatively detailed explanation is given at this point.

On this point, it is not wholly surprising that the divine hardening starts at the same time as do the 'plagues like none other'. Pharaoh has hardened himself against the earlier, lesser plagues that YHWH sent, plagues that were meant to get Pharaoh's acknowledgement of YHWH. However, they were plagues that could be copied initially, followed by heavier plagues. YHWH did not start with his strongest acts, but weaker ones. In doing so he created a deliberate ambiguity allowing choice, where Pharaoh was called upon to respond appropriately, but did not need to do so. There were signs that might have led him to the correct response, but were designed not to compel this. One might wonder why YHWH would not show him something unmistakable, in order to get him to release Israel. However, by the same token, if YHWH was only, or primarily, interested in getting Israel released, he did not need to bother with Pharaoh, and indeed, tells Pharaoh as much (9:15).[102] For some reason, YHWH seems interested in how Pharaoh responds. The explanation that he gives here is an explanation as to why things have taken so long (a similar function to that of 10:1-2).

We now come to the plagues like none other, plagues that one might expect to be irrefutable. They cannot be copied; nobody has ever seen the like of them. Surely even Pharaoh cannot fail to acknowledge YHWH as a

---

[101] Thus Greenberg: 'But the language [of 'all my plagues'] is hyperbolic and means only to convey the idea that henceforth restraint will be dropped. The Lord's incomparability will now be shown in blows of unprecedented severity...' (*UE,* 161).

Greenberg *UE,* 172 and Jacob *Exodus,* 187, suggest that one might expect this, the seventh plague, to be the last. However, in its place are this explanation, and a final triad of plagues, bringing the total up to ten, the next number signifying completeness after seven.

[102] The observation that YHWH wished to admonish or teach rather than destroy (cf. 9:15) goes back at least as far as Philo, who gives this response to the question of why YHWH used the gnat rather than more terrible creatures (*Mos.* I:110).

result of them? But he can, because YHWH 'hardens' him, or to be more precise, strengthens (וַיְחַזֵּק) his resolve against sending Israel. In other words, by stepping in to strengthen Pharaoh, YHWH is acting to maintain the ambiguity that he has set up. He has just given an explanation as to why the plagues have taken so long. Now he is taking steps to lengthen the procedure even more. The possibility is still held open for Pharaoh to refuse to acknowledge YHWH and to continue his policy of obstinacy in respect of the service of Israel.[103]

At this point, the reader may wish to object. Is the 'hardening' really designed in order to give Pharaoh a choice? Where it would appear that its purpose is to close down options, are we saying that it actually opens them up? This approach would appear to smell of special pleading, perhaps reading a 21st century individualistic (evangelical?) philosophy back into an ancient text.

There is some justice to these concerns. The 'hardening' is not portrayed as something that is meant to be beneficial to Pharaoh. We have noted that YHWH is not acting with humanitarian goals uppermost in his purposes, at least not in the short term. He is working upon Pharaoh, to increase the chances of his refusing to obey YHWH, and thus to suffer more plagues. We have noted that YHWH reverses the normal order of 'repentance' in removing the plagues before Pharaoh acts, and it is this removal that gives rise to Pharaoh's self-hardening. Thus, in one sense, YHWH's acts could be construed as being kind to be cruel.[104] Had he waited to remove the plagues until after Pharaoh had acted, then perhaps there would have been fewer plagues. However, this again may be importing views that are inappropriate. If we are to take 9:15 seriously, we need to assume that total destruction is something that YHWH not only could do, but would do.[105]

Moreover, the 'hardening' is not to be understood as YHWH allowing Pharaoh to be unaffected by the plagues, or to give him maximum flexibility in his choices. YHWH is working upon Pharaoh in order to influence his responses in a certain direction. Certain options are closed down, as the ambiguity in the encounters starts to break down.

---

[103] Interestingly, Durham suggests a version of this approach to explain why the divine hardening shifts from being simply implicit, to explicit after the collapse of the magi: 'It is difficult to imagine how Pharaoh could have held out so long, and inconceivable that he could hold out any longer, and so, at the ideal point, we are told plainly what has been implicit all along ... : YHWH has made obstinate the mind of Pharaoh' (122). Whatever one's view of the progression in the hardening, these plagues to come seem to be something different from the previous ones, something undeniable.

[104] One way of putting this might be as the dark side of 1Cor. 10:13. YHWH will not deal with someone beyond their capacity to refuse to accept it...

[105] Without bringing in other ANE texts, the OT provides examples of YHWH's ability and willingness to do such things. The supreme example would be the Flood (Gen. 6-8), although the total destruction of the Flood would never be repeated (Gen. 8:21-22).

The main point of the above analysis is to question whether the hardening would act as some kind of compulsion, or a means of removing the ambiguity that YHWH has allowed to arise. In other words, should we understand the divine hardening as removing Pharaoh's ability to obey YHWH, or simply reducing it? One could argue the former, suggesting that 9:13-19 is a paradigmatic watershed in the proceedings; before this Pharaoh had his own choices; after this, he becomes simply the means by which YHWH shows his power. However this appears unsatisfactory for a number of reasons.

First, this explanation, as one of the most detailed, comes after YHWH has hardened Pharaoh (9:12). If we take the context seriously and read it as an explanation *to Pharaoh* and not simply to the reader, then we have to ask what would be the point of giving this explanation to him at this point, rather than before. We have suggested that these explanations are given in order to promote a certain response, and it would be nonsensical to give it to one who was totally incapable of responding to it (because YHWH had prevented him from doing so). In particular the remonstration in 9:17 (cf. 10:3) would be very difficult to understand. We suggested that Moses would not have remonstrated with Pharaoh if he held out no hope of a response (8:25 [29]); would YHWH?[106]

Moreover, the plague is to be set upon Pharaoh's heart. This brings to mind the comments in 7:23 and 9:21 where 'not setting the heart upon something' is equated to a hard heart, and is opposed to fearing YHWH, respectively. Moreover, the reason for setting this plague upon Pharaoh's heart is so that he 'would know that there is none like me in all the earth'. This suggests that it is meant to teach Pharaoh something. In other words by being set upon Pharaoh's heart, the plague would appear to be opposing the hardening effect, rather than exacerbating it.[107]

Secondly, at the end of this plague, Pharaoh hardens himself once again. If he were incapable of doing anything else, because of the divine hardening, then this comment would be otiose.[108]

---

[106] This does leave the question of whether it is nonsensical for YHWH to 'explain' points to Pharaoh having just reduced the chance that he will listen. This is a fair point. Nevertheless, the model of Pharaoh's chances being reduced does not render the likes of 9:17 and 10:3 meaningless, as a removal of choice would arguably do.

[107] Cf. Noth, 80; Houtman, II 86; Schmidt, 418; contra Fretheim, 124.

[108] Against this one could suggest that the hardening only has effect at a certain point, the point of decision. However the comment that Pharaoh's heart 'remained' hard would seem to argue against this objection. Moreover it seems to be getting overly psychological. Pharaoh's 'hardness' is expressed in his attitude towards obeying YHWH and releasing Israel. The text only indicates any change of attitude by his agreements that Israel may go, and his reneging on such agreements.

This pattern of the hardening seems to fit with the model that we are developing of a progression of events, with a maintained, but increasingly-under-pressure ambiguity.

4.2.8.2 THE PLAGUE, MITIGATION AND AFTERMATH

Interestingly it is at this point that the only mitigation is offered to the Egyptians. Pharaoh has lost his magicians, and has been hardened by YHWH. Now he is offered the opportunity to respond to YHWH's word and save his livestock.[109]

This is also the first point where Pharaoh uses the language of contrition, after he has been 'hardened' by YHWH, and has seen the first 'incomparable' plague. His previous agreements to let Israel go had recognised YHWH (8:4 [8]), and broadly agreed the release after negotiations (8:24 [28]). However, in these cases, while Pharaoh is seemingly agreeing to a demand that he had initially rejected, the language is still that of a self-sufficient equal. Here Pharaoh starts with the confession that this time he has sinned (חָטָאתִי), followed by the comment that YHWH is righteous (הַצַּדִּיק) and that he and his people are wicked (הָרְשָׁעִים) (9:27-28).[110] The latter two terms tend to be used in contrast, often in terms of judgement between the two.[111] Finally he asks for intercession because the thunder is too much to bear. Pharaoh is expressing good theology here. He is acknowledging YHWH's superiority over him (both in terms of power and morality), and agreeing to a more practical response of acknowledgement by releasing the people and not delaying them any longer.

However, Moses is not convinced. He will do his part and intercede with YHWH so that the plague will stop. The reason for doing so is to gain a further acknowledgement from Pharaoh: that the land is YHWH's (9:29). He is not only in its midst (8:18 [22]) but it belongs to him. Moses is not convinced by Pharaoh's words. In 8:25 [29] his 'only' (רַק) showed that he was suspicious of Pharaoh after 8:4-11 [8-15]. Here he knows (יָדַע) that Pharaoh and his officials still do not fear YHWH, as YHWH knew (3:19)

---

[109] Once again, this suggests that Pharaoh would have been capable of doing so in some sense, unless the text is wishing to portray a god who only offers things that are unattainable.

More speculatively, we could suggest that this is a call and a chance for Pharaoh to do something useful. In terms of the division of labour theme, for once Pharaoh is being offered the chance to work with YHWH (in a similar sense to Moses), rather than being threatened with what will happen if he does not. This is in contrast to the previous responses where the magi had sought to copy the plagues, but had not done anything useful thereby, and arguably had increased the problems with the blood and the frogs.

[110] Cf. Schmidt, 414-45, on the peculiarities of the last three plagues, including admissions of guilt.

[111] E.g. Gen. 18:24-25; Ezek. 18:20, 24; Ps. 1; 37; Prov. 10-12.

that Pharaoh would not listen. The ambiguity that was coming under strain in 8:24-25 [28-29], is now almost broken for him, and he is letting Pharaoh know that he can see through his words. If Pharaoh will not follow YHWH's command with the result that he would save his livestock, why should anyone believe that he would follow YHWH's command with the result that he would lose his slaves?[112] In other words, Pharaoh may have correctly discerned the situation, and he may be using all the right language. However the acid test is whether he will respond correctly, and Moses *knows* that he will not.

Moses is correct. Yet once more Pharaoh sees the respite but chooses to use it as an opportunity to harden himself, rather than to acknowledge YHWH (9:34-35).

4.2.9 VIII: Locusts like None before (10:1-20)

Once again, we return to the area of previous study, to see how our discussion can be enhanced by reading 10:1-2 and the following plague in the light of what has gone before.

4.2.9.1 THE MESSAGE TO MOSES (VV1-2)

We have argued that 10:1-2 makes most sense as a response to Moses' statement in 9:30 in respect of Pharaoh's response and thus of the efficacy of the continual plagues in influencing Pharaoh. Looking back at the plagues narrative, although the focus has been on Pharaoh, we have seen Moses move from doubting the response of Pharaoh (8:25 [29]), to rejecting it (9:30). It is at this point that YHWH breaks his silence to Moses and engages with him, albeit briefly, in the manner of Ex. 3-7. Moses is to return to Pharaoh, and YHWH sets out his reasoning for this. It is not Moses that is being played with by Pharaoh (despite what Moses may think), but rather Pharaoh that is being played with by YHWH, and one day Moses will recount as much to his descendants.

4.2.9.2 THE MESSAGE TO PHARAOH (VV3-6)

In v3 the focus shifts back from Moses to Pharaoh. The announcement of the plague is preceded by YHWH's question of 'how long' Pharaoh will refuse to humble himself by releasing YHWH's people to serve him. Once again, YHWH confronts Pharaoh with the length of time that these encounters are taking. The explanations in 9:13-19 and 10:1-2 centre around this theme, and it forms a recurring theme in other plagues (7:16b

---

[112] In chapter 2 we linked Moses' certainty about Pharaoh's lack of 'fear of God' to the suggestion that he had not gathered in his livestock (9:21).

עַד־כֹּה ;9:2 and 17 עוֹדְךָ; 10:3 עַד־מָתַי).[113] Once again, the protest at
Pharaoh's recalcitrance leads to a plague.

This is the only speech to make explicit reference to another specific
plague.[114] The locusts will devour what the hail left (10:5b, 12b, 15a, cf.
9:31-32). Why is such a reference included here and nowhere else? One
way to explain it (and the strange 9:31-32), would be to refer to the idea of
the mitigation offered in the previous plague which, like this one, was a
unique occurrence (9:20-21). We noted that Pharaoh refuses to accept any
mitigation that involves following YHWH's word (9:30), and suggested
that this might well indicate the end of any such mitigation. This verse
could be read as eliminating any such mitigation. That which was saved
from the hail will now be wiped out. The pressure is raised that little bit
higher.[115]

4.2.9.3 RESPONSE BEFORE THE PLAGUE (VV7-11)

For the first and last time, Pharaoh responds positively to the mere threat of
a plague rather than to its execution. Up to this point the conditional nature
of YHWH's threats has not really been brought out. YHWH gives the
message to Moses (where there is one), and almost immediately afterwards
he speaks to Moses again to tell him to start the plague (7:18-19; 7:29-8:1
[8:4-5], 19-20 [23-24]; 9:5-6).[116] One has to assume in these cases that
Moses and Aaron presented the message to Pharaoh, and that Pharaoh
responded negatively. However, here we get to see a different picture. In
YHWH's initial words, the message for Moses takes the place of the
normal message for Moses to give to Pharaoh (vv1-2). When we do hear
the message, it is being given directly to Pharaoh (vv3-6). As a result, we

---

[113] 9:13-19 and 10:1-2 address the issue of why YHWH is letting matters carry on for so
long. However this is followed immediately in both cases with the same question being
asked of Pharaoh. We could also note the similar narratorial comments such as 9:34
with Pharaoh's refusal 'yet once more'.

[114] As previously discussed, one could add 9:15 to this, as referring to the cattle murrain.

[115] One could object that the mitigation that we identified in VII involved livestock over
and against crops, rather than different types of crops. However the narrative also
indicates that some crops were spared due to the time of year (9:31-32), and we could
see this as a form of mitigation, which did not require human intervention. Moreover,
locusts would not kill human slaves and livestock (9:20). However the last plague
would... (12:29).

[116] The previous plague of hail is different, because of the offered mitigation. The
normal pattern would run from v18 directly to v22. As with the earlier plagues, there is
no record of the giving of the message to Pharaoh, or his response. However there is a
record of the response of his servants.

also hear his response.[117] This response is due, in some part, to the reaction of the servants to Moses' message.

In a number of plagues, Pharaoh's court, be they servants or magicians, play a role in influencing Pharaoh's response, even where their acts are ultimately ignored by Pharaoh. Thus in these final plagues, Pharaoh's servants play a not dissimilar role to that of the magicians before them. There are a number of points of comparison between the magicians (in the serpent staff encounter, and plagues I, II, III, and VI) and the servants (in VII, VIII and X):

	Magicians	Servants
Reaction/response to Moses and Aaron	Copy plagues (serpent staff, I and II)[118]	Move livestock or ignore (VII – 9:20-21)
Confess 'defeat' to Pharaoh	'finger of (a) god' (III – 8:15 [19])	'Egypt is ruined' (VIII – 10:7)
Prostrate themselves before Moses (and Aaron)	Unable to stand (VI – 9:11)	Bow down before Moses (X – 11:8)

Here the servants confess defeat to Pharaoh, as the magicians did. However, whereas the magicians simply confess that this is 'the finger of god/a divine finger', the servants go further. [119]

First, they pick up YHWH's language of 'how long' (עַד־מָתַי 10:7, cf. 10:3), albeit changing the focus from Pharaoh to Moses, who is a 'snare' to Egypt. However, they also pick up the language of 'knowledge'. Does Pharaoh not yet know that Egypt is ruined? Here they resonate strongly with Moses' comments in 9:29-30 (10:7b תֵּדַע הֲטֶרֶם; 9:30 טֶרֶם כִּי יָדַעְתִּי). There, Pharaoh will acknowledge that the land is YHWH's but he does not yet fear YHWH. Here, Pharaoh is asked if he does not yet realise that the land is ruined. In light of the 'snare' reference, and their suggested remedy,

---

[117] This is not to suggest that we are to assume that there were similar discussions before the other plagues, which are unmentioned. The point is merely to counter any suggestion that there had been no *possibility* of Pharaoh responding like this in the past. The conditional nature of the threat is genuine.

[118] Albeit each time getting beaten (Aaron's staff eats theirs) or making things worse for Egypt (increasing the effect of I and II rather than diminishing them).

[119] Interestingly, the servants, who go further than the magi, are hardened when they come into focus in the story, whereas the magi are never hardened. On one level this is presumably because the magi are part of a prior, pre-9:12, stage of engagement with Pharaoh. Moreover the servants have just joined Pharaoh in receiving a choice of responses (9:20-21). Once again, this recalls the curious issue of more explanation and responses emerging *after* YHWH hardens Pharaoh (see above on VII).

they appear to be ascribing this ruination to YHWH through Moses. Thus where the magicians were correct, and yet potentially ambiguous as to the cause (אֱלֹהִים), the servants go beyond this. YHWH can ruin the land, and Pharaoh cannot stop him except by acquiescing to his demands. Thus the servants are acknowledging, in a practical sense at least, that 'the land is YHWH's'.

Secondly, they go beyond correct discernment and explicitly advocate a response, once again using YHWH's terminology (שַׁלַּח ... וְיַעַבְדֻנִי). Thus as well as acknowledging YHWH's power, they are urging Pharaoh to respond correctly, as YHWH has said.

Finally, unlike the magicians' confession, this one has a positive effect. Pharaoh's position 'softens' before the plague to the extent that he will recall Moses and Aaron to discuss this with them.

However, there is one new ambiguity in the servants' response to Pharaoh. In place of the normal עַם, they use הָאֲנָשִׁים. אֲנָשִׁים has the normal meaning of 'males', although it can often have the sense of 'humanity' or 'mortal', especially in comparison to God.[120] The servants could simply be using a different word, while still suggesting capitulation,[121] or they could be suggesting a cunning plan to allow Pharaoh to retain the people as a whole.[122] In line with the two possible meanings to שַׁלַּח אֶת־עַמִּי וְיַעַבְדֻנִי, the servants could be saying either 'release the people so that they can serve YHWH instead of you'; or 'why don't you let the *men* go and have their festival?'. As with the earlier discussion, it is impossible definitively to determine this ambiguity one way or the other.

However, whatever the servants intended, it is clear how Pharaoh understands it. Just as with his response in 8:21 [25], he chooses to understand this response as a method of keeping Israel under his control. He still maintains the picture of the three-day worship ceremony, and, as in 8:21 [25], he makes a clever response. Surely, if this is worship, only the adult men need to go? Why does Moses need the dependants as well?[123]

Moreover, as in 8:21-25 [24-29], while he uses ambiguity to his advantage, he indicates his dissatisfaction with Moses' position. As with Moses in 9:30, the doubts expressed with רַק (8:24 [28]) have moved on to certainty.[124] As Moses 'knows' that Pharaoh does not fear YHWH, so Pharaoh 'sees' that Moses is plotting evil. The ambiguity, and with it the chance for manoeuvre and response, is stretched to breaking point.

---

[120] N.P. Bratsiotis, אִישׁ, *TDOT* I 222-235. See examples 2a. and 2c. (223-224).

[121] Cf. Keil, 494.

[122] Cf. Ehrlich, 298; Jacob *Exodus*, 238.

[123] Cf. Childs, 159.

[124] Cf. Daube, 47. Ehrlich, 299 suggests that Pharaoh's 'this is what you seek' is ironic. By now he knows that the worship is only a ruse.

Whether or not Moses had a response to Pharaoh's words, as he did in 8:22-23 [26-27], he is driven out of Pharaoh's presence before he can speak. No 'deal' can be reached, at least not before the plague. Although Pharaoh rejects Moses' words, there is no hardening phrase here. Perhaps this is because it comes in the middle of a plague rather than at the end. Alternatively, there has already been a phrase at the beginning of the chapter (10:1).

4.2.9.4 RESPONSE AFTER THE PLAGUE (VV16-20)

As a result of the plague Pharaoh hurries to call Moses and Aaron to get the plague lifted (10:16-17). His language is similar to that used in 9:27-28, and even goes beyond it: he has sinned against them as well as YHWH (cf. 5:16). There is no reply from Moses to this offer, in contrast to previous ones (cf. 8:25 [29]; 9:30). At this point he simply goes out and intercedes, and YHWH ends the plague (10:18-19). Can we assume that Moses has given up responding to Pharaoh's 'offers', based on their total lack of execution to this point? In light of 9:27-28, Pharaoh's 'repentance' shows more desperation than resolve. As there, he seeks the removal of the plague before he will act appropriately. The only difference is that he begs Moses to ask YHWH to remove 'only this death' (10:17b). YHWH takes him at his word. This 'death' is the last one that is removed. After this, just as there is no mitigation among the Egyptians (after 9:20-21 and 9:30), so there is now no more intercession.[125] The plague of the firstborn looms closer. Thus it is no surprise when Pharaoh, once again, reneges on the deal, as YHWH hardens his heart (10:20).[126]

4.2.10 IX: Darkness that can be Felt (10:21-29)

As in the third and sixth plagues, there is no dialogue before the plague. Moses stretches his staff to the heavens and brings darkness upon the land, darkness that can be felt. However, once again, Goshen and the Israelites are exempted (10:21-23). Unlike in the two similar plagues, Pharaoh calls to Moses and Aaron, instead of the 'witness' being given by the magicians (10:24 cf. 8:15 [19]; 9:11). One might expect the servants to take their

---

[125] The plague of darkness does not invalidate this, as the darkness was always going to last for three days rather than an unlimited duration (10:22), even if Egypt were not aware of this. Cf. Propp, 339, who sees Pharaoh as unconsciously prophetic.

[126] This is not meant to indicate that 'YHWH hardened' should be understood as 'Pharaoh was not sincere', or 'Pharaoh hardened'. However, in light of 9:27-28 neither should it be understood as a truly repentant Pharaoh, desperately wanting to do the right thing, being prevented from doing so by YHWH's control. (For a reading along these lines see Gunn, 77ff.) We return to the image of YHWH strengthening Pharaoh, and the 'division of labour' theme.

place, as they have in the last two plagues. However, this is the last of the nine initial plagues, the last point of the 'negotiations' and thus it is fitting that Moses and Aaron are present.

It is also the point where the overall ambiguity collapses completely. The last condition from both sides are, at first viewing, ridiculous on any level. Pharaoh tells Moses that all the people may go, but that the animals must be left behind (10:24). Previously he has agreed that they may sacrifice to YHWH (זָבַח 8:4 [8]; 24 [28]). Now he agrees that they may עָבַד YHWH, but they cannot take any animals. If by עָבַד he means 'sacrifice', then this is nonsensical; what are they to sacrifice? If, however, he seems to be accepting a deeper meaning of 'serve', with the implication that they would not be coming back, then this condition is similar to that of retaining the dependants. They could not 'serve' YHWH, as they would have to return to serve Pharaoh because they could not survive in the wilderness without their livestock. [127]

Not to be outdone, Moses not only insists on some animals to sacrifice, which would be a reasonable demand. Instead, all the Israelite animals must be taken, as they will not know how to serve YHWH until they arrive (10:25-26). His words can even be read as indicating that Pharaoh must not only give up all the Israelites' animals, but also furnish them with sacrifices from his own herds, although this is not certain. [128] This counter-condition is as outrageous as Pharaoh's original condition. Even the alleged ignorance of Israel as to the necessary sacrifice would not necessitate taking all the animals.

---

[127] Alternatively, we could regard this as Pharaoh being more generous than in 10:10-11, as this time the dependants can go. (Thus Greenberg *UE*, 181, notes that as Pharaoh gets softer on the demands, Moses gets harder.) However this would presume that in the previous case neither the dependants nor the herds were allowed to go, whereas now at least one of them can go. Yet the herds are not discussed in 10:8-11. This view would fit with the general pattern that Pharaoh is being affected more and more by the plagues. However, instead of being more reasonable, it appears rather that Pharaoh is getting more desperate and losing his ability to answer cunningly. Thus in 10:8-11 Pharaoh had a reasonable point about the dependants not being necessary. However he has now given in to that demand. In its place he puts a demand that destroys any possible ambiguity. The only possible reason for retaining the herds is to prevent Israel from leaving permanently. The cunning ripostes of 'serve YHWH in the land' or 'only the men need to go, surely?' have now descended into an unsubtle final attempt to head off the exodus.

[128] This is without mentioning the point that Pharaoh's herds have already suffered under two plagues. However it would fit into the general outrageous nature of the final demands. Houtman, II 116, suggests that, if this is the case, then by supplying animals, Pharaoh would be serving and acknowledging YHWH in his own way. Thus Moses avoids Pharaoh's trap concerning the livestock, and sets his own in reply (cf. 9:20-21).

Thus the ambiguity, already stretched to breaking point at 9:30 and 10:10, has now collapsed. Both sides know that their conditions are outrageous, even in terms of a mere sacrifice. Both sides have set out their position in such a way that agreement by the other to that position would effectively concede defeat. Both have therefore effectively ruled out any further negotiation, any compromise position. This is the point at which the deeper issue of 'whom does Israel serve?' becomes unavoidable.[129]

YHWH then hardens Pharaoh's heart once more (10:27). Returning to our 'division of labour' model, we can now see how all three protagonists have effectively ended the process. Pharaoh has made an outrageous demand; as has Moses; and YHWH has strengthened Pharaoh's position. All that remains is for Pharaoh to set the seal on this impasse by threatening Moses with death if he ever appears before him again (10:28). For his part, Moses replies that if that is what Pharaoh wants, then he will never see him again (10:29).

Thus, at the end of the first triad, the ambiguity of the source of the plagues was removed; the magicians fail to replicate and confess that this is divine work. At the end of the second triad, the magicians bow out altogether and YHWH steps in and hardens Pharaoh, reducing any possibility of agreement. Here, at the end of the third triad, the negotiations break down altogether.[130] Yet, still, the people of Israel are servants of Pharaoh.[131] Something more is required.

4.2.11 X: Prelude to the Final Plague (11:1-10)[132]

We have seen possible shadows of the coming plague in the story so far.[133] Now it is spelled out.

---

[129] Thus Greenberg *UE*, 166, sees Pharaoh as willing to be 'godfearing', but within the bounds of his own sovereignty. Cf. Brueggemann 'Vassal', 40-41.

[130] Cf. Keil, 473.

[131] Durham, 144, notes that at this point one might ask 'has the process failed?'

[132] As with the discussion of the serpent staff episode in 7:8-13, we are not primarily interested in the form of this passage in comparison to the plagues narrative; or the question of whether it is part of that narrative or not. On this issue, see Bénédicte Lemmelijn, 'Setting and Function of Exod 11,1-10 in the Exodus Narrative', in Vervenne *Studies*: 443-460; and McCarthy 'Plagues', 144ff.

In its present form and context it appears to serve as an introduction to the final plague in a not totally dissimilar way to 7:14-17 and 9:13-18 introducing a new stage in the encounters.

[133] 4:21-23 (the message in 4:22-23 is set at this point); 9:7 (the 'lesser' death of cattle is not convincing for Pharaoh cf. Jacob *Exodus*, 180) and 9:30, 34 (mitigation not accepted).

4.2.11.1 MOSES (11:1-3)

The focus shifts back to Moses briefly, in a speech that makes two points.[134] First it returns to the language of 3:20 and 6:1, where Pharaoh *will* release the people, indeed he will drive them out (11:1). This part of the summary will be worked out as YHWH brings still (עוֹד) one more plague upon Egypt.

Secondly, it recapitulates YHWH's message in 3:21-22 (11:2-3).[135] This is now the time to put it into effect. As with the hardening, YHWH works through the responses of the people of Egypt, although in this case he 'softens' them, or gives them favour towards the Israelites. There is a great deal of discussion over the meaning of 3:21-22, specifically concerning the reason for Israel asking for and receiving the Egyptians' gold, silver and garments.[136] Thus it has been understood in light of Dt. 15:13 as Israel claiming the wages that they were due. However there is no mention of wages at any point in the narrative so this seems difficult.[137] Alternatively it has been seen as a trick. If 3:18 is understood as fooling Pharaoh into allowing a 'temporary' departure, then this could be Israel asking the Egyptians to 'loan' them items for this festival. In light of נָצַל it has also been understood as Israel despoiling Egypt as conquerors. At the point of the summary in 3:21-22 there is an ambiguity over what is meant. However by 11:1-3, as with the wider ambiguity over the demand to Pharaoh, this uncertainty is breaking down. After such a terrible plague that Pharaoh

---

[134] The position of 11:1-3 in this chapter has given rise to questions of placement. However these need not bother us unduly. 11:1-3 is not dissimilar to 10:1-2, as a message to Moses. With regard to its location, we can note that when Pharaoh speaks to Moses and Aaron during a plague (rather than before) there is always a comment about their departure, as Moses (with Aaron) goes out to pray to YHWH (8:8 [12], 26 [30]; 9:33; 10:18).

(There are also comments about Pharaoh leaving (7:23); and Moses and Aaron being driven out (10:10) but these are not the same context as Moses and Aaron leaving at the end of the plague. Nevertheless, the pattern remains that encounters during a plague always end with departure.)

Thus, if the darkness encounter ends at 10:29, it is anomalous, as there is no record of Moses departing. This suggests that 11:1-8 is set immediately after 10:29, and that 11:8 is the missing note of departure. Cf. Childs, 132-33, on this issue. (Also cf. Childs, 201 and Propp, 341-42, regarding the later encounter in 12:29ff in respect of this issue.)

[135] Cf. Durham, 147.

[136] In-depth discussion of this text is beyond our scope. For summaries of discussions see Houtman, I 382-386; Propp, 208; Childs, 175-178.

[137] In light of the strong similarity of Dt. 15:13 and Ex. 3:21 it may well be the case that one has influenced another, either the Dt. 15:13 passage being used within the exodus story, or the exodus story influencing the treatment of slaves, as is explicitly the case elsewhere. Cf. Daube, 79ff. However in the narrative itself one would still need to make sense of נָצַל and why the idea of wages is never mentioned.

drives them out (and compare 11:8), Egypt are unlikely to think that Israel would be returning (and thus are only borrowing the items).

4.2.11.2 PHARAOH (11:4-8)

Then the focus shifts back to Pharaoh (11:4-8). Moses gives Pharaoh his final message from YHWH, as the prelude to the final plague. This is the point at which the message of 4:22-23 was set; and here it is given, albeit in somewhat different terms. Three of the key themes of the plagues are then brought together.

First, there will be screams throughout Egypt, the like of which there has never been, nor will be again (11:6 cf. 9:18, 24; 10:6, 14). Secondly, this terrible unique happening will avoid the Israelites completely (11:7a). Thirdly, this is so that they[138] will acknowledge that YHWH distinguishes between Israel and Egypt, the final acknowledgement that Pharaoh is told that he will make (11:7b).

Finally Moses tells Pharaoh that his servants will come and bow before him and tell him to leave; and then he will go. Then he storms out (11:8).

4.2.11.3 ANOTHER CHANGE IN THE PLAGUES?

Thus we have the final plague set out. We can now look back at the progression in YHWH's acts throughout the encounters, and how it is linked to the responses of the human addressees.

The initial signs that YHWH gives Moses for Israel (4:1-9) were to deal with potential unbelief. Israel should believe the first sign, but if they do not there is another sign. If they *still* do not believe him there is a third sign.

7:16-17 introduces the initial triad of plagues, which the magicians can copy (excepting the last). These are more bothersome than catastrophic, and there is no indication that Goshen and the Israelites were exempted from them. At the end of this triad, the magicians realise that they are out of their depth, and confess 'this is the finger of god/a god'. This ends Pharaoh's ability to match the plagues (albeit not to get rid of them). However he still refuses to listen (8:14-15 [18-19]).

Therefore YHWH increases the power of the signs. The second triad begins with the plague of the swarm, the first plague that is 'heavy' (כָּבֵד), and the first to affect the land permanently (8:20 [24], cf. 9:3, 6 for the fifth). Goshen and Israel tend to be exempted. It finishes with the plague of boils where the magicians cannot even stand before Moses and Aaron. This time YHWH hardens Pharaoh.

---

[138] MT has תֵּדְעוּן, whereas LXX and Sam. Pent. have the singular that we might expect if this is addressed to Pharaoh (Propp, 309). The plural could refer to the court or the Egyptian people (cf. Ehrlich, 302). The next use of this formula certainly widens out to the Egyptians (14:4).

9:13-19 introduces the final triad where the plagues are incomparable in power, and YHWH explicitly hardens Pharaoh. Even though his servants remonstrate with him (10:7) and he appears to repent, Pharaoh refuses to release Israel.

Now, at the end we come to this, the last plague on a level of its own, with the differences and similarities to the previous ones.

Firstly, in contrast to all the preceding plagues, instead of sending the plague, YHWH himself is coming through Egypt.[139] As he comes, people will die. Thus far, although plagues have affected humans directly (9:11), and potentially killed servants (9:19), this is the first actually to seek human life, as well as animals.

Secondly, as with 7:16-17 and 9:13-19 there is no possibility of avoiding the plague. It is not conditional upon Pharaoh's lack of response; it *will* come. Unlike these previous cases, there is no comment on Pharaoh's previous lack of response as a reason for this.[140]

Thirdly, however, as with 9:19, there is a way to mitigate (or avoid) the plague, but this time it is only open to the Israelites, and this difference is held up to Pharaoh (11:7). Pharaoh is not told that Israel will need to act in order to avoid the tenth plague – for him this is no different from the other plagues that exempted Israel where they did not have to do anything. It is *Israel* that is told about the Passover regulations, because they are the ones that have to carry them out.[141] For Pharaoh, the exemption is to show that YHWH distinguishes Egypt and Israel.

Finally, unlike in most of YHWH's previous messages to Moses, there is no mention of Pharaoh being hard set against this.[142] Thus this last plague seems to be different from the last nine, as it *will* work.

Has YHWH now removed all restraint in his actions towards Egypt? The 'measure for measure' theme is stronger than, say, in 9:2-3. We have returned to 4:21-23 with the contrast of sons.[143]

---

[139] Cf. Keil, 473, 500.

[140] One could see the fact that Pharaoh had just permanently cut off negotiations as a good replacement for this. However, as with the changes in IV, there is not an identical pattern here.

[141] See 4.3.1.1 below on 12:1-27. However both explanations and the knowledge arising from it carry the same message: YHWH passed over the Israelites when he struck the Egyptians (11:7; 12:27). Thus for both Egypt and Israel it is the *exemption* that is as least as important as the occurrence of the plague itself.

[142] 4:21; 7:3; 7:14; 10:1.

[143] One could argue that there is still some restraint however, in light of 9:15. 4:22-23 has the unique use of 'son' rather than people here. YHWH could have said that because Pharaoh was holding onto YHWH's people, YHWH would kill Pharaoh's people. Instead, he restricts himself to killing only (!) the firstborn.

4.2.11.4 MOSES (11:9)

Then the focus shifts back again to Moses, now angry, presumably at Pharaoh's cessation of negotiations. YHWH tells him that Pharaoh will not listen, and that this will lead to YHWH's signs being made great.

The exact sense of the לְמַעַן here is debatable. One may assume that it is purposive as in 11:7b: 'Pharaoh will not listen so that …'. This would suggest that YHWH is ensuring that Pharaoh behaves thus in order to increase his wonders (as it is unlikely that Pharaoh's purpose would be to increase YHWH's wonders). However, there is no language of YHWH hardening as one might expect.

Alternatively, לְמַעַן can have a rhetorical consecutive function where an unintended result of an action is represented by לְמַעַן ironically as if it were intended.[144] The specific situation in which it is used is that of people acting against YHWH, which gives rise to YHWH's anger and/or action against them. Jer. 7:18; 32:29 are very similar to 11:9, as the message to a prophet.[145] This appears to fit the context of 11:9. If this is the case, 11:9 would have the sense of 'Pharaoh will not listen to you, but all he will do by that is increase my wonders'. Thus the 'change of perceptions' motif returns. Even here, perceptions are changed. Pharaoh's obstinacy will not lead to his glory, but rather to YHWH's.[146]

4.2.11.5 SUMMARY (11:10)

Finally, 11:10 returns us to the start of these sustained encounters in 7:6-7 as the second half of the inclusio. At this point the narrator summarises the plagues encounters in the words of 4:21 and 7:3, giving the final roles of all three groups: Moses and Aaron perform the signs, YHWH hardens Pharaoh's heart; Pharaoh does not send the people.[147]

We could also suggest that 7:6-7 and 11:10, as well as being an inclusio, are also in some sense parallel. They both end sections whose main focus is on whether Moses (Ex.3-7) and Pharaoh (Ex.7-11) respectively will do YHWH's will. Moses does (7:6); Pharaoh does not (11:10). The former passage shows the co-operative relationship between YHWH and Moses, the latter one the adversative equivalent between YHWH and Pharaoh.

---

[144] Joüon §169g; BDB p775 n.1.

[145] Cf. also Is. 30:1; 44:9; Jer. 27:10, 15; Hos. 8:4; Amos 2:7; Mic. 6:16; Ps. 51:6 [4].

[146] One does not need to see the imperfect as referring back to the plagues as a whole (contra Ehrlich, 302). As with the other speeches, YHWH is dealing with Moses' situation there and then.

[147] Childs, 161-62, notes the return to Ex. 7 so that the plagues are not seen as a failure.

4.3 Post Plagues Narrative – Passover, Red Sea[148] and Beyond (12:1-19:1)

4.3.1 12:1-13:22

4.3.1.1. 12:1-13

The main focus of this thesis is on the encounters between YHWH and Pharaoh in the plagues narrative. However, the overall encounter has not yet ended, and the exodus story has not reached its conclusion. Therefore it is appropriate to continue reading the text, albeit more briefly, concentrating on the explanations from YHWH.

Since 7:8, the text's focus has been almost entirely on Pharaoh, with a few brief exceptions. Now the focus shifts to Israel, where it will remain, barring a few brief returns to Pharaoh. We have already noted that this plague is different from the nine that precede it. As well as the differences in method, it is also distinguished by the fact that the details of the plague are woven about with instructions for the Israelites, both in respect of what they must do on this night, and also on how they will remember this night in the future.[149]

The fact that they themselves must act to prevent the plague from striking them is a departure from the previous plagues.[150] Formerly, Pharaoh or the reader has been told that the plague will exempt Goshen or the Israelites, but there has been no indication that Israel has had to do anything to accomplish this.

However, for these plagues, the recipient of YHWH's messages was Pharaoh. Thus for him the exemptions served as a sign from YHWH to demonstrate his power, character and so forth, designed to cause Pharaoh to respond appropriately and acknowledge him. Israel were simply the object of YHWH's protection and Pharaoh's stubbornness. Thus their responses were not at issue. Now the focus is on Israel, and they in their turn are called upon to respond appropriately to this event; they themselves are drawn into the plan of YHWH. As with Moses, and in contrast to Pharaoh, they are called to work with YHWH, albeit in avoiding the plague rather than bringing it about.

---

[148] The question of the location of a 'Re[e]d Sea' is not relevant here (see 1.4.1). We will retain the name 'Red Sea' for ease of use (although the literal Hebrew is 'sea of reeds'). Cf. Johnstone *Exodus OTG*, 203.

[149] The details of the Passover celebration, while extensively written upon, are not of central importance for our thesis. Therefore they will be passed over with a few comments.

[150] However, the fact that YHWH is willing to risk the lives of Israelites in this way supports the point that the first three plagues may well not have exempted Israel.

If we are seeing Ex. 3-7 as focussing on Moses and whether he will obey YHWH, with Ex. 7-11 asking the same question of Pharaoh, then we could see Ex. 12-15 (and afterwards) as Israel's equivalent. They are the recipients of the messages here.[151] Moses, as in Ex. 7-11, is the voice of YHWH; and Pharaoh returns to his role in Ex. 3-7 as one who is a problem or a rival focus for Moses (here Israel) instead of YHWH. Once again we need to guard against any firm drawing of boundaries. The story is more complicated and subtle than that. However, it appears that the overall focus may have shifted.

Israel, as well as Moses and Pharaoh, have been shown as those who will, or will not respond appropriately to YHWH's messages. Moses is initially more concerned with the response of Israel to his message rather than that of Pharaoh (3:13-4:9), although Israel's initial reaction is positive (4:31). However, when Pharaoh's reaction to Moses' message is to bring greater hardship upon them, the people turn against Moses and call on YHWH to judge him (5:20-21).[152] Ironically in doing so they are rejecting the one sent by YHWH. Although they speak of YHWH judging, their overall comments show that their focus is elsewhere. Moses and Aaron are to be judged because they have made Pharaoh so angry with Israel that he will kill them. For Israel, Pharaoh is the one who has the power, and their concern and focus is on him, rather than YHWH whom they call upon. Religious language is at odds with actual perception. Another irony is that YHWH *will* judge (6:6; 7:4; 12:12), but he will do so in the context of bringing Israel out of Egypt (the word that Moses has brought), and the objects of the judgement will be Egypt and its gods. When Moses returns with a renewed message from YHWH (6:2-8), Israel do not listen to him because of their lack of spirit and the oppressive work (6:9). Pharaoh's tactics appear to be working (5:8-9) and Israel are not interested in responding to Moses. After this point Israel disappear from the narrative, except as the object of Pharaoh and YHWH's encounters, and as those exempted by YHWH from the later more terrible plagues. It is at this point that they reappear as active participants in the narrative. Rather than simply being exempted by YHWH with no actions required from them, in this final plague they are required to act.[153]

---

[151] Thus Cassuto, 134, sees 11:9-10 as marking the change from Moses and Aaron being sent to Pharaoh, to them being sent to Israel.

[152] Cf. Gen. 31:50-54; Jdg. 11:27 for other uses of 'may YHWH judge'.

[153] Thus as with Moses (Ex. 3-7) and Pharaoh (Ex. 7-11) the basic point of YHWH's messages is the same: to change people's focus onto him, rather than themselves or another (Pharaoh in the case of Israel), so that they respond appropriately. Fokkelman contrasts 2:23-25 and 4:31 with 6:9, 12 and 14:30-31 with the double theme of 'God's concern with Israel versus the belief or unbelief of the people'. J. P. Fokkelman, "Exodus", in *The Literary Guide to the Bible*, Robert Alter and Frank Kermode eds.

Having described to Israel what they need to do (12:1-11), YHWH then sets out what he will do (12:12-13).[154] As mentioned in 11:4, YHWH himself will pass through the land of Egypt, and strike down every firstborn of Egypt. This is followed by the strange phrase that YHWH will 'perform judgements on all the gods of Egypt'. This phrase is repeated verbatim at Num. 33:4, detailing the itinerary of the Israelites from Egypt. Once again there it is linked to YHWH's smiting of the firstborn.

This is the only reference to YHWH acting against any other gods in these encounters, and it does not refer to what YHWH might have done to some gods (in the previous plagues), but what he will do to all of them. Thus this does not lend credence to the view that each plague targets a different god.[155] It is difficult to know exactly how to understand this obscure reference. Propp notes various suggestions about idols, but his suggestion is that YHWH will humiliate the Egyptian gods by having his way with them.[156] Noth suggests that we can no longer tell whether anything more specific than powerlessness is meant.[157] Hoffmeier notes that it was the responsibility of the Pharaoh to maintain *Maat*, or cosmic order, established by the creator god, and the plagues show his inability to do this. 'Rather it is Yahweh and his agents, Moses and Aaron, who overcome in the cosmic struggle, demonstrating who really controls the forces of nature.'[158] This idea of general humiliation and powerlessness seems to make good sense and to be about as far as we can go. To go further and allocate specific plagues as polemics against specific gods is problematic, not least because the vast number and overlapping responsibilities of the gods and goddesses in the Egyptian pantheon means that practically *any* plague, sign or natural occurrence could be understood as related to one (or indeed several) gods.

There are two other references to 'judgements' in this text (6:6; 7:4). Both of these refer to YHWH bringing Israel out of Egypt 'with great judgements', rather than the normal 'with a mighty hand (and an outstretched arm)'. Both are linked to YHWH bringing Israel out of Egypt, and one result of both is that Israel (6:7) and Egypt (7:5) will 'know that I am YHWH'.

(Cambridge, Mass.: Belknap Press of Harvard University Press, 1987): 56-65, 59. Cf. Wilson, 31-32 on 6:9 and 'Pharaoh did not listen'.

[154] The division of labour motif reappears.

[155] Propp, 400. Cf. Greenberg *UE,* 200-201. Kitchen, 253, suggests a couple of points but sees any attempt to go further as unjustified subjectivity. Cf. Zevit, 21.

[156] Cf. Houtman, II 184, suggesting that the death of the firstborn will show that the Egyptian gods are powerless. (He also cites other possibilities.) Cf. Sarna *Exodus,* 56, and Sarna *EE,* 78, on Jer. 46:25.

[157] Noth, 96.

[158] Hoffmeier *Israel,* 153; cf. 150-153.

Israel's later response picks up the thrust of 12:12: 'Who is like you amongst the gods, O YHWH?' (15:11). They, it seems, are acknowledging that 'I am YHWH'. There is no obvious Egyptian response along these lines (cf. 8:6 [10]; contrast Dan. 3:32-33 [4:1-2], 4:31-34 [34-37] and 6:26-28 [25-27] where the foreign rulers do acknowledge YHWH). There has been Pharaoh's response in 9:27, but 9:30 speaks against this. However the focus here is on Israel, not Egypt. They are the ones who hear 12:12, and the ones whom one would expect to respond.

However, in this judgement, Israel are to be spared, if they put the blood on the doors. The blood will be a sign for them (וְהָיָה הַדָּם לָכֶם לְאֹת) and, when he sees this blood, YHWH will pass over them.[159] After a number of signs for Egypt (10:2; 8:19 [23] etc), this is a sign for Israel. However, what sort of a sign is it?

One way to understand it is that the blood is a sign that the Israelites will set out for *YHWH*, so that he can see the sign and knows which houses not to enter (12:23). This could be understood as a sign of protection for Israel, in the manner of the sign of Cain in Gen. 4:15 (וַיָּשֶׂם יְהוָה לְקַיִן אוֹת) where the sign is 'for Cain' (לְקַיִן), and yet it is aimed at those who see Cain, rather than a sign for Cain himself.[160] The similar theme of protection might also argue for a connection,[161] although the complete phrase in Gen. 4 is לְ שִׂים, which is slightly different from הָיָה לְ, or simply לְ. However, if this is the meaning, it is an odd way to express it. One might expect YHWH to say 'this will be a sign for *me*...'.[162] Moreover, there are a number of other places in the Old Testament, which have the phrase לְךָ/לָכֶם אוֹת/אֹת, where the sign is for the addressee, not the addresser. In our passage, there is 3:12 (וְזֶה-לְּךָ הָאוֹת), where 'you' refers to Moses. In this case the sign is clearly not for YHWH, but for Moses, as a demonstration that YHWH is with him.[163] There is also 13:9 (וְהָיָה לְךָ לְאוֹת) where the unleavened bread is a sign for Israel, not YHWH.[164]

If we follow this argument, the blood on the doors is the sign for Israel, in the same way that the unleavened bread will be a sign for them (13:9),

---

[159] The debate over the exact meaning of פֶּסַח need not concern us here (see Childs, 183; Houtman, II 183; Propp, 401, for details). The main point is that YHWH will exempt Israel from the plague.

[160] Cf. Durham, 152, 'i.e., for the Israelites' benefit'.

[161] Cf. Helfmeyer, 'אוֹת' *TDOT* I, 176.

[162] Houtman, II 184-85, notes that Beer suggests reading לִי here.

[163] This will apply however one understands the content of the sign.

[164] Cf. also 1Sam. 2:34; Is. 37:30/2Kgs. 19:29; Is. 38:7/2Kgs. 20:9; Jer. 44:29. All of these have 'this will be a sign to you' and refer to a sign from YHWH for the people, rather than for YHWH. Cf. also Jos. 4:6; 1Sam. 10:7; Is. 7:14 (Lk. 2:12) for similar ideas. There is no place where 'this is a sign for you' refers to a sign which those signified by 'you' are to give to YHWH.

and the dedication of the firstborn will be a sign for them (13:16).[165] When
the focus was on Egypt there were signs for them (although the focus drew
back to show Israel watching the signs), just as Moses was given signs
when the focus was on him.[166] Now that the focus is on Israel, the activity
and the signs are for them.

One objection to this argument would be to point to 12:13b. The sign is
followed by the comment that YHWH will see the blood (the sign) and pass
over them. Does this not indicate that the sign is for YHWH? However, in
answer to this we can point to the distinction noted above. For this plague,
Israel have to respond appropriately to avoid it, unlike all the others. The
blood is a sign for them, a sign into which they enter, just as they enter into
the work with YHWH in this last plague. When YHWH sees their response
in putting up the blood, he will respond to their response by passing over
their dwelling.[167] This picks up a theme that has been running throughout
the plagues narrative. YHWH responds to people's responses, for good or
ill. (Compare 4:22-23; 7:16-17; 9:2-3; 9:13-19 where the focus is on
Pharaoh. This is the equivalent for Israel.)[168]

---

[165] The way that the Passover regulations combine the first night's ritual and the ongoing
celebration would bring this out, that this was to be a sign for Israel through all
generations (whether or not Israel continued to daub the blood on the doors in
subsequent Passovers). On this point Jacob *Exodus*, 312, notes that in all the Mechilta
discussions on where exactly the blood was to be placed, the assumption was that it was
a sign for Israel, not YHWH.

[166] The pattern is not exact, as 4:1-9 are signs for Israel. However, arguably they are
primarily in the context of reassuring Moses, and thus, in one sense, signs for him.
There is no suggestion in 4:31 that the people raise any of the issues that Moses
anticipates in 3:13-4:9.

[167] This is to make no claims with regard to putative earlier forms of the text/story, or
possible ancient apotropaic rituals. (For discussion and bibliography on this see, for
example, Houtman, II 153-66 and Propp, 434-44.) The point here is that the text, as it
stands, suggests that the sign is for Israel, rather than for YHWH. Thus, if it did arise
from an earlier version that had signs for YHWH, it has been changed to give a different
theological meaning.

[168] One could also compare 12:12-13 with 9:18-21. Israel can act to avoid this death as
Egypt could act to mitigate the hail. Obedience to YHWH brings life; disobedience
death. Cf. Propp, 'The blood, then, may be less for Yahweh's benefit than for Israel's,
who are thereby entitled to participate in their own redemption (Kaufmann 1942-56:
2.430). The paschal command is, as it were, both a test of Israel's obedience and a
demonstration of piety's rewards' (401). (However, Propp does go on to question
whether this is overly homiletical. He sees the idea of the blindly killing Destroyer
aspect of YHWH, repelled by magic, as a better tale.) Childs notes that the blood is a
sign both to Israel and to YHWH that no harm will befall the family (198). However he
does not expand this comment. Houtman, II 185, cites interpretations (Rashi; TgPsJ etc)
where YHWH regards Israel as having done their duty. It is slightly unfortunate that he
concludes simply that 'obviously the blood is not a sign (אוֹת, see 3:12) for the Israelites

4.3.1.2 12:14-28

The instructions are then joined to those of the feast of unleavened bread, together with a repetition of the instructions for the blood on the doorposts (12:14-23). This is to be a permanent ritual, and when one's son asks why this is done, the answer is that YHWH passed over the houses of Israel when he smote Egypt (12:24-27a). In this explanation, the focus is not on the fact that YHWH smote Egypt (in freeing Israel). Instead the point is that in smiting Egypt, he passed over Israel. Thus, just as for Pharaoh (11:7; cf. 8:18-19 [22-23]), YHWH is not to be known or acknowledged primarily as one who brings plagues, but as one who exempts from the plagues.

The people then acknowledge what has been said to them. They bow and worship (12:27b). Thus they have returned to the state of 4:31 from that of 5:21 and 6:9. Moreover, in an echo of 7:6, they go and do exactly what YHWH commanded Moses and Aaron (12:28). They respond correctly.

4.3.1.3 12:29-36

Israel having done their part, YHWH then does his, and smites all the firstborn in Egypt (12:29). Then Pharaoh and the Egyptians respond as the focus returns to them briefly.[169] This terrible plague, which leaves no house untouched, causes a scream unlike any ever heard in Egypt.

Pharaoh calls to Moses and Aaron and tells them to get out of the midst of his people, to go and serve YHWH, with the sons of Israel and all their herds, as they have said (12:30-32). The phrase 'as you said' is repeated twice, with regard to the manner of service (12:31) and the entirety of those leaving (12:32). Thus Pharaoh capitulates, and Moses' full demands are met. Pharaoh's final word to them is the request to 'bless me too'. After the previous 'repentance' (9:27-28; 10:16) it is not clear what to make of this. However the picture is of the mighty Pharaoh who did not know YHWH (5:2), and who subsequently fought his corner, now a broken man before YHWH's representatives.[170]

---

but for YHWH; adequately translating the Hebrew requires a 'free' rendering.' It is not obvious, at least to me, why this should be the case.

[169] Cf. Childs, 201.

[170] Cf. Brueggemann 'Vassal', 39; Noth, 98. Propp, 411 and Houtman, II 142, 199, see Pharaoh's words differently. Here 'as you said' is a reference back to the three-day journey, thus holding Moses to his original request, and avoiding total capitulation. However, the three day journey was last mentioned in 8:23 [27] (and even there Pharaoh is suspicious). After this Moses' words have been concerning who exactly would go (10:9, 25-26). Moreover, the second 'as you said' in v32 clearly refers to Moses' later words about the cattle, suggesting that the first 'as you said' in v31 does also. This would fit in with the general mood of panic suggested in vv33-36. Propp suggests that 14:5 argues against a full capitulation. However, to anticipate our discussion, 14:5 refers to a change of perception, rather than surprise.

This is followed immediately by the comment וַתֶּחֱזַק מִצְרַיִם ... (12:33). However, unlike the refrain to every other plague, this is not someone (here Egypt) 'strengthening' their hearts. Instead they are 'strongly urging/pressing' the people to leave before all Egypt is destroyed (cf. 6:1; 11:1).[171] To conclude this series of fulfilments, YHWH gives Israel favour in Egypt's eyes so that they can plunder the Egyptians (12:34-36; cf. 3:21-22; 11:2-3). At this point, any possible ambiguity regarding the Israelites borrowing the items has collapsed. In light of 12:33 it is unlikely that any Egyptian thinks that Israel are simply going out and will return shortly with the items. It is a sign of utter defeat.[172]

4.3.1.4 12:37-51

Finally, Pharaoh and the Egyptians having expelled them, the Israelites leave, a great number, together with their dependants, and very great herds (כָּבֵד מְאֹד),[173] as Moses had said.

4.3.1.5 13:1-16

In the middle of the exodus, there are two messages regarding further signs for Israel. To the already mentioned passover (12:13, 25-27), there is added the unleavened bread feast (13:3-10) and the dedication of the firstborn (13:1-2, 11-16). Both sections end in the same way, with an explanation, and a sign. The explanation is set on the lips of the parent, in response to a son's question as to why this is done. In both cases it is because of what YHWH did when he brought them out of Egypt. (13:8, 14b-15), as was the case with the Passover (12:27).

These three, together with the message in 10:2, form the 'explanations' given to Israel. However, as with all the other 'explanations', this is not merely a matter of abstract knowledge. The parents are enjoined to act; to pass this knowledge down, in the form of various rituals throughout all generations, and to explain their purpose to their children. In the latter three cases, this is described as a sign for Israel (13:9, 16; 12:13), thus something that is to point them to something else.[174] In contrast in 10:2 they are to recount how YHWH dealt with the Egyptians, where the signs were for them, not Israel; although Israel are to take note of this.

---

[171] Contrast this with 9:7 where Pharaoh 'sends...' but only to see if the Israelite cattle survived.

[172] Childs, 201.

[173] Cf. 9:3, 18, 24; 10:14. Cf. also Gen. 13:1-2.

[174] This theme is picked up strongly in Deuteronomy, especially the Shema (6:4-9) which is to be impressed upon one's children (Dt. 6:7), and bound as a sign upon the hand and the eyes (Dt. 6:8, cf. Ex. 13:16). The reason for obedience to the laws is to be explained to the son, as in Ex. 12-13, as based on YHWH's deeds in the exodus (Dt. 6:20-25).

Of particular interest is 13:15. 13:8 is a summary 'what YHWH did for me'; whereas 13:14-15 expands this. Pharaoh was stubborn (הִקְשָׁה cf. 1Kgs. 12:4; Job 9:4) about releasing Israel and YHWH killed all the firstborn. This is similar to the message in 4:22-23 to Pharaoh.

4.3.2 14:1-15:21

Our main focus is on the plagues narrative, rather than the Red Sea encounter. However, this chapter is the last encounter between YHWH and Pharaoh and it shares a number of similarities with the plagues encounters.

Ex. 14 could be seen as a microcosmic version of the encounters with Pharaoh in Ex. 3-14, with a number of similar features. There is the initial message from YHWH to Moses (vv1-4 cf. 3:18-20; 4:21-23 etc); the focus upon Pharaoh (vv5-9 cf. 5:1-18); the despair of the people and turn against Moses (vv10-14 cf. 5:21; 6:9); and YHWH's message to Moses (vv15-18 cf. 6:1/7:14 etc), which precedes his act (vv19-30 cf. plagues), leading to Israel's correct response (14:31-15:21 cf. 12:27-28). However there is one major difference. There is no interaction between YHWH and Pharaoh, no message, no demanded acknowledgement. Egypt will 'know that I am YHWH' in the events of the sea crossing, but, as in 7:5, this is told to Moses, not directly to the Egyptians themselves.

4.3.2.1 14:1-4

The Israelites are marching forth, but YHWH tells Moses to turn around and camp near the sea. This will convince Pharaoh that they are lost, and YHWH will harden his heart to pursue them. Thus YHWH will be glorified or glorify himself (וְאִכָּבְדָה) through Pharaoh and his army.

This speech recalls the earlier messages to Moses before the plagues. As then, it is given to him specifically. The same patterns are there, with the same division of labour. Moses is to act, prompting Pharaoh to act in a certain way, which will be influenced by YHWH. Finally YHWH will act. In terms of the purpose of this speech, it is less clear than in earlier speeches that Moses is in need of reassurance in order to get him to obey. One could note that turning around and heading back towards Egypt might not have been his preferred option, especially if the people were less than steady in resolve (cf. 14:11-12; 13:17). However, this is speculative.

As with the request for a 'three day journey' in 3:18, 5:3 etc, this move could be seen as a means of inducing Pharaoh to do something that he might not otherwise do.

Finally, the purpose of this, as with the plagues, is stated in terms of YHWH. He will receive כָּבוֹד over/through Pharaoh and his host, although at this stage the method is not specified. As with 3:18-20, it is a summary. Moreover, Egypt will acknowledge that 'I am YHWH' (cf. 7:5). Thus the one who did not know YHWH and thus would not listen to him (5:2) will become the reason for the whole of Egypt's acknowledgement of YHWH.

4.3.2.2 14:5-9

For the last time, the focus returns to Pharaoh, as we hear his words to his servants, and his plan. The news that is brought to Pharaoh is not identical to that of 14:3. He is told that the people have fled. However, the overall impression is the same. Those who were hurried out, on their terms, with Egypt's gold and goods (12:31-35), are now seen as fleeing from Egypt. Thus, as with the image of confusion in v3, they appear vulnerable. Pharaoh and his servants change their perception of Israel, leading to a change in their actions: pressure to leave (12:29-33) becomes pursuit.[175]

What exactly, should we make of וַיֵּהָפֵךְ? Pharaoh's heart was 'changed' or 'turned' (together with his servants). Is this the outworking of YHWH's comment that he will 'harden' Pharaoh, in v4? In favour of this is the previous usage of הָפַךְ in the narrative, where YHWH is always the ultimate cause (7:15, 17, 20; 10:19). However, there are some problems with this.

First, the verb is passive. In light of the above uses of הָפַךְ, and the move towards identifying YHWH with the hardening in the later plagues, one might expect YHWH as subject, as in 10:19. This is not insurmountable, as the earlier uses are all Niph'al in form, yet the cause is clearly YHWH. However, the other uses of the Niph'al of הָפַךְ, where the object is the heart, suggest otherwise. The closest parallel is probably Hos. 11:8 where YHWH's heart is 'changed' (נֶהְפַּךְ עָלַי לִבִּי) concerning what he will do to Israel. This strongly suggests a change from within, not due to influence from another. The only other use is in Lam. 1:20, where Zion's 'heart' is distressed over her actions (נֶהְפַּךְ לִבִּי בְּקִרְבִּי). Once again there is no suggestion of outside interference.[176]

Secondly there is the contrast of meaning between 'change' and 'harden'. Previously, Pharaoh had been hard set against Israel leaving, and his heart had remained strong, unresponsive or stubborn, or had been strengthened or made unresponsive. By 14:5, this resistance to Israel's departure had been smashed, as he had released them (12:31-33). Thus, here it requires a change of heart, as the verb הָפַךְ indicates. Pharaoh is responsive to the news, and he changes his mind, both the exact opposite of

---

[175] Thus Childs notes that in the integrated story, we see YHWH's plan to produce an effect on Pharaoh, followed by Pharaoh's plan as he regrets sending them. These contrasting perspectives differ in their view of Israel also (224).

[176] This is without considering the possibility that the Niph'al here is reflexive.

the various meanings of hardening. Thus if YHWH says that he will 'strengthen' (חָזַק), we would not expect him to 'change' (הָפַךְ).[177]

There is no message from YHWH to Pharaoh in 14:5-9, but there does not need to be. YHWH's demand has been fulfilled. It is the message as given to Pharaoh (presumably by his servants) that causes a reaction (compare 8:15 [19]; 10:7).

This change of mind is expressed in their words 'What have we done? We have released Israel from our service' (כִּי־שִׁלַּחְנוּ אֶת־יִשְׂרָאֵל מֵעָבְדֵנוּ). The demand of YHWH has been fulfilled, and Israel have been released to serve him (cf. 5:1). However, Egypt realise the consequences of this action. If Israel are serving YHWH, they will no longer be serving Egypt. As with the last plague, any ambiguity is now completely dead. If they want Israel back, they will have to pit their might against them (and their God). This is what they do (vv6-7).

At this point, the narrator informs us that YHWH hardened Pharaoh's heart, with a return to the refrain of 9:12; 10:20, 27. Pharaoh, having decided to pursue Israel, is strengthened in his resolve by YHWH, as he said that he would in v4. Thus, this is a better fit for v4 than the וַיֵּהָפֵךְ in v5. The same verb is used, and the action is the opposite of that in v5 (strengthening as opposed to changing). As with the plague narrative, YHWH sets up a situation that could provoke different responses, knowing which way Pharaoh will react. He then strengthens his resolve once it has changed. Thus Pharaoh sets out, and comes upon the Israelites, and the focus shifts for the last time.

4.3.2.3 14:10-18

The Israelites are true to form. When things are going well, they follow Moses (4:31; 12:27-28). However, when Pharaoh exercises his power, their focus shifts sharply to him. As in 5:21, they invoke YHWH's name, but their focus is on the power of Pharaoh, and they remonstrate with YHWH's servant for bringing down Pharaoh's might upon them. It is Pharaoh that Israel fear, and him that they choose to serve (v12). Cassuto notes the parallelism with Egypt's question in v5.[178]

v5 (Egypt)	מַה־זֹּאת עָשִׂינוּ כִּי־שִׁלַּחְנוּ אֶת־יִשְׂרָאֵל מֵעָבְדֵנוּ
vv11-12 (Israel)	מַה־זֹּאת עָשִׂיתָ לָּנוּ ... חֲדַל מִמֶּנּוּ וְנַעַבְדָה אֶת־מִצְרָיִם

Both change their view on what has happened, and prefer the previous situation of Israel's service, even though it was bringing death to both of them (5:21; 12:29-33). Israel even use the words that are to become the basis of their remembrance of the events: 'what have you done to us *to*

---

[177] Thus to say with Propp, '14:8 (P) reminds us, this is all Yahweh's doing' (484) is slightly too simple.

[178] Cassuto, 164; cf. Childs, 225-26.

bring us out of Egypt (לְהוֹצִיאָנוּ מִמִּצְרַיִם)?' (cf. Ex. 20:2). However here they are a term of reproach directed at Moses.

Moses reassures the people, telling them that their focus should be on YHWH (rather than on Pharaoh). They are not to fear, but rather to stand still and see the salvation that YHWH will bring; for YHWH will fight for them (vv13-14).

Finally YHWH speaks to Moses and gives an expansion of his comments in 14:4. Once again, Moses is to act, YHWH will strengthen the Egyptians, the Egyptians will act, and YHWH will be glorified in them, in such a way that YHWH is acknowledged.[179] Here the link is made clear. Egypt will 'know that I am YHWH' in his glorification (בְּהִכָּבְדִי cf. 7:17 בְּזֹאת, 7:5 בִּנְטֹתִי) over Pharaoh and his might.[180] As with the previous plagues, if they will not learn through one method, YHWH will use another, more terrible one, until the end is achieved. Furthermore, as in the previous plagues, there is a double emphasis here. The knowledge is linked to Pharaoh being totally and comprehensively beaten by YHWH. It is not linked specifically to either the sending of a plague, or removal/exemption of it. The sea encounter has, in one sense, the final exemption of Israel, as they walk across dry land while Egypt is swallowed by the water (cf. 11:7). However, it is more positive than an exemption, as the 'miraculous' element is the fact that they can walk through a body of water without being drowned, whereas the Egyptians suffer the fate one might expect from charging into it. However, the 'knowledge' is not phrased in terms of Israel's exemption, but of YHWH's glorification over Pharaoh. As with previous cases, the centrality of the knowledge focuses on YHWH, although the method of this acknowledgement is wrapped up with the salvation of Israel.

To put it another way, Jacob notes that כָּבֵד in the sense of 'glorify' re YHWH is not used in the 10 plagues, but only here where the king with his military might seeks to halt YHWH's efforts.[181] One could say that Pharaoh's כָּבֵד (stubbornness, albeit חָזַק is used here), leads to YHWH's כָּבֵד (glorification).[182] Once again, Pharaoh's seeming power and pre-eminence only leads to YHWH's power and pre-eminence (cf. 8:6 [10]; 11:9). Israel's perception of events will be irrevocably changed. YHWH will fight, and they will never see the Egyptians again (14:11-14).

4.3.2.4 14:19-15:21

The events unfold as YHWH has said. Israel are saved from Egypt, and Egypt are destroyed in the sea. As a result, Israel once again respond

---

[179] Cassuto, 166, notes the parallel of 'I' in v17 and 'you' in v16.

[180] Childs, 226, notes that Pharaoh's plan now becomes absorbed within YHWH's plan.

[181] Jacob *Exodus*, 392.

[182] Cf. Sarna *Exodus*, 71.

correctly (cf. 4:31; 12:26-27). They saw Egypt dead; they saw the great hand with which YHWH acted in Egypt, and they fear YHWH, and they believe in him and his servant Moses (14:30-31). Pharaoh is gone. YHWH is the one to fear and trust. Moses is his servant, through whom he speaks. This is demonstrated in a great hymn of praise focussing on YHWH (15:1-21), on which note the initial exodus story ends.

4.3.3 *15:22-18:12 and 19:1ff*

4.3.3.1 15:22-16:36

However, this great hymn of praise is not the last word on Israel's response. The subsequent passages speak of Israel, when faced with problems, adopting the same approach as in 14:10. There is no Pharaoh for them to focus on anymore, but there is a lack of water (15:22-27) or food (16:1-36). In the first case they simply grumble, and are told that if they listen to YHWH, he will not bring upon them the diseases of Egypt. In the next story, they explicitly wish to have been killed by YHWH in Egypt, where they had much to eat (16:2-3). YHWH tells Moses that he will provide bread from heaven, and Moses responds to the people with the words: 'in the evening you will know (וִידַעְתֶּם) that YHWH brought you out of the land of Egypt, and in the morning you will see the glory (כְּבוֹד) of YHWH in his hearing (בִּשְׁמְעוֹ – cf. 14:18; 7:17 etc) your murmurings against him' (16:6-7).

The language of the plagues narrative returns, but this time it is the Israelites who are at fault. While they speak of dying at YHWH's hand and thus use pious language, their focus is on their present situation and their displeasure with Moses and Aaron, YHWH's representatives (cf. 5:21; 4:1, contrast 14:31). In reality, they are told, they are not rejecting Moses, but rejecting YHWH. Thus they will know that YHWH brought them out and will see his glory; a combination of יָדַע and כָּבֵד that recalls 14:18, except here the knowledge comes through succour rather than defeat. YHWH is not known in his glorification over Israel (cf. 14:18, 7:17), but in his listening to them (16:6-7).[183]

---

[183] In some ways it is not so different from Ex. 14. There YHWH is known as he acts in a way that will save Israel (as noted above, the miraculous point is that Israel can walk through the sea on dry land). Moreover, in the story of the quail in Num. 11, YHWH's actions include both succour, and striking; in a way not wholly dissimilar from the plagues narrative with the sending, exempting and removing of the plagues.

4.3.3.2 18:1-12

Finally, in this section, we can note the first third party reaction to the news of the exodus.[184] Jethro returns to the scene, hears of what YHWH has done for Israel's sake. His reaction is: 'now I know that YHWH is greater than all gods, because of what he did to those who acted arrogantly against them' (18:11),[185] and he sacrifices to YHWH. Thus, as in 15:11, YHWH's incomparability is shown by his treatment of his people, and Jethro acknowledges it.

4.3.3.3 19:1FF

The impact of the events of the exodus is not limited to their immediate aftermath. The recollection of these events, and the responses that this recollection is meant to engender, become a constant theme throughout the rest of Israel's scriptures. However, we will end this chapter with the people about to receive the law and covenant at Sinai. The next chapter will deal with the understanding of the exodus events among the people, as the people of YHWH. How is one meant to respond to the knowledge of what YHWH has done? What does YHWH require of them?

---

[184] One could point to 15:15-16. However this is, presumably, a reaction set in the future, when the Israelites will encounter these nations.

[185] The Hebrew is כִּי בַדָּבָר אֲשֶׁר זָדוּ עֲלֵיהֶם. For the Qal use of זִיד cf. Jer. 50:29 (Babylon); Neh. 9:10 (Egypt), 16, 29 (Israel). Israel, it seems, can be like Egypt.

Chapter 5

Giving Glory to YHWH – Exodus, the Wider OT and 1 Samuel 4-7

5.1 Introduction

An important part of our interpretation of the plagues narratives has been the realisation that Pharaoh and Moses are called upon to respond to YHWH correctly. However we have also noted that Israel are also called upon to respond to YHWH, both in the messages in the plagues narratives (10:2; 12:1-27; 13:3-10, 11-16), and in the beginnings of the wilderness wanderings (15:22-18:27).[1] In chapter 1 we noted the large number of uses of the exodus tradition in the Old Testament. Therefore it seems appropriate in our final chapter to widen the focus once more and consider whether the points made in the previous chapters might apply to some of the wider uses of the exodus. There are already discussions of these wider uses.[2] As in the preceding chapters, our discussion will focus on the way that these wider references are used, and what function(s) they appear to have in their contexts, before moving to our investigation of 1Sam. 4-7.[3] We can summarise briefly some of the main categories of use.[4]

The predominant use of the tradition concerns obedience to YHWH, his laws, and his covenant. It is held up as a reason to obey YHWH's laws and covenant,[5] especially in the context of faithfulness to YHWH as against idolatry or serving other gods.[6] 'I am YHWH who brought you out... therefore...'. As well as this being the response expected of Israel to what YHWH has done for them, it is connected to their status as the holy, loved people of YHWH.[7] It is also the reason for observances.[8]

---

[1] The relevant discussions were at the end of chapters 3 and 4 respectively.

[2] For example, Daube, cf. 12, on exodus pre-eminence; also Zakovitch, and chapter 10 of Fishbane *Text* (The "Exodus" Motif/The Paradigm of Historical Renewal, 121-140).

[3] The reasons for selecting 1Sam. 4-7 for study in this chapter were set out in the Introduction.

[4] This is not an attempt to categorise all uses. Moreover, some of those mentioned may fit into more than one category.

[5] Lev. 18:3; 19:36; 22:33; 26:13; Num. 15:40-41; Dt. 6:21-24; 8:14; 11:1-4.

[6] Dt. 6:12; 13:5-6 [4-5], 11 [10]; 29:1 [2], 15 [16]; 1Sam. 12:8; Jos. 24.

[7] Ex. 19:4-6; 29:46; Lev. 11:45; Dt. 4:19-20; 34-35; 7:7-8.

[8] Firstborn - Num. 3:13; 8:17; Passover/Mazzot – Ex. 23:15; 34:18; Dt. 16:1-6; Firstfruits – Dt. 26:5-10; Booths – Lev. 23:42-43.

However, Israel often fell short of this response, and the exodus is often held up as a reproach to them. They forsook or disobeyed YHWH, even though he was the one who brought them out of slavery in Egypt to the promised land.[9] As well as a reproach, this contrast in Israel's behaviour to that of YHWH is often raised as an explanation of why a calamity is coming upon Israel: 'it is *because* you/they forsook YHWH who brought you/them out... that this is happening'; or as a warning of what will happen if they do behave in such a way.[10] In some cases, the punishment for such offences is a return to Egypt.[11] In spite of this, YHWH's actions in the exodus also form an important element of intercessions for the sins of the people.[12]

There are a number of different contexts and genres where the references to the exodus appear: in narrative, recapitulations of history, legal codes, prophets, and psalms.[13] This obedience to YHWH, or lack of it, is the one category of use that spans all of these genres. It is expressed primarily by upholding the covenant that he made with them after he had brought them out of Egypt (cf. 19:4; 20:2).

The exodus is also cited as a reason to focus upon YHWH. Israel are to have confidence in him rather than focussing on the problems ahead.[14] The exodus is also used to show YHWH's incomparability and by extension the incomparability both of Israel, inasmuch as he brought them out, and of Moses as the one sent by YHWH.[15] It is also a reason for praising YHWH.[16] It is something witnessed by non-Israelites which often influences their opinion of YHWH and hence their actions towards Israel.[17]

It is held up as an event which signifies Israel's origin 'ever since the time...',[18] and as a precedent or comparative to later events.[19] The sicknesses of Egypt in particular are remembered either for good or ill.[20]

---

[9] Ex. 32:7-8 (cf. 1Kgs. 12:28); Dt. 9:7, 12; Jdg. 2:1-2; 1Sam. 8:8; 10:18-19; 2Kgs. 17:35-41; Ps. 78:12-17, 44-58; 81:11-12 [10-11]; 106:7, 21; Jer. 2:6; 7:22-26; 11:4-8; Mic. 6:3-4.

[10] Num. 14:11-12, 20-23; Dt. 29:23-28 [24-29]; Jdg. 2:11-15; 6:8-10, 13; 10:11-13; 1Kgs. 9:9; 2Kgs. 17:7; 21:15; 2Chr. 7:22; Jer. 34:13-17; Ezek. 20; Hos. 12:14-15 [13-14]; Amos 2:10-16; 3:1-2.

[11] Dt. 28:68; Hos. 8:13; 9:3; 11:5 (correction).

[12] Ex. 32:11-12 (cf. Dt. 9:26-28); Num. 14:13-20; 1Kgs. 8:51-53; Ps. 80:9 [8]; Jer. 32:20-21; Dan. 9:15.

[13] It does not appear in wisdom literature (outside of the Psalms), but this is unsurprising.

[14] Dt. 1:30; 7:18-19; 20:1.

[15] Dt. 4:34; 2Sam. 7:23 (albeit possibly corrupt); 1Kgs. 8:51-53; Dt. 34:11.

[16] Ps. 114:1; 135:8-9; 136:10.

[17] Ex. 18:1, 8-12; Num. 23:22; 24:8; Jos. 2:10-11; 9:9; 1Sam. 4:8; 6:6. Contrast these with 5:2.

[18] Jdg. 19:30; 2Sam. 7:6; 1Kgs. 6:1; 8:16, 21; 2Chr. 6:5.

Finally it is given as the reason for decent treatment of slaves, although only Hebrew slaves, as Levenson points out.[21] The reason is either the remembrance that they had been slaves in Egypt from where YHWH had freed them, or the remembrance that they themselves were slaves of YHWH.[22]

Thus the prime use of the exodus tradition elsewhere in the Old Testament concerns the response of Israel to YHWH's acts in the exodus. As with YHWH's words and acts within the exodus itself, that response should be the acknowledgement of these acts. Thus arguably the vast majority of the uses of the exodus tradition in the wider Old Testament are in the context of seeking a certain response to it, mainly from Israel, and mainly with regard to their relationship with YHWH.[23] This response is to come from a focus on YHWH and his actions on behalf of Israel in the exodus.

Thus far our comments on the plagues narratives would seem to be of relevance to the wider use of the tradition as well. However the above analysis is necessarily very brief. To permit a more detailed comparison, we will restrict ourselves to one specific place in the Old Testament that uses the exodus narrative: the story of the capture and return of the Ark in 1Sam. 4-7. The reasons for selecting 1Sam. 4-7 out of all of the different uses of the exodus tradition in the Old Testament were set out in chapter 1. As the focus of this chapter is on 1 Samuel and not on Exodus, for this chapter alone references to Exodus will contain the 'Ex.' prefix, while references to 1 Samuel will appear without prefix (e.g. 4:8; 6:6).

5.2 Some Previous Studies and their Views on YHWH

Before setting out our approach, and as a contrast to it, there follows a brief summary of various monographs on the subject which have been written for various purposes. As with our hardening taxonomy, in the brief space here we are unable to do justice to these scholars' arguments, and can only summarise their position. Their arguments on points relevant to our investigation will be picked up as appropriate. Also, as with the hardening,

---

[19] Is. 10:24, 26; 11:15-16; 52:4; Jer. 16:14; 23:7; 31:32; Hos. 2:17 [15]; Mic. 7:15. cf. Bernhard W. Anderson 'Exodus typology in Second Isaiah' in *Israel's Prophetic Heritage: Essays in Honor of James Muilenburg*, ed. Bernhard W. Anderson and Walter Harrison (London: SCM, 1962): 177f.

[20] Good for Israel Ex. 15:26; Dt. 7:15; Bad for Israel – Dt. 28:27, 60; Amos 4:10.

[21] Levenson, *Hebrew Bible*, 136, 152.

[22] Ex. 22:20 [21]; 23:9; Lev. 19:34; 25:37-38, 42, 55; Dt. 5:15; 15:15; 16:12; 24:22; Jer. 34:13 (cf. Dt. 10:19; 24:17-18 on similar points re treatment of the sojourner, widow and orphan).

[23] This is arguably even the case where judgement is declared, if we understand at least part of the function of such a declaration to be an attempt to get the hearers to respond.

the questions that one asks of a text may be influential in the understanding which one gets from it. For example, the way one understands the theology of the passage will depend upon what one includes within the passage.[24]

In his monograph *The Succession to the Throne of David*[25] Leonard Rost put forward the thesis that the majority of 1Sam. 4-6 together with 2Sam. 6 contained an independent 'ark narrative' which was the ἱερός λόγος, or cult legend, of the shrine of the ark in Jerusalem.[26]

> Our narrator sees Yahweh as the fearful destroyer. The ark is regarded as a symbol of his presence, but he is not restricted to it. ... If we can come to any conclusion now, it is that the narrator himself sees God's activity everywhere, and would like everyone to share the same point of view.[27]

After Rost, several monographs and commentaries have linked discussion of the scope of this 'ark narrative' to its purpose and theological position, two of which are those by Campbell,[28] and Miller and Roberts.[29]

Anthony Campbell gives a useful summary of the position pre- and post-Rost, and generally follows Rost's division of the text.[30] He asks three questions of the text: what sort of text it is (genre); what sort of a situation it would have arisen from (setting); and why it was composed (intention).[31] The most relevant question for us is the last one. Instead of an ἱερός λόγος, he sees the narrative as concerning YHWH breaking from his people. Chapters 4-6 give no obvious reason for this. [32] YHWH then releases himself from Philistia and makes his own way back to Israel where he chooses to return eventually to the people. Even when he does return it has

---

[24] Anthony F. Campbell, 'Yahweh and the Ark: A Case Study in Narrative', *JBL* 98/1 (1979): 31-43, henceforth 'Campbell 'Yahweh'', 33, 43.

[25] Leonard Rost, *The Succession to the Throne of David,* trans. Michael D. Rutter and David M. Gunn, HTIBS I (Sheffield: Almond Press, 1982), henceforth 'Rost'.

[26] Rost, 26.

[27] Rost, 33.

[28] Anthony F. Campbell, *The Ark Narrative (1Sam 4-6; 2Sam 6) A Form-Critical and Traditio-historical study,* SBLDS 16 (Missoula: Scholars' Press University of Montana, 1975), henceforth 'Campbell *Ark*'.

[29] Patrick D. Miller Jr. and J. J. M. Roberts, *The Hand of the Lord: A Reassessment of the 'Ark Narrative' of 1 Samuel,* JHNES (Baltimore: Johns Hopkins University Press, 1977), henceforth 'Miller and Roberts'.

[30] Campbell *Ark*, chapter 1. This was followed up by Campbell 'Yahweh', summarising his work and that of Miller and Roberts (see below), and Franz Schicklberger: *Die Ladeerzählungen des ersten Samuel-Buches, Eine literaturwissenschaftliche und theologiegeschichtliche Untersuchung*, Forschung zur Bibel 7 (Würzburg: Echter, 1973). Here Campbell is mainly concerned with the scope of the narrative and the effect on its purpose.

[31] Campbell *Ark*, 2.

[32] Campbell *Ark*, 197-200.

dubious consequences for Israel (Jeconiah's descendants and Uzzah).[33] Thus Campbell summarises the theology of the ark narrative:

> This is the message that is constantly reiterated from 1Sam. 5:2 through 2Sam. 6:11. Yahweh cannot be controlled, Yahweh cannot be manipulated, Yahweh retains for himself complete freedom of initiative.[34]

Following Campbell, Miller and Roberts retain the link between scope and purpose, asking: 'where does it begin, where does it end, and what secondary accretions must be removed from the narrative?'[35] However, they reassess the scope of the ark narrative. They argue for the inclusion of part of 1Sam. 2 (vv12-17, 22-25, 27-36) in the earlier narrative, and for the exclusion of 2Sam. 6. They discuss Campbell but argue that the question of YHWH's sovereignty does not answer the Israelite question in 4:3.[36] Thus they argue that the mention of the Elides requires an earlier section to introduce them. Moreover, the defeat of Israel would be inexplicable without the judgement motif found in 1Sam. 2.[37] They also see the end of the narrative as 1Sam. 7:1 where YHWH is victorious, the ark is returned and a new 'keeper' of the ark is sanctified.[38] They see the motif of the 'hand' of YHWH as binding together the passage,[39] and debate the appropriateness of the title 'ark narrative':

> The subject of the narrative is Yahweh, and not the ark. The issue is not what happens to the ark, but what Yahweh is doing among his people. Not the ark, but Yahweh's power and purpose is what the story is about.[40]

The story, concerned with these events, acts as an early example of theodicy.[41]

---

[33] Campbell *Ark*, 205-206.

[34] Campbell *Ark*, 206.

[35] Miller and Roberts, 18.

[36] Miller and Roberts, 7-9. They also discuss Schicklberger. They reject his central premise of 1Sam. 4 representing an old 'catastrophe narrative' as there are no other examples of such a narrative. Moreover they are unconvinced by his reason for such a narrative being written; to tell people what happened without any explanation whatever (p2-6).

[37] Miller and Roberts, 18-22. They note the arguments of John Willis, 'An Anti-Elide Narrative Tradition from a Prophetic Circle at the Ramah Sanctuary' *JBL* 90 (1971): 288-308, henceforth 'Willis', that 1Sam. 1-7 was originally a unity. Although disagreeing with him on the originality of the Samuel narratives, they do accept his arguments that 1Sam. 4-6 needs an introduction, and that 2Sam. 6 was not part of the original.

[38] Miller and Roberts, 23-27.

[39] Miller and Roberts, 48-49.

[40] Miller and Roberts, 60.

[41] Miller and Roberts, 73.

In a move away from seeking the original 'ark narrative', Lyle Eslinger has carried out a close reading of 1Sam. 1-12.[42] His main focus in on the crisis of YHWH's kingship in 1Sam. 8-12. However, he argues that one needs to read 1Sam. 1-7 before this in order to understand the whole.[43] His reading of the actions of YHWH in 4-6 is almost wholly negative. YHWH is in total control, and does as he pleases (1Sam. 3:18). However his actions are inappropriately large (such as killing so many Israelites simply to exterminate two sinful priests); and at times inexplicable (killing men for simply looking at the ark, who were celebrating its return).[44] The 'new exodus' in chapter 6 is a disappointment, and by the end of the story (with its concealed criticism of YHWH's actions) we feel empathy with Israel and move away from YHWH.[45] Therefore chapters 4-6 are necessary to undermine the otherwise powerful rhetoric of Samuel and YHWH in chps 8-12.[46]

> The presentation of chs. 4-6 neutralises the theological-political prejudices of the reader (that God rightly and justly rules Israel) so that the reader can approach the request [for a king] in chp 8 with an appreciation of its legitimacy.[47]

This negative picture mirrors the exodus:

> Yahweh's personal motivation is the same as his purpose in Exodus. He sends minor plagues at first, not wanting to crush 'the opposition' straightaway so that he can give an extended demonstration of his power. God's ultimate aim, of course, is to spread his reputation...[48]

As part of his investigation into narrative art and poetry in Samuel, Fokkelman splits 1Sam. 1-12 into three acts. He argues that 1Sam. 4 should be taken with 1Sam.1-3 rather than as part of 4-6, seeing 1-4 as a scheme of announcement and fulfilment.[49] 1Sam. 5-7 is then taken together as the

---

[42] Lyle M. Eslinger, *Kingship of God in Crisis. A close reading of 1Sam 1-12*, BLS (Sheffield: Almond Press, 1985), henceforth 'Eslinger *KGC*'.

[43] Eslinger *KGC*, 40, 45. Contrast this with Hermann Timm, 'Die Ladeerzählung (1. Sam. 4-6; 2. Sam. 6) und das Kerygma des deuteronomistischen Geschichtswerks', *EvT* 26 (1966): 509-26, henceforth 'Timm'. Timm also sees chps 4-7 as important for understanding chps 8-12, but sees them as part of the deuteronomic understanding of the exile (518).

[44] Eslinger *KGC*, 194, 217, where he sees concealed criticism of YHWH's actions in the text cf. also 185, 193-94, 196, 199, 201, 220, 223, 225 etc. This is very much a key theme for Eslinger.

[45] Eslinger *KGC*, 199-201.

[46] Eslinger *KGC*, 217, 200.

[47] Eslinger *KGC*, 201.

[48] Eslinger *KGC*, 198.

[49] J.P. Fokkelman, *Vow and Desire (1Sam. 1-12)*. Vol IV of *Narrative Art and Poetry in the Books of Samuel: a full interpretation based on stylistic and structural analyses*,

'second act'. As Fokkelman's rich discussion primarily concerns the narrative form, it is quite difficult to summarise any overall theological position. His comments will be of use primarily on individual sections.

Finally, most recently, Brueggemann has discussed the passage in the light of what the church does when it stands before a biblical text.[50] He takes a very different position from Eslinger, emphasising the vulnerability of YHWH. His focus is on the glory (*kābôd*) of YHWH. YHWH loses it (and therefore his power) because of the sin of Israel and is beaten by Dagon as a result.[51] The defeat in chapter 4 is therefore a real defeat of YHWH. He then regains his *kābôd* from Dagon after a short while, and exercises it on the Philistines by his 'alien work' of tumours[52]:

> YHWH – the one who is "heavy", whose glory has departed and whose glory is now again visible in the world of the Philistines – is a glory-seeking, glory-getting God.[53]

This story, far from showing a similar God to that of the exodus, actually deconstructs it:

> The Philistines expect – perhaps require – YHWH to be engaged in the conventional contest of domination. This present narrative undermines an overreading of the Exodus narrative, as though Israelite faith is always, everywhere, about winning. Exodus is not so readily replicated, and this God is now seen to be more nuanced ... and more vulnerable ... than a flat Exodus doxology might allow. The narrative, so to say, deconstructs the God of the exodus.[54]

5.3 Our Approach to the 'Ark Narrative'

Our general approach to the 1 Samuel narrative is the same as the approach to the Exodus plagues narrative. We will be looking at the story in its context within 1 Samuel, trying to find any explanations for YHWH's acts in this narrative. The point is accepted that this may well have been an older story, although not all agree on the exact boundaries of the story. The point is also accepted that if, say, 4:1-7:1 were read on their own, or perhaps together with 2Sam. 6, this might give a different understanding or

---

SSN, trans. L Waaning-Wardle (Assen: Van Gorcum, 1993), henceforth 'Fokkelman *Narrative*', 194.

[50] Walter Brueggemann, *Ichabod Towards Home – The journey of God's glory* (Grand Rapids: Eerdmans, 2002), henceforth 'Brueggemann *Ichabod*'.

[51] Brueggemann *Ichabod*, 14.

[52] Brueggemann *Ichabod*, 34, 56.

[53] Brueggemann *Ichabod*, 39.

[54] Brueggemann *Ichabod*, 11.

understandings.[55] However the story as we have it forms part of the wider story in 1 Samuel, and it will be read as such. Thus we will be drawing on passages in 1Sam. 2-3 and 7 in our understanding of YHWH's acts here.

However there is one key difference in respect of our approach. In the plagues narrative there were an abundance of explanations both in speeches from YHWH and in information from the narrator in respect of why events occurred as they did. Thus these formed, to a greater or lesser extent, the basis of our understanding of the passage. However, in this narrative, there are no speeches from YHWH at all, only deeds. Moreover the narrator is dispassionate and laconic in the information given.[56] Thus we appear to be looking at different narrative conventions here. How, therefore, are we to approach the text?

There are a number of speeches by groups of people in our text (Israelites elders; Philistine leaders; members of a city; priests and diviners; Israelite villagers; Samuel). In many of these, the speakers comment on what is happening and consider what they need to do. The longest speech, containing the fullest 'explanation' of events is that of the Philistine priests in 6:2-9, where they set out how the ark is to be returned and appear to come up with an answer that works. The fact that foreign priests can come up with the clearest explanation, and one which accords with good Yahwistic theology, suggests that, although divine speeches may be lacking, these human speeches may provide a way to understand the story.

Thus our approach will be to consider four speeches. Each of these occurs at an important moment, and arguably sums up a section of the story by considering what response the speakers should make to what is perceived to be an act or acts of YHWH. When the response is made, it leads to a consequence, either positive or negative, which offers us a means of judging the appropriateness or otherwise of the response. In each case we can also suggest a cause for YHWH's actions, related to the prior behaviour of these humans, although this is often implicit rather than explicit.

The speeches and corresponding sections are:

---

[55] See, for example, Campbell's reading of the defeat in 1Sam. 4 without the preceding 1Sam. 2-3. However note also his comments in Campbell 'Yahweh', 43 on the need for interpretation at every level including the most identifiable level of the present context.
[56] Cf. Hans Wilhelm Herzberg, *1 & II Samuel – A commentary* (London: SCM, 1960), henceforth 'Herzberg' 49; Campbell *Ark*, 64-65, 209; Kellenberger *Hardening*, 3; Brueggemann *Ichabod*, 29.

Speech	Context	Section
4:3	Israel's response to their initial defeat	4:1-22
5:7-8	Philistines' response to Dagon's fall and initial plagues	5:1-10
6:2-9	Philistines' response to continuing plagues	5:11-6:18
7:3	Israel's response to the return of the ark	6:19-7:14

This division also brings out the 'story within a story' nature of the narrative with the move from Israel to Philistia and back, following the ark.

One caveat should be made before we begin. It has already been noted that, as with the plagues narrative, this is a 'difficult' story to understand in relation to YHWH's acts. This difficulty needs to be respected if one is to appreciate the story and any possible 'messages' that it carries. Inevitably any one framework is unlikely to do full justice to these complexities. Some of the exact boundaries between sections are fluid and the above delineations are unavoidably abstract (for example, should the third and fourth sections change at 6:13 or 6:18?). Some of the above sections contain multiple speeches or acts.[57] 4:12-22 will hardly be covered in our discussion, but it forms part of the story in spelling out the consequences of Israel's defeat and the grief that it causes.

Moreover the fact that there are few if any explicit statements as to why something has happened does create a sense of puzzlement amongst the grief (cf. 4:3, 20-21; 5:11-12; 6:20).[58] In the plagues narrative we saw that there were possible ambiguities in understanding for those involved. Here the lack of explicit explanation extends that ambiguity to the reader as well as the participants. Nevertheless, as with the plagues narrative, this discussion will suggest that some conclusions and understanding can be reached. Whether it succeeds or not may be determined afterwards by the reader going back and rereading the story in 1Sam. 4-7 again without the 'scaffolding' provided here. Illumination of the story (or lack of it) must be the real test of success.

5.3.1 First Speech: 4:3 (4:1-22) 'Why has YHWH struck us...?'

וַיָּבֹא הָעָם אֶל־הַמַּחֲנֶה וַיֹּאמְרוּ זִקְנֵי יִשְׂרָאֵל לָמָּה נְגָפָנוּ יְהוָה הַיּוֹם לִפְנֵי
פְלִשְׁתִּים נִקְחָה אֵלֵינוּ מִשִּׁלֹה אֶת־אֲרוֹן בְּרִית יְהוָה וְיָבֹא בְקִרְבֵּנוּ
וְיֹשִׁעֵנוּ מִכַּף אֹיְבֵינוּ

The people came to the camp, and the elders of Israel said 'Why has YHWH struck us today before the Philistines? Let us fetch from Shiloh to us the ark of the

---

[57] For example 5:1-5 and 6:18-7:1.

[58] On this see especially Brueggemann *Ichabod* (e.g. 112-113 concerning his differences with Childs, even if our discussion may end up in a more Childs-like position).

covenant of YHWH so that it/he may come into our midst and may save us from the hand of our enemies.'

5.3.1.1 SITUATION

The Philistines have just fought with Israel, beaten them, and killed four thousand men (4:2). The elders are gathering to consider what has happened, and what they can do about it. The actual description of the battle simply says that the Israelites were struck (Niph'al נגף); but the elders have no doubts that this was YHWH smiting them (Qal נגף).

5.3.1.2 RESPONSE

Their response is to bring the ark of the covenant from Shiloh into the camp so that it or YHWH will save them from their enemies. The Hebrew could refer either to the ark or to YHWH saving Israel. On the face of it, this seems to be a strange response. If YHWH has struck them, why would bringing his ark along help matters?[59] Their view is not simply that YHWH is absent, or has not helped them, but that he himself has struck them.[60] Eslinger suggests that in bringing the ark, they are reminding YHWH of his covenantal obligations: he should be smiting *Philistines*, not Israelites![61]

While the detailed reasons for their action may not be clear, the overall purpose is clear: 'bring the ark, and that will sort out the problem'. There is no consultation with YHWH, and no attempt to ponder the real implications of the question 'why...' that they have asked (compare Jos. 9:14 and contrast Jos. 7:6-9; 1Sam. 14:36-46). They simply want a way to deal with the issue.[62]

---

[59] Fokkelman *Narrative*, 201. He disagrees with Eslinger's view (*KGC* 163-66) that the narrator agrees with the elders' attribution of the cause of the defeat, saying rather that it is 'highly unlikely that the narrator backs their position'. Eslinger argues that the Niph'al 'defeated before' suggests that it is not ultimately the Philistines' responsibility, and that refusal to accept the judgement of 4:3 is a refusal to accept the narrative conventions. Cf. Miller and Roberts, 33; A. Stirrup "'Why has Yahweh defeated us today before the Philistines?' The question of the ark narrative", *TynBul* 51.1 (2000): 81-103, henceforth 'Stirrup', 88. At this point we do not need to make a firm decision. The question here is how the elders react to what they *perceive* to be the case.

[60] Cf. Robert P. Gordon, *I & II Samuel A commentary*, LBI (Grand Rapids: Zondervan, 1986), henceforth 'Gordon', 93. Campbell *Ark*, 66, 148, emphasises this point, arguing against any diminution in its gravity (e.g. by saying 'YHWH *allowed* them to be defeated').

[61] Eslinger *KGC*, 165-66.

[62] The deeper implications of the question are not always seen to be relevant. Fokkelman *Narrative*, 201, sees the question as a vehicle of indignation. P. Kyle McCarter Jr., *1 Samuel*, AB (New York: Doubleday, 1980), henceforth 'McCarter', 105, understands it as a rhetorical question seeing YHWH as agent due to the lack of the ark. Campbell *Ark*, 149, sees this as the mentality of Num. 14:42 and Dt. 1:42. Noting that no answer is

Thus they bring the ark, along with Hophni and Phinehas from Shiloh (v4). When it reaches the camp, their roar of joy alerts the Philistines that something is happening, and we hear their reaction (v5-9). 'Gods have come into the camp' they say, seeming to equate the presence of the ark with the gods of Israel who presumably were absent in the previous engagement.[63] This spells potential doom for the Philistines. 'Who can save us from the hand of these mighty gods?' they ask, knowing that these are not just any gods, but the gods who beat the mighty Egyptians (4:8 cf. Ex. 15:14).[64] The only thing that they can do is fight as hard as they can. Their reaction is similar to the Israelites: the mere presence of the ark will have its effect and swing the conflict away from them.

5.3.1.3 CONSEQUENCE

The two sides engage once more. Everything in 1Sam. 4 to this point has suggested that Israel should now win, as both sides have acknowledged. The ark of the god who beat the Egyptians is here, the god who also has a covenant with Israel.

However, against such expectations we get a series of short statements that the Philistines fought; struck Israel (נגף as before); each man fled to his tent;[65] the smiting was great; thirty thousand Israelite footsoldiers fell; the ark of God was taken; and the two sons of Eli, Hophni and Phinehas were killed. This unexpected catalogue of disasters jars the reader. This defeat is far worse than the previous one. Something has gone terribly wrong, but there is no explicit word as to what or why. This is followed by a passage which recounts the despair that falls upon Israel as a whole (vv12-13, contrast vv13b-14 with vv5-6), and upon the Elide family in particular (vv14-22). The fact that things have gone so very wrong suggests that something was wrong with the preceding speeches and actions. But what was it?

The Philistines' formulation is crude (it is a god, not gods; he did not smite Egypt in the wilderness; and it is uncertain whether he has physically come into the camp). However their question 'who can deliver us?' and the

---

given and that the ark is simply brought, he says that 'to draw moralising consequences from this procedure is exegetically out of place' (66). However it seems odd that, if we take the force of 'YHWH striking' seriously, as Campbell rightly argues, we should not expect someone to try to answer the question in 4:3. Even if, as Eslinger *KGC*, 165, suggests, this question suggests that the elders are not aware of any sin, the preceding chapters have shown that such sin, and therefore a possible answer to the question, exists.

[63] Eslinger *KGC*, 170.

[64] On אֱלֹהִים as plural, see Driver *Samuel*, 37.

[65] This is a phrase for the dispersion of fighters. When used with נוס, as here, it describes a defeat and rout (2Sam. 18:17; 19:9 [8]; 2Kgs. 14:12/2Chr. 25:22).

exodus references agree with our analysis of the exodus story.[66] The Israelite perception is more difficult, as it is not stated that YHWH smote them. However if the Philistines' perception of the situation was crudely correct, this argues for the possibility that the Israelites' perception was similarly correct. What we know to be incorrect are the implications that both sides drew from their perceptions. Bringing the ark did not save the Israelites or defeat the Philistines, which raises the question of why this was the case.

5.3.1.4 CAUSE?

Three possibilities suggest themselves at this point.

First, YHWH has been defeated by the Philistines. This is the impression that 4:10-22 might well give. It would certainly be a realistic assumption in the culture of the time.[67] Brueggemann's first chapter gives the most in-depth engagement with this possibility.[68] Miller and Roberts note the use of נִגְלָה here: the ark has been forcibly carried off.[69]

However the idea that a defeat of Israel entails a defeat of YHWH would be practically unique in the Old Testament, at least as an underlying view of the text rather than a view of the humans within it. Brueggemann notes that people have tried many ways to avoid accepting such a unusual conclusion here.[70] However, while it is a fair point that uniqueness should not automatically lead to rejection, such uniqueness does place the burden of proof upon those who support it.

Secondly, as there is no reason given, perhaps we should not try to find a reason when none is intended, but simply recognise the event itself: 'it is not an end, "because" – it is simply an end.'[71]

Thirdly, we can return to the Israelites' question in 4:3. Although they may not have sought an answer as to why YHWH might smite his people, we can. Reading it in the wider context of 1 Samuel as we are, there is one obvious reason: the behaviour of the Elide priesthood at Shiloh, in particular Hophni and Phinehas (cf. 2:12-17, 22-25, 27-36). This terrible defeat, capture of the ark, and death of the priests would certainly be something that would make the hearers' ears tingle (3:11-14; cf. 2:34).[72]

---

[66] 'Nothing like this has happened before' reminds us of the last plagues (cf. Ex. 9:18; 10:6; 11:6). It is *this* god that they are facing, and they know it (contrast Ex. 5:2).

[67] Cf. Campbell *Ark*, 154 n.1, although he sees 5:2-5 as discounting this.

[68] Brueggemann *Ichabod*, 1-25.

[69] Miller and Roberts, 42. They compare Hos. 10:5 and contrast Ezek. 10-11. This is their view of what is *implied* by chapter 4.

[70] Brueggemann *Ichabod*, 22.

[71] Campbell *Ark*, 200.

[72] Miller and Roberts argue that this was part of the original story, as it explains the emphasis on Hophni and Phinehas and their death in 4:1-22, where without elements of 1Sam. 2 we would not know why they were mentioned (19-22, 66-66). Against this

YHWH striking thirty-four thousand Israelites for the sins of two men appears disproportionate to some.[73] However this formulation may understate the problem in Israel. The greatest tragedy portrayed here is arguably the loss of the ark. It is mentioned last in the list in 4:10-11; the news of its capture is what kills Eli rather than that of the death of his sons in v18 (cf. v14); and this is what prompts the comment from Phinehas' wife that the glory has gone from Israel in v21-22. In the same way, the corruption of the priesthood and thus the mechanisms for dealing with YHWH (2:25a) suggest dire consequences. The idea that *serious* malpractice in the relationship with YHWH would lead to mass death and disaster is by no means unique to this passage.[74] Moreover, the idea that the sin of those in positions of authority affects those under them is also present in the Old Testament. We can compare the plagues of Egypt, where Pharaoh's obstinacy led to the destruction of Egypt, in terms of crops, livestock, firstborn and army.[75]

The following events and speeches will build up our understanding of the cause further.

5.3.2 Second Speech: 5:7-8 (5:1-10) 'YHWH's hand is heavy upon us and our god'

וַיִּרְאוּ אַנְשֵׁי־אַשְׁדּוֹד כִּי־כֵן וְאָמְרוּ לֹא־יֵשֵׁב אֲרוֹן אֱלֹהֵי יִשְׂרָאֵל עִמָּנוּ
כִּי־קָשְׁתָה יָדוֹ עָלֵינוּ וְעַל דָּגוֹן אֱלֹהֵינוּ [8] וַיִּשְׁלְחוּ וַיַּאַסְפוּ אֶת־כָּל־סַרְנֵי

Campbell notes the lack of any negative comments on Hophni and Phinehas in 1Sam. 4 (for general problems with the connection of 1Sam. 2-3 and 4-6, see Campbell *Ark*, 174-77; "Yahweh" 34-37). On this point the LXX has an addition to 4:1 which speaks of the sins of Hophni and Phinehas (cf. McCarter, 103). However this looks to be a response to such a concern rather than something lost from the MT.

However we understand any previous versions, in the text as we have it 1Sam. 2-3 seems to give the reason for 1Sam. 4 (cf. Eslinger *KGC*, 164; McCarter, 109; Aage Bentzen, 'The Cultic Use of the Story of the Ark in Samuel', *JBL* LXVII (1948): 37-53, henceforth 'Bentzen', 46-47).

[73] Campbell *Ark*, 35, uses this as an argument against seeing the Elides as the reason (cf. Brueggemann, 8). Eslinger *KGC*, 175, 193-94, sees it as the reason, but a totally disproportionate one. We will accept אֶלֶף as thousand here rather than discussing other possible meanings. The main point is that this is a terrible tragedy for Israel. However Miller and Roberts argue that 'it is not difficult to assume that their [Hophni and Phinehas'] death would be meted out in the course of their duties, and that Israel might endure tragedy as a consequence' (22 cf. 29).

[74] Leaving aside the larger matter of the Exile(s), see Ex. 32:10, 28, 35; Num. 16:31-35, 17:6-15 [16:41-50]; 25:1-9.

[75] Another connection with Pharaoh is the idea in 2:25b that Hophni and Phinehas' wickedness had reached the point of no return in YHWH's eyes and he would destroy them for it.

פְּלִשְׁתִּים אֲלֵיהֶם וַיֹּאמְרוּ מַה־נַּעֲשֶׂה לַאֲרוֹן אֱלֹהֵי יִשְׂרָאֵל וַיֹּאמְרוּ גַּת
יִסֹּב אֲרוֹן אֱלֹהֵי יִשְׂרָאֵל

> The men of Ashdod saw that this was the case, and they said,[76] 'The ark of the god of Israel shall not stay with us, for his hand is heavy upon us and upon Dagon our god.' They sent and gathered all the rulers of the Philistines to them and said, 'What shall we do with the ark of the god of Israel?' and they said, 'Let the ark of the god of Israel be moved round to Gath.'

In this section there are two main events, responses and consequences (the fall of Dagon and the plagues), so we will split the discussion accordingly.[77]

5.3.2.1 EVENT 1: THE FALL OF DAGON

5.3.2.2 SITUATION

With the ark's capture, the story moves with it from Israel to Philistia. As in the plagues narrative there follows a section where the focus is on non-Israel and where Israel do not appear.[78]

The victorious Philistines take the ark to Ashdod (5:1) and place it in the temple of their god, Dagon, just in front of Dagon's statue (v2).[79] However when they return in the morning, the statue has fallen over in front of the ark (v3a).

5.3.2.3 RESPONSE

There is no speech here. The people just pick him up and put him back (v3b).

5.3.2.4 CONSEQUENCE

Once again, when they come back the next morning Dagon is lying on the floor. This time however, his hands and head have broken off and are lying on the threshold. (v4). (This is explained as the origin of the custom of jumping over Dagon's threshold.[80])

---

[76] On וְאָמְרוּ see Joüon §119z.

[77] We could say that there are three, as there are multiple plagues. However the main point is how the Philistines respond to the plagues initially. The next section will discuss how they ultimately respond in 5:11-6:18.

4:1-22 could also be said to have two main events, being the two defeats in 4:2 and 4:10-11. However there is no obvious response in 4:12-22 except the cry (v13) and the deaths from the news (vv18-20).

[78] Cf. Eslinger *KGC*, 87-88.

[79] This could be treating it as booty, or as an idol to worship. Cf. Miller and Roberts, 9-17; Campbell *Ark*, 188; Gordon, 98. The text, however, is silent on their motivations.

[80] This passage is not, however, thought to be primarily an etiology: Campbell *Ark*, 156 n1; Zakovitch, 53.

There is no explicit explanation given as to why Dagon fell either time, just as there is no explicit reason given for Israel's two previous defeats.[81] However, as with the previous section, the fact that the response leads to something worse happening suggests that the response was incorrect.

5.3.2.5 CAUSE?

There is little doubt as to the reason for Dagon's double fall. YHWH's ark has been placed in his temple. However each time he falls, it is 'before the ark of YHWH' (נֹפֵל לְפָנָיו אַרְצָה לִפְנֵי אֲרוֹן יְהוָה 5:3, 4). The original position of the two 'gods' is reversed. This fall could be seen as an act of worship. However in light of the previous use of נָפַל to describe Israel 'falling' (4:10) and being struck 'before the Philistines' (לִפְנֵי פְלִשְׁתִּים 4:2-3), its use here suggests that just as the Philistines defeated Israel, so YHWH has defeated Dagon.[82] Moreover, just as in the previous chapter, when the two are brought together again, the loser gets even more conclusively beaten (Israel lose the ark that was meant to bring them victory, Dagon loses his head and hands).[83] The initial encounter had enough ambiguity in it to allow different responses. The second encounter makes the point more forcefully. In neither case is a third encounter even considered.[84]

However this is not a 'battle of the gods', inasmuch as Dagon does nothing apart from falling over.[85] As with the 'gods of Egypt' (Ex. 12:12) his only role is to be acted upon. As with other portrayals in the Old Testament, YHWH acts while other gods do nothing.[86] Perhaps a better comparison would be with Pharaoh's magicians. While they appear the equal of Moses and Aaron at first, small inequalities soon escalate. Aaron's staff eats theirs. Then they are unable to reverse the first two plagues. This develops into a failure even to copy the third plague, and the admission that 'this is the finger of god' (Ex. 8:15 [19]). However Pharaoh's inability to listen to this (compare the Philistines' picking up of the statue), leads to the

---

[81] Brueggemann *Ichabod*, 26, notes that it happens in the night (as with the last plague of the exodus). He suggests that the Philistines kept worshipping Dagon during the day even after picking him up (28).

[82] Cf. Miller and Roberts, 44-45. They note the two options and favour defeat, mentioning 1Sam. 17:49; Baal and Yam; and Anat collecting heads and hands. In light of our discussions of 'acknowledgement' we could see Dagon here acknowledging YHWH (cf. Stirrup, 93). However this does not appear to be the primary meaning.

[83] Cf. Campbell *Ark*, 87.

[84] Cf. Brueggemann *Ichabod*, 29.

[85] Even if this lies behind our story (cf. Miller and Roberts, 69; Bentzen, 45), it is not portrayed thus here.

[86] 1Kgs. 18:20-29 presents a similar picture where such a 'contest' or 'battle' is totally one-sided. This contrast is, of course, a repeated theme of the prophets (cf. Is. 40:12-20; 41:1-7, 21-29; 44:6-20; 45:20-46:7 etc; Jer. 2:9-13; 10:2-16).

final humiliation where they, as Pharaoh's representatives cannot even stand before Moses and Aaron as YHWH's representatives.

This passage removes any idea that Dagon may have been responsible for the Philistines' victories and thus superior to YHWH.[87] However we should note that even in 4:8-9 there is no mention of Dagon. They just speak of strengthening themselves (הִתְחַזְּקוּ) and being men.[88]

5.3.2.6 EVENT 2: ASHDOD, GATH AND EKRON UNDER YHWH'S HAND

5.3.2.7 SITUATION

YHWH does not only strike the god of the Philistines, but the people as well. Tumours break out on the inhabitants of Ashdod, and this is explicitly said to be the work of YHWH, as his hand is heavy upon them (v6 cf. Ex. 9:3).

5.3.2.8 RESPONSE

Here we have the main speech of the section, which bears a number of similarities to 4:3. The Philistines have suffered reverses and they attribute the events to YHWH, which is certainly correct in terms of the plagues and almost certainly so in terms of Dagon.[89] They consider how they may deal with these problems. As with Israel they do not consult anyone about what to do, but decide on the quick solution of moving the ark of YHWH, in this case from Ashdod to Gath. In contrast to Israel they want to remove it rather than bring it. However for Philistia, the presence of Israel's god is something to be avoided rather than welcomed (compare 4:5 and 4:6-9). For both Israel and Philistia it is thought that moving the ark will get rid of the problem.

Ironically, as with Israel, they have the answer in their speech but do not follow up on it. That the ark 'should not stay with us' is entirely correct, and is the eventual solution.[90] However the response that follows understands 'us' too narrowly in terms of Ashdod, not Philistia; just as

---

[87] See especially Campbell *Ark*, 156 n1. Cf. Miller and Roberts 47, 67; Campbell *Ark*, 92, 100-101; Eslinger *KGC*, 189. Brueggemann *Ichabod*, sees YHWH as regaining his 'glory' and thus being able to beat Dagon (34). However it is not clear how or why YHWH regains it, especially with his ark in another god's temple.

[88] Cf. Eslinger *KGC*, 171.

[89] This suggests that the recipients of YHWH's actions are able to discern what is happening, making the attribution to YHWH in 4:3 more likely.

[90] To anticipate, if we understand מַה־נַּעֲשֶׂה לַאֲרוֹן in a propitiatory sense in 6:2-9: 'what shall we do *for*...', then the relevant issue is raised even more clearly here and yet misunderstood.

Israel's perceptive question 'why has YHWH struck us' was ignored in favour of bringing the ark.[91]

5.3.2.9 CONSEQUENCE

In another similarity with Israel, and with the previous Dagon event, their response simply leads to the problem being increased in magnitude. As the ark moves to Gath, so the plagues move with it (v9). Now there are two Philistine areas infected rather than one. They try once more, but the Ekronites have seen what happened to Gath, and refuse to accept it, realising that it means death for them (v10). Clearly the response of simply moving the ark around is no better here than it was in 4:4.

5.3.2.10 CAUSE?

Apart from the fact that YHWH is behind the plagues, the cause is not spelt out at this point. It does remove any idea that the Philistines (rather than Dagon) were more powerful than YHWH as they had beaten his people. Not only their god, but also they themselves are shown to be inferior to YHWH.

However, in light of 4:1-22 we cannot view this (or what follows) simply as Israelite *Schadenfreude* over a defeated foe. The YHWH who strikes Philistia, previously struck Israel. 'Any triumphalism in the plague stories must needs be tempered by the presence of an unspoken but menacing implication for Israel.'[92]

5.3.3 Third Speech: 6:2-9 (5:11-6:18) 'If you are returning the ark...'

The Philistines called for the priests and diviners, saying, 'What shall we do with the ark of YHWH? Inform us with what we shall send it to its place.' They said, 'If you are sending (מְשַׁלְּחִים) the ark of the god of Israel, do not send it empty (אַל־תְּשַׁלְּחוּ אֹתוֹ רֵיקָם), but definitely return an offering (אָשָׁם) to him. Then you will be healed and it will be known to you why his hand does not turn away from you.' They said, 'What is the offering that we will return to him?'. They said, 'The number of the lords of the Philistines, five gold tumours and five gold mice, for one plague was upon you all and your lords. You will make images of the tumours and images of the mice, the destroyers of the land, and you will give glory (כָּבוֹד) to the god of Israel. Perhaps he will lighten (יָקֵל) his hand from upon you, your gods and your land. Why should you harden (תְכַבְּדוּ) your hearts as Egypt and Pharaoh hardened (כִּבְּדוּ) their hearts? Was it not when he toyed with (הִתְעַלֵּל) them that they sent (וַיְשַׁלְּחוּם) them and they went? Now take and prepare one new cart and two heifers giving suck that have not been yoked. Attach the heifers to the cart but take their calves away from them, back home.

---

[91] To anticipate, when Israel eventually do deal with this issue (7:2-3) the difference in results is clear.

[92] Campbell *Ark*, 100-01.

Take the ark of YHWH, place it upon the cart, and put the items of gold that you will have returned[93] to him as an offering in a box by its side; then sent it and it will go. Watch; if it goes up the road to its territory to Beth Shemesh then he did this great evil to us; but, if not, then we will know that it was not his hand that struck us; it happened to us by chance.'[94]

5.3.3.1 SITUATION

Ashdod, Gath, and, it seems, Ekron (v11-12) have fallen under YHWH's plague. The terms used show the escalation. The hand of YHWH is heavy upon Ashdod, although there is no mention of panic, and they simply send the ark on. In Gath the hand of YHWH is against them and there is a very great panic. However in Ekron there is a deathly panic; the hand of YHWH is very heavy (כָּבְדָה מְאֹד) there; all who do not die are stricken with the tumours and the cry of the city rises up to the heavens (cf. Ex. 2:23).[95] However, in contrast to Ex. 2:23 (but as in Ex. 11:6 and 12:30), there is nobody to respond.[96]

The immediate response of the Ekronites is clear. They recognise the danger of the situation, and that YHWH is its cause. Their response is that the ark of Israel's god should not be sent around (סָבַב) Philistia. Instead it should be sent to its place, i.e. Israel. However, rather than just sending it around, they call in the experts, the priests and diviners, to ask how this should be done.

5.3.3.2 RESPONSE

This is the longest speech in the whole narrative, contains the most extended interpretation of events in relation to YHWH and is arguably the key to the narrative. Therefore we will investigate this speech in more detail than the other speeches here, although in light of the points made there.

The lords ask the priests two questions. What they are to do to (or for)[97] YHWH's ark? How they are to return it to its place? (6:2)

---

[93] The verb is in the perfect tense. Smith suggests that 'the perfect indicates that in intention they have already given the recompense'; Henry Preserved Smith, *A Critical and Exegetical Commentary on the Books of Samuel*, ICC (Edinburgh: T&T Clark, 1899), 45.

[94] Due to its length, citing the whole speech in Hebrew and English would be unwieldy. Hebrew phrases of particular significance have been given.

[95] Cf. Stirrup, 94; McCarter, 124.

[96] Cf. Brueggemann *Ichabod*, 36; Tony W. Cartledge, *1&2 Samuel*, SHBC (Macon: S&H Publishing, 2001), henceforth 'Cartledge', 85.

[97] עָשָׂה לְ can mean to do something *to* one (Gen. 20:9; Jdg. 9:56), or to do something *for* one (Gen. 30:31; 1Kgs. 11:8) – BDB p793. The sense here is not clear. If it means 'do for' then it could have a propitiatory sense to it, as 6:3-5 suggests. Perhaps the ambiguity here feeds back to the incorrect response to the same question in 5:8.

In response, the priests say that if the lords are going to return the ark, they should not return it empty (רֵיקָם), but rather they should return to him an offering (אָשָׁם). Then they will be healed and it will be known to them why he has not turned his hand from them (6:3).

רֵיקָם has the general sense of 'empty'.[98] The closest parallel uses to 6:3 are Ex. 3:21 and Dt. 15:13:

כִּי תֵלֵכוּן לֹא תֵלְכוּ רֵיקָם   (Ex. 3:21)

וְכִי־תְשַׁלְּחֶנּוּ חָפְשִׁי מֵעִמָּךְ לֹא תְשַׁלְּחֶנּוּ רֵיקָם (Dt. 15:13)

אִם־מְשַׁלְּחִים אֶת־אֲרוֹן אֱלֹהֵי יִשְׂרָאֵל אַל־תְּשַׁלְּחוּ אֹתוֹ רֵיקָם (1Sam. 6:3)

In all three cases someone or something is leaving captivity in some sense. However the one stipulation is that when (or if) they leave they are not to leave רֵיקָם. Israel take Egypt's silver, gold and clothing. The servant is to be liberally provided with animals, food and wine (cf. Dt. 15:14). As well as the similarities in vocabulary and form, the context is also similar, dealing with the release from captivity, either of a people, a slave, or the ark.

Here the contrast to sending the ark רֵיקָם is to return an אָשָׁם. The majority of the uses of אָשָׁם in the Old Testament are in a cultic setting where it refers to an offering or a gift made in respect of guilt.[99] However the use here is different from the majority, having the sense of 'propitiatory sacrifice, compensation, indemnification' or 'rehabilitation and restitution'.[100] A situation has been created that needs to be dealt with by means of making a gift. The two things that the Philistines have done previously that could qualify are the defeat of Israel and the treatment of the ark. The second of these is far more probably the reason.[101] Israel at least understand the defeat as being caused by YHWH rather than the Philistines, and 5:1-8 seem to emphasise this point. Moreover, the plagues follow the ark, and it is the ark that must be returned and an offering made to YHWH. Israel feature nowhere in this reckoning of אָשָׁם. The offering is to be made to YHWH.[102]

The exact meaning of the end of the verse is difficult to understand. However, it appears to refer in some sense to the Philistines being healed

---

[98] Nobody is to appear before YHWH at feasts 'empty-handed' (Ex. 23:15; 34:20; Dt. 16:16). People can return empty (Jer. 14:3; Ruth 1:21). Words or weapons do not return to someone 'empty', 'in vain' or 'unfulfilled' (2Sam. 1:22; Is. 55:11; Jer. 50:9).

[99] D. Kellermann 'אָשָׁם', *TDOT* I, 429-437, 431ff; R. Knierim 'אשם' *TLOT* 1, 191-195, 191ff.

[100] *TDOT* I, 431 and *TLOT* 1 193 respectively. The LXX is unhelpful here, rendering אָשָׁם with βάσανος, 'pain' or 'torment'. This presumably refers to the images as effectively representing the torments.

[101] Driver *Samuel*, 43; Campbell *Ark*, 160.

[102] We could compare the uses in Gen. 26:10 where the אָשָׁם is in respect of Rebekah. Daube, 82-83 sees the idea of returning misappropriated objects with additional payment and sacrifice, as here, underlying Lev. 5:20-26 [6:1-7] and Num. 5:5-10.

and 'knowing'. They ask why YHWH would not lift his hand from them. This is odd. Amending the pointing could give: 'you will know why he did not lift his hand from you [previously]'. Moving the ark by itself was not enough, it required an אָשָׁם.[103] However it is understood, the general sense is that this אָשָׁם would have positive results.

Thus the sense of the priests' response in 6:3 appears to be 'if you are going to do this, then do it *properly*'. The comments in 5:11 and 6:2 leave us in little doubt that the Philistine lords have decided to get rid of the ark back to Israel, so the 'if' would not indicate that the issue was still open.[104] They are the experts called to advise on how the ark is to be returned (in contrast to the previous attempts).

In response to this statement of principle, the lords ask for more details. Exactly what sort of an offering should they return to YHWH? The priests respond that the offering should be five golden models of both tumours and rats, one for each of the lords (6:4). Although we have not heard that Gaza or Ashkelon have yet been affected, the whole of the Philistine nation is to be symbolically represented in this offering.

However they then go further than this, giving an explanation for what this would (hopefully) achieve (6:5), and an exhortation as to why the lords should do it (6:6). Sending the ark with the golden models, they explain, will give כָּבוֹד to Israel's god. Perhaps then he will lighten (קָלַל) his hand from them, their gods and their land.[105]

כָּבֵד/כָּבוֹד:The Key to the Narrative?

We have already met the multiple senses of כָּבֵד in the exodus story. Pharaoh made the work 'hard' upon Israel (Ex. 5:9); his heart was 'unresponsive' to YHWH's signs or demand (Ex. 7:14; 8:11 [15], 28 [32]; 9:7, 34; 10:1), in response to which YHWH's plagues became 'heavy' or very 'heavy' (Ex. 8:20 [24]; 9:3, 18, 24; 10:14). Finally YHWH would 'glorify himself' over Pharaoh and his hosts at the Red sea encounter (Ex. 14:4, 17-18).

---

[103] Cf. Herzberg, 56. Miller and Roberts, 53-54, offer a different translation in light of the plague prayers of Mursili II. They see it as a pair of alternatives: either you will be healed or you will know why YHWH has not lifted his hand from you [and therefore what you need to do about it]. However this would require understanding וֹ as 'or'. Once again, LXX does not help, changing וְנוֹדַע to ἐξιλασθήσεται 'be propitiated', possibly picking up the sense of אָשָׁם above.

[104] Cf. Fokkelman *Narrative*, 262, on the implications of 6:1 also.

[105] אוּלַי often expresses a 'more or less hesitant hope' for the outcome suggested. When it is YHWH's will that gives rise to the uncertainty, אוּלַי expresses not so much 'one's uncertainty with respect to a moody despot, but a consciously humble attitude of one who takes into account the sovereign freedom of God.' E. Jenni, 'אוּלַי' *TLOT* 1, 59-60. See Gen. 18:24-32; Num. 23:3, 27; Josh. 14:12; 1Sam. 9:6; 2Kgs. 19:4.

כָּבוֹד is also a theme that runs throughout our current story. As she dies, Phinehas' wife names her son Ichabod (אִי־כָבוֹד 4:21-22) 'alas the כָּבוֹד' or 'where is the כָּבוֹד?'. We are told that she said this because her husband was killed, but primarily because the ark was taken. In the next chapter we see where the כָּבוֹד has gone. It has moved with the ark to Philistia, and YHWH's hand is 'heavy' upon that land (5:6, 11).[106] As with the ark, the Israelites mourn the loss of the כָּבוֹד, whereas the Philistines come to mourn its presence.

It is with this in mind that we read the explanation of the priests to the Philistines. YHWH's hand is heavy upon them and they know this. If they wish YHWH to lighten (קלל) his hand upon them, then they must give him כָּבוֹד. This כָּבוֹד has its concrete expression in the אָשָׁם of the golden images. Thus by giving YHWH כָּבוֹד they hope to remove the כָּבוֹד that is upon them. Brueggemann sums it up as:

> The *kabod* of YHWH has been heavy against the Philistines. If, however, the Philistines willingly give *kabod* to YHWH, YHWH may not need to claim *kabod* so violently, and can ease up on the Philistines.[107]

It is at this point that the priests make reference to Egypt hardening (כִּבְּדוּ) their hearts. The Philistine lords are urged not to behave like Pharaoh, a symbol of opposition to YHWH, by hardening their hearts as Pharaoh did. The priests point out the foolishness of this position based on what happened to him. YHWH 'toyed with' (הִתְעַלֵּל) them, after which they let the people go anyway. They do not need to draw any comparisons as they are reasonably obvious to anyone who knows the exodus story.[108] Pharaoh had something belonging to YHWH but refused to release it. As a result YHWH's plagues got worse until he was broken down (Ex. 12:29-30).

At this point we could ask why this exhortation is mentioned at all. There is no mention of the Philistine lords hardening their hearts, or opposing the return.[109] Indeed, it appears that they have decided to return the ark before

---

[106] 5:7 uses קָשָׁה, but as in Exodus, the terms are similar in meaning.

[107] Brueggemann *Ichabod*, 55. His study picks up the importance of כָּבוֹד in the story, albeit seeing it as lost to YHWH and then returning: 'It is all heavy! It is all *kabod*! It is all about glory! "Ichabod" is banished. The glory has returned and the news is not good for the Philistines.' (36 on 5:11; cf. 55, 59). The importance of כָּבוֹד has been noted in recent studies (Fokkelman *Narrative*, 250, 266, 280; Stirrup, 87, 94, 96-97; although note also Herzberg, 59).

[108] This point should not be taken as raising any claims regarding historicity. The point is that *this narrative portrays* the Philistines as being clearly aware of the events of the exodus not only in general (4:8) but even more specifically (6:6 where they know of YHWH's speech to Moses and the message for Israel in Ex. 10:2).

[109] Cf. Eslinger *KGC*, 88; Campbell *Ark*, 113-114. Both note the possibility that this is simply a device for the reader to put the exodus idea into the narrative. Miller and

even speaking to the priests, unlike Pharaoh who never seemed genuine in his agreement that Israel could leave.

However, we can make sense of this statement in its immediate and wider context. The priests are dealing with the question of the אָשָׁם, what it should be, and what it would mean. It would bring כָּבוֹד to YHWH. Immediately after this they tell the Philistines not to harden (כָּבֵד) their hearts like Pharaoh. The use of this key term in the passage suggests a link with the previous uses. The כָּבוֹד should be YHWH's, not theirs. If returning the ark with an אָשָׁם would give כָּבוֹד to YHWH, would not returning it empty suggest that the כָּבוֹד stays with Philistia? Miller and Roberts discuss the treatment of captured images and possible methods of return, including those where a victor could return something to show his superiority.[110] This suggests that returning the ark would not *automatically* have been a symbol of defeat.[111] The method of return could have given very different messages (magnanimity or simple superiority) which the אָשָׁם prevents. However this is not obviously picked up in the text.

Previously the Philistines have discerned correctly, but have not responded correctly. At this point they have seen how כָּבֵד YHWH can be on them and even on their gods, much more כָּבֵד than they can be. We can see a wordplay between the different senses of √כבד here. A refusal to give YHWH כָּבוֹד (glory or acknowledgement) is extremely stupid, indicating that their hearts (or wills) are unresponsive (or heavy) כָּבוֹד to the situation. All it would lead to is YHWH's כָּבוֹד (power or presence) remaining with them and הִתְעַלֵּל. Eventually they would have to do what YHWH wanted, just like Pharaoh did. We could sum this up by saying that the כָּבוֹד belongs with YHWH. If they are going to send the ark, then they need to send it properly, i.e. with their acknowledgement of this fact, via the images.[112]

Brueggemann also links the כָּבוֹד in 6:5 with the images:

> In Egypt Israel stole the silverware (Exod. 11:2). Here the proposal is that YHWH should not be made to steal the gold of the Philistines. Rather, the Philistines should freely and gladly give YHWH the gold. The concession to YHWH is in part cunning, in part prudence, and in part theological awareness that the God of Israel is indeed the God of the Philistines who will be worshipped. The condition of hard-heartedness is most often coupled with the coveting of gold commodities, a non-starter with YHWH, surely not worth the effort.[113]

Roberts, 55 suggest that the exodus typology shows that the divine warrior has made sport of any enemy. However Daube, 82, argues that it is not a secondary addition, as exodus ideas permeate the whole episode. The question for us is whether this statement can be understood in the context of the priests' speech.

[110] Miller and Roberts, 9-16.

[111] Contra Bentzen, 52.

[112] Cf. Fokkelman *Narrative*, 268.

[113] Brueggemann *Ichabod*, 55.

However there are a couple of significant differences to our reading. It is not clear that hard-heartedness is often linked to covetousness. In our reading it is not the gold that is the issue, but what it represents in terms of acknowledgement. However this acknowledgement is not that YHWH should be worshipped by the Philistines. They are not YHWH's people and like Pharaoh their response and acknowledgement should be different from that of Israel. Pharaoh was not called to serve YHWH, but to send Israel out of Egypt so that they could serve him. Although YHWH was 'in the midst of the land', it was not appropriate for Israel to serve him there (Ex. 8:21-25 [25-29]). Likewise here, YHWH is clearly present in the land and able to act. However the Philistines are not told to build a shrine for the ark and worship YHWH here. Their one attempt at amalgamating YHWH into their religion in whatever fashion had dire consequences (5:1-5). Keeping the ark had failed. What they must do is send it away (Pi'el שָׁלַח, compare Ex. 5:1 etc.) 'to its place' (5:11, 6:2), which is not Philistia.

This still leaves the objection that the Philistines have not shown any obvious signs of refusing or balking, which would necessitate the comment in 6:6. However, the wordplay above suggests that this comment is linked to the priests' initial point on returning the ark. Previously they had tried to get rid of the problem by moving the ark on, but keeping it in Philistia. Now they realise that this is untenable, so they simply want to get rid of it, and want to know how. Pharaoh himself, when *in extremis*, appeared to say all the right things and promised to let Israel go. It was after the plague that he reneged and hardened his heart, not backing up his words with actions. The comparison made with him and the double use of כָּבֵד suggest that this אָשָׁם, this acknowledgement of YHWH, may be the point at which the Philistines, like Pharaoh, balk.

Consider our discussion of Ex. 10:24-29. It is when Pharaoh has conclusively to give up, and show that he has totally given up Israel, that the negotiations cease. Furthermore, compare 6:6 with Ex. 9:30. In neither case is there any obvious sign in the immediate context that the addressee is unwilling to perform the necessary action. Yet at least in Ex. 9:30-34, it is not wholly surprising when Pharaoh reneges 'once again' (cf. Ex. 8:25 [29]; 9:20-21). It is to this moment that the Philistine priests point, perhaps drawing some comparisons between the Philistine lords' previous attempts to get rid of the problem and Pharaoh's previous 'agreements'. They have to change their focus from 'getting rid of the problem' to dealing with, and acknowledging YHWH.

This is somewhat speculative, but we can find support for this position in the wider story. In 6:5 there is the contrast between כָּבֵד and קָלַל. קָלַל is an antonym of כָּבֵד having a similar range of meanings from physically 'light' to figuratively 'slight', 'insignificance' (thus 'lack of glory or honour').[114]

---

[114] *TDOT* VII, 23.

This contrast appears in one other place in our story, in a message from YHWH to Eli in 2:30. There, Eli is told of the end of the Elide priestly line. YHWH chose them out of all Israel (1Sam. 2:28). However his response was to kick against (בָּעַט cf. Dt. 32:15) YHWH's sacrifices by honouring (כָּבֵד) his sons more than YHWH, and making them fat on YHWH's sacrifices. 2:12-17 shows how Hophni and Phinehas had treated YHWH's offerings with contempt (נָאַץ cf. Num. 16:30). Later, Samuel's message from YHWH speaks of the sons 'belittling' themselves (מְקַלְלִים לָהֶם). If we accept the *tiqqun sopherim*, they were belittling God (מְקַלְלִים אֱלֹהִים). Once again, Eli did not restrain them (3:13).[115] Therefore, although YHWH had declared that they would hold the position forever, he now revokes that, giving the following reason:

כִּי־מְכַבְּדַי אֲכַבֵּד וּבֹזַי יֵקָלּוּ

'For those who honour me I will honour, but those who despise me will be of little account.' (2:30)

The principle is a clear one. As people treat YHWH, so will they be treated. Fokkelman notes that this 'mirror principle' is used previously in respect of the treatment of YHWH's people (Gen. 12:3; 27:29; Num. 24:9). However this is the first time that it is used of the attitude towards YHWH himself. Also it is preceded by a unique use of חָלִילָה לִּי on the lips of YHWH himself, rather than a human.[116] This all suggests that this statement is one of theological significance.

This suggests the answer to the Israelites' question in 4:3. YHWH is treating Israel as Israel (through their priests) have treated him. YHWH has not been given כָּבוֹד and thus his כָּבוֹד will neither fight for Israel, nor stay with them (4:22). It also exposes the folly of bringing the ark from Shiloh, especially with Hophni and Phinehas in attendance. If the people's engagement with YHWH was not bringing him כָּבוֹד (glory), then simply bringing the ark along would not guarantee his כָּבוֹד (presence) to fight for them.[117]

Thus we return to the situation in 6:2-9. Philistia have not given YHWH כָּבוֹד and thus they have received כָּבוֹד that they did not want. The message

---

[115] Cf. Fokkelman *Narrative*, 250, on קָלַל/כָּבֵד.

[116] Fokkelman *Narrative*, 143. He notes the rabbinic phrase *midda k'neged midda* used to describe this, but does not elaborate further.

[117] One comparable passage is the story of Achan in Jos. 7. Because the Israelites have transgressed YHWH's commands, YHWH is not with them when they assault Ai. When Joshua comes before YHWH he is told of this transgression. When Achan is uncovered as the culprit, Joshua's words to him are: 'my son, give glory to YHWH the god of Israel, and give to him thanskgiving (שִׂים־נָא כָבוֹד לַיהוָה אֱלֹהֵי יִשְׂרָאֵל וְתֶן־לוֹ תוֹדָה). Recount to me what you have done…' (Jos. 7:19). There the 'giving glory' was bound up with confession so that the sin could be removed. In returning the ark *with the images*, the Philistines could be seen to be doing something similar.

of the priests to the Philistine lords deals with this situation: 'If you are going to return the ark, then do it *properly*! Give the כָּבוֹד to YHWH! Don't allow your own כָּבוֹד to get in the way!'[118]

Once again we can compare this to the exodus story. The mistake that Philistia (and Israel) made was seeing the ark and YHWH simply in terms of power and raw force (4:3, 8; 5:7-8) which can be summoned or removed. Instead of power in these terms, it is about כָּבוֹד and how one deals with YHWH. Likewise Pharaoh had to learn what YHWH's power actually meant (power expressed rather differently than his own understanding, cf. Ex. 9:16), and how he should acknowledge it.

After this explanation and exhortation come the specific instructions on what they are to do (6:7-9). They are to send the ark back in a way so contrary to nature that, if it does return to Israel, they will know that YHWH was behind the events that have befallen them, rather than them having happening by chance. As in the plagues narrative YHWH's acts are to be a sign (cf. 2:34).

5.3.3.3 CONSEQUENCE

The test is set up, and the ark returns with the Philistines following it (6:10-12). Thus they know that YHWH was behind the plagues, and they return to their lands (6:16).[119]

The fact that YHWH could direct the cart thus suggests that he could have returned the ark at a time of his choosing, rather than waiting for seven months (6:1). Anyone who tried to impede it would presumably have suffered Uzzah's fate (2Sam. 6:6-7). However he did not do this. Rather he sent plagues upon the Philistines to 'persuade' them to return it. As in the exodus story, YHWH is concerned that even non-Israelites respond correctly and acknowledge him. There is no explicit demand from YHWH, but this fits with the nature of the story where there are no messages from YHWH, at least none that are spoken.

We are not told whether or not the return of the ark with the אָשָׁם has the desired effect of ending the plagues. Thus we cannot use this as proof that their response this time was the correct one. However perhaps this is being too rigid in our categories. The nature of the ark's return (6:10-12) is a

---

[118] Cf. Kellenberger *Hardening*, 6-7, Brueggemann *Ichabod*, 55. On the negative use of כָּבוֹד see Fokkelman *Narrative*, 226, on Eli's 'heaviness' (4:18).

[119] One could speculate that, inasmuch as the cart reaching Israel meant that the offerings would be taken to YHWH, יָדַע in 6:9 also has the secondary implication of 'acknowledge'. If the cart had not gone to Israel, presumably the Philistines would have taken back the gold images and thus there would have been no acknowledgement of YHWH. This would explain the seeming anomaly of testing something (i.e. YHWH as cause of the plagues), of which they are already, correctly, convinced (5:7, 10-11; 6:5-6).

consequence of sorts, and it clearly shows that YHWH was behind the plagues, and (presumably) that he wants the ark back in Israel. As we move with the ark to Beth-Shemesh, the focus shifts from Philistia to Israel, and the Philistines' problems are no longer relevant.[120] On the assumption that giving כָּבוֹד to YHWH was correct, we might expect the plagues to cease when the ark left. At the least, the Philistines are not wiped out by them, as they are able to attack Israel in twenty years time if not before.[121]

5.3.3.4 CAUSE?

The test in vv7-9 and its execution prove that the cause of the plagues was YHWH, if such proof were needed. The reason for YHWH's action is set out in 6:5-6, which resonates with a similar message to Eli (and by extension, to Israel) in 2:30. Those who honour YHWH will be honoured. Those who dishonour YHWH will be despised. Philistia have not given YHWH כָּבוֹד in their treatment of the ark. If they wish him to lighten (קָלַל) his כָּבוֹד from them, they must give him the כָּבוֹד that he deserves. We could compare this to the idea that YHWH is 'being a Pharaoh to Pharaoh' in Ex.10:2, which is cited here by the Philistine priests. As people do, so shall it be done to them.

However there is one striking difference between 6:6 and Ex. 10:2. The combination of כָּבֵד and הִתְעַלֵּל shows that the comments in 6:6 relate to this particular text in the plagues narrative. However while in Ex. 10:2 YHWH says that *he* has hardened the hearts of Pharaoh and his servants, in 1Sam. 6:6 the priests exhort the Philistines 'do not harden your hearts as *the Egyptians and Pharaoh* hardened their hearts...'. Why has the author of the hardening been changed? As with the plagues narrative, the context may be of help. The priests are appealing to the Philistines to do the right (and smart) thing. The Philistines stand in the position of Egypt/Pharaoh in this story. YHWH's messages to Pharaoh focussed upon his responsibility for his obdurate state, rather than YHWH's hardening. Thus, in a similar context, the priests call upon the Philistines to act appropriately. Focussing on YHWH's hardening would be inappropriate, given the purpose of their comments.

In this light, we can return to the previously mentioned Ps. 105:25. Here the initial acts of Egypt against Israel are ascribed to YHWH's influence, whereas in Ex. 1-2, YHWH is noticeably absent. The context here is a psalm of praise, where the focus is wholly upon YHWH's deeds. Therefore everything is understood as originating from him. The difference between the summaries of the 'hardening' in these two verses can be explained by their context and their purpose.

---

[120] Cf. Brueggemann *Ichabod*, 57.

[121] There is no record of whether they attacked over the period covered by 7:2 as it is not relevant to the story.

More widely we could mention Paul's use of Ex. 9:16 in Rom. 9:17. His context is the assertion that 'it is not as if the word of God had failed', even though his people are not following Christ (Rom. 9:6). The context is similar to that of Moses facing setbacks in his work (cf. Ex. 5:22; 9:30). Paul takes the message of Ex. 9:16 (remonstrance) and uses it in the sense of Ex. 10:2 (reassurance), just as the Philistine priests take the message of Ex. 10:2 (reassurance) and use it in the sense of Ex. 9:16 (remonstrance).[122]

5.3.4 Fourth Speech: 7:3 (6:19-7:14) 'If you are returning to YHWH...'

וַיֹּאמֶר שְׁמוּאֵל אֶל־כָּל־בֵּית יִשְׂרָאֵל לֵאמֹר אִם־בְּכָל־לְבַבְכֶם אַתֶּם שָׁבִים
אֶל־יְהוָה הָסִירוּ אֶת־אֱלֹהֵי הַנֵּכָר מִתּוֹכְכֶם וְהָעַשְׁתָּרוֹת וְהָכִינוּ לְבַבְכֶם
אֶל־יְהוָה וְעִבְדֻהוּ לְבַדּוֹ וְיַצֵּל אֶתְכֶם מִיַּד פְּלִשְׁתִּים

And Samuel spoke to all the house of Israel, saying 'If it is with all your hearts that you are returning to YHWH then put away the foreign gods from your midst and the ashtoreths. Fix your hearts upon YHWH and serve him alone, that he may deliver you from the hand of the Philistines.'

5.3.4.1 EVENT 1: SLAUGHTER AT BESH-SHEMESH

5.3.4.2 SITUATION

The ark has returned to Israel. The Philistine lords have seen this, realised its implications for them, and returned. Some of the men of Beth-shemesh looked into or at the ark and were killed, turning the mood from rejoicing at the ark's return into mourning because of the slaughter. The ark has returned, but this does not equate to joy for Israel (6:19).

5.3.4.3 RESPONSE

The people's response to this is to ask 'who can stand before YHWH, this holy God? To whom shall he go up from upon us?' (6:20 cf. 5:7-8). They then send messengers to Kiriath-jearim, whose inhabitants take the ark, and consecrate a priest for it (6:21).

5.3.4.4 CONSEQUENCE

The ark stays in Kiriath-jearim for twenty years. Sending the ark to Kiriath-jearim does not lead to slaughter there, as happened in Philistia (compare

---

[122] This is to make no assertions or assumptions about which exodus traditions the various authors had available to them, or about any hermeneutical methods that they used. However it does suggest a way in which the various different uses can be read together as part of Scripture.

6:21 with 5:8b).[123] However for twenty years Israel lament after YHWH
(7:2). The position has not changed noticeably from that of 4:12-22.

5.3.4.5 CAUSE?

This passage is difficult to understand, not merely due to the odd
numbers,[124] but also in terms of YHWH's actions. If רָאוּ בַּאֲרוֹן is
understood to mean 'looked *in* the ark' we could understand the slaughter
as YHWH's response to disrespectful treatment of the ark (on a par with
what has just happened to the Philistines). However the more probable
reading of רָאָה בְּ is 'looked at' rather than 'looked in'.[125] As a result there
is nothing obviously negative in the people's responses to explain such an
act by YHWH; rather they rejoice and offer sacrifices. The LXX would
give us a possible reason, where those who do not celebrate are condemned,
but for now we will stay with the more difficult MT.

We can compare the shock of 6:19, expressed in 6:20, with that of 4:10-
11, expressed in 4:12-22. In both cases what should have been a positive
engagement with the ark seemingly inexplicably turns into an
overwhelmingly negative one. There is nothing obviously wrong with
either bringing the ark into battle, or celebrating its return. If we accept the
larger number in 6:19, then the deaths in 4:3, 4:10 and 6:19 get
progressively larger. The question of 6:20 recalls the similar question of
4:3. If we have concluded that YHWH's actions in 4:3 and 4:10-11 were
due to a deeper problem in Israel (1Sam. 2-3), then we have to ask the
question of what has changed in Israel between 4:22 and 6:13 when the ark
returns. In other words, should we (or Israel) be so surprised that the
coming of the ark is not a matter of joy for Israel?

We can also compare 6:19-20 with the initial acts of YHWH against the
Philistines. The Beth-shemeshites' question in 6:20 is very similar to that of
the Philistines in 5:7-8. They realise that they cannot cope with this God, or
his ark, and they want to get rid of it.[126] On both occasions the ark has come

---

[123] Perhaps the difference is due to the fact that they consecrated a priest for it, or that
keeping the ark in Israel is not inappropriate in and of itself, as it was in Philistia. The
story is not overly concerned with this.

[124] The MT reads that YHWH smote 'seventy men, five thousand men'. The LXX
expands this to say that the men of Jeconiah amongst the Beth-Shemeshites did not
rejoice to see the ark, so YHWH struck them down, retaining the 'seventy, five
thousand'.

[125] Driver *Samuel*, 46; Campbell *Ark*, 161; Eslinger *KGC*, 217, 452-54 n10; Fokkelman
Narrative, 289 n40. Driver and especially Eslinger provide support for this. In line with
his overall thesis, Eslinger views this episode as an example of YHWH's overbearing
power (Eslinger *KGC* 217-223).

[126] Eslinger *KGC*, 224, and Fokkelman *Narrative*, 291, see the expression 'this holy
God' in 6:20 as indicating distance or alienation from this God. Fokkelman compares it
to 4:8.

into the possession of a group of people, who initially view this fact positively. (This is a presumption in respect of the Philistines' attitude, but in light of the victory that precedes and their depositing of the ark in their temple, this seems reasonable.) However in both cases the recipients of this ark get a (fatal) shock on receiving the ark.

In both cases this appears linked to their misunderstanding of their relationship to it. The Philistines may think that they have captured it; the Israelites may think that they have 'their' ark back. However in both cases, the ark's movement has nothing to do with the *recipients*, but rather to do with YHWH's engagement with those who have lost it. The ark went to Philistia because of Israel's lack of כָּבוֹד for YHWH, and it returned to Israel as an attempt by the Philistines to give him כָּבוֹד.[127] The fact that they now hold the ark, in either case, does not confer any automatic authority or rights in respect of it.[128] YHWH cannot be presumed upon, and both the Israelites and the Philistines have to learn how to deal with him.

5.3.4.6 EVENT 2: DELIVERANCE AT MIZPAH

5.3.4.7 SITUATION

The ark has remained in Kiriath-jearim for twenty years while Israel lamented after YHWH. Now Samuel, the faithful priest, comes forward with a message (7:2-3; compare 6:1-2).

5.3.4.8 RESPONSE

If the question in 6:20 is similar to that of 5:8 or 5:10-11, and possibly also the initial question of 4:3, then Samuel's message is quite similar to that of the Philistine priests in 6:2-9.

In 6:3 the priests said 'If you are returning the ark, then *do it properly* – send an אָשָׁם and therefore give the glory to YHWH.'

In 7:3 Samuel says 'If you are truly returning (שָׁבִים) to YHWH, then *do it properly* – get rid of the foreign gods and serve YHWH only.'

In both cases there is no point in trying to deal with YHWH unless they do it properly. There is no point in discerning things and making gestures unless they back up their understanding with appropriate actions. The Philistines had to provide propitiation in the form of golden images. The Israelites have to get rid of their images and serve YHWH alone. Moreover in both cases, it is only if they respond properly and positively, that YHWH

---

[127] The Philistines are right in 4:8 to fear YHWH's power. They conquered, not due to their superior power, but because of YHWH's actions against Israel. Similarly, Israel here have done nothing to deserve the ark back.

[128] Cf. Miller and Roberts, 59; Campbell *Ark*, 162; Fokkelman *Narrative*, 249. Another way to put this, at least in respect of Israel, is that this is the ark of YHWH's *covenant*, with all the implications that this holds.

can be expected to respond positively: 'perhaps he may lift his hand' and 'he will deliver you from the hand of the Philistines' respectively.

Once again, the underlying theme is the same for both. Both tried simply to move the ark around initially, presumably having the view that this would solve their problems. Both are subsequently told that YHWH does not work like that. They have to engage with him properly. However, the actual mechanics of doing so differ from group to group. Egypt/Pharaoh and the Philistines (not YHWH's people) are to 'send...[Israel or the ark]'. Israel (YHWH's people) are to 'serve...[YHWH]'. Moreover, in the plagues narrative the explanations and actions of YHWH may have appeared different to Pharaoh/Egypt and Moses/Israel, but the underlying message was the same: respond to YHWH correctly.[129]

One objection to this could be that the words of Samuel here do not mention the ark, in contrast to the other three sections. Moreover the issues are not the same as in 2:12-36. Priestly malpractice, primarily in the sacrificial system, has changed to the more common issue of idolatrous worship of 'other gods'. In response to this we have noted above that 1Sam. 4-7 may contain an older story that has been put in the text at this point. However the comparisons drawn above suggest that if it is older, it has been used within and interwoven with the current text, to create new patterns and messages as a result.

Thus we have a contrast between the views of the Israelites elders and Philistines lords ('send/bring the ark'), and the views of the priests, Samuel and (it seems) the narrator ('deal with YHWH').

5.3.4.9 CONSEQUENCE

The people follow Samuel's words (7:4). While Samuel is judging them the Philistines attack them at Mizpah. Samuel, at the people's entreaty, calls upon YHWH (7:5-9a). This time, in contrast to 4:10-11, YHWH answers as they hope.[130] He routs the Philistines before Israel and they flee (7:9b-11). This is followed by the setting up of Ebenezer (compare 7:12 with 4:1)[131] and the report that the Philistines were subdued during Samuel's leadership of the people.

If the first two speeches and responses were judged incorrect by their consequences, and the third assumed to be correct due to 6:10-12, then the

---

[129] This similarity between the words of Samuel and of the Philistine priests underlines the point that the narrator does not seem to have a problem with the non-Israelite priests setting out good Yahwistic theology.

[130] Rather than comparing 6:19-20 with 4:10-22 we could compare it to 4:2-3, and then compare 7:4-14 with 4:10-22. Both have an initial setback, caused by YHWH; but the response and consequence are very different.

[131] Cf. Fokkelman *Narrative*, 198; Willis, 304.

events of 7:9-14 vindicate Samuel's words and the people's actions in 7:3-8.

5.3.4.10 CAUSE?

For once the cause is not in any real doubt. The people have responded appropriately to YHWH, and he responds to them accordingly.[132] The pattern of 2:30 continues.

5.4 1 Samuel 4-7 in the Old Testament – Jeremiah's Temple Sermon

We have considered 1Sam. 4-7 as a place in the Old Testament where the exodus story, and more specifically the plagues narrative, is both referred to explicitly and resonates implicitly. As a final test of our observations we will consider the use of 1Sam. 4-7 itself in the Old Testament, to see if such use supports our comments on this text.

Perhaps the strongest use comes in the double presentation of Jeremiah's 'temple sermon' in Jer. 7 and 26. The speech in Jer. 7 is the longer of the two and thus will be our focus.[133]

There is no explicit link between Jer. 7 and 1Sam. 4-7. 1Sam. 4 makes no mention of the destruction of Shiloh (although interestingly the question in 6:20 suggests that returning the ark to Shiloh was not obvious for some reason). In Jer. 7 there is no mention of the ark (unlike Ps. 78:60 cf. v67). However the lack of any references to Shiloh as a worship centre after 1Sam. 4 in contrast to the situation before, would connect these two events to the reader of the text, even if not necessarily to Jeremiah's original hearers.[134]

Jeremiah stands at the gate of the temple and speaks YHWH's message to the people. He sets up a contrast. The people are urged to mend their ways, rather than trusting in the deceitful words 'This is YHWH's temple, YHWH's temple, YHWH's temple.' (Jer. 7:4). *If* they amend their ways, both in terms of acting justly to each other and towards YHWH, then he

---

[132] One might question the fate of the Philistines – they are defeated although they had previously dealt with YHWH correctly. Leaving aside the twenty year gap, the position here is similar to that of Ex. 14. The focus is back with Israel again, and Philistia are the enemy who oppose them. *Israel* act correctly towards YHWH, and YHWH responds to *Israel.*

[133] I am grateful for the sight of a draft of RWL Moberly's forthcoming book *Prophecy and Discernment*, which contains a section on this passage.

[134] Shiloh is mentioned several times in Jos. 18-22 and Jdg. 18-21 as well as 1Sam. 1-4 (e.g. Jos. 18:1; Jdg. 18:31; 1Sam. 1:3; 3-4). However, after our story, it is mentioned only a few times either as a dwelling place (1Sam. 14:3; 1Kgs. 14:2, 4; Jer. 41:5), or as a reference to its fate or to that of the Elide priesthood there, in wholly negative terms (1Kgs. 2:27; Ps. 78:60; Jer. 7:12, 14; 26:6, 9). Nowhere in the Old Testament is there any mention of a separate destruction of Shiloh.

will dwell with them here (Jer. 7:5-7). Yet they seem to think that they can act unjustly and idolatrously and then come to the temple and say 'we are safe' (Jer. 7:8-11).[135] However they are mistaken...

Even before we get to the reference to Shiloh, the parallels are clear. The symbol of YHWH's presence, now the temple rather than the ark, is being viewed as a method of ensuring safety and YHWH's help. 'This is the temple of YHWH... We are safe!' (Jer. 7:4, 10) sounds suspiciously like 'bring the ark of YHWH so that he will save us...' (1Sam. 4:3). In both cases they were facing an enemy and the threat of exile, be it the ark and the 'glory' to Philistia, or the people to Babylon.

Jeremiah then raises Shiloh as a warning to them. They are urged to go and see what happened to the place where YHWH's name first dwelt, and what he did to it because of the people's wickedness (Jer. 7:12-13). But Judah now are like Israel then, and therefore YHWH will do to his present house what he did to the previous one, and to current Judah what happened to past Israel (Jer. 7:14-15).

Unlike 1Sam. 4-7, both options are placed side by side here. The people can either treat YHWH with lipservice and see his temple as a means of automatic protection, as they did with the ark; or they can truly engage with YHWH, as they did at Mizpah. Jeremiah, as a prophet of YHWH, is bringing YHWH's words to the people in order to get them to respond appropriately. Although he does not use the words, one can almost hear the echoes of Samuel and the Philistine priests: 'if you are going to engage with YHWH, then do it *properly*!'

YHWH's acts in the exodus were intended to get the correct response from the people. The tradition and remembrance of those acts in the wider Old Testament, and in 1Sam. 6:6 in particular are used for exactly the same purpose: to get the correct response. Now here we see that even YHWH's acts at Shiloh were both intended at the time to provoke the right response, and reused years later for exactly the same reason. In each case those who hear and see these things have multiple possible responses, but this does not mean that all responses are equally appropriate.[136]

---

[135] Craigie, 121 notes the mention of theft, murder, adultery, perjury and other gods as an assault on the ten commandments (Peter C. Craigie; Page H. Kelley; Joel F. Drinkard Jr., *Jeremiah 1-25*, WBC 26 (Waco: Word, 1998)).

[136] We could finish with a light-hearted modern-day equivalent of the use of 1Sam. 4-7 by noticing how it is picked up in two modern films. In *Raiders of the Lost Ark*, the hero Indiana Jones is consulted about a Nazi plot to find the lost ark of the covenant. They seek it because it will make any army that carries it invulnerable. Quite whether the irony of a Nazi army trying to use a Jewish holy object was appreciated is unclear. The view of both sides in this appears to be that this is a very powerful object that the other must not get; very similar to the view of the Israelite elders and Philistine lords. Perhaps if the worried American military had consulted an Old Testament (or Tanakh)

theologian (rather than an archaeologist), he or she would have pointed them to this passage and saved everyone a lot of bother...

In contrast, in the film *Chariots of Fire*, the Olympian 100m runner Eric Liddell refuses to run in the 100m as it was on a Sunday, backing up his beliefs with action. Instead he entered the 400m, which was not his distance. It is said that before the race he was handed a piece of paper on which was written 'Those who honour me, I will honour'. Liddell went on to claim the gold in a record-breaking time. Samuel, the priests and Jeremiah might well have approved.

However, as with the 1Sam. 4-7 story, this is more than simply a mechanical formula. Afterwards Liddell dedicated his life to being a missionary in China, and died in a Japanese prison camp. The patterns that we have seen in 1Sam. 4-7 are accompanied by seemingly dark and confusing events. Yet if one chooses, explanations can be seen in a larger picture of God dealing with humanity.

Chapter 6

Concluding Remarks

The importance of the exodus story, together with the rich depths that we have only begun to sound, give warrant for far greater exploration. However, as this particular study necessarily draws to a close, it will be useful to draw together the threads of our discussion. This study started with a brief summary of the theological issues arising in the plagues narrative, and a representation of different views on the hardening of the heart, which is probably the most complicated and certainly the most discussed of these issues. In light of our discussions we can return to these issues and make the following points:

The initial summary of 'issues' in the plagues narratives gave a confusing and possibly contradictory picture of this God. However in our discussions, we have argued for a different, more cohesive picture: a God who responds to human actions and acts himself in order to seek the appropriate response from them in turn. This seeking of response is brought about by the sending of signs, which point beyond themselves, and the giving of explanations. Each explanation needs to be read in its context, rather than trying to abstract it, as the content and the context (including that of the recipient of the message) need to be understood together. They are not simply explanations, but rather are designed to bring about a certain response, often by changing the focus of the recipient.

This change of perceptions is often towards a more theocentric focus; and this theocentrism stands out as the reason for YHWH's actions. Israel and Egypt will 'know that I am YHWH'. This, rather than any specifically humanitarian motive, is given as the purpose behind YHWH's actions. However, when we look in detail at this focus on YHWH and his power, it does not indicate a disregard for the humans involved. Rather it is expressed in ways that give insight into what kind of God this is. This is a God who shows signs of his power through restraint, and through salvation, as well as through plagues. Moreover, this change of focus should not negate or lessen the role of the humans who are encountering him. Instead this knowledge of YHWH should lead to an appropriate acknowledgement of him in their actions. This response of the humans who encounter YHWH, whether appropriate or inappropriate, often leads to a further response from YHWH which takes the human action into account.

We can return to the specific issues of the length and nature of the plagues and the interaction of YHWH with Pharaoh, with the hardening as a key issue. Reconsidering these oddities or difficulties in the light of the above picture, it is possible to make sense of them in the story. The narrative shows that although YHWH has the ability to make the required human response, or the need for it, obvious from the start, this does not happen. At the beginning of the various encounters there are ambiguities allowing different possibilities of response to YHWH. However it is made clear that not all understandings or interpretations of YHWH's words and deeds are equally valid. Some are explicitly rejected. Some lead to worsening conditions. Often the initial ambiguities are whittled down through the subsequent encounters, and as a result of the responses of the humans, until the situation becomes clearer, with less possibility of alternate actions. Yet throughout all of this, YHWH remains concerned that the human or humans encountered make the appropriate response. Often this response is the one thing that they would not choose to do, and we see their attempts to get around this. However YHWH continues to move them towards his aim, rather than either ignoring them and acting unilaterally, or allowing the humans to do as they like.

Thus what is perhaps the most important explanation in the plagues narrative (9:13-19) is a message for Pharaoh, drawing attention to what YHWH could have done, what he has done instead, how Pharaoh has answered this, and what YHWH will do in response. This exemplifies a pattern that flows throughout the encounters between YHWH and Pharaoh. YHWH makes the continual demand 'send ... serve', but Pharaoh refuses to heed it. Initially he dismisses YHWH and his right to demand such a response, and at the end of each encounter this hard-set opposition is either maintained or strengthened if it has softened. YHWH's response to this is the increasing or worsening of signs/plagues designed to achieve the knowledge or acknowledgement of YHWH from Pharaoh and Egypt. If YHWH's acts to date will not cause Pharaoh to respond appropriately, then YHWH will increase them. This is seen most clearly at 7:14-17 and 9:13-19. With the former comes the commencement of the plagues. With the latter comes the commencement of the divine hardening of Pharaoh.

Pharaoh, however, is not the only person that YHWH encounters in the story. Moses, YHWH's chosen messenger, has encounters with YHWH not wholly dissimilar to Pharaoh, before the plagues narrative commences. His unwillingness to obey YHWH (due either to perceived inadequacy or reverses suffered) is dealt with by explanation and sign, focussing on the facts that YHWH will be with him, that he will provide him with signs and a spokesman, and that, even when Pharaoh does not respond appropriately, YHWH will still be acting. While the focus moves to Pharaoh rather than Moses in the plagues narrative (crudely Ex. 7-11 after Ex. 3-7), there is still a sub-current of engagement between YHWH and Moses where required, as 10:1-2 shows. Moses is given summaries of what he is to do, what Pharaoh will do, and what YHWH will do. For him, the focus is on the power of YHWH, not in an adversative sense as with Pharaoh, but in a context of reassurance, and the hardening of Pharaoh forms an important part of this.

Israel as well, although absent for much of the plagues narrative, have their own responses to the word and signs of YHWH. This does not end at the Red Sea, or Mt. Sinai, as the exodus tradition recurs throughout the whole Old Testament, often in the context of Israel's response to it, whether appropriate or (as is often the case) inappropriate. It is given as a reason to follow YHWH, as a rebuke for failing to follow, as a reason for YHWH's response to this failure in terms of exile, and in the intercessions made to YHWH on Israel's behalf. One particular story resonates with the exodus narrative; that of the capture of YHWH's ark by the Philistines at the beginning of 1 Samuel. As with Pharaoh, Egypt, Moses and Israel, so Israel and the Philistines have to learn how to respond correctly to YHWH.

Our discussion was set up in light of the struggle that one may have in reading what is an important and yet difficult text from the position of one who follows this God, attempting to walk the line between an outright rejection of 'problematic' texts or alternatively a naïf embrace of them. The picture of YHWH that has emerged may not be entirely appealing or comfortable, but this would accord with the reactions of those who encountered YHWH in the narrative. Encounters with YHWH are not portrayed as comfortable experiences, but rather ones where the one encountered is challenged by YHWH, where the 'explanations' that he gives are intended to provoke a reaction, often one which is not initially palatable. This is the case for both those within the narrative (predominantly Moses and Pharaoh), and also its hearers, such as Israel. Inasmuch as these stories form part of Scripture, they continue to be read and heard in contexts very different from those of the exodus or later Israel. Any detailed discussion of how the points made here may feed in to the wider discussions of the reading of Scripture must be left for another time. However some brief comments may be made in conclusion.

The different messages, explanations and rationales offered in different contexts, with their ambiguities and possibilities of multiple interpretations, show the need for some sophistication in a reading of the text. Attempts to flatten out the different messages into one meaning or abstract them as propositions would lose the contextual understanding that is so important in grasping the above points. Moses and Pharaoh are encountered differently in their different contexts, and the context of the reader is different again.[1]

---

[1] Thus if one, standing in a position similar to Pharaoh, were to read the text and appropriate the messages to Moses (or vice versa), this could lead to all manner of misappropriations. One interesting discussion of this is the thesis proposed by Dykstra.

However, this emphasis on contextualisation should not close down, but rather open up the possibility of the reader being addressed by the text. In the story the messages are given in the context of challenging the hearer's own position and actions. If, as this reader, one approaches the text in the hope that one may, in some sense, be addressed by it, and the One who stands behind it, then these are points that one needs to ponder.

She argues that first world readers of the exodus should read the story not from the point of view of the Israelites, but rather from the point of view of the Egyptians, being those who are part of a system that oppresses others.

Appendix I - Important Hebrew Words and Phrases[1]

Hebrew	Transliteration	Meaning(s)
כָּבֵד (v./a.)	kāḇēḏ	harden/be hard, make/be heavy, glorify (v.); heavy, hard, abundant (a.)
כָּבוֹד (n.)	kāḇôḏ	abundance, honour, glory
חָזַק חָזֵק (v.) (a.)	ḥāzaq/ḥāzāq	be/make strong/hard, grasp(v.) Strong/hard(a.)
קָשָׁה	āšāʰ	be/make stubborn, hard, difficult
שַׁלַּח	allaḥ	send/release!
עַמִּי	ʿammî	my people
וְיַעַבְדֻנִי/עָבַד (v.)	ʿāḇaḏ/ wəyaʿaḇḏūnî	serve, work, worship/'that they may serve me'
עֲבֹדָה/עֶבֶד	ʿeḇeḏ/ʿāḇōḏāʰ	slave, servant/service, work
יָדַע כִּי/יָדַע	yāḏaʿ/yāḏaʿ kî	know(acknowledge)/know that
כִּי עַתָּה שָׁלַחְתִּי	kî ʿattāʰ šālaḥtî	'For by now I could have sent'
הֶעֱמַדְתִּיךָ	heʿĕmaḏtîḵā	'I have sustained you'
(וַ)אֲנִי	(wa)ʾănî	(and) I
כַּאֲשֶׁר דִּבֶּר יְהוָה	kaʾăšer dibber yhwh	'as YHWH said'
הִתְעַלַּלְתִּי	hiṯʿallaltî	'I have toyed with/sported with/abused'
אֹתֹתַי/אוֹת	ʾôṯ/ʾōṯōṯay	sign/my signs
הָפַךְ	hāp̄aḵ	change/overturn
רֵיקָם	êqām	empty
אָשָׁם	ʾāšām	(guilt) offering
קָלַל	ālal	be light/lighten, be lightly esteemed
יְהוָה	yhwh(ʾăḏōnāy)	YHWH(the LORD)
מֹשֶׁה	ōšeʰ	Moses
פַּרְעֹה	parʿōʰ	Pharaoh

---

[1] This is meant as a basic aid for those who do not read Hebrew. Therefore distinctions e.g. of verb mood between Qal, Niph'al etc. are not covered. Neither are the meanings given meant to be exhaustive. In the transliteration, broadly a line under a consonant indicates soft pronounciation, and a line over a vowel indicates a long vowel, while š is pronounced 'sh'.

Appendix II - יָדַע and יָדַע כִּי in the Exodus Story

Ref	Context[1]	Statement

יָדַע

Ref	Context	Statement
1:8	Narrator	A new king arose who did not know Joseph
2:4	Narrator	His sister stood distant to know what would happen…
2:14	Ms' thoughts	'Surely the thing has become known.'
2:25	Narrator	God saw the sons of Israel and God knew.
3:7	Y to M	'I know their [Israel's] sufferings'
5:2	P to M	'I do not know YHWH and Israel I will not send.'
6:3	Y to M	'But by my name YHWH I did not make myself known to them [Abraham, Isaac and Jacob].'
10:26	M to P	'We will not know how to serve YHWH until we arrive.'

יָדַע כִּי

Ref	Context	Statement
3:19	Y to M	'I know that Pharaoh will not allow you [Israel] to go, except by a strong hand.'
4:14	Y to M	'I know that he [Aaron] can certainly speak.'
6:7	Y(M) to Israel	'You will know that I am YHWH, who brought you out from under the burdens of Egypt.'
7:5	Y to M	'The Egyptians will know that I am YHWH as I send my hand against Egypt and bring out the sons of Israel from their midst.'
7:17	Y(M) to P	'By this you will know that I am YHWH…'
8:6 [10]	Y(M) to P	'As you say, so that you will know that there is none like YHWH our God.'
8:18 [22]	Y(M) to P	'You will know that I am YHWH in the midst of the land.'
9:14	Y(M) to P	'You will know that there is none like me in all the land/earth.'
9:29	Y(M) to P	'You will know that the land is YHWH's.'
9:30	M to P	'I know that you [Pharaoh] do not yet fear YHWH God.'

---

[1] Y - YHWH, M - Moses, P - Pharaoh. Y(M) signifies that the message is being given by YHWH to Israel or Pharaoh through the agency of Moses. He is told the message, but as YHWH's spokesman. It is not ultimately for him.

10:2	Y(M) to Israel	'You will know that that I am YHWH.'
10:7	Servants to P	'Do you not yet know that Egypt is ruined?'
11:7	Y(M) to P	'You will know that YHWH separates between Egypt and Israel.'
14:4	Y to M	'The Egyptians will know that I am YHWH'
14:18	Y to M	'The Egyptians will know that I am YHWH in my glorification over Pharaoh, his chariots and horsemen.'

Appendix III - Comparison of Narratorial Refrains

Encounter	Hardening Refrain Concluding Encounter	Change in Pharaoh's Position/ State during that Encounter.	Event Immediately Preceding Hardening
Initial	*None*	*5:2, 4, 6-9, 17-18 Hardset*	*N/A*

I. Pharaoh's Heart *Remains Hard*

Encounter	Hardening Refrain Concluding Encounter	Change in Pharaoh's Position/ State during that Encounter.	Event Immediately Preceding Hardening
Serpent Staff	וַיֶּחֱזַק לֵב פַּרְעֹה (Qal) 7:13 cf. 7:14	No change from Ex.5	Magi copy Moses and Aaron (7:11-12)
Blood River	וַיֶּחֱזַק לֵב־פַּרְעֹה (Qal) 7:22 cf. 7:23	No change from 7:13-14	Magi copy Moses and Aaron (7:22)
Dust to Gnats	וַיֶּחֱזַק לֵב־פַּרְעֹה (Qal) 8:15 [19]	No change from 8:11 [15]	Magi fail to copy (8:14 [18]) and confess (8:15 [19])
Livestock Death	וַיִּכְבַּד לֵב פַּרְעֹה (Qal) 9:7	No change from 8:28 [32]	Pharaoh finds no dead Israelite cattle (9:7)
Hail and Storm	וַיֶּחֱזַק לֵב פַּרְעֹה (Qal) 9:35	Follows 9:34.	Follows 9:34

II. *Pharaoh* Hardens his Heart

Frog Invasion	וְהַכְבֵּד אֶת־לִבּוֹ (Hiph'il) 8:11 [15]	8:4 [8] – 'softening' - will let them go	8:11 [15] Pharaoh sees respite from the plague
The Swarm	וַיַּכְבֵּד פַּרְעֹה אֶת־לִבּוֹ (Hiph'il) 8:28 [32]	8:21 [25], 24 [28] – 'softening' – will let them go	8:28 [32] Plague removed
Hail and Storm	וַיַּכְבֵּד לִבּוֹ הוּא וַעֲבָדָיו (Hiph'il) 9:34	9:27-28 – 'softening' - will let them go	9:34 Pharaoh sees respite from the plague

III. *YHWH* Hardens Pharaoh's Heart

Boils and Sores	וַיְחַזֵּק יְהוָה אֶת־לֵב פַּרְעֹה (Pi'el) 9:12	No change from 9:7	9:11 Magi unable to stand before Moses and Aaron
Locusts	וַיְחַזֵּק יְהוָה אֶת־לֵב פַּרְעֹה (Pi'el) 10:20	10:16-17 – 'softening' - will let them go	10:19 Plague removed
Darkness	וַיְחַזֵּק יְהוָה אֶת־לֵב פַּרְעֹה (Pi'el) 10:27	10:24 - 'softening' - will let them go	10:25-26 Moses counters Pharaoh's offer

Bibliography

Albrektson, Bertil. *History and the Gods – An Essay on the Idea of Historical Events as Divine Manifestations in the Ancient Near East and Israel.* CBOTS 1, Lund: CWK Gleerup, 1967.

Althann, R. 'פדת in Exodus 8:19', in *Exodus 1-15: Text and Context.* Edited by J. J. Burden. OTWSA/OTSSA 29 (1986): 73-79.

Anderson, Bernhard W. 'Exodus typology in Second Isaiah' in *Israel's Prophetic Heritage: Essays in Honor of James Muilenburg.* Edited by Bernhard W. Anderson and Walter Harrison, London: SCM, 1962: 177f.

Auld, A. G. *Amos.* OTG, Sheffield: Sheffield Academic Press, 1995.

Baentsch, Bruno. *Exodus, Leviticus und Numeri.* HKAT I.2. Göttingen: Vandenhoek und Ruprecht, 1903.

Bailey, Randall C. '"And they shall know that I am YHWH!": The P Recasting of the Plagues Narratives in Exodus 7-11.' *JITC* 22 (1994): 1-17.

Barclay, John. *The Politics of Contempt: Judeans and Egyptians in Josephus' Against Apion.* [cited 30 August 2004]. Online: http://josephus.yorku.ca/pdf/barclay2000.pdf

Barth, Karl. *Church Dogmatics.* Translated by G. T. Thomson et al. Edinburgh: T&T Clark, 1956-1969.

Baskin, Judith R. *Pharaoh's Counsellors – Job, Jethro and Balaam in Rabbinic and Patristic Tradition.* BJS 47, Chico, California: Scholars Press, 1983.

Beale, G. K. 'An Exegetical and Theological Consideration of the Hardening of Pharaoh's Heart in Exodus 4-14 and Romans 9.' *TrinJ* 5 (1984): 129-154.

Bellis, Alice Ogden, and Joel S. Kaminsky, eds. *Jews, Christians and the Theology of the Hebrew Scriptures,* SBLSymS 8, Atlanta: SBL, 2000.

Bentzen, Aage. 'The Cultic Use of the Story of the Ark in Samuel.' *JBL* LXVII (1948): 37-53.

Bertman, S. 'A note on the reversible miracle.' *HR* 3 (1964): 523-37.

Brown, Francis., S. R. Driver and Charles A. Briggs, *The New Brown-Driver-Briggs-Gesenius Hebrew and English Lexicon.* Peabody: Hendrickson, 1979, based on the original 1907 edition.

Brueggemann, Walter. 'Pharaoh as Vassal: A Study of a Political Metaphor.' *CBQ* 57.1 (1995): 27-51.

– *First and Second Samuel.* IBC, Louisville: John Knox Press, 1990.

– *Ichabod Towards Home – The journey of God's glory* Grand Rapids: Eerdmans, 2002.

Byron, John. *Slaves of God and Christ. A Traditio-Historical and Exegetical Examination of Slavery Metaphors in Early Judaism and Pauline Christianity.* Ph.D. dissertation. University of Durham, 2002.

Campbell, Anthony F. 'Yahweh and the Ark: A Case Study in Narrative.' *JBL* 98/1 (1979): 31-43.

– *The Ark Narrative (1Sam 4-6; 2Sam 6) A Form-Critical and Traditio-historical study*. SBLDS 16 (Missoula: Scholars' Press University of Montana, 1975.

Cartledge, Tony W. *1&2 Samuel*. SHBC, Macon: S&H Publishing, 2001.

Cassuto, U. *A Commentary on the book of Exodus*. Translated by Israel Abrahams, Jerusalem: Magnes Press, 1974.

Chacko, Modayil Mani. *Liberation and Service of God: A Theological Evaluation of Exodus 1-15:21*. Delhi: Indian Society for the Promotion of Christian Knowledge, 2002.

Childs, Brevard S. *The Book of Exodus. A Critical Theological Commentary*. OTL, Louisville: The Westminster Press, 1974.

Clines, D. J. A. *Job 1-20*. WBC 17, Dallas: Word, 1989.

– *Interested Parties – The Ideology of Writers and Readers of the Hebrew Bible*. Sheffield: Sheffield Academic Press, 1995.

Cooke, G. A. *A Critical and Exegetical Commentary on the Book of Ezekiel*. ICC, Edinburgh: T&T Clark, 1970.

Cornell, Vincent J. '"I am Your Lord Most High": Pharaoh and the Sin of Hubris in the Qur'an.' *JSR* 2.2 (2002). No pages [cited 18 August 2004]. Online: http://etext.virginia.edu/journals/ssr/issues/volume2/number2/

Couroyer, B. 'Le Doigt de Dieu.' *RB* 63 (1956): 481-495.

Craigie, Peter C.; Page H. Kelley; and Joel F. Drinkard Jr., *Jeremiah 1-25*. WBC 26, Waco: Word, 1998.

Croatto, J. Severino. *Exodus - A Hermeneutics of Freedom*. Salvator Attanasio trans. Maryknoll: Orbis, 1981.

Danby, Herbert. *The Mishnah*. London: Oxford University Press, 1933.

Daube, David. *The Exodus Pattern in the Bible*. ASS II, London: Faber & Faber, 1963.

Davies, G. I. 'The Hebrew Text of Exodus VIII 19 (EVV. 23) An Emendation.', *VT* 24 (1974): 489-492.

Davis, Ellen F. 'Critical Traditioning' in *The Art of Reading Scripture*. Edited by Ellen F Davis and Richard B. Hays, Grand Rapids: Eerdmans, 2003: 163-180.

Davis, John J. *Moses and the Gods of Egypt: Studies in Exodus*. Winona Lake, Indiana: BMH Books, 1986.

Deist, F. E. 'Who is to blame: The Pharaoh, Yahweh or circumstance? On human responsibility and divine ordinance in Exodus 1-14.' in *Exodus 1-15: Text and Context*. Edited by J. J. Burden. OTWSA/OTSSA 29 (1986): 91-112.

Dillenberger, John, Editor. *Martin Luther: Selections from his Writings*. New York: Anchor, Doubleday, 1962.

Dillmann, August. *Die Bücher Exodus und Leviticus*. Leipzig: S. Hirzel, 1880.

Dozeman, Thomas B. *God at War. Power in the Exodus Tradition*. New York: Oxford University Press, 1996.

Driver, S. R. *Notes on the Hebrew Text of the Books of Samuel*. Oxford: Clarendon Press, 1890.

– *The Book of Exodus*. CBSC, Cambridge: Cambridge University Press, 1918.

Dumermuth, Fritz. ‚Folkloristisches in der Erzählung von den Ägyptischen Plagen.‘ *ZAW* 76 (1964): 323-325.

Durham, John I. *Exodus*. WBC 3, Waco: Word, 1987.

Dykstra, Laurel A. *Set Them Free – The other side of Exodus*. Maryknoll: Orbis Books, 2002.

Ehrlich, Arnold B. *Randglossen zur Hebräische Bibel: Erster Band Genesis und Exodus*. Hildesheim: Georg Olms Verlagsbuchhandlung, 1968.

Eslinger, Lyle M. *Kingship of God in Crisis. A close reading of 1Sam 1-12*. BLS, Sheffield: Almond Press, 1985.

– ‘Freedom or Knowledge? Perspective and Purpose in the Exodus Narrative (Exodus 1-15).’ *JSOT* 52 (1991): 43-60.

Fishbane, Michael. *Text and Texture – Close Readings of Selected Biblical Texts*. New York: Schocken Books, 1979.

Fokkelman, J. P. ‘Exodus’ in *The Literary Guide to the Bible*. Edited by Robert Alter and Frank Kermode. Cambridge, Mass.: Belknap Press of Harvard University Press, 1987: 56-65.

– *Vow and Desire (1Sam 1-12). Vol IV of Narrative Art and Poetry in the Books of Samuel: a full interpretation based on stylistic and structural analyses*. Translated by L. Waaning-Wardle, SSN, Assen: Van Gorcum, 1993.

Fretheim, Terence E. *Exodus*. IBC, Louisville: John Knox Press, 1991.

Gibson, J.C.L. *Davidson's Introductory Hebrew Grammar ~ Syntax*. Edinburgh: T&T Clark, 1994.

Ginzberg, Louis. *The Legends of the Jews*. Philadelphia: Jewish Publication Society, 1967.

Goldingay, John. *Old Testament Theology. Volume 1: Israel's Gospel*. Downers Grove: IVP, 2003.

– ‘"That you may know that Yahweh is God" A Study in the relationship between theology and historical truth in the Old Testament’ *TynBul* 23 (1972): 58-93.

Gordon, Robert P. *1 & II Samuel A commentary*. LBI, Grand Rapids: Zondervan, 1986.

Gowan, Donald E. *Theology in Exodus – Biblical Theology in the form of a commentary*. Louisville: Westminster/John Knox Press, 1994.

Gray, George Buchanan. *A Critical and Exegetical Commentary on Numbers*. ICC, Edinburgh: T&T Clark, 1903.

Greenberg, Moshe. ‘The Thematic Unity of Exodus III-XI.’ *Fourth World Congress of Jewish Studies Papers*, Vol 1. Jerusalem, 1967: 151-154.

– *Understanding Exodus*, The Heritage of Biblical Israel. Vol II part I of the Melton Research Center Series, New York: Behrman House, 1969.

Gunn, David M. 'The "hardening of Pharaoh's heart": Plot, character and theology in Exodus 1-14', in *Art and Meaning: Rhetoric in Biblical Literature*. Edited by David J. A .Clines, David M. Gunn, and Alan J. Hauser, JSOTsup19, Sheffield: Sheffield Academic Press, 1982: 72-96.

Heither, Theresia. *Schriftauslegung – Das Buch Exodus bei den Kirchenvätern*. NSKAT 33/4, Stuttgart: Verlag Katholisches Bibelwerk, 2002.

Herzberg, Hans William. *I & II Samuel – A commentary*. London: SCM, 1960.

Hesse, Franz. *Das Verstockungsproblem im Alten Testament: Eine Frömmigkeitsgeschichtliche Untersuchung*. BZAW 74, Berlin: Alfred Töpelmann, 1955.

Hoffmeier, James K. 'The Arm of God versus the Arm of Pharaoh in the Exodus Narratives', *Biblica* 67 (1986): 378-87.

– *Israel in Egypt: The Evidence for the Authenticity of the Exodus Tradition*, Oxford: Oxford University Press, 1996.

Hornung , Erik. *Conceptions of God in Ancient Egypt: The One and the Many*. Translated by John Baines, New York: Cornell University Press, 1982.

Hort, Greta. 'The Plagues of Egypt', *ZAW* 69 (1957): 84-103; 70 (1958): 48-59.

Houtman, Cornelis. *Exodus*. Translated by Sierd Woudstra, HCOT, Kampen: Kok, 1993, 1996.

Humphreys, Colin J. *The Miracles of Egypt. A Scientist's Discovery of the Extraordinary Natural Causes of the Biblical Stories*. London: Continuum, 2003.

Hyatt, J. P. *Exodus*. NCB, London: Marshall, Morgan & Scott, 1971.

Ibn Ezra's commentary on the Pentateuch – Exodus. H. Norman Strickman and Arthur M. Silver, New York: Menorah Publishing Company, 1996.

Jacob, Benno. 'Gott und Pharao', *MGWJ* LXVIII (1923): 118ff, 202ff, 268ff.

– *The Second Book of the Bible. Exodus*. Translated by Walter Jacob, New Jersey: Ktav Publishing House Inc, 1992.

Janzen, J. Gerald. *Exodus*. Louisville: Westminster/John Knox Press, 1997.

Jeffrey, David Lyle. 'Exodus' and 'Plagues of Egypt' in *A Dictionary of Biblical Tradition in English Literature*. Edited by David Lyle Jeffrey. Grand Rapids: Eerdmans, 1992.

Johnstone, William. 'Exodus' in John W. Rogerson, R. W. L. Moberly and William Johnstone, *Genesis and Exodus*. Sheffield: Sheffield Academic Press, 2001: 182-276.

– *Chronicles and Exodus: An Analogy and its Application*. JSOTSup 275, Sheffield: Sheffield Academic Press, 1998.

Josephus. *The Life Against Apion*. Translated by H. St.J. Thackeray, LCL Josephus I, London: William Heinemann Ltd, 1961.

Joyce, Paul M. *Divine Initiative and Human Response in Ezekiel*. JSOTSup 51, Sheffield: Sheffield Academic Press, 1989.

Kaufmann, Yehezkel. *The Religion of Israel. From its Beginnings to the Babylonian Exile.* Translated and abridged by Moshe Greenberg. London: George Allen & Unwin, 1961.

Kautzsch E. and A. E. Cowley, *Gesenius' Hebrew Grammar.* Oxford: Clarendon, 1990.

Keil, C. F. and F. Delitzsch *Biblical Commentary on the Old Testament. Vol I: The Pentateuch.* Translated by James Martin. CFTL XXII, Edinburgh: T&T Clark, 1864.

Kellenberger, Edgar. 'Pharaoh's Hardening and the Hardening of the Philistines: A Comparison of Ex.4-14 and 1Sam 4-6.' An unpublished English transcript of a paper presented at the meeting of the International SBL, Cambridge, 21 July 2003.

– *Die Verstockung Pharaos: Exegetische und auslegungsgeschichtliche Untersuchungen zu Exodus 1-15.* BWANT 171, Stuttgart: Kohlhammer, 2006.

Kitchen, K. A. *On the Reliability of the Old Testament,* Grand Rapids: Eerdmans, 2003.

Knight, George F. A. *Theology as Narrative: A Commentary on the Book of Exodus.* Edinburgh: Handsel Press, 1976.

Kohata, Fujiko. *Jahwist und Priesterschrift in Exodus 3-14.* BZAW 166. Berlin: de Gruyter, 1986.

Krašovec, Jože. *Reward, Punishment and Forgiveness – The Thinking and Beliefs of Ancient Israel in the Light of Greek and Modern Views.* VTSup LXXVIII, Leiden: Brill, 1999.

Kuyper, Lester J. 'The Hardness of Heart according to Biblical Perspective.' *SJT* 27 (1974): 459-474.

Lapide, Pinchas. 'Exodus in the Jewish Tradition' in *Exodus – A Lasting Paradigm.* Bas van Iersel and Anton Weiler eds., Concilium 189 (1987): 47-55.

Larrson, Göran. *Bound for Freedom: The Book of Exodus in Jewish and Christian Traditions.* Peabody: Hendrickson, 1999.

Leibowitz, Nehama. *New Studies in Shemot (Exodus) Part I.* Translated by Aryeh Newman. Jerusalem: Haomanian Press, 1995.

Lemmelijn, Bénédicte. 'Setting and Function of Exod 11,1-10 in the Exodus Narrative' in *Studies in the Book of Exodus; Redaction – Reception – Interpretation.* Edited by Marc Vervenne. BETL CXXVI, Leuven: Leuven University Press, 1996: 443-460.

Levenson, Jon. D. *The Death and Resurrection of the Beloved Son.* New Haven: Yale University Press, 1993.

– *The Hebrew Bible, the Old Testament, and Historical Criticism: Jews and Christians in Biblical Studies.* Louisville: Westminster/John Knox Press, 1993.

Lindström, Fredrik. *God and the Origin of Evil – A Contextual Analysis of Alleged Monistic Evidence in the Old Testament.* CBOTS 21, Lund: CWK Gleerup, 1983.

Macintosh, A. A. 'Exodus VIII 19, Distinct Redemption and the Hebrew Roots פדה and פדד.' *VT* 21 (1971): 112-114.

McCarter Jr., P. Kyle. *1 Samuel.* AB, New York: Doubleday, 1980.

McCarthy, Dennis J. 'Moses' Dealings with Pharaoh: Ex.7,8-10,27.' *CBQ* 27 (1965): 336-347.

– 'Plagues and Sea of Reeds: Exodus 5-14', *JBL* 85 (1966): 137-158.

McKane, William. *A Critical and Exegetical Commentary on Jeremiah.* ICC, Edinburgh: T&T Clark, 1996.

Milgrom, Jacob. *Numbers.* JPSTC, Philadelphia: Jewish Publication Society, 1990.

Miller Jr, Patrick D. and J. J. M. Roberts, *The Hand of the Lord: A Reassessment of the 'Ark Narrative' of 1 Samuel.* JHNES, Baltimore: Johns Hopkins University Press, 1977

Moberly, R. W. L. *The Bible, Theology and Faith – A study of Abraham and Jesus.* CSCD, Cambridge: Cambridge University Press, 2000.

– *The Old Testament of the Old Testament: Patriarchal Narratives and Mosaic Yahwism.* OBT, Minneapolis: Fortress Press, 1992.

Murphy, Roland. *Ecclesiastes.* WBC 23a, Dallas: Word, 1998.

Noth, Martin. *Exodus.* Translated by J.S. Bowden, OTL, London: SCM Press, 1962.

Ogden, G. S. 'Notes on the use of היוה in Ex. IX 3.' *VT* 17 (1967): 483-484.

Origen Homilies on Genesis and Exodus. Translated by Ronald E. Heine, FC 71, Washington: The Catholic University of America Press, 1981.

Passover Hagadah with the commentary of Rabbi Dr Marcus Lehrmann. London: Honigson Publishing Co, 1969.

Paton, Corrine. '"I myself gave them laws that were not good": Ezekiel 20 and the Exodus Tradition.' *JSOT* 69 (1996): 73-90.

Pedersen, Johannes. 'Passahfest und Passahlegende.' *ZAW* 52 (1934): 161-175.

Philo. *De vita Mosis.* Translated by F. H. Colson, LCL Philo VI, London: William Heineman, 1959.

Pixley, George V. *On Exodus – a liberation perspective.* Maryknoll: Orbis, 1987.

Plastaras, James. *The God of Exodus: The Theology of the Exodus Narratives.* Milwaukee: Bruce Publishing, 1966.

Polak, Frank. 'Theophany and Mediator' in *Studies in the Book of Exodus: Redaction – Reception – Interpretation.* Edited by Marc Vervenne, BETL LXXVI, Leuven: Leuven University Press, 1996: 113-147.

Propp, William H. C. *Exodus 1-18. A New Translation with Introduction and Commentary.* AB, New York: Doubleday, 1998.

Räisänen, Heikki. *The Idea of Divine Hardening. A Comparative Study of the notion of divine hardening, leading astray and inciting to evil in the Bible and the Qur'an*. Publications of the Finnish Exegetical Society 25, Helsinki, 1976.

Rashbam's Commentary on Exodus - An Annotated Translation. Edited and translated by Martin I. Lockshin, BJS 310, Atlanta: Scholars Press, 1997.

Rosen, Norma. *Biblical Women Unbound: Counter-tales*. Philadelphia: Jewish Publication Society, 1996.

Rost, Leonard. *The Succession to the Throne of David*. Translated by Michael D. Rutter and David M. Gunn, HTIBS I, Sheffield: Almond Press, 1982.

Saggs, H. W. F. *The Encounter with the Divine in Mesopotamia and Israel*. London: The Athlone Press, University of London, 1978.

Sanderson, Judith E. *An Exodus Scroll from Qumran: 4QpaleoExod^m and the Samaritan Tradition*. HSS 30. Atlanta: Scholars Press: 1986.

Sarna, Nahum M. *Exodus*. JPSTC, Philadelphia: Jewish Publication Society, 1991.

– *Exploring Exodus: The Heritage of Biblical Israel*. New York: Schoken Books, 1986.

Sauter, Gerhard. ''Exodus' and 'Liberation' as Theological Metaphors: A Critical Case-Study of the Use of Allegory and Misunderstood Analogies in Ethics.' *SJT* 34 (1981): 481-507.

Schmidt, Werner H. *Exodus*. BKAT 2, Neukirchen-Vluyn: Neukirchener Verlag, 1988, 1995, 1999.

Ska, Jean Louis. 'Note sur la traduction de welo' en exode III 19b', *VT* XLIV (1994): 60-65.

Skehan, Patrick W. et al. *Discoveries in the Judaean Desert IX Qumran Cave 4 IV Paleao-Hebrew and Greek Biblical Manuscripts*. Oxford: Clarendon Press, 1992.

Smith, Henry Preserved. *A Critical and Exegetical Commentary on the Books of Samuel*, ICC. Edinburgh: T&T Clark, 1899.

Stirrup, A. ''Why has Yahweh defeated us today before the Philistines?' The question of the ark narrative.' *TynBul* 51.1 (2000): 81-103.

Stuart, Douglas. *Hosea-Jonah*. WBC 31, Dallas: Word Books, 1998.

Sugirtharajah, R. S. ed., *Voices from the Margin – Interpreting the Bible in the Third World*. London: SPCK, 1991.

Talmon, S. 'Textual Criticism: The Ancient Versions' in *Text in Context: Essays by Members of the Society of Old Testament Study*. Edited by A. D. H. Mayes. Oxford: Oxford University Press, 2000: 141-170.

Targums Neofiti 1 and Pseudo-Jonathan: Exodus. Targum Neofiti translation by Martin McNamara, notes by Robert Hayward. Targum Pseudo-Jonathan translation and notes by Michael Maher. ArBib 2, Edinburgh: T&T Clark, 1994.

Timm, Hermann. ,Die Ladeerzählung (1. Sam. 4-6; 2. Sam. 6) und das Kerygma des deuteronomistischen Geschichtswerks.' *EvT* 26 (1966): 509-26.

Tov, Emanuel. *Textual Criticism of the Hebrew Bible.* Minneapolis: Fortress Press, 1992.

Trible, Phyllis. *Texts of Terror.* OBT 13, Philadelphia: Fortress Press, 1984.

Ulrich, Eugene et al. *Discoveries in the Judaean Desert XII: Qumran Cave 4 VII Genesis to Numbers.* Oxford: Clarendon Press: 1994.

Van Seters, John. 'The Plagues of Egypt: Ancient Tradition or Literary Invention?' *ZAW* 98 (1986): 31-39.

Vater, Ann. M. 'A Plague on both our houses: Observations in Exodus 7-11' in *Art and Meaning: Rhetoric in Biblical Literature.* Edited by David J. A .Clines, David M. Gunn, and Alan J. Hauser, JSOTsup19, Sheffield: Sheffield Academic Press, 1982: 62-71.

Vervenne, Marc. 'Current Tendencies and Developments in the Study of the Book of Exodus' in *Studies in the Book of Exodus: Redaction – Reception – Interpretation.* Edited by Marc Vervenne, BETL LXXVI, Leuven: Leuven University Press, 1996: 21-55.

Von Rad, Gerhard. *Old Testament Theology. Vol II.* Translated by D.M.G. Stalker from the German original of 1960. London: SCM, 1965.

Walzer, Michael. *Exodus and Revolution,* New York: Basic Books, 1985.

Warrior, Robert Allen. 'Canaanites, Cowboys and Indians: Deliverance, Conquest and Liberation Theology Today', in *The Postmodern Bible Reader.* Edited by David Jobling, Tina Pippin, and Ronald Schliefer, Oxford: Blackwell, 2001: 188-194.

Warshaver, G. '"The Hardening of Pharaoh's Heart" in the Bible and Qumranic Literature.' *BIJS* 1 (1973): 1-12.

Weisel, Elie. ‚The Crisis of Hope' in *Die Hebräische Bibel und ihre zweifache Nachgeschichte: Festschrift für Rolf Rendtorff zum 65. Geburtstag,* herausgegeben von Erhard Blum, Christian Macholz und Ekkehard W. Stegemann, Neukirchen-Vluyn: Neukirchener Verlag, 1990: 717-724.

Wevers, John William. *Notes on the Greek Text of Exodus.* SBLSCS 30, Atlanta: Scholars Press, 1990.

Williamson, H. G. M. 'Do we still need commentaries?' Presidential paper to the winter meeting of the Society of Old Testament Study, 5-7 Jan 2004.

Willis, John. 'An Anti-Elide Narrative Tradition from a Prophetic Circle at the Ramah Sanctuary.' *JBL* 90 (1971): 288-308.

Wilson, Robert R. 'The Hardening of Pharaoh's Heart.' *CBQ* 41 (1979): 18-36.

Zakovitch, Yair. *"AND YOU SHALL TELL YOUR SON" The Concept of the Exodus in the Bible.* Jerusalem: The Magnes Press, 1991.

Zevit, Ziony. 'Three Ways to Look at the Ten Plagues.' *BR* 6.3 (1990): 16-23, 42-44.

Zimmerli, W. *I am Yahweh.* Translated by Douglas W. Stott and edited by Walter Brueggemann, Atlanta: John Knox Press, 1982.

Index of Names

Index of Scriptural References

Index of Subjects

Paternoster Biblical Monographs

(All titles uniform with this volume)
Dates in bold are of projected publication

Joseph Abraham
Eve: Accused or Acquitted?
A Reconsideration of Feminist Readings of the Creation Narrative Texts in Genesis 1–3

Two contrary views dominate contemporary feminist biblical scholarship. One finds in the Bible an unequivocal equality between the sexes from the very creation of humanity, whilst the other sees the biblical text as irredeemably patriarchal and androcentric. Dr Abraham enters into dialogue with both camps as well as introducing his own method of approach. An invaluable tool for any one who is interested in this contemporary debate.

2002 / 0-85364-971-5 / xxiv + 272pp

Octavian D. Baban
Mimesis and Luke's on the Road Encounters in Luke-Acts
Luke's Theology of the Way and its Literary Representation

The book argues on theological and literary (mimetic) grounds that Luke's on-the-road encounters, especially those belonging to the post-Easter period, are part of his complex theology of the Way. Jesus' teaching and that of the apostles is presented by Luke as a challenging answer to the Hellenistic reader's thirst for adventure, good literature, and existential paradigms.

2005 / 1-84227-253-5 / approx. 374pp

Paul Barker
The Triumph of Grace in Deuteronomy

This book is a textual and theological analysis of the interaction between the sin and faithlessness of Israel and the grace of Yahweh in response, looking especially at Deuteronomy chapters 1–3, 8–10 and 29–30. The author argues that the grace of Yahweh is determinative for the ongoing relationship between Yahweh and Israel and that Deuteronomy anticipates and fully expects Israel to be faithless.

2004 / 1-84227-226-8 / xxii + 270pp

Jonathan F. Bayes
The Weakness of the Law
God's Law and the Christian in New Testament Perspective

A study of the four New Testament books which refer to the law as weak (Acts, Romans, Galatians, Hebrews) leads to a defence of the third use in the Reformed debate about the law in the life of the believer.

2000 / 0-85364-957-X / xii + 244pp

Mark Bonnington
The Antioch Episode of Galatians 2:11-14 in Historical and Cultural Context

The Galatians 2 'incident' in Antioch over table-fellowship suggests significant disagreement between the leading apostles. This book analyses the background to the disagreement by locating the incident within the dynamics of social interaction between Jews and Gentiles. It proposes a new way of understanding the relationship between the individuals and issues involved.

2005 / 1-84227-050-8 / approx. 350pp

David Bostock
A Portrayal of Trust
The Theme of Faith in the Hezekiah Narratives

This study provides detailed and sensitive readings of the Hezekiah narratives (2 Kings 18–20 and Isaiah 36–39) from a theological perspective. It concentrates on the theme of faith, using narrative criticism as its methodology. Attention is paid especially to setting, plot, point of view and characterization within the narratives. A largely positive portrayal of Hezekiah emerges that underlines the importance and relevance of scripture.

2005 / 1-84227-314-0 / approx. 300pp

Mark Bredin
Jesus, Revolutionary of Peace
A Non-violent Christology in the Book of Revelation

This book aims to demonstrate that the figure of Jesus in the Book of Revelation can best be understood as an active non-violent revolutionary.

2003 / 1-84227-153-9 / xviii + 262pp

Robinson Butarbutar
Paul and Conflict Resolution
An Exegetical Study of Paul's Apostolic Paradigm in 1 Corinthians 9

The author sees the apostolic paradigm in 1 Corinthians 9 as part of Paul's unified arguments in 1 Corinthians 8–10 in which he seeks to mediate in the dispute over the issue of food offered to idols. The book also sees its relevance for dispute-resolution today, taking the conflict within the author's church as an example.

2006 / 1-84227-315-9 / approx. 280pp

Daniel J-S Chae
Paul as Apostle to the Gentiles
*His Apostolic Self-awareness and its Influence on the Soteriological Argument
in Romans*
Opposing 'the post-Holocaust interpretation of Romans', Daniel Chae competently demonstrates that Paul argues for the equality of Jew and Gentile in Romans. Chae's fresh exegetical interpretation is academically outstanding and spiritually encouraging.
1997 / 0-85364-829-8 / xiv + 378pp

Luke L. Cheung
The Genre, Composition and Hermeneutics of the Epistle of James
The present work examines the employment of the wisdom genre with a certain compositional structure and the interpretation of the law through the Jesus tradition of the double love command by the author of the Epistle of James to serve his purpose in promoting perfection and warning against doubleness among the eschatologically renewed people of God in the Diaspora.
2003 / 1-84227-062-1 / xvi + 372pp

Youngmo Cho
Spirit and Kingdom in the Writings of Luke and Paul
The relationship between Spirit and Kingdom is a relatively unexplored area in Lukan and Pauline studies. This book offers a fresh perspective of two biblical writers on the subject. It explores the difference between Luke's and Paul's understanding of the Spirit by examining the specific question of the relationship of the concept of the Spirit to the concept of the Kingdom of God in each writer.
2005 / 1-84227-316-7 / approx. 270pp

Andrew C. Clark
Parallel Lives
The Relation of Paul to the Apostles in the Lucan Perspective
This study of the Peter-Paul parallels in Acts argues that their purpose was to emphasize the themes of continuity in salvation history and the unity of the Jewish and Gentile missions. New light is shed on Luke's literary techniques, partly through a comparison with Plutarch.
2001 / 1-84227-035-4 / xviii + 386pp

Andrew D. Clarke
Secular and Christian Leadership in Corinth
A Socio-Historical and Exegetical Study of 1 Corinthians 1–6
This volume is an investigation into the leadership structures and dynamics of first-century Roman Corinth. These are compared with the practice of leadership in the Corinthian Christian community which are reflected in 1 Corinthians 1–6, and contrasted with Paul's own principles of Christian leadership.
2005 / 1-84227-229-2 / 200pp

Stephen Finamore
God, Order and Chaos
René Girard and the Apocalypse
Readers are often disturbed by the images of destruction in the book of Revelation and unsure why they are unleashed after the exaltation of Jesus. This book examines past approaches to these texts and uses René Girard's theories to revive some old ideas and propose some new ones.
2005 / 1-84227-197-0 / approx. 344pp

David G. Firth
Surrendering Retribution in the Psalms
Responses to Violence in the Individual Complaints
In *Surrendering Retribution in the Psalms*, David Firth examines the ways in which the book of Psalms inculcates a model response to violence through the repetition of standard patterns of prayer. Rather than seeking justification for retributive violence, Psalms encourages not only a surrender of the right of retribution to Yahweh, but also sets limits on the retribution that can be sought in imprecations. Arising initially from the author's experience in South Africa, the possibilities of this model to a particular context of violence is then briefly explored.
2005 / 1-84227-337-X / xviii + 154pp

Scott J. Hafemann
Suffering and Ministry in the Spirit
Paul's Defence of His Ministry in II Corinthians 2:14–3:3
Shedding new light on the way Paul defended his apostleship, the author offers a careful, detailed study of 2 Corinthians 2:14–3:3 linked with other key passages throughout 1 and 2 Corinthians. Demonstrating the unity and coherence of Paul's argument in this passage, the author shows that Paul's suffering served as the vehicle for revealing God's power and glory through the Spirit.
2000 / 0-85364-967-7 / xiv + 262pp

Scott J. Hafemann
Paul, Moses and the History of Israel
The Letter/Spirit Contrast and the Argument from Scripture in 2 Corinthians 3
An exegetical study of the call of Moses, the second giving of the Law (Exodus 32–34), the new covenant, and the prophetic understanding of the history of Israel in 2 Corinthians 3. Hafemann's work demonstrates Paul's contextual use of the Old Testament and the essential unity between the Law and the Gospel within the context of the distinctive ministries of Moses and Paul.
2005 / 1-84227-317-5 / xii + 498pp

Douglas S. McComiskey
Lukan Theology in the Light of the Gospel's Literary Structure
Luke's Gospel was purposefully written with theology embedded in its patterned literary structure. A critical analysis of this cyclical structure provides new windows into Luke's interpretation of the individual pericopes comprising the Gospel and illuminates several of his theological interests.
2004 / 1-84227-148-2 / xviii + 388pp

Stephen Motyer
Your Father the Devil?
A New Approach to John and 'The Jews'
Who are 'the Jews' in John's Gospel? Defending John against the charge of antisemitism, Motyer argues that, far from demonising the Jews, the Gospel seeks to present Jesus as 'Good News for Jews' in a late first century setting.
1997 / 0-85364-832-8 / xiv + 260pp

Esther Ng
Reconstructing Christian Origins?
The Feminist Theology of Elizabeth Schüssler Fiorenza: An Evaluation
In a detailed evaluation, the author challenges Elizabeth Schüssler Fiorenza's reconstruction of early Christian origins and her underlying presuppositions. The author also presents her own views on women's roles both then and now.
2002 / 1-84227-055-9 / xxiv + 468pp

Robin Parry
Old Testament Story and Christian Ethics
The Rape of Dinah as a Case Study

What is the role of story in ethics and, more particularly, what is the role of Old Testament story in Christian ethics? This book, drawing on the work of contemporary philosophers, argues that narrative is crucial in the ethical shaping of people and, drawing on the work of contemporary Old Testament scholars, that story plays a key role in Old Testament ethics. Parry then argues that when situated in canonical context Old Testament stories can be reappropriated by Christian readers in their own ethical formation. The shocking story of the rape of Dinah and the massacre of the Shechemites provides a fascinating case study for exploring the parameters within which Christian ethical appropriations of Old Testament stories can live.

2004 / 1-84227-210-1 / xx + 350pp

Ian Paul
Power to See the World Anew
The Value of Paul Ricoeur's Hermeneutic of Metaphor in Interpreting the Symbolism of Revelation 12 and 13

This book is a study of the hermeneutics of metaphor of Paul Ricoeur, one of the most important writers on hermeneutics and metaphor of the last century. It sets out the key points of his theory, important criticisms of his work, and how his approach, modified in the light of these criticisms, offers a methodological framework for reading apocalyptic texts.

2006 / 1-84227-056-7 / approx. 350pp

Robert L. Plummer
Paul's Understanding of the Church's Mission
Did the Apostle Paul Expect the Early Christian Communities to Evangelize?

This book engages in a careful study of Paul's letters to determine if the apostle expected the communities to which he wrote to engage in missionary activity. It helpfully summarizes the discussion on this debated issue, judiciously handling contested texts, and provides a way forward in addressing this critical question. While admitting that Paul rarely explicitly commands the communities he founded to evangelize, Plummer amasses significant incidental data to provide a convincing case that Paul did indeed expect his churches to engage in mission activity. Throughout the study, Plummer progressively builds a theological basis for the church's mission that is both distinctively Pauline and compelling.

2006 / 1-84227-333-7 / approx. 324pp

David Powys
'Hell': A Hard Look at a Hard Question
The Fate of the Unrighteous in New Testament Thought
This comprehensive treatment seeks to unlock the original meaning of terms and phrases long thought to support the traditional doctrine of hell. It concludes that there is an alternative—one which is more biblical, and which can positively revive the rationale for Christian mission.
1997 / 0-85364-831-X / xxii + 478pp

Sorin Sabou
Between Horror and Hope
Paul's Metaphorical Language of Death in Romans 6.1-11
This book argues that Paul's metaphorical language of death in Romans 6.1-11 conveys two aspects: horror and hope. The 'horror' aspect is conveyed by the 'crucifixion' language, and the 'hope' aspect by 'burial' language. The life of the Christian believer is understood, as relationship with sin is concerned ('death to sin'), between these two realities: horror and hope.
2005 / 1-84227-322-1 / approx. 224pp

Rosalind Selby
The Comical Doctrine
The Epistemology of New Testament Hermeneutics
This book argues that the gospel breaks through postmodernity's critique of truth and the referential possibilities of textuality with its gift of grace. With a rigorous, philosophical challenge to modernist and postmodernist assumptions, Selby offers an alternative epistemology to all who would still read with faith *and* with academic credibility.
2005 / 1-84227-212-8 / approx. 350pp

Kiwoong Son
Zion Symbolism in Hebrews
Hebrews 12.18-24 as a Hermeneutical Key to the Epistle
This book challenges the general tendency of understanding the Epistle to the Hebrews against a Hellenistic background and suggests that the Epistle should be understood in the light of the Jewish apocalyptic tradition. The author especially argues for the importance of the theological symbolism of Sinai and Zion (Heb. 12:18-24) as it provides the Epistle's theological background as well as the rhetorical basis of the superiority motif of Jesus throughout the Epistle.
2005 / 1-84227-368-X / approx. 280pp

Kevin Walton
Thou Traveller Unknown
The Presence and Absence of God in the Jacob Narrative
The author offers a fresh reading of the story of Jacob in the book of Genesis through the paradox of divine presence and absence. The work also seeks to make a contribution to Pentateuchal studies by bringing together a close reading of the final text with historical critical insights, doing justice to the text's historical depth, final form and canonical status.
2003 / 1-84227-059-1 / xvi + 238pp

George M. Wieland
The Significance of Salvation
A Study of Salvation Language in the Pastoral Epistles
The language and ideas of salvation pervade the three Pastoral Epistles. This study offers a close examination of their soteriological statements. In all three letters the idea of salvation is found to play a vital paraenetic role, but each also exhibits distinctive soteriological emphases. The results challenge common assumptions about the Pastoral Epistles as a corpus.
2005 / 1-84227-257-8 / approx. 324pp

Alistair Wilson
When Will These Things Happen?
A Study of Jesus as Judge in Matthew 21–25
This study seeks to allow Matthew's carefully constructed presentation of Jesus to be given full weight in the modern evaluation of Jesus' eschatology. Careful analysis of the text of Matthew 21–25 reveals Jesus to be standing firmly in the Jewish prophetic and wisdom traditions as he proclaims and enacts imminent judgement on the Jewish authorities then boldly claims the central role in the final and universal judgement.
2004 / 1-84227-146-6 / xxii + 272pp

Lindsay Wilson
Joseph Wise and Otherwise
The Intersection of Covenant and Wisdom in Genesis 37–50
This book offers a careful literary reading of Genesis 37–50 that argues that the Joseph story contains both strong covenant themes and many wisdom-like elements. The connections between the two helps to explore how covenant and wisdom might intersect in an integrated biblical theology.
2004 / 1-84227-140-7 / xvi + 340pp

Stephen I. Wright
The Voice of Jesus
Studies in the Interpretation of Six Gospel Parables
This literary study considers how the 'voice' of Jesus has been heard in different
periods of parable interpretation, and how the categories of figure and trope may
help us towards a sensitive reading of the parables today.
2000 / 0-85364-975-8 / xiv + 280pp

Paternoster
9 Holdom Avenue,
Bletchley,
Milton Keynes MK1 1QR,
United Kingdom
Web: www.authenticmedia.co.uk/paternoster

July 2005

Paternoster Theological Monographs

(All titles uniform with this volume)
Dates in bold are of projected publication

Emil Bartos
Deification in Eastern Orthodox Theology
An Evaluation and Critique of the Theology of Dumitru Staniloae
Bartos studies a fundamental yet neglected aspect of Orthodox theology: deification. By examining the doctrines of anthropology, christology, soteriology and ecclesiology as they relate to deification, he provides an important contribution to contemporary dialogue between Eastern and Western theologians.

1999 / 0-85364-956-1 / xii + 370pp

Graham Buxton
The Trinity, Creation and Pastoral Ministry
Imaging the Perichoretic God
In this book the author proposes a three-way conversation between theology, science and pastoral ministry. His approach draws on a Trinitarian understanding of God as a relational being of love, whose life 'spills over' into all created reality, human and non-human. By locating human meaning and purpose within God's 'creation-community' this book offers the possibility of a transforming engagement between those in pastoral ministry and the scientific community.

2005 */ 1-84227-369-8 / approx. 380 pp*

Iain D. Campbell
Fixing the Indemnity
The Life and Work of George Adam Smith
When Old Testament scholar George Adam Smith (1856–1942) delivered the Lyman Beecher lectures at Yale University in 1899, he confidently declared that 'modern criticism has won its war against traditional theories. It only remains to fix the amount of the indemnity.' In this biography, Iain D. Campbell assesses Smith's critical approach to the Old Testament and evaluates its consequences, showing that Smith's life and work still raises questions about the relationship between biblical scholarship and evangelical faith.

2004 / 1-84227-228-4 / xx + 256pp

Tim Chester
Mission and the Coming of God
Eschatology, the Trinity and Mission in the Theology of Jürgen Moltmann
This book explores the theology and missiology of the influential contemporary theologian, Jürgen Moltmann. It highlights the important contribution Moltmann has made while offering a critique of his thought from an evangelical perspective. In so doing, it touches on pertinent issues for evangelical missiology. The conclusion takes Calvin as a starting point, proposing 'an eschatology of the cross' which offers a critique of the over-realised eschatologies in liberation theology and certain forms of evangelicalism.
2006 / 1-84227-320-5 / approx. 224pp

Sylvia Wilkey Collinson
Making Disciples
The Significance of Jesus' Educational Strategy for Today's Church
This study examines the biblical practice of discipling, formulates a definition, and makes comparisons with modern models of education. A recommendation is made for greater attention to its practice today.
2004 / 1-84227-116-4 / xiv + 278pp

Darrell Cosden
A Theology of Work
Work and the New Creation
Through dialogue with Moltmann, Pope John Paul II and others, this book develops a genitive 'theology of work', presenting a theological definition of work and a model for a theological ethics of work that shows work's nature, value and meaning now and eschatologically. Work is shown to be a transformative activity consisting of three dynamically inter-related dimensions: the instrumental, relational and ontological.
2005 / 1-84227-332-9 / xvi + 208pp

Stephen M. Dunning
The Crisis and the Quest
A Kierkegaardian Reading of Charles Williams
Employing Kierkegaardian categories and analysis, this study investigates both the central crisis in Charles Williams's authorship between hermetism and Christianity (Kierkegaard's Religions A and B), and the quest to resolve this crisis, a quest that ultimately presses the bounds of orthodoxy.
2000 / 0-85364-985-5 / xxiv + 254pp

Keith Ferdinando
The Triumph of Christ in African Perspective
A Study of Demonology and Redemption in the African Context
The book explores the implications of the gospel for traditional African fears of occult aggression. It analyses such traditional approaches to suffering and biblical responses to fears of demonic evil, concluding with an evaluation of African beliefs from the perspective of the gospel.

1999 / 0-85364-830-1 / xviii + 450pp

Andrew Goddard
Living the Word, Resisting the World
The Life and Thought of Jacques Ellul
This work offers a definitive study of both the life and thought of the French Reformed thinker Jacques Ellul (1912-1994). It will prove an indispensable resource for those interested in this influential theologian and sociologist and for Christian ethics and political thought generally.

2002 / 1-84227-053-2 / xxiv + 378pp

David Hilborn
The Words of our Lips
Language-Use in Free Church Worship
Studies of liturgical language have tended to focus on the written canons of Roman Catholic and Anglican communities. By contrast, David Hilborn analyses the more extemporary approach of English Nonconformity. Drawing on recent developments in linguistic pragmatics, he explores similarities and differences between 'fixed' and 'free' worship, and argues for the interdependence of each.

2006 / 0-85364-977-4 / approx. 350pp

Roger Hitching
The Church and Deaf People
A Study of Identity, Communication and Relationships with Special Reference to the Ecclesiology of Jürgen Moltmann
In *The Church and Deaf People* Roger Hitching sensitively examines the history and present experience of deaf people and finds similarities between aspects of sign language and Moltmann's theological method that 'open up' new ways of understanding theological concepts.

2003 / 1-84227-222-5 / xxii + 236pp

John G. Kelly
One God, One People
*The Differentiated Unity of the People of God in the Theology of
Jürgen Moltmann*
The author expounds and critiques Moltmann's doctrine of God and highlights
the systematic connections between it and Moltmann's influential discussion of
Israel. He then proposes a fresh approach to Jewish–Christian relations building
on Moltmann's work using insights from Habermas and Rawls.
2005 / 0-85346-969-3 / approx. 350pp

Mark F.W. Lovatt
Confronting the Will-to-Power
A Reconsideration of the Theology of Reinhold Niebuhr
Confronting the Will-to-Power is an analysis of the theology of Reinhold
Niebuhr, arguing that his work is an attempt to identify, and provide a practical
theological answer to, the existence and nature of human evil.
2001 / 1-84227-054-0 / xviii + 216pp

Neil B. MacDonald
Karl Barth and the Strange New World within the Bible
Barth, Wittgenstein, and the Metadilemmas of the Enlightenment
Barth's discovery of the strange new world within the Bible is examined in the
context of Kant, Hume, Overbeck, and, most importantly, Wittgenstein.
MacDonald covers some fundamental issues in theology today: epistemology,
the final form of the text and biblical truth-claims.
2000 / 0-85364-970-7 / xxvi + 374pp

Keith A. Mascord
Alvin Plantinga and Christian Apologetics
This book draws together the contributions of the philosopher Alvin Plantinga to
the major contemporary challenges to Christian belief, highlighting in particular
his ground-breaking work in epistemology and the problem of evil. Plantinga's
theory that both theistic and Christian belief is warrantedly basic is explored and
critiqued, and an assessment offered as to the significance of his work for
apologetic theory and practice.
2005 / 1-84227-256-X / approx. 304pp

Gillian McCulloch
The Deconstruction of Dualism in Theology
With Reference to Ecofeminist Theology and New Age Spirituality
This book challenges eco-theological anti-dualism in Christian theology, arguing that dualism has a twofold function in Christian religious discourse. Firstly, it enables us to express the discontinuities and divisions that are part of the process of reality. Secondly, dualistic language allows us to express the mysteries of divine transcendence/immanence and the survival of the soul without collapsing into monism and materialism, both of which are problematic for Christian epistemology.

2002 / 1-84227-044-3 / xii + 282pp

Leslie McCurdy
Attributes and Atonement
The Holy Love of God in the Theology of P.T. Forsyth
Attributes and Atonement is an intriguing full-length study of P.T. Forsyth's doctrine of the cross as it relates particularly to God's holy love. It includes an unparalleled bibliography of both primary and secondary material relating to Forsyth.

1999 / 0-85364-833-6 / xiv + 328pp

Nozomu Miyahira
Towards a Theology of the Concord of God
A Japanese Perspective on the Trinity
This book introduces a new Japanese theology and a unique Trinitarian formula based on the Japanese intellectual climate: three betweennesses and one concord. It also presents a new interpretation of the Trinity, a co-subordinationism, which is in line with orthodox Trinitarianism; each single person of the Trinity is eternally and equally subordinate (or serviceable) to the other persons, so that they retain the mutual dynamic equality.

2000 / 0-85364-863-8 / xiv + 256pp

Eddy José Muskus
The Origins and Early Development of Liberation Theology in Latin America
With Particular Reference to Gustavo Gutiérrez
This work challenges the fundamental premise of Liberation Theology, 'opting for the poor', and its claim that Christ is found in them. It also argues that Liberation Theology emerged as a direct result of the failure of the Roman Catholic Church in Latin America.

2002 / 0-85364-974-X / xiv + 296pp

Jim Purves
The Triune God and the Charismatic Movement
A Critical Appraisal from a Scottish Perspective
All emotion and no theology? Or a fundamental challenge to reappraise and realign our trinitarian theology in the light of Christian experience? This study of charismatic renewal as it found expression within Scotland at the end of the twentieth century evaluates the use of Patristic, Reformed and contemporary models of the Trinity in explaining the workings of the Holy Spirit.
2004 / 1-84227-321-3 / xxiv + 246pp

Anna Robbins
Methods in the Madness
Diversity in Twentieth-Century Christian Social Ethics
The author compares the ethical methods of Walter Rauschenbusch, Reinhold Niebuhr and others. She argues that unless Christians are clear about the ways that theology and philosophy are expressed practically they may lose the ability to discuss social ethics across contexts, let alone reach effective agreements.
2004 / 1-84227-211-X / xx + 294pp

Ed Rybarczyk
Beyond Salvation
Eastern Orthodoxy and Classical Pentecostalism on Becoming Like Christ
At first glance eastern Orthodoxy and classical Pentecostalism seem quite distinct. This ground-breaking study shows they share much in common, especially as it concerns the experiential elements of following Christ. Both traditions assert that authentic Christianity transcends the wooden categories of modernism.
2004 / 1-84227-144-X / xii + 356pp

Signe Sandsmark
Is World View Neutral Education Possible and Desirable?
A Christian Response to Liberal Arguments
(Published jointly with The Stapleford Centre)
This book discusses reasons for belief in world view neutrality, and argues that 'neutral' education will have a hidden, but strong world view influence. It discusses the place for Christian education in the common school.
2000 / 0-85364-973-1 / xiv + 182pp

Hazel Sherman
Reading Zechariah
The Allegorical Tradition of Biblical Interpretation through the Commentary of
Didymus the Blind and Theodore of Mopsuestia
A close reading of the commentary on Zechariah by Didymus the Blind
alongside that of Theodore of Mopsuestia suggests that popular categorising of
Antiochene and Alexandrian biblical exegesis as 'historical' or 'allegorical' is
inadequate and misleading.
2005 / 1-84227-213-6 / approx. 280pp

Andrew Sloane
On Being a Christian in the Academy
Nicholas Wolterstorff and the Practice of Christian Scholarship
An exposition and critical appraisal of Nicholas Wolterstorff's epistemology in
the light of the philosophy of science, and an application of his thought to the
practice of Christian scholarship.
2003 / 1-84227-058-3 / xvi + 274pp

Damon W.K. So
Jesus' Revelation of His Father
A Narrative-Conceptual Study of the Trinity with Special Reference to
Karl Barth
This book explores the trinitarian dynamics in the context of Jesus' revelation of
his Father in his earthly ministry with references to key passages in Matthew's
Gospel. It develops from the exegeses of these passages a non-linear concept of
revelation which links Jesus' communion with his Father to his revelatory words
and actions through a nuanced understanding of the Holy Spirit, with references
to K. Barth, G.W.H. Lampe, J.D.G. Dunn and E. Irving.
2005 / 1-84227-323-X / approx. 380pp

Daniel Strange
The Possibility of Salvation Among the Unevangelised
An Analysis of Inclusivism in Recent Evangelical Theology
For evangelical theologians the 'fate of the unevangelised' impinges upon
fundamental tenets of evangelical identity. The position known as 'inclusivism',
defined by the belief that the unevangelised can be ontologically saved by Christ
whilst being epistemologically unaware of him, has been defended most
vigorously by the Canadian evangelical Clark H. Pinnock. Through a detailed
analysis and critique of Pinnock's work, this book examines a cluster of issues
surrounding the unevangelised and its implications for christology, soteriology
and the doctrine of revelation.
2002 / 1-84227-047-8 / xviii + 362pp

Scott Swain
God According to the Gospel
Biblical Narrative and the Identity of God in the Theology of Robert W. Jenson
Robert W. Jenson is one of the leading voices in contemporary Trinitarian theology. His boldest contribution in this area concerns his use of biblical narrative both to ground and explicate the Christian doctrine of God. *God According to the Gospel* critically examines Jenson's proposal and suggests an alternative way of reading the biblical portrayal of the triune God.
2006 / 1-84227-258-6 / approx. 180pp

Justyn Terry
The Justifying Judgement of God
A Reassessment of the Place of Judgement in the Saving Work of Christ
The argument of this book is that judgement, understood as the whole process of bringing justice, is the primary metaphor of atonement, with others, such as victory, redemption and sacrifice, subordinate to it. Judgement also provides the proper context for understanding penal substitution and the call to repentance, baptism, eucharist and holiness.
2005 / 1-84227-370-1 / approx. 274 pp

Graham Tomlin
The Power of the Cross
Theology and the Death of Christ in Paul, Luther and Pascal
This book explores the theology of the cross in St Paul, Luther and Pascal. It offers new perspectives on the theology of each, and some implications for the nature of power, apologetics, theology and church life in a postmodern context.
1999 / 0-85364-984-7 / xiv + 344pp

Adonis Vidu
Postliberal Theological Method
A Critical Study
The postliberal theology of Hans Frei, George Lindbeck, Ronald Thiemann, John Milbank and others is one of the more influential contemporary options. This book focuses on several aspects pertaining to its theological method, specifically its understanding of background, hermeneutics, epistemic justification, ontology, the nature of doctrine and, finally, Christological method.
2005 / 1-84227-395-7 / approx. 324pp

Graham J. Watts
Revelation and the Spirit
A Comparative Study of the Relationship between the Doctrine of Revelation and Pneumatology in the Theology of Eberhard Jüngel and of Wolfhart Pannenberg

The relationship between revelation and pneumatology is relatively unexplored. This approach offers a fresh angle on two important twentieth century theologians and raises pneumatological questions which are theologically crucial and relevant to mission in a postmodern culture.

2005 / 1-84227-104-0 / xxii + 232pp

Nigel G. Wright
Disavowing Constantine
Mission, Church and the Social Order in the Theologies of John Howard Yoder and Jürgen Moltmann

This book is a timely restatement of a radical theology of church and state in the Anabaptist and Baptist tradition. Dr Wright constructs his argument in dialogue and debate with Yoder and Moltmann, major contributors to a free church perspective.

2000 / 0-85364-978-2 / xvi + 252pp

Paternoster:
thinking faith

Paternoster
9 Holdom Avenue,
Bletchley,
Milton Keynes MK1 1QR,
United Kingdom
Web: www.authenticmedia.co.uk/paternoster

July 2005

Made in the USA
Las Vegas, NV
27 July 2023